Ulster Emigration

to

Colonial America

1718–1775

by

R. J. DICKSON

with a New

INTRODUCTION

by

G. E. KIRKHAM

ULSTER HISTORICAL FOUNDATION

BELFAST

First published 1966
by Routledge & Kegan Paul Ltd
on behalf of
Ulster Historical Foundation (UHF)
12 College Square East, Belfast BT1 6DD
Email: enquiry@uhf.org.uk
Website: www.ancestryireland.com

First reprint by UHF 1976
Second reprint by UHF 1988
Third reprint by UHF 1996
Fourth reprint by UHF 2001
© R.J. Dickson, 1966

Printed by ColourBooks Ltd

ISBN: 978-0-901905-17-8

Cover: 'Londonderry' from an original sketch by John Nixon
circa 1793, in the possession of Mr R. Adams.

Contents

Introduction

IT is more than twenty years since R. J. Dickson's *Ulster Emigration to Colonial America 1718-1775* was first published, and forty years since the research on which it was based was undertaken. With the passage of time it is easy to overlook the extent to which his work broke new ground and established new standards for this field of study. Much of the earlier literature dealing with Ulster emigration (and some more recent) was primarily concerned with the debate over the 'Scotch-Irish' and their contribution to the pioneering and settlement and the military and political development of colonial and revolutionary America. Most of these works were based on a limited and undiscriminating use of source material; the economic and social background to emigration and the operation of the emigrant trade itself were sketchily drawn and often woefully in error. Religious and political factors were heavily emphasised as the primary causes of the outflow of population, while economic stimuli to migration were perceived most often only in terms of 'oppression' by landlords, bishops and government.

By contrast, *Ulster Emigration to Colonial America* provided for the first time a balanced and professional study of the entire emigration phenomenon, a history rather than a filio-pietist tract. It was based on a carefully analytical approach, closely and critically argued; it employed a wide range of historical sources and utilised a variety of techniques in assessing them; and it carefully examined the religious and political context of emigration. The major thrust of Dickson's conclusions on causation was founded on his work on changes in the Ulster economy over the period. This was in many respects pioneering for at the time of his research Irish economic history, particularly regional studies, was generally undeveloped. At the time of publication both Dickson's approach and his findings represented a major historiographical achievement.

Inevitably, advances in research since that period have modified or superseded certain of his conclusions, while others may now be amplified or supported with additional evidence. The quantity and variety of primary material accessible to the historian of emigration has increased dramatically and the considerable progress of research

Introduction

in recent years on various aspects of Ulster history has provided a much more detailed view of the background to the period. Emigration itself has attracted further academic attention. This introduction to a new edition of Dickson's study is intended to provide a brief outline of the more important revisions to the subject, of which those approaching the topic should be aware.[1]

In his account of the wider economic background to emigration Dickson was necessarily guided by the orthodoxies of an older generation of historians, which held that the Irish economy was severely retarded before the later decades of the eighteenth century. The resultant emphasis on backwardness and underdevelopment can now be seen as having considerably understated the real vitality of economic change, particularly in Ulster. Over much of the first half of the century the agrarian economy was indeed relatively depressed, but the rise of domestic industry and the opening of other specific avenues of economic opportunity to the northern population resulted in a considerable degree of development. This was reflected not only in a substantial increase in output from the province but also in a significant rise in material standards of living. In the mid-seventeenth century Ulster had been the poorest province of Ireland; by the middle of the eighteenth century it was undoubtedly the most prosperous.[2]

Dickson presented the Ulster economy during his period as essentially agricultural, to which the linen industry provided an 'appendix', a 'means to supplement the meagre profits of farming'; only in the latter years of his period does he accord the manufacture of linen more than subsidiary importance. In fact, it is clear that the progress of change was rather more complex. In many areas of east Ulster — that is, counties Antrim, Armagh, Down and Monaghan, and the eastern portions of Londonderry, Tyrone and Cavan —

1 The research on which this introductory essay is based was partly carried out under the auspices of the Garfield Weston Research Project, 'Emigration from Ulster to North America', at the University of Ulster at Coleraine, 1982-85.
References given are intended to provide a basic guide to relevant secondary material and are not exhaustive. Where no reference is cited the material is derived either from works previously cited or from the author's research in progress.
2 L. M. Cullen, 'Economic Development, 1691-1750' and 'Economic Development, 1750-1800', in T. W. Moody and W. E. Vaughan, eds., *A New History of Ireland, IV: Eighteenth-Century Ireland 1691-1800* (Oxford, 1986), pp.123-158, 159-95; W. H. Crawford, 'Ulster as a Mirror of the Two Societies', in T. M. Devine and David Dickson, eds., *Ireland and Scotland 1600-1850: Parallels and Contrasts in Economic and Social Development* (Edinburgh, 1983), pp.60-9.

Introduction

domestic linen weaving became the dominant element in the popular economy well before the mid-eighteenth century, and was the primary mode of economic activity through almost the whole of this region by the 1770s. For a large part of the population household labour was directed towards work at the loom, spinning, cultivation and preparation of small flax crops, and provision of basic domestic subsistence food supplies rather than market-oriented agriculture. Indeed, from at least the 1730s much of the population was dependent for a significant portion of their diet on foodstuffs imported into the region. The primacy of linen production had profound effects in shaping the economy of this area, producing greater domestic incomes, higher rent levels and smaller holding sizes than in other parts of the province. Considerable additional employment was generated by the industry in bleaching and other textile finishing processes, in commerce, transport, retailing and the whole complex of urban and rural crafts and services. Population density was also greater than in other parts of Ulster: the east of the province contained not only a majority of all the inhabitants of the north but, more specifically, much the largest proportion of the Protestant population, from which most of the emigrants of the period derived.[3]

In west Ulster weaving did not become an important element in the regional economy until late in the century, except in a few localised pockets in the Foyle area. There the pace of economic change was undoubtedly slower, and the level of popular prosperity rather lower than in the east, but there was nonetheless a notable vitality in the course of development. The most widespread form of economic activity was the domestic spinning of linen yarn, predominantly for export to the textile manufacturing region of north-west England. A good indication of the major growth which this form of domestic industry underwent is given by the increase on yarn shipments from the port of Derry; these soared from an annual average for about 500 cwt. in the first two decades of the century to

3 W. H. Crawford, 'The Origins of the Linen Industry in North Armagh and the Lagan Valley', *Ulster Folklife*, XVII (1971), pp.42-51; 'The Market Book of Thomas Greer, A Dungannon Linendraper, 1758-59', *Ulster Folklife*, XIII (1967), pp.54-60; 'Economy and Society in South Ulster in the Eighteenth Century', *Clogher Record*, VIII, 3 (1975), pp.241-58; *Domestic Industry in Ireland: The Experience of the Linen Industry* (Dublin, 1972); J. H. Andrews, 'Land and People, c.1780', in Moody and Vaughan, eds., *New History of Ireland, IV*, pp.236-64. A useful model of domestic linen manufacture in Ulster is outlined in Brenda Collins, 'Proto-Industrialisation and Pre-Famine Emigration', *Social History*, VII, 2 (1982), pp.127-46.

Introduction

reach almost 18,000 cwt. per annum in the 1760s. Earnings from spinning provided a sizeable and essential component in household incomes throughout the region. Further opportunities were offered by the rises of two specific aspects of the agricultural economy. The development of a substantial whiskey distilling industry, both legal and illicit, in the west of the province provided an expanding and profitable market for surpluses of grain, particularly barley, from which many farmers in the region were able to benefit. West Ulster also contained extensive areas of rough pasture, which were increasingly exploited from the 1720s and 1730s for the rearing of lean beef cattle, sold for fattening and slaughter outside Ulster, and of milch cows for the weaving population of the east.[4]

In addition to these major elements in the northern economy there were other more localised forms of activity which provided employment and income for portions of the population in areas throughout the province. The economic background was thus both more diverse and considerably more developed then Dickson's account suggests. As in other pre-industrial European societies, however, the Ulster economy was vulnerable and subject to considerable fluctuations from year to year. Dickson drew attention to the importance of harvest failures as a major cause of emigration during his period, but the effects of poor seasons were not simply those of a reduction in subsistence. Deficient harvests were usually accompanied by a more general short-term economic recession, specifically a slump in demand and prices for linen, yarn and other elements of output (other than grain) on which domestic economies were founded. In these circumstances household incomes were severely reduced and the necessary purchase of supplementary foodstuffs at much increased prices rendered more difficult. The coincident failure of flax crops and the death of cattle in bad years exacerbated the problems of subsequent recovery.

The economy was also vulnerable to recessions in the external markets from which demand for its major products came. Thus, credit crises or failures in business confidence amongst, for example, the cattle graziers of Cork or Meath, the yarn buyers of

---

4 G. Kirkham, 'Economic Diversification in a Marginal Economy: A Case Study', in P. Roebuck, ed., *Plantation to Partition: Essays in Ulster History in Honour of J. L. McCracken* (Belfast, 1981), pp.64-81; '"To pay the Rent and Lay Up Riches": Economic Opportunity in Eighteenth-Century North-West Ulster', in Rosalind Mitchison and Peter Roebuck, eds., *Economy and Society in Scotland and Ireland, 1500-1939* (Edinburgh, 1988).

Introduction

Manchester, or the linen merchants of London, Chester or Dublin, could seriously undermine the economic well-being of a large proportion of the Ulster population.

Another crucial element in the background to emigration was land tenure, particularly the impact of rising rent levels. Dickson was considerably more reserved in his judgements on these aspects of the economy than most of his predecessors, for whom the reputed greed and rapacity of landlords were among the most noted 'oppressions' of emigrants. Recent studies have shown, however, that the role of proprietors in pushing up rent levels was relatively minor; indeed, the historical development of the landholding system in Ulster resulted in a situation in which many estate owners had little effective short-term control over their properties. In the mid-seventeenth century much of the province had been sparsely populated. Economic development was weak and the returns from land small. The immigration of large numbers of settlers from England and Scotland in the period before 1700 brought a substantial increase in population and a marked upturn in economic activity, but in order to attract and keep tenants on their estates Ulster landlords had of necessity to offer advantageous terms of tenure. Many features of the system established during this period persisted through much of the eighteenth century. Thus, lands were normally set by proprietors on leases of 21 or 31 years, or for the duration of the lives of three individuals; agreements of the latter type often lasted for more than 50 years. Although there were, as Dickson noted, contemporary protests about the shortness of lease terms, these were in fact beneficial forms of tenure for those holding land directly from the proprietor. However, landlords did require some evidence of the future security of their rent payments, and substantial tenants able to provide this were scarce. Considerable quantities of land were therefore let to groups of individuals holding leases in partnership, and jointly responsible for the rent, or to prosperous 'middleman' tenants. The latter took large proportions of land, often at a beneficially low rate, and re-set it at a profit to a number of undertenants. Rents paid to the landowner remained fixed during the term of the lease, but demands made on undertenants by middlemen usually increased more rapidly, in line with the rising market value of farm holdings. The practice of undersetting was widespread throughout the landholding system: those who held land from a middleman could themselves sublet portions

Introduction

of their farms at a higher rate, thereby reducing the real cost of the land they actually worked. As Dickson pointed out, and as subsequent research has amply confirmed, many of the criticisms levelled at the land system in Ulster resulted from the proliferation of this hierarchy of tenure through multiple levels.[5]

It was evident to proprietors that under this form of landholding they received only a fraction of the current market value of their properties, and from mid-century there was an increasing tendency to grant leases directly to the occupiers of lands rather than to intermediate tenants. The time-lag introduced by long leases meant that middleman tenures persisted over a much longer period, but the large increase evident in many estate rentals during the 1760s, 1770s and subsequent decades must be attributed in part to the effects of the policy; occupying tenants at the lower levels of the hierarchy of tenure must have been paying comparably higher rents from a rather earlier period. The new tenurial policy benefited not only landlords' incomes but also the much increased number of households for whom the level of rent payments would remain fixed over a period of their lease. One of the major factors underlying the Hearts of Steel unrest in the early 1770s was the disappointment of large numbers of undertenants of their expectations of receiving direct leases.

Other factors also tended to moderate any inclination of proprietors to seek unreasonably high rents. One of these was the knowledge that any subsequent economic crisis might cause numbers of overburdened tenants to 'break', leaving farms untenanted and rents unpaid. Another was the persistence of the popular observance of 'tenant right', the customary perception that an occupying tenant had a prior and prescriptive right to negotiate for renewal of his lease on its expiry, and that such negotiations should be seen to have failed before others would bid for the land. It is true that in certain

5 W. H. Crawford, 'Landlord-Tenant Relations in Ulster, 1609-1820', *Irish Economic & Social History*, II (1975), pp.5-21; P. Roebuck, 'Rent Movement, Proprietorial Incomes and Agricultural Development, 1730-1830', in Roebuck, ed., *Plantation to Partition*, pp.82-101; 'Landlord Indebtedness in Ulster in the Seventeenth and Eighteenth Centuries', in J. M. Goldstrom and L. A. Clarkson, eds., *Irish Population, Economy and Society: Essays in Honour of the late K. H. Connell* (Oxford, 1981), pp.135-54; David Dickson, 'Middlemen', in Thomas Bartlett and D. W. Hayton, eds., *Penal Era and Golden Age: Essays in Irish History 1690-1800* (Belfast, 1979), pp.162-85; W. A. Maguire, 'Lord Donegall and the Hearts of Steel', *Irish Historical Studies*, XXI, 84 (1979), pp.351-76; J. S. Donnelly, 'Hearts of Oak, Hearts of Steel', *Studia Hibernica*, XXI (1981), pp.7-73.

Introduction

areas of extreme competition for holdings some landowners introduced the practice of 'canting' out-of-lease farms — that is, the seeking of competitive written proposals for new rents, allowing no specific advantage to the sitting tenants — but this method of letting was by no means universal and was strongly resisted. Over much of the province the continuing balance of power towards leaseholders in landlord-tenant relations is shown by the existence of an active market in lease 'interests'; the purchaser of an interest obtained both occupation of a holding during the unexpired term of the lease and the 'tenant right' to negotiate subsequent renewal. Such sales realised substantial sums, amounting to several times the annual rent of a farm, and were often used to provide the outgoing household with a capital stake prior to emigration.

Dickson rightly concluded that the primary causes of increasing rents in Ulster during the period were competition for land and the influence of domestic industry, coupled with the effects of middleman tenures and subsidiary undersetting. He suggested, however, that the scale of the increase in the cost of access to land was 'unreasonable', in terms of the burden it imposed on domestic incomes, because it outpaced both growth of productivity and the long-term rise in prices for the major products of the province. The second of these points is undoubtedly true, but the first is questionable. Over the period covered by *Ulster Emigration to Colonial America* the number of households (that is, landholding units) in the province at least doubled. The resultant increase in demand for holdings was concentrated in areas of better land in proximity to markets, and was particularly marked in the region in which linen manufacture predominated. Dickson's examples of increases in rent levels were drawn from the east of the province where all of these effects operated most strongly; subsequent studies have shown considerably greater variation in both the scale and timing of rent movements across Ulster than was indicated by his evidence. More importantly, however, the increasing vitality of the economy provided a developing range of economic opportunities from which the population could derive an income; these opportunities were considerably greater at the end of the period than they had been at the beginning.[6]

6 On population change see D. Dickson, C. Ó Grada and S. Daultrey, 'Hearth Tax, Household Size and Irish Population Change, 1672-1821', *Procs. Royal Irish Academy*, LXXXII, C, 6 (1982), pp.125-81; W. Macafee and V. Morgan, 'Population in Ulster, 1660-1760', in Roebuck, ed., *Plantation to Partition*, pp.46-63.

Introduction

The emphasis on domestic industry as a major source of earnings also facilitated a progressive reduction in the size of holdings, either by subdivision between family members or through the profitable parcelling off of small portions to subtenants. Considerable areas of marginal land within farms were reclaimed through settlement of additional households. Thus, although the cost of access to land certainly climbed steeply to levels well above its national value for purely agricultural use during this period, the productivity of a given farm in, say, the 1720s had also risen substantially by the 1770s in terms of the output of the increased number of households based on it, from whose much increased incomes the rent was paid. It is possible that by the latter part of the period an increasing proportion of the population was becoming marginalised as labourers or cottiers, although there is as yet no clear evidence on this point. However, contemporary observers emphasised the growing material prosperity of the inhabitants of Ulster, and this, together with the marked leisure preference displayed by the population, suggests that for most families the growth of income more than kept pace with increases in rent and other demands such as tithes.

This is not to suggest that rents and the pressures of competition in the landholding system were not frequently burdensome, or to reduce the importance of these factors as principal elements in the background to emigration. Just as the vigour of economic development enabled rents to climb as they did, so there were corresponding difficulties for the population when the economy was temporarily disrupted by dearth or recession. Contemporary complaints about rent levels almost all date from such periods of crisis. It is of more than passing significance that conditions of land tenure were a major aspect of the grievances expressed by the Hearts of Steel in the troubled years of the early 1770s, but were a minor concern of the agrarian protesters known as Oakboys in the 'average' year of 1763.

The stimulus towards emigration which land and rents created, however, would not have been nearly as great without the contrast which local conditions in Ulster offered when compared with the information available to prospective migrants on the situation in America. Dickson noted the role of press advertisements, emigration agents and the masters of emigrant vessels in extolling the easy availability, size, fertility, freedom from restriction and above all cheapness of the holdings to be obtained by emigrants. A

Introduction

further, and almost certainly more important, source of information was letters from previous emigrants to relatives and friends in Ireland. Only a few examples of these were available to Dickson, but it is clear from the substantial collection compiled in recent years by the Public Record Office of Northern Ireland as well as from examples available in other archives that such correspondence must have been extremely persuasive. Many letters provided detailed accounts (from individuals known and trusted by the recipients) of the experiences, fortunes and improved circumstances of those who had emigrated, and in many cases offered practical aid to those who would follow them. Examples of return letters from Ulster to America indicate that such information was readily accepted, and many of these urge their correspondents to provide greater detail. The very fact that those previous emigrants did not simply 'disappear' once they left home and took ship must in itself have made the prospect of the journey and the promise of the destination more appealing to those left behind.[7]

Perhaps the greatest single problem presented by the study of eighteenth-century Irish emigration is assessment of the overall numbers of individuals who departed. Dickson's cautious and methodical analysis was based on a far wider range of sources than were used by his predecessors and he produced a series of detailed although in some cases inconclusive arguments on the volume of emigration during various phases of his period. For the years 1750-75 he constructed a detailed series of figures for the numbers of sailings of emigrant vessels from Ulster ports, derived from an exhaustive combing of Irish newspaper sources, on which he based his conclusion. Many of his findings on specific aspects of the emigration process remain unchallenged, but it is now clear that even the much expanded range of material he utilised for his estimates of

---

7 E. R. R. Green, 'Ulster Emigrants' Letters', in E. R. R. Green, *Essays in Scotch-Irish History* (Belfast, 1969), pp.87-103; Alun C. Davies, '"As Good A Country As Any Man Needs to Dwell In"; Letters from a Scotch-Irish Immigrant in Pennsylvania, 1766, 1767 and 1784', *Pennsylvania History*, L, 4 (1983), pp.313-22. K. A. Miller has made extensive use of emigrant letters, and provides location details for a large number of examples, in *Emigrants and Exiles: Ireland and the Irish Exodus to North America* (Oxford, 1985).

Introduction

emigrants' numbers was misleading and deficient in certain respects. There is, for example, considerable doubt about the comprehensiveness of the data presented by the *Belfast News Letter*, Ulster's only newspaper until the early 1770s and one of Dickson's major sources for emigrant sailings from ports other than Belfast. In the 1750s, a period for which the *News Letter* files are in any case only partly complete, American newspapers certainly recorded the arrival of much greater numbers of vessels from Derry, for example, than Dickson was able to identify.

No detailed re-examination has yet been made of emigration levels after the mid-century, although it seems certain that some upward revision of the figures presented in *Ulster Emigration to Colonial America* will be necessary for at least part of the period. Recent research on the four decades before 1750, using data on emigrant voyages derived from American sources, has significantly expanded Dickson's assessment of the population flow during this earlier period. He concluded that after the surges of emigration he documented for the late 1710s and 1720s the trade continued at a substantially lower and unspectacular level over several decades. In fact, emigrant voyages during the 1730s and 1740s ran at more than double the levels of the two preceding decades; this period was therefore one of major expansion for the trade, and one in which the exodus to America became a regular and established element in Ulster life. Additionally, Dickson and other previous writers underestimated the scale of emigration in the late 1710s. It was previously understood that sailings during this peak were primarily directed to New England, but it is apparent from the new data that voyages to north-eastern ports actually comprised less than half of passages from Ulster in the years 1717-19, with a larger number, additional to those previously identified, directed to New York, the Delaware ports, and to South Carolina.

The overall volume of emigration during the pre-1750 period was therefore substantially greater than was apparent to Dickson. Nonetheless, the detailed annual figures for sailings during these years do confirm the emphasis he placed on economic factors, especially poor harvests and economic crises, in prompting migration. There were marked peaks in the number of voyages, not only in 1718-19 and 1727-29, but also in 1735-36, 1740-41 and 1745-46, all of which were to a greater or lesser extent periods of dearth and recession. These crisis years total only a quarter of the time span of his study but account for more than half of the sailings identified.

The 'crisis' characteristic of the emigrant trade continued over much of the eighteenth century, and provides an additional argument against the major emphasis in older writings on religious and political 'oppressions' as primary motivations for emigration. For the vast majority of Ulster Presbyterians specific disabilities on grounds of religion had ceased to be important by c.1720 and, as Dickson suggested, the older perception of the emigrant population as universally 'Scotch-Irish' — Presbyterian and of direct Scottish ancestry — was in any case certainly in error. Recent studies have provided evidence of the mixed religious and ethnic composition of the exodus, which included not only Presbyterians but also substantial numbers of native Irish Catholics and adherents of the Established Church who were of English descent. The extent of Catholic emigration is particularly difficult to assess because many native Irish migrants appear to have abandoned a specifically Catholic identity once in America; many runaway servants with distinctively 'Irish' names, for example, assumed aliases which concealed their origins. Presbyterians certainly formed a majority amongst emigrants, but this was not the direct result of burdens specific to this group. The much larger number of Catholic inhabitants of Ulster were disadvantaged to a considerably greater extent, both by specific legal disabilities and in their general economic and social status. Attempts have been made to explain the differing propensities of these groups to emigrate in terms of particular world views or mentalities, including the argument that Protestantism, particularly in its Nonconformist variants, represented a 'modern' culture which encouraged achievement and an active response to adversity; the 'traditional' culture of Catholicism being marked by a greater degree of acceptance, fatalism and pragmatic adaptation in the face of difficulty. Such arguments are attractive, but are ultimately difficult to verify; other factors such as the discouragement to Catholics presented by the strongly Protestant ethos of colonial America and the attractions to different groups within the Catholic population of migration to England or Continental Europe may also have been important. More significantly perhaps, the flow of information on America and the popular perception of it as a 'promised land' were considerably less accessible to the Catholic population because of substantially lower literacy rates, widespread use of the Irish language and the relatively small numbers of previous emigrants from this group.[8]

Very many aspects of the emigration phenomenon remain obscure and demand further research; more detailed definition of the emigrant population as a whole is perhaps the most pressing of these. As this work continues, however, the major contribution of R. J. Dickson to the field, both in his findings and in his approach to the problems, will continue to be acknowledged. The continuing academic reputation of *Ulster Emigration to Colonial America* has been supplemented by the growth of wide popular interest in its subject matter. Publication of this new edition to meet this demand is a tribute to the enduring qualities of his scholarship.

Graeme Kirkham

---

[8] D. N. Doyle, *Ireland, Irishmen and Revolutionary America, 1760-1820* (Dublin, 1981); K. A. Miller, with Bruce Boling and D. N. Doyle, 'Emigrants and Exiles: Irish Cultures and Irish Emigration to Northern America, 1790-1922', *Irish Historical Studies*, XIII, 86 (1980), pp.97-125. Also of some relevance is the debate on the ethnic origins of the American population at the time of the first census. For a review see 'The Population of the United States'.

Author's Preface

THE hundreds of thousands of Irish emigrants to colonial America have been overshadowed by the millions who emigrated from Ireland in the second half of the nineteenth century. Yet it was of those half-forgotten emigrants that it was said in the Irish parliament in 1784, 'America was lost by Irish emigrants'.[1] Historians, rightly, have not adopted this explanation of the loss of the American colonies but the fact that the Irish element in America was singled out for its part in the Revolution is an indication of the contribution of eighteenth century Irish immigrants to the growth of the American colonies and the founding of the infant republic.

It is, therefore, surprising that no comprehensive account of emigration from Ireland to colonial America has yet been written, though the paucity of material has undoubtedly acted as a deterrent to the undertaking of such a study. Historians have not ignored the subject but, when dealing with it, their eyes have been focused elsewhere. W. E. H. Lecky's interest was centred in Dublin Castle, not merchants' offices at outlying ports.[2] To him, the *Freemason*, the Chester packet, with its statesmen and bishops was of greater interest than the *Freemason* of Newry which carried, far to the west, hundreds of much less distinguished people. To J. A. Froude, presbyterian emigration was but the result of the short-sighted and disastrous policy of episcopacy that seemed determined to accomplish its own ruin by driving its natural allies across the seas.[3] American historians have examined some aspects of Irish emigration more closely, yet it cannot be said that it was on Irish emigration that their eyes were fixed. Naturally, they viewed the Irish as immigrants into America rather than as emigrants from Ireland. The effects of Irish immigration on the colonies and its influence on the Revolution hold the centre of the stage and crowd

[1] *The parliamentary register, or history of the proceedings and debates of the house of commons of Ireland*, iii. 125.
[2] *History of Ireland in the eighteenth century* (2nd ed., London, 1892). Further remarks on this and the other works named in this introduction will be found in the bibliography and in footnotes in the body of the book.
[3] *The English in Ireland in the eighteenth century*.

xix

the Irish scene into the wings. This point is illustrated by the title of one of the best works on the subject, *The Scotch-Irish in America*, by H. J. Ford. This limitation as a contribution to Irish history is even more apparent in the works of avowedly Irish-American and Ulster-American historians such as M. J. O'Brien[1] and C. A. Hanna[2] for, because of the religious and political bias of the authors, the emigrant becomes not merely an extra on the stage but a pawn in a game he sought no part in. O'Brien minimised the extent of emigration from the protestant north in order to exaggerate that from the Roman catholic south. Even the name *Scotch-Irish*, the 'kailyard hyphen',[3] angered him, so it is not to be expected that his work should be an objective analysis of the Irish element in pre-Revolutionary America. Hanna's concern was the presbyterian, whether in Scotland, Ireland or America. Celt and Roman catholic held no interest for him, least of all as competitors for the glory won by the Irish in the Revolution. This attitude, combined with a rather puzzling system of arrangement, reduces the value of Hanna's work from an argued synthesis to a mine of interesting and detailed information. It is useful to study the writings of O'Brien and Hanna as complementary to each other, though the sharp conflict of opinions is chastening rather than instructive.

In other words, the Irish emigrant to colonial America has failed to attract the attention he deserves purely as an emigrant. The object of this book is to fill in part of that gap in Irish history by examining emigration to colonial America from the northern ports of Ireland, for it was from those ports that a substantial number of America-bound emigrants sailed. Emigration must be viewed against the background of a larger scene but the central figure of this investigation is the Ulster emigrant of the period prior to the American Revolution.

The preparation of this book was spread over several years and during that time I was fortunate enough to meet many people who were most helpful at all times and whose patience I have come to regard, in retrospect, as astonishing. I am very conscious of the debt which I owe to the staffs of the libraries of the Queen's University of Belfast, the Linenhall Library, Belfast, the National

---

[1] *George Washington's associations with the Irish*; *Pioneer Irish in New England*; *A hidden phase of American history*; *Ireland's part in America's struggle for liberty*; and various articles in the *Journal of the American Irish Historical Society* as listed in the bibliography.
[2] *The Scotch Irish: or, the Scot in North Britain, North Ireland, and North America.*
[3] *Washington's Irish assoc.*, pp. 72–3.

Author's Preface

Library, Dublin, and Magee University College, Londonderry, and to the staffs of the Public Record Offices in Belfast, Dublin and London and of the British Museum. I owe a special debt, however, to Professor J. W. Blake, formerly Senior Lecturer in the Department of History of the Queen's University of Belfast, and now Vice-Chancellor of Basutoland University, for his advice and guidance in the collection of material and to Mr K. Darwin, the Deputy Keeper of the Public Records of Northern Ireland, and Professor J. C. Beckett, Professor of Irish History at the Queen's University of Belfast, for their seemingly endless patience during the time when the material was being prepared for publication.

I am honoured by the fact that my work on emigration from Ulster to America was selected by the Ulster-Scot Historical Society to be the first book to be published in its series and I must express my gratitude to the Duke of Abercorn, the President of the Society, and to Sir William Scott, the Chairman, for the personal interest they showed during the preparation of this book.

R. J. DICKSON

Strangarry,
Mullaghmore,
Omagh, Co. Tyrone.

Abbreviations used in the footnotes

Acts privy council (col.)	*Acts of the privy council, colonial series*
Amer. Ir. Hist. Soc. Jn.	*Journal of the American Irish Historical Society*
B.M., Add.MS(S)	British Museum, Additional Manuscript(s)
B.N.L.	*Belfast News Letter*
Boulter letters	*Letters written by* . . . . *Hugh Boulter, D.D., lord primate of all Ireland*
Cal. H.O. pap.	*Calendar of home office papers*
Cal. S.P. Amer. & W. Ind.	*Calendar of state papers, colonial series America and West Indies*
Cal. S.P. Ire.	*Calendar of state papers relating to Ireland*
Cal. treas. bks. & papers	*Calendar of treasury books and papers*
C.E.P.	*Cork Evening Post*
C.O.	Colonial office papers in the Public Record Office of England
C.M.H.	*Cambridge modern history*
Commons' jn.	*Journals of the house of commons of Great Britain*
Commons' jn. Ire.	*Journals of the house of commons of Ireland*
Commons' reports (G.B.)	*Reports from committees of the house of commons* (Great Britain)
Customs	Customs papers in the Public Record Office of England
D.A.B.	*Dictionary of American biography*
D.N.B.	*Dictionary of national biography*
F.D.J.	*Faulkner's Dublin Journal*
Froude, *Ire.*	J. A. Froude, *The English in Ireland in the eighteenth century*
Lecky, *Ire.*	W. E. H. Lecky, *History of Ireland in the eighteenth century*
L.J.	*Londonderry Journal*
Lords' jn.	*Journals of the house of lords of Great Britain*
Lords' jn. Ire.	*Journals of the house of lords of Ireland*
M.T. Co. P.	Papers of the Merchant Taylors Company, London
M.T. Co. P.(T.)	Transcripts of the papers of the Merchant Taylors Company in the

	Public Record Office of Northern Ireland
n.d.	undated
Parliamentary Debates	*Parliamentary history of England from the earliest period to the year 1803*
P.C.	Privy council papers in the Public Record Office of England
Proc. and Trans. Roy. Soc. Can.	*Proceedings and Transactions of the Royal Society of Canada*
P.R.O.N.I., rep. D.K.	*Report of the Deputy Keeper of the Public Records of Northern Ireland*
P.R.O.N.I., D.	Deposited original documents in the Public Record Office of Northern Ireland
P.R.O.N.I., T.	Transcripts in the Public Record Office of Northern Ireland
R.S.A.I. Jn.	*Journal of the Royal Society of Antiquaries of Ireland*
Rec. gen. syn.	*Records of the general synod of Ulster*
Revill, S.C.	J. Revill, *A Compilation of the Original Lists of Protestant Immigrants to South Carolina 1763–1773*
Scot. Hist. Rev.	*Scottish Historical Review*
Scotch-Ir. in Amer.	*The Scotch-Irish in America; Proceedings of the Scotch Irish Congress*
S.P.	State Papers in the Public Record Office of England
Treasury	Treasury papers in the Public Record Office of England
T.S.P.I.	Transcripts in Public Record Office of Northern Ireland of state papers relating to Ireland
U.J.A.	*Ulster Journal of Archaeology*

CHAPTER I

The Background

THE desire to emigrate is no fundamental part of the natural make-up of man. Through the ties of home and family and through the love of familiar things and distrust or fear of the new, mankind as a whole tends to settle in a groove. As an anonymous eighteenth century author wrote, emigration 'is never produced . . . without great pangs and struggles'.[1] Nevertheless, two of the greatest motivating forces in human development have at times turned man's eyes from his native country and sometimes even from his friends and family. One of the minimum demands of man has always been personal economic stability, and economic advancement has been the goal of most. The religious appetite of man is no less potent a force than his physical appetite. Religious toleration is now regarded as the right of all in most countries and by most people: in the sixteenth and seventeenth centuries and, in a less militant form in the eighteenth century, the struggle for religious supremacy was a force which sometimes surpassed the economic as a rallying point of the people. At times the quest for a free conscience and a full stomach seemed unavailing in the homeland and the bold went far afield in search of their own green acres and their own God.

It follows that it is a truism to say that the religious and economic history of Ireland in the eighteenth century determined the heights and depths of Irish emigration of that period. An examination of this connection will be found later in these pages but it is relevant to paint first the scene against which was to be played the tragedy

[1] *Observations on the popery laws* [1771], pp. 52–3.

I

of emigration—a true tragedy for in it hope and despair inter-mingled.

Ulster which had been the despair of the Tudors became the stronghold of the Irish protestant interest and the British connec-tion under the Stuarts. This transformation was accomplished early in the seventeenth century by the plantation of part of Ulster, the most fertile lands of which passed by degrees into the hands of English and Scottish settlers leaving generally only the mountain-ous regions to the native Irish. As was to be expected, most of the people of this migration had been prompted to leave Scotland and England by 'poverty, scandalous lives, or . . . adventurous seeking of better accommodation' and their classification as 'the scum of the earth' was, doubtless, a harsh judgment of poverty and could be applied with equal justice to most migrations.[1]

The northern part of the Ulster settlement became more and more Scottish as the seventeenth century progressed, partly because of the proximity of the two countries and partly because of the greater sufferings of the Scottish presbyterians when compared with the lot of their co-religionists in Ireland.[2] Even after the driving force of persecution ended with the accession of William III, the movement from Scotland continued in order to take advantage of cheap Ulster lands which had been left tenantless after the campaigns of 1688 and 1689.[3] This seventeenth-century stream of Scottish immigrants, a stream that at times reached flood proportions and was seldom dry, left its mark on the character and outlook of the presbyterians of eighteenth century Ireland. To them, the tie of their adopted country was weak and the tradition of emigration strong. To many, the survival of the episcopal establishment and increasing economic distress in Ireland made their sojourn there appear as but a resting place on the journey to the land of promise. This tradition of emigration, as well as their locally superior numbers and their peculiar grievances, may partly

---

[1] See T. W. Moody, *The Londonderry plantation 1609-41. The city of London and the plantation in Ulster*; W. F. T. Butler, *Confiscation in Irish history*; J. S. Reid, *History of the presbyterian church in Ireland*, ed. J. W. Killen (2nd ed. 1853), i. 92–3; Rev. Andrew Stewart, *The history of the church of Ireland since the Scots were naturalised* (Supplement to Rev. Patrick Adair, *A true narrative of the rise and progress of the presbyterian church in Ireland, 1623-70*, ed. W. D. Killen (1866), pp. 315-21).
[2] Reid, *Pres. ch. Ire.*, ii.307-8; W. T. Latimer. *A history of the Irish presbyterians*, pp. 156-8.
[3] J. Harrison, *The Scot in Ulster*, p.87.

explain the preponderance of presbyterians among north Irish emigrants of the period studied.[1]

A second effect of a century of immigration from Scotland was, naturally, an increase in the strength of presbyterianism in Ireland. By 1640, 100,000 Scots and 20,000 English had settled in Ulster.[2] The 1641 rebellion greatly reduced those numbers but the renewal of settlement in Cromwellian and Restoration times compensated for the protestant losses and, in 1672, 100,000 Scots, concentrated in Ulster, and 200,000 English, scattered over the four provinces, were numbered among Ireland's 1,100,000 inhabitants.[3] The number of Scotch-Irish was further augmented by the thousands who fled from Scotland during the reigns of Charles II and James II and by the immigration into Ulster of about 50,000 Scots in the fifteen years which followed the victory at the Boyne. This immigration together with the approximate doubling in the number of presbyterian congregations between 1660 and 1715 would suggest that Ulster's population, numbering about 600,000 in 1715—out of a total Irish population of about 2,100,000— included about 200,000 presbyterians. Rather more than half the others were Roman Catholics and the remainder protestant episcopalians.[4] By 1715, however, Scotland had ceased to be a breeding ground for the Ulster settlement—by that time presbyterianism had triumphed in Scotland, the days of cheap land in Ulster were over and growing Scotch-American trade opened a more attractive outlet for Scottish dissidents.

Some indication has already been given of the causes of the preponderance of presbyterians among the emigrants from north

---

[1] See Chapter II.

[2] R. Bagwell, *Ireland under the Stuarts*, i. 241; Lord Ernest Hamilton, *The Irish rebellion of 1641*, p. 67; W. F. T. Butler, *Confiscation and plantation in Ireland*, p. 49. See also *Cal. S.P. Ire.*, 1660–2, p. 165.

[3] Sir Wm. Petty, *The political anatomy of Ireland* (1672), p. 7. This estimate of Ireland's population has been challenged as too low (*Transactions of the Royal Irish Academy*, iii. 145) and Petty himself raised his estimate to 1,300,000 (*A treatise of Ireland* (1687), p. 610 in *The economic writings of Sir William Petty*, ed. C. H. Hull). See also A. Dobbs, *An essay upon the trade and improvement of Ireland* (1729), pp. 409–18 in second volume of *A collection of tracts and treatises illustrative of the natural history, antiquities, and the political and social state of Ireland*, and Butler, op. cit., pp. 48–51.

[4] Ed. Synge, abp. of Tuam: B.M., Add. MS 6117, p. 50; Reid, *Pres. ch. Ire.*, iii, 2; cf. Hanna, *Scotch-Irish*, i., 620; C. Wyndham, Lord chancellor of Ireland, to Sir C. Yorke, 19 Jan. 1731/2, B.M., Add.MS 35585, p. 150; Nicholls, *History of the Irish poor law*, pp. 11–12; G. O'Brien, *Economic history of Ireland in the eighteenth century*, pp. 9–12; T. Newenham, *Statistical and historical enquiry into the magnitude of the population of Ireland*, pp. 309–10.

Irish ports in the sixty years which followed 1715 but it is relevant to isolate another cause of that preponderance now that it has been pointed out that the presbyterians formed a minority of the inhabitants of Ulster. The province was no citadel of presbyterianism unsullied by the presence of any substantial rival element and so it does not follow that emigration was necessarily presbyterian. It was not Ulster that was overwhelmingly presbyterian but those parts of Ulster which were served by the chief north Irish ports. Four of these ports—Londonderry, Portrush, Larne, and Belfast—lay in such districts, serving counties Londonderry and Antrim, the east of county Donegal and the north of county Down. The fifth port, Newry, served part of the remainder of Ulster and probably shared the bulk of Ulster's non-presbyterian emigrants with Sligo, Drogheda and Dublin and smaller ports on the western coast of county Donegal. It is clear that presbyterian emigration from Ulster was much greater than the comparative strength of the presbyterians in the province but, because of the isolation of non-presbyterian districts from the northern ports, the number of non-presbyterian emigrants from Ulster may have been greater than has been generally thought and was certainly greater than the number of non-presbyterians who emigrated through the five ports with which this investigation is concerned.

The rapid increase in the number of presbyterians in the north of Ireland was some guarantee of the permanency of the supremacy of the protestant interest in that region. That very guarantee reacted at times against the people who had helped to secure it, for complacency as to protestant strength led to the narrowing of protestant supremacy to the supremacy of the established church. Three phases of this process are apparent, each, significantly, following the reimposition of protestant control after a period of Roman catholic resurgence. With the initial success of the plantation ended the period when the episcopal authorities permitted the Scottish ministers to have their own churches and to collect tithes: Wentworth and persecution succeeded the broadminded Archbishop Ussher and the common perils of the first years of the plantation.[1] A quarter of a century later the presbyterians had reason to expect thanks from the restored Charles II for their loyalty to him during his travels and for their steadfastness against the onslaught of the native Irish counter-attack on the plantation.

[1] Reid, *Pres. ch. Ire.*, i. 98, 154–6.

4

The Background

Instead, presbyterian ministers were expelled from their churches and acts similar to those enacted in England were passed by the Dublin parliament and, ironically, relief came only with the measures of James II to help the Roman catholics.[1] The third testing time of the strength of the Ulster plantation came with the Glorious Revolution and then, too, the presbyterians fought no less bravely than their fellow protestants for the success of the Williamite cause. Yet the completeness of their victory led not to religious equality for Irish presbyterians but to the failure of the English government's attempt to secure more toleration for them and to the extension of the sacramental test to Ireland.[2] The 'zeal and steadiness' to the Hanoverians that was remarked of the presbyterians in 1715[3] was but a continuation of a century of faithfulness to the protestant interest in Ireland and yet even in 1718, the year in which large scale north Irish emigration to the American colonies began, the Irish presbyterians worshipped on suffrance and were excluded from all posts in the government they had helped to preserve.

The strength and compactness of the presbyterian *bloc* and the reality of the hold of the presbyterian church over the daily lives of its members had an important effect on both the attitude of the established church to toleration and on the volume of presbyterian emigration. On the one hand, many were convinced that the granting of toleration to such a body would be but the prelude to a presbyterian bid for supremacy.[4] On the other, just as coals burn more brightly when in contact with one another, so did resentment rise among the closely-knit and numerically dominant presbyterian congregations in north-eastern Ireland. If that resentment did not of itself produce emigration, it helped the waverers to make their decision and lived in many minds long after temporal hardships were forgotten. Emigration in such a community was likely to be as contagious as a fever in an insanitary town: it was liable to become a local epidemic if the minister sponsored it.

---

[1] *Cal. S. P. Ire.*, 1669–1670, pp. 149, 226, 242, 649; Reid, *Pres. ch. Ire.*, ii. 229; J. C. Beckett, *Protestant dissent in Ireland 1687–1780*, pp. 20–4.
[2] 2 Anne c.6 (Ireland); Beckett, *Prot. dissent in Ire.*, pp. 17–8.
[3] Wm. Conolly, speaker of the Irish house of commons to the lord lieutenant, 9 Aug. 1715 (T.S.P.I., T.448, p. 90). See also H. Lynn to Stanhope, 27 Dec. 1715 (ibid. p. 185). For a more detailed account of presbyterian disabilities see Chapter III.
[4] C. K. Bolton, *Scotch Irish pioneers in Ulster and America*, pp. 126–7; Beckett, *Prot. dissent in Ire.*, pp. 17–8.

Tradition has it that the Scotch-Irishman is noted for keeping the Sabbath and everything else he can lay his hands on. If so, economic conditions in Ireland were no more appealing to him than religious conditions during the century prior to the American Revolution.

Ireland's economic stability was effectively undermined in the half-century prior to 1715. It was to be expected that the prosperity and well-being of Ireland would have been the special concern of the English authorities. Ireland had not only the claims of a colony on England's goodwill but had the additional claim of a country whose safe-keeping was vital for England's defence. In the eyes of the Stuarts and the Hanoverians the most dependable weapon in that defence was the maintenance of protestant supremacy in Dublin, backed by a hard core of protestant yeomen. Yet it was in the second half of the seventeenth century, after the insecurity of protestant supremacy had been demonstrated, that the English and subservient Irish parliaments passed a series of acts which delivered Irish interests as a sacrifice to the English commercial and agricultural classes—measures which struck at least as hard against England's natural friends as they did against her natural enemies.[1] By 1715, the importation into Great Britain of all Irish livestock and livestock products except wool was forbidden as was the export from Ireland of raw wool or of any article of woollen manufacture to any country except England. Thus, within sight of the British shore, Ireland suffered from the mercantilist mentality more than did the American colonies three thousand miles beyond the Atlantic horizon. Though free to export linen goods and provisions to the colonies, she was, in practice, denied the privilege of inter-colonial trading, a privilege denied to no other British colony: she did not even enjoy with foreign countries the right to import non-enumerated goods from the American colonies. One instance, without comment, will suffice to illustrate the motive behind this 'two-pence halfpenny' attitude to empire and justify Ireland's bitterness against the restrictions. In 1715 the mayor and corporation of Bideford petitioned the king for measures to prevent the smuggling of wool from Ireland to France when

---

[1] 12 Car. II, c.4; 15 Car. II, c.7; 18 Car. II, c.2; 20 Car. II, c.7; 22 and 23 Car. II, c.26; 25 Car. II, c.6; 32 Car. II, c.2; 1 Wm. and Mary, c.32; 7 and 8 Wm. III, c. 22; 7 and 8 Wm. III, c.28; 10 and 11 Wm. III, c.10; 10 Wm. III, c.5 (Ire.). All except the last were English acts.

England was, by law, the only open market. With honest indignation his honour explained that such smuggling had so raised the
price of Irish wool that English merchants could not purchase it.[1]
More attention was paid to this and similar protests than to the
address of the Irish commons to Queen Anne in 1703 in which
members expressed their concern to discover 'by what methods
this country might be preserved from utter ruin'.[2] These laws were
modified in a few details as the eighteenth century progressed.
After a hard fight by the Earl of Carteret, then lord lieutenant, and
others, Ireland was granted permission to import non-enumerated
commodities from America.[3] Later, the importation into Britain
of woollen bay yarn and of most raw hides was permitted.[4] With
these exceptions, all the restrictions which have been mentioned
remained to cripple Irish trade till after the outbreak of revolution
in America.

The discouragement of cattle and sheep farming was eventually
beneficial to the rapidly increasing population of Ireland but the
restrictions on the manufacture of woollens had not even the
redeeming feature of unintentional benefit. Many of those engaged
in the woollen trade were protestant planters who had brought the
craft with them from Britain: the thirty thousand people whom
restrictions on the manufacture are said to have driven to emigrate
in the years before 1715 must have included many such non-Irish
subjects.[5]

By 1715 the Irish woollen manufacture was but a memory, yet its
ghost remained to haunt Ireland long after the body had departed.
The active discouragement of the woollen and other manufactures
led to a growing resistance to the absorption of Ireland's increasing
population. Only the manufacture of linen was tolerated and this
led in the north to an unhealthy dependence on that trade to

---

[1] T.S.P.I., T.448, p. 4 (20 Jan. 1714/5).
[2] *Commons jn. Ire.*, xvi. 389.
[3] 4 Geo. II, c.15 (Eng.); Memorial, Dublin merchants to Carteret, n.d. (C.O. 388/87,
pp. 28-9); Memorial, master wardens and brethren of Trinity guild, Dublin, recvd.
25 Feb. 1730/1 (ibid., pp. 52-3); Duke of Newcastle to—, 29 Nov. 1726 (P.R.O.
Index 8310, entry 46); Carteret to Ed. Southwell, 9 Dec. 1729 (B.M., Add.MS 38016);
B.T. representation to the King, 18 March 1730/1 (B.M., Add.MS 38497, pp. 15-6).
By 5 Geo. III, c.45, Ireland shared with parts of Europe the right to import American
lumber and iron.
[4] 12 Geo. II, c.21; 9 Geo. III, c.39; 14 Geo. III c.9. All were English acts.
[5] O'Brien, *Econ. hist. Ire. 18th cent.*, pp. 183-4. P. J. Temple, in the preface to O'Brien's
Pioneer Irish, states that, in 1689, 42,000 protestant families and 14 Roman catholic
families were engaged in the woollen trade (p. xii).

supplement the meagre profits of farming. The extent of the rise of the linen trade was a measure of the total extent of the rise of industry in the north of Ireland: when this single line of economic defence was breached, poverty swept over a land which had gambled its security on that defence. A second industry would not have prevented a linen decline but it would have lessened the effects of that decline.

The linen industry was allowed to prosper in Ireland 'since it can be of no prejudice to Great Britain and . . . is in a manner all that is left to Ireland and ought therefore to be encouraged as much as possible'.[1] Permission rather than encouragement was given by the English government in the eighteenth century, encouragement being reserved for the developing English and Scottish branches of the trade. The burden of giving practical assistance to the establishment and development of the linen manufacture fell on the Irish tax-payer. A linen board was set up in 1711 and, through bounties, aided the importation of flaxseed and the perfection of technical skill till after the opening of the American Revolution. The total sum spent on encouraging the linen industry in this way between 1700 and 1775 was over one and a quarter million pounds, most of which went to the north, the main seat of the Irish linen manufacture. This policy achieved its desired end, for the annual value of Irish exports of linen cloth and yarn rose from an average of £270,752 in the period 1715–19 to £1,467,294 in the period 1766–70. Throughout most of the eighteenth century linen exports comprised about half the total value of Ireland's exports.[2]

Thanks mainly to the impetus given by the settlement of Louis Crommelin and other Huguenot weavers in county Antrim, the linen manufacture became most firmly rooted in the northern counties of Ireland though the linen board encouraged it equally in all parts of the country. As early as 1728 the northern counties were spoken of as 'the seat of [the Irish] linen manufacture' and by 1770 that area produced more than four-fifths of the total quantity of linen marketed in Ireland.[3]

---

[1] Sunderland to Stanhope, 4 June 1715 (T.S.P.I., T.448, p. 51).
[2] C. Gill, *The rise of the Irish linen industry*, pp. 72–3, 94, 178; A. Young, *A tour in Ireland: with observations on the present state of that kingdom* (2nd ed. 1780), ii. 212; *Commons' jn. Ire.*, xvi. 405–8; Lords justices to lord lieutenant, 23 Nov. 1728 (P.C. 1/48).
[3] Hugh Boulter, abp. of Armagh, to Newcastle, 23 Nov. 1728. (*Boulter letters*, i. 210); Gill, *Irish linen industry*, pp. 160–1. Only about one-third of the Irish exports of linen in 1773 took place through north Irish ports (Young, *Tour*, ii. 180). This apparent

The linen industry was still a cottage industry at the time of the American Revolution, though capitalism had by then obtained a foothold in it. Linen weaving in the north of Ireland was in the hands of about 35,000 people of whom about 10,000 were employed by large or small manufacturers. Weaving and farming shared the energies of the remainder, to the detriment of the latter occupation in Young's opinion.[1] A pamphleteer of 1760 who described the effect of the growth of the linen industry did not share Young's view. He wrote,

> The north of Ireland began to wear an aspect entirely new; and from being (through lack of industry, business, and tillage) the almost exhausted nursery of our American plantations, soon became a populous scene of improvement, traffic, wealth, and plenty; and is at this day a well-planted district, considerable for numbers of well-affected, useful, and industrious subjects.[2]

Yet linen, seemingly poverty's cure, brought hardship in its wake—hardship on which the emigration trade was to thrive. The greater margin of security promised by an additional income from linen was nullified by increased rents. One sentence from a letter serves to blast the fantasy of linen as the salvation of the north. 'Should the linen manufacture decline', wrote an observer from the Merchant Taylors' lands in county Londonderry, 'be assured many parts of the proportion will not stand at the rents they now pay'. As a Newry writer put it in 1774 'the price of land . . . kept pace with the linen manufacture to the summit.'[3] Non-linen workers had to compete for land with those who combined the linen manufacture with farming and so the price of all land rose

---

contradiction of what has been said can be explained in two ways. First, Dublin was the commercial capital of Ireland and linen was by far the largest single Irish export and so it is reasonable to suppose that the Dublin factors did not confine themselves to the southern market towns. Second, 1773 was a year of depression in the linen trade and stocks in the hands of the Dublin merchants were ten times more than normal. (Infra, Chapter V). A more accurate guide to the distribution of the linen trade is the amount of flaxseed imported into the various ports. Of the 39,344 hogsheads of flaxseed imported into Ireland during the year ended March 1773, 28,524½ entered through the ports of Belfast, Coleraine, Londonderry and Newry (Customs, 15/76).

[1] Gill, op. cit., p. 162; Young, *Tour*, ii. 305.
[2] *Ancient and modern state of Ireland* (1760), pp. 49–50.
[3] J. McAlester to —, Coleraine, Mar. 1758 (M.T.Co. P., Box 126, no. 33); *Commons' jn. Ire.*, xvi. 41–7.

in linen districts. When the progress of the linen manufacture was halted, even if only for a year or two, rents absorbed much more than an economical share of the proceeds of farming, and poverty resulted.

Not only were fluctuations in the linen trade partly responsible for emigration from the north of Ireland to the American colonies but, ironically, the growth of that trade provided means of emigration for those who desired to go to America. By 1775, flaxseed was by far the principal north Irish import from America. In 1768, one of the last of the normal years prior to the great boom and temporary collapse of the linen trade in the early 'seventies, flaxseed comprised half the value of Irish imports from the American colonies, including Newfoundland, Bahamas, and Bermuda.[1] As most of this flaxseed was imported into the north of Ireland, that item must have accounted for about three-quarters of the total exports from America to the north Irish ports. Thus a regular trade was established between America and the north of Ireland and year by year the flaxseed fleets from Philadelphia and New York anchored in the five north Irish ports in the early spring. Linen goods were the chief cargo on the return journey to America. For example, in the financial year 1772, linen goods comprised two-fifths of the value of Belfast's total exports to the colonies and eleven-twelfths and five-sixths of those of Newry and Londonderry, respectively.[2] With the substitution of linen goods for bulky flaxseed there was ample space for emigrants in the outgoing vessels.

Rising rents had such important effects on eighteenth century Ulster that they call for much more than the passing reference which has been made to them. One effect of the Williamite wars was the letting of the decimated lands of the north on easy leases.[3] Unfortunately, most of the leases were for terms of only

---

[1] B.M., Add. MS 15485, pp. 30–2. The total Irish imports were £60,278. 12s. 3d., those of flaxseed being £29,508 14s. Ireland possessed a virtual monopoly of the American flaxseed trade for, in 1768, the value of the flaxseed exported to countries other than Ireland was only £2,080. 14s. 1d.

[2] Customs, 15/76. The approximate figures were:

Belfast	:	linen exports £2,500	:	other exports £6,500.
Newry	:	linen exports £6,500	:	other exports £600.
Londonderry	:	linen exports £6,000	:	other exports £1,200.

[3] Abp. Boulter to bp. of London, 13 March 1728/9 (*Boulter letters*, i. 233). In a rent roll of 1694 of the manor of St John Baptist in the Merchant Taylors' proportion in county Londonderry, the rentals of three farms are entered thus:

twenty-one or thirty-one years. Before these terms expired, settled conditions, heavy immigration from Scotland and the improvements which had been made during the period of the leases served to drive rents upward, a trend which continued for over a century and a half with few respites. The experience of the inhabitants of the Mercers' proportion in county Londonderry was typical of what was happening in at least those parts of the north of Ireland for which details of rents are available. The proportion was let not to the immediate tenants but to the Jackson family of Coleraine in 1663 for an annual rent of £300, together with an initial fine of £500. The records of the neighbouring Merchant Taylors' proportion indicate that the value of these lands in 1695 was about what it was in 1663, the improvements made in the interval being balanced by the fall in the value of land during and after the wars. By 1714 the lease of the Mercers' proportion was renewed to the Jacksons for 37 years, the rent rising to £420 and the fine to £6,000. In other words, under the 1663 lease, the average annual rent was £310: in 1714 it rose to £582.[1] Such a rise would be reflected, at least as sharply, in the rents paid by the under-tenants.

Rising rents are not *per se* a proof of increasing poverty—indeed, they are normally an indication of prosperity—but rents in the north of Ireland increased during the eighteenth century at a pace which far out-distanced the growth of productivity and the prices obtained for farm produce. It will be suggested that rents quintupled in parts of the area during the half-century prior to the American Revolution[2] but the *Belfast News Letter* reports of the prices of wheat and oats—the main crop of the north of Ireland— reflect no corresponding rise. There is no indication of the development in the north of Ireland before 1775 of an increasingly efficient husbandry that would have produced heavier yields to compensate for this lag in prices. Indeed, Young found in districts where the linen manufacture was carried on that concentration on linen and the resulting reduction in the size of farms had caused such a

---

'£8. 10s. this is worth if it were lett to best advantage £20 p.Ann.
    £30   these lands were lett before the Warr for £52
    £13   were worth before the troubles £21'.
(M.T.Co.P. (T), T.656, no. 40).
[1] J. W. Kernohan, *Two Ulster parishes: Kilrea and Tamlaght O'Crilly*, p. 19.
[2] See Chapter V.

decline in farming efficiency that the occupiers scarcely deserved the name of farmers.[1] The rise of the linen industry as an appendix to farming in the north of Ireland is explained, in some measure, by the greater profits that were to be derived from this combination than from orthodox farming, but, in the linen industry also, there was no spectacular rise either in efficiency or in prices. Between 1710 and 1770, for example, the average price of Irish linen cloth advanced by only twenty per cent.[2] The nearest approach to a balance between the gross profits of farming and the rising rents was to be obtained by concentrating on the cultivation of flax which offered more than twice the proceeds of other crops. The realisation of this fact caused a gradual increase in the amount of flaxseed and a fall in the quantity of undressed flax imported into the north of Ireland, but the severity of flax on the soil and the growing of other crops for family subsistence on the small and largely self-supporting farms limited the extension of an obviously beneficial rearrangement of cropping.[3]

One of the chief reasons for the relatively small rise in the cost of provisions was the continuing lowness of wages. An eighteenth century writer stated that wages in Ireland did not rise between the time of Elizabeth and the middle of the eighteenth century.[4] In the quarter-century that followed they advanced little. A correspondent of the *Belfast News Letter* estimated that they increased by five per cent. during that period, and he had no reason to minimise the figure for he was concerned with defending the rise in the cost of provisions. Certainly, a comparison between the daily wage of nine pence offered to a labourer in 1756 and sixteen pence offered to a journeyman tailor in 1775 does not indicate that, in the interval, the ability to pay higher prices for food kept pace with the increase in rents.[5]

Eighteenth century rents in the north of Ireland were forced to unreasonable heights by keen competition for land. The influx of Scots after 1691 and the resurgence of Roman catholic competition

[1] *Tour*, ii. 101. Young's statement that five or six acres was considered 'a good farm' in the north of Ireland was supported by a writer at the beginning of the nineteenth century when it was observed that the average size of farms in county Londonderry was between five acres and twenty acres, before sub-leasing (G. V. Sampson, *Statistical survey of the county of Londonderry*, p. 249).
[2] *Commons' jn. Ire.*, xvi. 396; D. Macpherson, *Annals of commerce*, iii. 515.
[3] Young, *Tour*, ii. 295–6.
[4] Hamilton, *Earliest times*, p. 317.
[5] B.N.L., 24 Dec. 1772, 18 June 1756, 12 May 1775.

for land[1] after the first sharp blast of the penal days forced rents up to the margin of subsistence, leaving that margin more then ever at the mercy of the seasons. It did not take extraordinarily bad seasons to produce poverty. The shortness of leases continually adjusted the balance between rents and demand for land so finely that the 'least accident' in the harvest was sufficient to produce 'little less than a famine every other year'.[2] Those who gambled on linen profits to meet rising rents merely gave another hostage to fate and added the caprice of trade to the uncertainty of nature.

Rents, prices and wages formed a mighty triumvirate in determining the extent of north Irish emigration. The growing gap between rents and prices weighed heavily on the farming class and was an ever present incentive to emigrate. On the other hand, the failure of prices in normal times to accompany rents in their rapid ascent was a boon to the labouring class and helped to retain that class in the homeland. In time of scarcity the roles were reversed. Poor crops meant unemployment to many labourers and dearer provisions slashed the real wages of those who continued to be employed. The farmer at such times generally managed to subsist by continuing to weave his linen and produce sufficient food for his own family. Scarcities did not ease his lot but they did not burden him so heavily as they did the labourer. During normal times, the farming class formed the bulk of Ulster emigrants but during periods of shortage the lead was taken by the labouring poor.

The effects of rack-renting would have been partially off-set had a considerable part of the proceeds been spent locally. Unfortunately, as much Irish land was in English ownership, the proportion of rents transferred abroad was abnormally high.[3] In 1729 it was

[1] Roman catholic tenants were preferred by many landlords because of their apparent docility and their willingness to offer high rents in their anxiety to repossess part of the land. 'Popish tenants are daily preferred, and protestants rejected, either for the sake of swelling a rental or adding some more duties which protestants will not submit to' (1745 pamphlet, in Hanna, *Scotch-Irish*, i. 622). A similar opinion was held by William King, archbishop of Dublin, who wrote, 'The papists will always outbid a protestant . . . most of the farms of Ireland are got into their hands, and as leases expire, it is probable the rest will go the same way' (to abp. of Canterbury, 2 June 1719, C. S. King, *A great archbishop of Dublin*, pp. 301–2). Further references to the pressure of population will be found in Chapter III.
[2] Boulter to Carteret, 20 July 1727 and to Newcastle, 25 May 1728 (*Boulter letters*, i. 151, 194).
[3] Young, *Tour*, ii. 190.

estimated that about £600,000 was transmitted abroad each year, a sum equal to about one-third of the total rents in Ireland[1] and that figure doubled in half a century.[2] Absenteeism was denounced by all classes except the absentees themselves. Townshend, when lord lieutenant, believed that it was one of the main causes of Irish poverty and that emigration was partly due to the 'absence of the nobility and gentry whose incomes are drained from hence'.[3] Arthur Young lamented that many Irish landlords knew nothing more about their lands other than the remittance of their rents.[4] The Hearts of Steel, rising in protest in the 'seventies against ever-rising rents, denounced those landlords who went abroad in search of luxury and lavished away the sweat of thousands of tenants.[5] Irish anger against the absentees was epitomised in a newspaper comment of 1771:

> So unfortunately is this poor country situated with respect to absentees that we are informed there are no less than one hundred and thirty six Irish families now at Bath, spending the product of thousands of poor people here; besides, the vast numbers in other parts of England, France, etc. Poor Ireland! how is it possible you should grow rich, or your manufacturers have employment.[6]

The effects on Ireland's economy of a system of absentee land-lordism which laid the country 'under a continual yearly pillage to vanity and luxury' and which successfully denied to the exchequer even the proceeds of a land tax are obvious,[7] but it would be wrong

---

[1] *Seasonable reflections* (1729), p. 25; [J. Swift], *An humble address to both houses of parliament*, in *The drapier's letters to the people of Ireland concerning Wood's halfpence*, ed. H. Davis, p. 156.

[2] Hely Hutchinson, *Commercial restraints*, p. 81. If this and the 1729 estimate are correct, it would follow that there was no increase in absenteeism in the intervening half-century as rents had at least doubled or trebled during that period. (See, Chapter VI.) For other estimates of the extent of absenteeism in the eighteenth century see Anon., *List of the absentees of Ireland* (1767); Young, *Tour*, ii. 194; and T. Prior, *A list of the absentees of Ireland and the yearly value of their estates and money spent abroad* (3rd ed., 1745).

[3] To Weymouth, 23 Nov. 1770 (S.P. 63/432, no. 53); to Rochford, 18 July 1773 (S.P. 63/440, no. 50). A Dr John Hothan writing from Dublin to Lord George Germaine spoke of absentees as 'Ireland's first and greatest enemies'. 1 Dec. 1777 (*Sackville MSS*, p. 248).

[4] *Tour*, ii. 194.

[5] Enclosure, Townshend to Rochford, 27 Mar. 1772 (S.P. 63/435, no. 63g).

[6] *B.N.L.*, 30 Jan. 1771.

[7] *List of the absentees of Ireland*, p. 30; Hunt, *Irish parliament*, pp. xxiii–xxv; O'Brien,

to lay at the door of the absentees a major share of the responsibility for emigration from Ulster. For one thing, absenteeism was much less common in Ulster than elsewhere in the country. Moreover, there is no evidence that, as a class, the agents of the absentees oppressed the people more than did resident landlords or their agents. The rack-renting of the earl of Donegall in the Belfast district is castigated as the worst example of the effects of absenteeism on the every-day lives of the people[1] but the discontent that culminated in the Hearts of Steel orginated in the oppressions of the resident Clotworthy Upton in south Antrim as much as in the oppressions of the absentee Donegall.[2] Again, one of the best landlords in eighteenth century Ulster was the first earl of Hillsborough who rebuilt the town of Hillsborough, encouraged the linen trade in the vicinity and was mainly responsible for the notable prosperity of the region, yet he was listed as one of the absentees 'who live generally abroad and visit Ireland occasionally, for a very short time'.[3] The effects of absenteeism on the social structure and the economy of Ireland were both great and detrimental but the Ulster tenant's hardships were, in part, the result of landlordism rather than absenteeism and were often due more to a rapacious land agent than to a landowner, whether he resided on his estate, in Dublin or in London.

A study of emigration embracing only accounts of discouragement and hardship would be deceptively ill-balanced. The forces which induce emigration are two-fold in character: as well as pressure from within a country there must be attraction from without, whether that attraction is a shining light in its own right or merely made so by the darkness of home conditions. Opinions as to the comparative influence of these factors have varied. On the one hand, it has been stated that conditions in Europe were chiefly responsible for European emigration to America: others have

---

Econ. hist. Ire., 18th cent., pp. 6-25. Details of the proposal to levy a tax of 2s. in the £ on the lands of absentees and of the agitation against it may be found in S.P. 63/437B, pp. 17-25 and in *The correspondence of King George III from 1760 to December 1783*, ed. Sir J. W. Fortescue, iii. nos. 1310, 1311, 1330, 1333, 1336, 1338-44.
[1] Townshend to Rochford, 15 Apr. 1772 (S.P. 63/435, nos. 82 a, b, c); *F.D.J.*, 11 Nov. 1773; *Public Journal*, 5 Aug. 1772.
[2] See Chapter V. W. F. Adams, *Ireland and Irish emigration to the New World from 1815 to the Famine*, p. 7; Young, *Tour*, ii. 194; Earl of Selkirk, *Highland emigration*, p. 20.
[3] Gill, *Irish linen industry*, p. 28; *List of the absentees of Ireland*, p. 7.

believed that it was the attraction of American conditions that induced European emigration.[1]

Forces inducing immigration into the American colonies as well as forces encouraging emigration from Great Britain and Ireland were at work in the eighteenth century. Some light is thrown on the influence of the attraction of America in that century by the replies of the port authorities in response to the order of 1773 requiring them to make weekly returns to the Treasury of the number of emigrants and the causes of their emigration. These returns show that of the 518 passengers who sailed in four vessels from Britain to Nova Scotia in 1774, 298 emigrated because of 'the desire to seek a better livelihood and employment.'[2] This reply implied a conscious comparison in the minds of the emigrants between conditions in Britain and those in America and shows that the latter consideration was at least as important as the former in inducing more than half of the passengers in the four vessels to emigrate. A similar conclusion may be drawn from the return of the port authorities of Wigtown who reported of their examination of emigrants that

> the only reason they gave for their emigration was that they were informed and understood they could live much better and with more ease in the country to which they were going than they could in this country. These persons and some others who had gone to north America having wrote letters to their relations and friends in this country advising of their beneficial settlements there, and of their having purchased for a trifling sum the property of a considerable extent of lands that produce plentifully the necessaries and comforts of life have raised a spirit of emigration amongst others of the like station in the country next to madness.[3]

Similar details of emigration from Ireland were not kept at any time in the eighteenth century but it is clear that shipping advertisements and letters from emigrants encouraged the people of the north of Ireland to think of a better land, even during periods when the pressure of poverty had temporarily ceased to give the most direct impetus to emigration. The activities of agents who, as early as 1729, were described as seeking to 'entice and ensnare

[1] I. Ferenzi, *International migrations*, ed. W. P. Willcox, i. 83; see Adams, *Irish emig. in 19th cent.*, p. 7.
[2] Treasury 47/9–12; see Chapter V.
[3] Treasury 1/500 (5 Jan. 1774).

the unwary people'[1] will be described later, as will be the actual conditions awaiting immigrants in the new heaven and the new earth across the Atlantic, but examples of shipping advertisements and emigrants' letters will serve to show the siege under which the ties of homeland were laid. An addendum was added to the advertisement of the *Hopewell*, which sailed from Londonderry to Nova Scotia in 1766. This declared:

'It would swell the advertisement to too great a length to enumerate all the blessings those people enjoy who have already removed from this country to said province, it may suffice to say, that from tenants they are become landlords, from working for others they now work for themselves, and enjoy the fruits of their own industry'.[2]

Three months later, the *Falls*, sailing from Belfast to Nova Scotia, called upon people to embrace

'such a favourable opportunity of settling themselves to advantage by a removal to that country, a removal which cannot fail to give freedom, peace, and plenty to those who now wish to enjoy those blessings, as well as secure the same in the highest degree for their posterity'.[3]

The whole spirit of such advertisements was summed up by the agents of the *Britannia* who, in announcing the date of the vessel's departure, declared that 'The ship, by the blessing of God, will then proceed on her intended voyage for the Land of Promise'.[4]

More convincing to the people than these eulogies were letters received from friends who had already emigrated. Many emigrants whose experiences had not been happy ones may have written with yearning of the land they had left but some shipmasters were, it was asserted, not averse to censoring the letters they carried and making sure that unfavourable reports of America never reached their destinations.[5] Newspapers and other documents of the time contain a tantalising abundance of allusions to letters that could not have failed to receive approval after such a scrutiny but, with few exceptions, they contain nothing more concrete than allusions. For this reason, a letter of 1737 from James Murray, an Ulster emigrant to New York, to a presbyterian minister in county

1 *Dublin Weekly Journal*, 7 June 1729.
2 B.N.L., 3 June 1766.
3 Ibid., 12 Aug. 1766.
4 Ibid., 14 April 1767.
5 Ibid., 22 Feb. 1774.

Tyrone is of more than usual interest.[1] Murray gave a most flattering description of New York and stressed, as did the shipping agents, the cheapness and fertility of American lands and the superiority of the American colonies over Ireland from the viewpoint of labourers and tradesmen. Though unusual in its survival, the letter was probably typical of thousands that brought unsettling news of prosperity to within hailing distance of most homes in the north of Ireland.

When emigrants arrived in America they may have found that conditions were not what shipping advertisements and letters from friends had led them to expect. It was, however, those romantic advertisements and letters that represented, in Ireland, the actuality of American life, and their brightness attracted eyes that hardship had dimmed.

[1] Crimmins, *Irish-American historical miscellany*, pp. 61–6.

CHAPTER II

The First Phase: 1718–1720

LITTLE emigration took place from the north of Ireland to the American colonies during Stuart times. The absence of sustained persecution and the abundance of land attracted Scottish immigrants to Ulster and tended to keep them there. Nevertheless, on two occasions a large-scale exodus seemed imminent. Under Wentworth, Ireland experienced some of the persecution that was helping to promote emigration from the neighbouring island and, in 1636, 140 persons, 'considering how precious a thing the public liberty of pure ordinances was', set out from Belfast lough for New England on board the *Eagle Wing*. Storms persuaded the would-be emigrants that their project had not divine favour and they returned to Ireland after having been more than half-way across the Atlantic.[1] It cannot be doubted that their failure had a profound influence on the spirit of emigration in the north of Ireland in the middle part of the century. The inclination to emigrate was in no way diminished by Wentworth's continued activities and by the terrible release of pent-up Irish anger that followed soon after the relief of his recall but, to the devout, the will of God had been clearly expressed in the *Eagle Wing* episode and the wrath of the sea had spoken to the scoffer with a no less certain voice. The success of the *Eagle Wing* would have been an encouragement to further emigration but its failure

[1] Exodus xix. 4. 'I bare you on eagles' wings, and brought you unto myself.' The *Eagle Wing* episode is described in Ford, *Scotch-Irish in Am.*, pp. 165–7; Hanna, *Scotch-Irish*, i. 562–3; Bolton, *Scotch Irish pioneers*, pp. 7–10; M. J. Murphy, 'Ulster settlers in America. Some of the early colonists—their service in the American revolution', in *U.J.A.*, ii. no. 1, p. 17 (1896).

acted as a deterrent during the decades that followed. During those same years, however, increasing trade with the colonies gradually minimised the terrors of the deep and usage made the Atlantic a pathway for women and children rather than a scene worthy only of the exploits of a Drake. Poverty and the renewal of episcopal aggression following the Restoration rekindled the spirit of emigration and from about 1680 a trickle of north Irish emigrants arrived in the American colonies. The movement was both small in extent and narrow in origin, being apparently mainly confined to the Laggan (co. Donegal) and Foyle valleys and directed to the lands bordering on Chesapeake bay.[1] Emigration acquired a firm hold over the minds of the ministers of the Laggan presbytery because of active persecution in the region[2] and of contacts the presbytery had with the American colonies. William Traill, the first presbyterian minister in America of whom there is certain knowledge, and Francis Makamie, 'the father of American presbyterianism', were members of the Laggan presbytery before they emigrated in the 'eighties.[3] Though specific reference was made during this period to Scotch-Irish settlements in Maryland, it is certain that the extent of emigration from Ulster was not comparable with the proportion of presbyterian ministers who emigrated, as many of the latter went to America without companions in answer to calls from settlers, whether Scots or Scotch-Irish, already there.[4] It would be impossible to ascertain with any degree of accuracy the number of north Irish emigrants prior to 1718 but they could probably be numbered in hundreds. Significantly, when laws discouraging the immigration of Roman catholics were passed in South Carolina in 1698 and in Maryland in 1704 and 1715, the laws excluded or imposed duties on the importation of all *Irish* servants without distinguishing protestant from Roman

---

[1] Ford, *Scotch-Irish in Am.*, pp. 170–81. Emigration was not, of course, confined to the one district nor did the emigrants go exclusively to the Chesapeake region. For example, James Logan, later William Penn's secretary, and other quakers emigrated from Lurgan to Pennsylvania (Murphy, *U.J.A.*, ii. no. 1, p. 18), and Irish were noted among the inhabitants of South Carolina in 1682 (Samuel Wilson, *Account of Carolina* (1682), in *North Carolina history told by contemporaries*, ed. H. T. Lefler, p. 29; Bolton, *Scotch Irish pioneers*, pp. 31–5; L. C. Gray, *History of agriculture in the southern United States to 1860*, i. 328).

[2] Reid, *Pres. ch. Ire.*, ii. 321–4; A. G. Lecky, *The Laggan and its presbyterianism*, pp. 19–23.
[3] Bolton, *Scotch Irish pioneers*, p. 21; G. S. Klett, *Presbyterians in colonial Pennsylvania*, p. 39.
[4] Bolton, *Scotch Irish pioneers*, pp. 21–8; Ford, *Scotch-Irish in America*, pp. 171–8.

catholic,[1] so suggesting that only a negligible minority, if any, of those servants were north Irish protestants.

A small number of people from the north of Ireland arrived at Boston between 1715 and 1717[2] but it was after the latter date that emigration rose to such a pitch that Macaulay wrote that the north-eastern counties of Ireland were almost drained of their protestant inhabitants in the half century that followed.[3] The first step was taken when a group of over 300 ministers and people from places as far apart as Cavan and Bushmills petitioned Samuel Shute, governor of New England, for a grant of land in that region. The negotiations were entrusted to William Boyd, presbyterian minister of Macosquin in county Londonderry, who crossed to Boston in 1718. Assurances of support were given by Shute who was to prove a steadfast friend of those who emigrated, encouraged by Boyd's reception. It is uncertain how many of the petitioners actually emigrated on Boyd's return but it is known that neither Boyd nor any of the eleven ministers who signed the petition did so.[4] In spite of this strange lack of response, Shute's assurances were not unavailing. On 31 October 1718 a petition for a grant of land was presented to the house of representatives of Massachusetts by James McGregor and Archibald Boyd—possibly related to William Boyd—on behalf of themselves and twenty-six others already arrived in Boston and forty more families who were about to emigrate from Ireland.[5] James McGregor had been presbyterian minister of Aghadowey in the Bann valley about six miles from Coleraine, the district in which lived the great majority of the signatories of the original petition to Shute. It is not known why he did not sign the first petition to Shute but he must have known of its existence and Shute's favourable response to it either induced him to emigrate or encouraged his already-formed resolution to do so.

Emigration was not confined to the Bann valley, for a similar

1 H. W. Farnam, *Chapters in the social legislation of the United States to 1860*, p. 56; J. C Hurd, *The law of freedom and bondage in the United States*, i. 251.

2 Bolton, *Scotch Irish pioneers*, pp. 317-9.

3 Quoted, Maude Glasgow, *The Scotch Irish in north Ireland and in the American colonies*, p. 157. No reference given.

4 Ford, *Scotch-Irish in Am.*, pp. 190-2; R. C. Mack, *The Londonderry* [N.H.] *celebration, 10 June 1869*, p. 124; Bolton, *Scotch Irish pioneers*, pp. 324-30, and T. Witherow, *Historical and literary memorials of presbyterianism in Ireland*, ii. 5-7.

5 *Journal of the house of representatives of Massachusetts*, 31 Oct. 1718. Biographical details of McGregor may be found in Bolton, *Scotch Irish pioneers*, pp. 106-8.

movement was taking place at the same time through the port of Londonderry. It has been suggested that it was through Robert Homes, the captain of a merchant vessel and the son of a presbyterian minister who had emigrated from Strabane in 1714, that the people of the Foyle valley learned of the opportunities of removing to New England.[1] Robert Homes may have contributed to this knowledge as did the activities of New England companies such as the Pejepscot company and the Lincolnshire proprietors,[2] but much about America must have already been known in the area because of the links forged between the Foyle presbyteries and American presbyterianism at the end of the seventeenth century. It has already been seen that presbyterian ministers acted as spokesmen for the Bann emigrants and they played a similar role in the case of the Londonderry emigration of 1718. James Woodside, a presbyterian minister, led one of the largest companies of emigrants —their numbers being variously stated as 100 and 160 persons[3]— to leave the north of Ireland in that year. These emigrants sailed from Londonderry in the *Maccullum* (or *McCallom*) and arrived in Boston in September 1718 only to leave a week later for Casco bay in Maine where Indians gave them a most unenviable time.[4]

It would be easy to exaggerate the number of emigrants from the north of Ireland to the American colonies between 1718 and 1720. For example, it has been stated that 6,800 Scotch-Irish immigrants landed at Boston in 1718.[5] Again, Thomas Lechmere, the surveyor-general of the customs at Boston, expected the arrival of twenty ministers with their congregations in the spring of 1719[6] and Cotton Mather, the leading New England divine of the time, mentioned in his diary in 1718 'the great number of people that are transporting themselves thither from the north of Ireland'.[7] The view that a really substantial movement of people occurred in the

[1] Ford, *Scotch-Irish in Am.*, pp. 189–90. Robert Homes later married the sister of Benjamin Franklin.
[2] R. H. Akagi, *The town proprietors of the New England colonies*, pp. 244, 245, 248, 259–61; Bolton, *Scotch Irish pioneers*, pp. 140, 219; S. S. Green, *The Scotch-Irish in America*, p. 11 fn.
[3] C.O. 5/848, f. 82; Petition, Woodside to the king, n.d. [c.1722] (C.O. 5/752).
[4] G. F. Donovan, *The pre-Revolutionary Irish in Massachusetts, 1620–1775*, p. 23; Akagi, op. cit., p. 259.
[5] I. F. Mackinnon, *Settlements and churches in Nova Scotia, 1749–76*, p. 29 fn.; Akagi, *The town proprietors of the New England colonies*, p. 269.
[6] To John Winthrop, his brother-in-law, n.d. [1718] in Ford, *Scotch-Irish in Am.*, p. 193.
[7] 7 Aug. 1718 (ibid.).

period is further strengthened by the fact that in 1719 Shute referred to the Massachusetts assembly the heavy charge falling on the New England authorities because of the immigration of 'poor people from abroad, especially those that come from Ireland'.[1]

The statement that 6,800 north Irish immigrants arrived at Boston in 1718 is readily disproved by the physical impossibility of such a number being carried by the shipping engaged in trade between the north of Ireland and New England. Four of the six vessels listed in the incomplete Boston port records as having arrived from Ireland during the year had left northern ports and one hundred immigrants arrived on each of two of them.[2] Boston newspapers show that fifteen vessels arrived from Ireland in 1718[3] and, if the port records that remain are a cross-section of the year's arrivals, it would appear that approximately one thousand north Irish people disembarked from ten vessels at Boston in 1718.

The statements of Lechmere and Mather were shaped by expectations as much as by events. When Lechmere wrote of the approaching immigration of twenty ministers he had certainly in mind Boyd's mission to Shute but not one of those ministers actually emigrated and the number of ships arriving in Boston from Ireland dropped from fifteen in 1718 to ten in 1719, the year of the expected influx of ministers and their congregations. A further thirteen vessels arrived from Ireland in 1720 and, even if conditions in 1719 and 1720 remained as in 1718, the number of emigrants carried in those three years from north Irish ports to New England probably did not exceed 2,600.[4]

Emigration during the period was not directed exclusively towards New England. Reference was made in 1720 to immigration into Pennsylvania and New York from the north of Ireland[5] and it

---

[1] *Journal of the house of representatives of Massachusetts.*, 4 Nov. 1719, ii. 174–5. See also ibid., 2 Dec. 1718, p. 104 and 4 Nov. 1719, pp. 172–3. op. cit., p. 269.
[2] C.O. 5/848, f. 65, *William and Elizabeth*, 40 tons, from Londonderry with passengers and provisions; f. 81, *William and Mary*, 30 tons, from Coleraine with passengers and provisions; f. 82, *Dolphin*, 70 tons, from Dublin with 34 servants; ibid., *McCallom*, 70 tons, from Londonderry, with 100 passengers and some linen; f. 83, *Mary and Elizabeth*, 45 tons, from Londonderry, with some linen and 100 passengers; ibid., *Beginning*, 30 tons, from Waterford with passengers and servants.
[3] Bolton, *Scotch Irish pioneers*, pp. 319–21.
[4] Bolton, *Scotch Irish pioneers*, pp. 321–3.
[5] J. F. Watson, *Annals of Philadelphia and Pennsylvania*, ii. 259; *Cal. S.P. Am. & W. Ind.*, 1720–1, p. 656.

has also been stated that five hundred north Irish settlers were placed at about this time on lands in South Carolina vacated by the Yamassee Indians.[1] Despite these indications that north Irish eyes were not fixed exclusively on Boston, it was to that port that most emigrants of the period sailed and when the lords justices of Ireland reported on emigration to the lord lieutenant, New England was the only part of America named in their report.[2]

The importance of this first period of emigration cannot be measured merely in terms of numbers. From the official viewpoint, the most alarming feature about it was that the emigrants were from a region 'well affected to his majesty's person and government' and events were to show that the damage done by the 1718–20 movement was much more serious than the loss of a few thousand protestants. The significance of 1718 is that, after the efforts and dashed hopes of close on a century, the flood gates of emigration were opened for the first time as an outlet for the distressed and discontented. For the first time, thousands of north Irish people had successfully transplanted themselves across the Atlantic: and had shown the tens of thousands of relations and friends they had left behind in the Bann and Foyle valleys that, for ordinary people like themselves, life in America was a practical alternative to life in Ireland.

It is usually obvious which of the two factors, religious or economic, was the more important in a particular episode of emigration. The would-be emigrants on board the *Eagle Wing* and their puritan contemporaries from England were more concerned with the urges of the soul than with the comforts of the body: religion did not motivate the Roman catholics who emigrated in the nineteenth century from countries such as Ireland, Italy and the south German states to the protestant United States of America. Often, however, there was an intermingling of motives. To the popular mind, the Pilgrim Fathers are the best known of all English emigrants who sailed to America in the name of religion. Their original emigration to Amsterdam in 1593 was undoubtedly inspired by religious sentiments but it was their poverty in a land

---

[1] *An historical account of the rise and progress of the colonies of South Carolina and Georgia* (1779), i. 229–30; E. Sanford, *A history of the United States before the Revolution*, p. 111. The proprietors reclaimed the grants and many of the Irish are stated to have perished and the remainder moved northward out of the colony.

[2] N.d. [1718], in Latimer, 'Ulster emigration to America', in R.S.A.I. *Jn.*, series 5, xii. 387.

ravaged by war that turned their eyes to the Virginia company and to Guiana and the Dutch West Indies. In fact, in order to placate possible hostility in England they were prepared to sacrifice one of their most vital independent tenets—the denial of the supremacy of the state in religious matters.[1]

Feeding the roots of the emigration movement in the north of Ireland were poverty and religious grievances. It is difficult to strike a balance between the relative importance of the two factors, not merely because of the changing circumstances in the half-century of extensive emigration but because of the conflicting views advanced by each of the various factions concerned—presbyterians, episcopalians and landlords—to further its own interest.

One thing is clear and that is that the vast majority of the north Irish emigrants to the American colonies were presbyterians. At both the beginning and the end of the period of heavy emigration, observers who were not presbyterians agreed on this point. William King, archbishop of Dublin, determined as he was to minimise the extent of presbyterian emigration in order that it should not be used as a lever against the test act, admitted the preponderance of presbyterians among the Irish emigrants, though he claimed that emigration among the other protestant denominations of the north was proportionally just as great as among presbyterians.[2] Writing a few years after the great climax of emigration of the 'seventies, Arthur Young stated that the spirit of emigration had been confined to the presbyterians.[3]

This has led some writers to the illogical conclusion that the emigrants left Ireland because they were presbyterians—that they emigrated because of the trials their faith was undergoing. To Hanna, the villains of the piece were the mitred gentry who enjoyed their ill-gotten tithes in the palaces of Ireland or languished in the pavilions of Bath.[4] To J. P. MacLean, the historian of the Scottish highlanders in America, the Irish presbyterian emigrants

---

[1] *C.M.H.*, vii. 12–13.
[2] King to Wm. Wake, abp. of Canterbury, 2 June 1719 (King, *A great abp.*, p. 302). The qualification was a contradiction of the main statement unless emigration was confined to counties Antrim and Londonderry where the presbyterians had an absolute majority.
[3] *Tour*, ii. 131.
[4] Hanna devotes 10 pages to an account of the religious causes of the presbyterian emigration, and 3 pages to the economic causes (*Scotch-Irish*, i. 614–21, ii. 172–5).

were 'martyrs for conscience sake', though he does add that 'there were other causes which assisted'.[1] F. J. Bigger, in a surprising remission from his battle against landlords, ancient and modern, wrote of these emigrants that 'It is quite evident that these pioneer colonists left on religious grounds, preferring to risk their lives in a new country, to exercise in the fullest extent their religious opinions, rather than live in Ireland, where their sect was not the dominant party.'[2]

Some colour is given to these conclusions by an episode at Coleraine in 1718 prior to the embarkation of part of the Aghadowey dissenting congregation under their minister, James McGregor, at the beginning of what was to be the first large settlement of Scotch-Irish in America. The gravity of such an occasion naturally called for explanation and this McGregor gave in a farewell sermon. Friends and native land were to be left behind by the emigrants who sought thereby to avoid oppression and cruel bondage, to shun persecution and designed ruin, to withdraw from the communion of idolators and to have an opportunity of worshipping God according to the dictates of conscience and the rules of His inspired Word.[3] To the emigrants, the wilderness had become an ocean and Moses an Ulster-Scot.

McGregor's sermon was a parting broadside at episcopacy rather than a reasoned evaluation of the motives that had inspired his followers to emigrate to America. By 1718, the days were gone when the doors of presbyterian churches were nailed and presbyterian ministers imprisoned in Ireland. The accession of the Hanoverians in 1714 had not only laid low Tory supremacy in England but had delivered the Irish presbyterians from the hands of their spiritual enemies. The Irish presbyterians had shown more enthusiasm for the Hanoverians than had the Irish episcopalians[4]

---

[1] *An historical account of the settlements of the Scotch Highlanders in America prior to the peace of 1763*, p. 45.
[2] In a note on the article by M. J. Murphy, 'Ulster settlers in America', in *U.J.A.*, ii. no. 1. Similar views are expressed in Mack, *Londonderry celebration*, p. 17; W. A. Carrothers, *Emigration from the British Isles with special reference to the development of the British dominions*, p. 2; E. McCrady, *The history of South Carolina under the royal government*, p. 314; Glasgow, *Scotch Irish*, p. 134.
[3] E. L. Parker, *Londonderry* (N.H.), p. 34; T. Witherow, *Presbyterian memorials*, ii. 2.
[4] Lords justices to the earl of Stanhope, 26 Jan. 1716 (T.S.P.I., T. 448, p. 208); R. Mant, *History of the church from the revolution to the union of the churches of England and Ireland*, p. 275; Reid, *Pres. ch. Ire.*, iii. 106.

and in return, the English whigs restored and enlarged the *regium donum* and abandoned the attempt that had been made in the reign of Anne to enforce an abjuration oath in which a few sensitive ears detected an anti-presbyterian ring.[1] Though it was not till 1719 that legal toleration was granted to the Irish protestant dissenters,[2] toleration had been an actual fact for the preceding five years: toleration was as wide in Aghadowey when McGregor left in 1718 as it was after the toleration act reached the statute book in the following year. The merely confirmatory nature of the toleration act explains, in part at least, the surprising inaction and apparent indifference of the presbyterian church in the events which led up to it. Indeed, the presbyterians were by now becoming more concerned with dissensions within their church rather than with attacks from outside.[3]

It is informative to compare with those of McGregor the reasons given by another presbyterian minister for his decision to emigrate from the north of Ireland to America in 1720. In that year Isaac Taylor, the minister of Ardstraw, asked the presbytery of Strabane for permission to leave his congregation as he wished to settle in America. There was considerable opposition to his request, both from the presbytery and from his congregation, so it is significant that the most weighty reason he could offer was not persecution, great or petty, but 'the want of a necessary support at Ardstraw'. Such want in Ardstraw was not confined to the minister as he had already agreed to take other emigrants with him. Had the current wave of emigration been motivated by religious unrest, one would have expected the Strabane presbytery to sympathise with a soul that would not be chained: instead, reluctant and conditional permission was given to Taylor and a vote of censure was passed

---

[1] Beckett, *Prot. dissent in Ire.*, pp. 64–71.

[2] 6 Geo. I, c.5 (Ire.). The main provisions of the act were to permit worship in protestant dissenting churches and the celebration of the sacrament of the Lord's Supper by protestant dissenting ministers who adhered to the doctrine of the Holy Trinity. The conditions attaching to the toleration were not such as would have offended the presbyterians. An oath of allegiance was to be taken, together with an oath of abjuration of the pretender and an oath of abjuration of the papal power to depose sovereigns, and a declaration against doctrines such as transubstantiation had to be signed.

[3] Beckett, *Prot. dissent in Ire.*, pp. 76, 78; abp. King to abp. Wake of Canterbury, 2 June 1719 (Mant, *Church of Ireland*, pp. 333 ff); Rec. gen. syn., i. 539–40; Allen, R. *Scottish ecclesiastical influence upon Irish presbyterians from the non-subscription controversy to the union of the synods*, pp. 41 ff.; Reid. *Pres. ch. Ire.*, iii. 155 ff.

against his undertaking.[1] The debate over Taylor's plans is more convincingly objective than McGregor's sermon. The latter was intended to be heard in Dublin and London, while Taylor's case was confined to the ears of the presbyterian ministers and elders of the Strabane presbytery. Moreover, direct evidence that sheer want drove some presbyterian ministers to America is to be found in the records of the general synod of the presbyterian church. In a letter addressed to the presbyterian people in 1720, in which the synod appealed for financial support for the ministers of the church, it was stated that 'It is melancholly to hear that many of our Brethren are wanting ev'n the necessaries of life; others are forc'd to lay down their charge; and others to transport themselves to America.'[2]

McGregor's charges may be challenged by an examination of the actual position of presbyterians but even surer grounds for doubt are supplied by a survey of the state of economic life in the Aghadowey district at the time of the emigration. McGregor had not found life there easy and, like Taylor, had found a 'necessary support' lacking. The arrears due to him by his congregation, prior to his departure for America, were proved to be over eighty pounds, but the congregational funds in 1719, before any settlement of this debt was made, were but a single shilling.[3] Such a state of affairs was symptomatic of the difficult times that had been the lot of the emigrants during their last two or three years in Aghadowey. In common with the rest of the north of Ireland, they had experienced a series of crop failures and other blows at the hands of nature. Between 1715 and 1720 a series of natural calamities

[1] Minutes of the presbytery of Strabane, 6 April, 27 May, 1 August 1720. Taylor returned to Ireland, as the presbytery had insisted that he should do, in 1722 (ibid., 1 Aug. 1722), and joined the established church seven years later (ibid., 10 June 1729). A rather different picture of Taylor as an emigrant was given in a letter from one Ezekiel Stewart of Portstewart to judge Michael Ward of Bangor: 'The Presbiteirin ministers have taken their shear of pains to seduce their poor Ignorant heerers, by Bellowing from their pulpits against ye Landlords and ye Clargey, calling them Rackers of Rents and Scruers of Tythes . . . . . . There are two of these Preachers caryed this affair to such a length that they went themselves to New England and caryed numbers with them, their names are Cornwell & Taylour, ye first minister of Clougher and ye latter minister of Astraw both in ye County of Tyrone, but these gentlemen not finding their acct in ye project, returned themselves but left their Cargoes behind . . . . . .'. (25 March 1729, in J. Stevenson, *Two centuries of life in Down 1600–1800*, pp. 237–8).
[2] *Rec. gen. syn.*, i. 530.
[3] Aghadowey session book, 29 April 1719.

intensified the effect of the restrictions on Irish economy that were, for a century, a millstone round the country's neck. Those five years were spanned by a drought that ruined crops and farmers and drove the price of food far above the means of many of the poorer people. The worry caused by these events besieged the minds, while small-pox and other diseases laid claim to the bodies of the people with uncommon insistence.[1]

On top of these trials came rising rents, the *coup de grâce* for many who were already flinching beneath their burdens. Aghadowey formed part of the Clothworkers proportion which had been leased to Richard Jackson of Coleraine. The leases of some, but not all, of the farms in seventeen townlands of the proportion expired in May 1717 and Jackson took the opportunity to increase rents with the result that the total rental of these townlands rose from £200. 10s. to £234. 10s. A rise of one-sixth may not seem startling, but it must be remembered that times were bad and that the increase in the case of the farms for which new leases were granted was much greater than one-sixth as the rental includes many leases that did not expire in 1717. A more accurate idea of the extent by which rents were increased when leases expired is gained from the fact that the total rental of the Clothworkers proportion rose from £528. 7s. in 1716 to £1,002. 16s. 6d. in 1736 by which time most of the seventeenth century leases—but few of the post-1716 ones—had expired. The rental of the proportion had, therefore, approximately doubled in the course of one turnover of leases.[2] McGregor stressed religious disabilities as the mainspring of the Aghadowey emigration but an observer informed the Clothworkers and Merchant Taylors companies that 'one reason they give for their going is the raising of the rent of the land to such a high rate that they cannot support their families thereon with the greatest industry'.[3] In the view of a later secretary to the Irish Society, the effect of Jackson's action in raising his rents was to produce 'an almost total emigration'.[4] The thoughts of the Aghadowey

---

[1] T. Meldycott to E. Southwell, 3 Apr. 1721 (B.M., Add. MS 34778); Lords justices of Ireland to Stanhope, 20 Jan. 1715/6 (T.S.P.I., T. 448, p. 202); Rutty, *Weather and seasons*, p. 12; Bolton, *Scotch Irish pioneers*, pp. 43–4.

[2] M.T.Co.P. (T.), T.656, nos 44 and 57. Cf. Jos. Marriott to —, 25 Apr. 1718. '. . . [on Jackson's land] severall Farms have been raised to double some treble the value they were of before the Revolution' (M.T.Co.P. Box 126, bundle 33).

[3] Jos. Marriott, 12 Aug. 1718 (M.T.Co.P. Box 126, bundle 16).

[4] R. Slade, *Narrative of a journey to the north of Ireland in the year 1802*, p. 57.

emigrants were probably on the Jackson mansion while McGregor denounced more remote gentlemen.

This early phase of emigration was not confined to Aghadowey nor was Jackson the only landlord who raised his rents. King believed that rents had doubled or trebled in 'most places' in the north of Ireland and attributed emigration to oppression by 'excessive rents and other temporal hardships'.[1] King was not an unprejudiced observer but the evidence that has already been detailed concerning the Aghadowey emigration supports his conclusion, as do Swift's references to rents. He declared in 1720 that 'the screwing and racking of tenants has reduced the people to worse conditions than Poland';[2] and it was probably he who had written four years earlier, '[The people] have already given their bread, their flesh, their butter, their shoes, their stockings, their beds, their house furniture and houses to pay their landlords and taxes. I cannot see how any more can be got from them, except we take away their potatoes and buttermilk, or flay them and sell their skins.'[3]

The meeting-house certificate carried by a Cork quaker who sailed to Pennsylvania in 1710 is of some importance in showing the weight of the economic factor in Irish emigration of the period. The certificate stated that the motives for this individual emigration were high rents and the difficulty of supporting a family in Ireland.[4] It is dangerous to generalise from a particular case but the prominence given in the certificate to the influence of rents is significant as one would have expected some reference to the religious factor. Quakers were, if anything, rather less favoured than the other Irish protestant dissenters in early Hanoverian times[5] and could anticipate a welcome in Pennsylvania, particularly if they entered the colony as people who had sacrificed home and homeland rather than capitulate to religious tyranny.

Large-scale emigration of Irish presbyterians did not commence till after the dawn of a better day for their church but it would be

[1] To abp. of Canterbury, 2 June 1719 (King, *A great abp.*, p. 302).
[2] *Proposal for a universal use of manufactures*, p. 25.
[3] *Hist. MSS. Comm.*, 2nd report, p. 257.
[4] A. C. Myers, *Immigration of the Irish quakers into Pennsylvania, 1682–1750, with their early history in Ireland*, p. 48.
[5] See A. Fuller and T. Holms, *A compendious view of some extraordinary sufferings of the people called quakers, both in person and substance, in the kingdom of Ireland; from the year 1655 to the end of the reign of King George I* (1731).

unwise to dismiss lightly the religious aspect of the movement. Man may normally be a rational creature but—in the north of Ireland at least—he may often be irrational in matters concerning religion. Even to-day there is a latent suspicion between the presbyterian and episcopalian churches, a suspicion that might have deepened into hostility but for the fear of both of weakening the protestant interest against the Roman catholic element. Almost a century after the disestablishment of the episcopal church it is only too evident that the past is not entirely forgiven or forgotten: how much greater must have been presbyterian resentment when all that had been granted was a legal toleration of worship, and that against the bitter opposition of the majority of the prelates,[1] and while presbyterians were still barred from public posts, while their schools were illegal, and while the validity of their marriages was challenged in the ecclesiastical courts. These disabilities were of practical consequence to few presbyterians but they branded all presbyterians with the mark of inferiority. Of itself, such resentment would not have caused emigration but, when the poverty of a known life and the hopefulness of an unknown life were being weighed in the balance, it may have in many cases tipped the balance in favour of a new world where presbyterians could worship in liberty rather than on sufferance.

---

[1] When the bill came up for the third reading in the lords, Abp. Lindsay, the primate, concluded his speech against it by 'assuring their lordships that schism was a damnable sin' (E. Webster, Irish secretary, to Delafay, 22 Oct. 1719, T.S.P.I., T.519, p. 230). Of the nine bishops who voted against the final reading, seven were natives of Ireland: of the seven bishops who voted for it, only one was an Irishman and possibly another whose identity is unknown (*Lords' jn. Ire.*, ii. 663); Beckett, *Prot. dissent in Ire.*, p. 77; Reid, *Pres. ch. Ire.*, iii. 151). The bitterness of the opposition to the bill can be judged from Abp. King's despair after its passage: 'The bill could not have passed if our brethren that came to us from your side of the water, had not deserted us and gone over to the adverse party. I fear we shall all feel the effects of it; and, in truth, I can't see how our church can stand here, if God do not, by a peculiar and unforseen providence, support it' (Abp. King to Abp. Wake, 10 Nov. 1719, in Mant, *Church of Ireland*, p. 337, and King, *A great archbishop*, p. 220). See also T.S.P.I., T. 519, pp. 146, 147, 149, 153, 172.

CHAPTER III

Religion and Emigration: 1721–1730

AFTER an apparent lull, north Irish emigration on a considerable scale resumed about 1724, though it was now directed mainly to Newcastle and Philadelphia and not to the New England ports. Early in 1725, James Logan, the secretary of Pennsylvania, noted a growth in the number of Scotch-Irish in that colony.[1] Three years later it was reported that 20,000 people had declared their intention of emigrating from the north of Ireland in 1729.[2] By 1730 the force of this second phase of the movement was spent and the volume of emigration declined even more rapidly than it had risen six years previously.

Five thousand people, including 3,500 from Ulster, are said to have landed in America from Ireland between 1725 and 1727.[3] The records on which these figures are said to have been based are unspecified but the Irish total is a reasonable one, though possibly on the high side. Hugh Boulter, the primate of Ireland, numbered Irish emigrants in 1726 and 1727 at 1,100[4] but this estimate was certainly too low though Boulter had no reason for deliberately under-estimating the extent of emigration as his purpose was to impress on the English authorities the seriousness of the problem. The arrival of eight or nine vessels with Irish immigrants at Newcastle in 1727[5] would suggest that close on one thousand

---

[1] Logan papers, *Letter books*, ii. 247 (Klett, *Pres. in Pa.*, p. 32).
[2] Lords justices of Ireland to lord lieutenant, 23 Nov., 1728 (P.C.2/91, p. 401).
[3] W. H. G. Flood, 'Irish emigration to the American colonies, 1723–73', in *Amer. Ir. Hist. Soc. Jn.*, XXXI, 204–6.
[4] To Newcastle, 23 Nov. 1728 (*Boulter letters*, 2nd ed., 1770, i. 209–11).
[5] Logan papers, *Letter books*, iv. 153–4 (Klett, *Pres. in Pa.*, p. 32).

landed at that port within a single season and that the total number of Irish immigrants at all American ports in 1727 exceeded Boulter's figure for that year together with the preceding one.

It was in 1728 that the number of Irish emigrants to the American colonies first reached the 3,000 mark in a single year. An 'infatuation' for emigration swept over the north of Ireland like a contagious disease.[1] Boulter's conservative estimate of the extent of emigration in 1726–7 gives credence to his statement that 3,100 Irish left for America in 1728,[2] a figure which seems to be borne out by the evidence of a Thomas Whitney, probably a seaman, that thirteen vessels at north of Ireland ports in July of that year were preparing to take emigrants on board.[3] Certainly, emigration reached such proportions that the first approach was made to London at the end of the year for powers to put an end to it.[4]

The infatuation that Boulter had mentioned in 1728 gave way to a 'frenzy' that seemed about to lead to 'a great desertion'[5] in the following year. In March, seven vessels were at Belfast carrying off one thousand people and, in July, twenty-five ships were stated to have already left or were preparing to leave the port of Londonderry for America with 3,500 emigrants.[6] The number of Irish who landed at the Delaware ports in 1729 probably exceeded 4,000, for 1,155 of the 1,708 immigrants who landed at Philadelphia in that year were Irish and the 4,500 who landed at Newcastle were described as 'chiefly from Ireland'.[7]

---

[1] Boulter to Newcastle, 23 Nov. 1728 (*Boulter letters*, i. 209–11), and same to Carteret 17 Dec. 1728 (ibid., i. 216).

[2] Same to Newcastle, 23 Nov. 1728 (ibid., i. 209–11).

[3] To—, 27 July 1728 (T.S.P.I., T.659, pp. 52–3). Whitney, who wrote from Larne, also stated that four emigrant vessels were preparing to leave Sligo and that 40,000 people had emigrated from Ulster and the vicinity of Sligo since 1720. This figure would appear to be a gross exaggeration as it is incredible that Boulter could have under-estimated the number of emigrants by five-sixths. Thomas Prior, in his *List of the absentees of Ireland* (3rd ed., 1745, p. 13), estimated that 3,000 people emigrated annually from Ireland in the late 'twenties.

[4] Newcastle to Boulter, 5 Dec. 1728 (T.S.P.I., T.659, pp. 59–60); See Chapter IX.

[5] Boulter to abp. of Canterbury, 13 Feb. 1728/9 (*Boulter letters*, i. 223–4).

[6] Same to Newcastle, 13 Mar. 1728/9 (ibid., i. 231); *Pa. Gazette*, 17 Nov. 1729 (Klett, *Pres. in Pa.*, p. 20).

[7] *Pa. Gazette*, 6–13 Jan. 1729/30 (Klett, *Pres. in Pa.*, p. 32). O'Brien assumes without explanation that 4,445 of the 4,500 immigrants were Irish and so concludes that 5,600 Irish landed at the two ports (*Hidden phase*, p. 269). The period covered by these returns was the year ended Christmas 1729, but O'Brien refers to is at the calendar year 1728 and P. H. Bagenal as 1727 (*The American Irish and their influence on Irish politics*, p. 8).

Irish emigration during 1729 was not directed exclusively to the Delaware ports. From an entry in a Boston newspaper it would appear, indeed, that 5,655 Irish—and less than one-tenth of that number from other countries—immigrated through Boston in that year.[1] No confirmation of that figure or anything approaching it has been found. When the house of representatives of Massachusetts referred in the autumn of 1729 to Irish immigration it stated that 'several' ships, most of them transporting 'a number of passengers', had arrived from Ireland during the summer.[2] Such language does not suggest the arrival of the forty or fifty vessels that would have been required to transport 5,655 people. Moreover, G. F. Donovan, the historian of the Irish in colonial Massachusetts, makes no mention of substantial Irish immigration into the colony between the 1718-20 period and the late 'thirties.[3]

Emigration on an even greater scale than in 1729 was predicted for the following year. A memorial of the noblemen of Ireland to the lords justices declared that, by the autumn of 1729, twenty thousand people had announced their intention to emigrate in the spring of 1730.[4] Events confounded the prophets for, in March of the latter year, the English privy council was able to decline to adopt coercive measures to stop emigration on the ground that reports from Ireland had shown that few people were actually emigrating.[5]

Two points remain to be considered in this review of the extent of emigration in the 'twenties: first, the total number of Irish emigrants in the decade, and second, how many of those people left through the northern ports. From the material available, it seems reasonable to assume that about two-thirds of those who emigrated from Ireland in these years entered America by way of the Delaware ports and so the total number of Irish emigrants to the continental colonies was probably in the region of 15,000. This number includes those who emigrated from the south of Ireland but it is clear that most were from the north of the country for there is ample evidence to substantiate Boulter's statement that

---

[1] *New England Weekly Journal*, 30 Mar. 1730 (O'Brien, *Hidden phase*, p. 270). A comparison with the Newcastle and Philadelphia returns noted above shows a remarkably close resemblance to this figure.
[2] *Journal of the house of representatives of Massachusetts*, viii. 98-9.
[3] *The pre-Revolutionary Irish in Massachusetts*, pp. 24-6.
[4] *Pa. Gazette*, 17 Nov. 1729 (Klett, *Pres. in Pa.*, pp. 20-1).
[5] P.C. 2/91, p. 193.

emigration affected only protestants and raged chiefly in the north.[1]
A report of the lieutenant governor of Pennsylvania in 1731 spoke
of 'those from the north of Ireland and Germans of both of which
we have considerable numbers',[2] while, three years before, the
lords justices of Ireland had written of 'the great numbers of
protestant subjects who have lately transported themselves from
the north of Ireland to the plantations on the continent of America'.[3]
Roman catholics undoubtedly emigrated to America during the
decade but most of them appear to have gone to the West Indies
where their growing numbers caused disquiet.[4]

Protestant emigration caused near-panic among the ruling
classes. King's main concern in connection with the 1718 emigration was that 'No papists stir . . . . . . The papists being already
five or six to one, and being a breeding people, you may imagine
in what condition we are like to be in.'[5] The same concern was felt
in the late 'twenties. A memorial from 'the noblemen and gentlemen of Ireland' to the lords justices on the subject of emigration
expressed fear of 'a dangerous superiority of our inveterate
enemies the papists, who openly and avowedly rejoice at this
impending calamity and use all means and artifices to encourage
and persuade the protestants to leave the nation, and cannot refrain
from boasting that they shall by this means have again all the lands
of this kingdom in their possession'.[6]

The fear, common to Irish protestants of all classes and sects, of
any increase in the relative strength of the Roman catholic element
of the population was exploited to the full by presbyterian spokesmen. In an address to the king, three southern Irish presbyterian
ministers attributed emigration solely to the sacramental test.
After preparing the ground by pointing out that the Irish Roman
catholics, 'these dangerous and unwearied enemies', were daily
growing in wealth, in power and in insolence and were already
much superior in strength and number to the protestants of all
denominations, the memorialists reached their main point:

> The inconveniences arising from the continuance of [the sacra-
> mental test] have been so many and the hardships and oppressions

---

1 To Newcastle, 23 Nov. 1728 (*Boulter letters*, i. 209–11).
2 P. Gordon to B.T., 10 Nov. 1731 (C.O. 5/1268, f.35).
3 To Carteret, 4 Dec. 1728 (P.C. 2/90, p. 401).
4 *Cal. S.P.Amer. and W.Ind.*, 1730, p. 302; ibid., 1731, pp. 25, 168, 292.
5 To abp. Wake, 6 Feb. 1717/8 (King, *A great abp.*, pp. 207–8).
6 Printed in *Pa. Gazette*, 17 Nov. 1729 (Klett, *Pres. in Pa.*, p. 21).

which the protestant dissenters in this your Majesty's kingdom have laboured under upon account of it are so very grievous that they have in great numbers transported themselves to the American plantations for the sake of that liberty and ease which they have been denied in their native country, and we have too much reason to fear that many more will soon follow if the occasion of their grievances should not be timely removed. . . . . . .[1]

This memorial was directed at an English government which had already intervened in Dublin on behalf of the Irish presbyterians, a government which was at the time relieving British dissenters by acts of indemnity and which considered that 'no distinctions should be kept up among protestants which might be an occasion of disuniting them, considering the great disproportion in number that there is between them and the papists'.[2]

In the spring of 1729 in response to a request from the lords justices of Ireland, Craghead and Iredell—two of the three memorialists—gave more complex reasons for emigration. Dublin Castle, much less sympathetic than London to the presbyterians and more familiar with the true causes of the happenings in the north, was told that emigration had been caused by bad seasons, high rents, uncertainty of tenure and the encouragement held out by those who had already emigrated as well as by 'the peculiar discouragements' suffered by presbyterians.[3] Yet, when Craghead was in London a few months afterwards, he appears to have reverted to the purely religious theme, representing 'that the uneasiness of the people of the north is occasioned by the continuance of the sacramental test and the not allowing the legality of their marriages'.[4] Presbyterian hopes lay in London, not in Dublin, and to London they directed the plea that was most likely to evoke the desired response—the plea that the loyal protestant interest in Ireland was being irreparably harmed by the continuance of an act that drove to America the most loyal subjects the Hanoverians had in Ireland.

Iredell and Craghead detailed four presbyterian grievances in their letter to the lords justices. The removal of one of these

---

[1] N.d. [1728] (T.S.P.I., T.659, pp. 20–3). The memorial was signed by Francis Iredell, Richard Choppin and Robert Craghead.
[2] Newcastle to Boulter, 5 Feb. 1731/2 (T.S.P.I., T.722, pp. 25–7).
[3] N.d. [between 11 Mar. 1728/9 and 9 Apr. 1729] (Latimer, 'Ulster emigration to America', in *R.S.A.I. Jn.*, series 5, xii. 289–92).
[4] Marmaduke Coghill to Ed. Southwell, 7 Aug. 1729 (B.M., Add.MS 21122).

grievances—the alleged insertion in leases of clauses forbidding the erection of presbyterian meeting houses—was not within the recognised province of an eighteenth-century government. The other disabilities which were claimed as having been important causes of emigration were the inability of presbyterians to occupy public posts, the illegality of presbyterian marriages and the prohibition of all schools other than those conducted by teachers licensed by bishops.

That these three grievances had led to emigration was an allegation that could be readily disproved. Iredell and Craghead acknowledged that prosecutions on account of presbyterian marriages and schools 'have not been so frequent or so violent as formerly'. An indignant Boulter claimed that no molestation had been offered to presbyterian marriages 'for some time' and, as for presbyterian schools, he 'had never heard any such grievance till [he] saw it in their memorial'.[1] Iredell and Craghead were on somewhat firmer ground when they complained of the effect of the test act on the employment of presbyterians in even the most humble official posts. Yet even this grievance had little real meaning to the mass of the people—for instance, few presbyterians had the material qualification for membership of the judicial bench. They were the 'middle and meaner sort of people', untroubled by hopes of preferment.[2] The official posts to which such people could have aspired in the eighteenth century were so few that the vast majority of people of all denominations probably never thought of the possibility of securing one of them. Of those that did exist, the northern presbyterians would seem to have had their share in spite of the sacramental test.[3]

It was natural that the presbyterian clergy should stress the religious rather than the economic causes of the migration. As members of a church they had cause to be indignant at the stigma placed upon them by the test act but, as individuals, the yoke of the sacramental test fell lightly on them. It might have been good

[1] To bp. of London, 13 Mar. 1728/9 (*Boulter letters*, pp. 231–6).

[2] T.S.P.I., T.448, p. 280. Abp. Synge estimated that there were not more than four presbyterians who were large landowners in Ireland in 1715 (B.M., Add.MS 6117, p. 35). Boulter, in 1732, believed that, in all Ireland, there were not twenty presbyterians having sufficient substance to qualify as justices of the peace. To Newcastle, 15 Jan. 1731/2 (T.S.P.I., T.722, pp. 10–4).

[3] J. Wainwright wrote in 1734 that the people in the north of Ireland 'dreaded an innundation of their brethren from North Britain to fill the little employments of the excise and customs'. To—, 16 Jan. 1733/4 (T.S.P.I., T.756, p. 7).

pulpit rhetoric but it certainly was not historical fact to state that, by settling and defending Ulster, the presbyterians 'forged their own chains, which in time became so firmly rivetted that, to get rid of them, they were obliged in great numbers to abandon that very country where they had made a comfortable habitation'.[1] Religious persecution may lead to migration but it is doubtful if that result would be caused by legal niceties of practical concern to few people. The badge of inferiority was galling to the majority church of the extreme northern counties of Ireland as it would have been to any church regardless of its strength, but in Hanoverian Ireland the presbyterians had legal toleration, the anti-presbyterian laws were enforced with laxity or not at all and a series of indemnity acts was passed between 1719 and the repeal of the sacramental test in 1780.[2] The presbyterians were subject to pin-pricks but, far from being persecuted, they lived unmolested and enjoyed absolute freedom of worship. It was a presbyterian minister who asked, in 1749,

> Is it not good then that we enjoy truth as well as peace; that the most sacred of all rights, that of conscience and private judgment, is preserved to us; that we have the liberty of . . . . . professing our religious sentiments without molestation? And dissenters in particular, when they look back upon former times and consider the hardships their forefathers suffered in every reign from the Reformation to the Revolution (or I should say, the taking place of the Hanoverian succession) certainly have special reason to rejoice and be thankful for the freedom and tranquility they enjoy.[3]

Shipping advertisements form a useful barometer of the relative influence of the several factors leading to emigration. In the forty years following the failure of the attempt to secure the repeal of the test act in 1733, references to rents and other temporal hardships

---

[1] Rev. S. Barber, *Remarks on a pamphlet entitled, the present state of the church of England by Richard lord bishop of Cloyne*, p. 37.
[2] Beckett, *Prot. dissent in Ire.*, pp. 97–105.
[3] Rev. Gilbert Kennedy, jnr. (Witherow, *Presbyterian memorials*, ii. 68). Letters in similar vein were inserted by various presbyterian congregations in the *B.N.L.* in 1772 during agrarian troubles. For example, the Aghadowey presbyterians wrote of 'the mildness of the present administration' (*B.N.L.*, April 17) and the Kilmore (county Down) presbyterians condemned 'the blackest ingratitude to that so indulgent government, under which the firm protection and enjoyment of their civil and religious liberty is so well provided for' (ibid., April 14).

were frequent in these advertisements but references to religion were rare. One of these few references appeared in the notice advertising the sailing of the *Charming Molly* to Maryland in 1773, and the description of Baltimore as 'a place where all kinds of religion are tolerated'[1] may, indeed, have been a reflection on religious intolerance in some of the colonies rather than in Ireland. Shipping agents respected neither bishops nor landlords: they were interested in persuading people to emigrate and this they did by painting the American scene in its brightest colours and stressing all that could be found fault with at home. The 'chains' that angered Barber must not have weighed heavily on prospective emigrants if they failed to attract the questing eyes of agents and ship masters. Moreover, no further attempt was made after 1733 to pin responsibility for emigration on the continued existence of the test act which was not repealed until 1780.[2] One must conclude that though the test act was denounced by many of those who left the north of Ireland for America it had little influence on their decision to emigrate.[3]

There can be no doubt, on the other hand, that tithes were a genuine cause of resentment to the presbyterian farmer. The injustice of being obliged to maintain a church whose services the majority of the people did not attend and whose clergy were often absentees needs no elaboration,[4] but of even greater importance to all farmers, whether presbyterian or not, was the fact that tithes bit deeply into the margin of subsistence left by high and increasing rents. Boulter asserted that, after a tenant had paid his rent, seldom more than a third and often only a fifth of his profits remained and concluded from this that 'it is plain from what side the hardship arises'[5] but in the eyes of the people there was little to choose between landlords and rectors. One was a leech in his own name, the other in the name of God. One collected a rent, part of which the people acknowledged to be his just due; the other collected a rent, which he called a tithe, to which he had no right in the opinion of those who had to pay it. It was cold comfort for the Irish farmer to know that tithes in Ireland, especially in the north, were generally

---

[1] *B.N.L.*, 27 July 1773.
[2] 19 and 20 Geo. III, c.6 (Ire.).
[3] Cf. Beckett, *Prot. dissent in Ire.*, pp. 87–91.
[4] See O'Brien, *Econ. hist. Ire. 18th cent.*, ch. XIV.
[5] Boulter to bp. of London, 13 Mar. 1728/9 (*Boulter letters*, i. 233).

lower than in England.[1] The parson whose tithes were gleaned from a people who were poor after the landlord had reaped his harvest left poverty where frugality had been.

The system of canting tithes to tithe farmers[2] made an obnoxious system doubly pernicious. This evil system of selling the right to collect tithes to the highest bidder was still the same in the 'seventies when the Hearts of Steel singled out tithe farmers for special note when complaining about 'the exorbitancies of high tithes'. They wrote, 'We wanted and want (if it might possibly be obtained) that there be no tithe farmers, but all rectors to dwell in their own parishes and agree and receive their tithes themselves: for we really imagine the tithes may be as well paid the rector as to any tithe farmer'.[3] Had the rector collected his own tithes instead of employing this man 'destitute of compunction', this 'species of wolf left behind by the shepherd to take care of the flock in his absence',[4] he could have reduced the amount paid by the farmer for tithes, sometimes by as much as half,[5] and still received the same money as previously. Such a reduction would have made a great difference to the farming community, especially in years of poor crops or of low prices. Arthur Young's observations support this point. He believed that tithes were reasonably rated in Ireland and that the evils of the system were mostly due to tithe farmers who 'screw up the tenants and poor people very severely'.[6] The exactions of tithe farmers, 'very ill men', were given by two Lisburn farmers who emigrated to America in 1729 as one of the causes of their removal and other emigrants in the same year cited

[1] Young, *Tour*, ii. 185–6; Adams, *Irish emig. in 19th cent.*, p.29; O'Brien, *Econ. hist. Ire., 18th cent.*, p. 148. Though potatoes and flax were usually exempt from tithes in the north, this was not universally so. A pamphleteer of 1742 spoke of the flax tithe as 'that terrible tax of ten shillings an acre which now it pays to the clergy in all parts of the kingdom' (*A scheme for utterly abolishing the present heavy and vexatious tax of tithe*, p. 13).
[2] Advertisements asking for bids were inserted in the newspapers. Within a month, the setting of the rectorial tithes of the parishes of Donegore and Killbride, Seagoe, Donacloney and Magherawley were thus advertised (*B.N.L.*, 11 May and 15 June 1770).
[3] Humble address of the Steel Society of county Londonderry, 23 Mar. 1772 (Londonderry estate office papers P.R.O.N.I., D. 654).
[4] *The speeches of the Rt. Hon. Henry Grattan* (2nd ed. 1853), ed. D. A. Madden, p. 123.
[5] Young, *Tour*, ii. 185.
[6] Ibid., ii. 179. The duke of Rutland, when lord lieutenant, believed that the real grievance of the people with regard to tithes was the manner of their collection (B.M., Add.MS 24138, f. 110).

the same reason in an address to the justices of the north-eastern circuit of Ireland.[1]

Resentful as the presbyterians were at the payment of tithes it was scarcity of food and increases in rents that drove people from Ireland in the 'twenties to a land where poverty was said to be unknown and where every man could become his own landlord. During the decade, as at all other times during the century, all non-landlord groups—emigrants, bishops, lord lieutenants and presbyterians—agreed on the close connection between rising rents and rising emigration. The effect of the expiration in the second decade of the century of the twenty-one year leases granted after the Williamite wars has already been examined. The thirty-one year leases expired with similar results in the 'twenties. The revenue of the Southwell estate in the vicinity of Downpatrick was £1,244 in 1713: in 1731 it had risen to £2,254.[2] The rental of 34 farms on the Hertford estate, near Lisburn, was £90 5s. 6d. in 1719: in 1728 the same farms were let for £222. 16s. 7d.[3] In other words, rents doubled in the process of a single turnover of leases. Such increases were but examples of a process that continued for the remainder of the century and, when combined with periods of low yields or low prices for farm produce, formed an ever present and ever pressing reason for emigration.

The statement by Hugh Wyndham that the emigration of the 1728 period was 'said and believed by many to have taken its rise from contracts between landlords and tenants'[4] received ample support from other observers in closer touch with events in the north. Letters explaining the causes of north Irish emigration to America appeared in a Dublin newspaper in 1729. The writers agreed that tithes, bad seasons, and the belief that America was a new Eden contributed to the emigration movement, but they were particularly emphatic when they discussed the part played by the 'intolerable' burden of excessive rents and the 'griping avarice of estated gentlemen'.[5] Increased rents were reported to the justices of the north-western circuit of Ireland as a cause of emigration in 1728 and it was again alleged that protestant tenants were being

---

1 *Dublin Weekly Journal*, 5 June 1729; Enclosure, Carteret to Newcastle, 26 June 1729 (T.S.P.I., T.659, p. 74).
2 *P.R.O.N.I. rep. D.K. 1931*, p. 19.
3 P.R.O.N.I., D. 427, nos. 1 (receipt book, 1719) and 2 (rent roll, 1728).
4 To—, 11 Jan. 1728/9 (T.S.P.I., T.656, p. 65).
5 *Dublin Weekly Journal*, June 7 and July 5.

replaced by Roman catholics who were prepared to contract for higher rents.[1]

In the eyes of some observers, the shortness of leases was as influential as high rents in causing emigration. Leases for twenty-one or thirty-one years did not provide the necessary inducement to improve the land and yet only improvement could have made the increased rents economical. Landowners had replied to charges that high rents were one of the main causes of emigration by pointing out that many people who held land at low rents had sold the interests of their leases and had emigrated to America with the proceeds.[2] Iredell and Craghead agreed that this had occurred but stated that the main reason for it was that those concerned were merely anticipating the inevitable. Leases were so short that those who were paying low rents realised that they, in turn, were bound to 'quickly sink . . . into the same abject poverty to which they had seen others reduced from flourishing circumstances by the like methods'.[3] The north-western justices gave as much prominence to complaints about short leases as they did to complaints about high rents. Special mention was made of church lands where the usual term was only seven years.[4]

It was singularly unfortunate that, as had happened ten years before, near-famine struck Ireland as the rents rose. The new rents could have been paid in years of normal crop yields but 1727 and the following two years were so abnormal that the awe-stricken people believed them to be either heralds of eternity or vehicles of the wrath of God.[5]

Famine was no stranger to the people of Ireland. Memories and fears kept alive the feeling of insecurity even in a year of abundance for such a year was usually followed by one of shortage.[6] Boulter attributed these recurring catastrophies to the increasing area of pasturage but this tendency must have been comparatively slight in the north.[7] The fundamental explanation was a simpler one.

[1] John St. Leger and Michael Ward. Enclosure, Carteret to Newcastle, 26 June 1729 (T.S.P.I., T.659, p. 76).
[2] Memorial, landowners of Ireland, printed in *Pa. Gazette*, 17 Nov. 1729 (Klett, *Pres. in Pa.*, p. 21).
[3] Iredell and Craghead to lords justices, n.d. (1729) (Latimer, 'Ulster emigration to America', in *R.S.A.I. Jn.*, series 5, xii. 389).
[4] Enclosure, Carteret to Newcastle, 26 June 1729 (T.S.P.I., T.659, p. 77).
[5] *Dublin Weekly Journal*, 7 June and 5 July 1729; Rutty, *Weather and seasons*, pp. 8–18.
[6] Boulter to Newcastle, 25 May 1728 (*Boulter letters*, i. 193–4).
[7] To abp. of Canterbury, 24 Feb. 1727/8 (ibid., i.175–8). This opinion may have been

Bad seasons in 1727 and 1728 seriously reduced the crops in Ireland in common with the rest of the British Isles and matters were made worse in Ireland by the purchase of some of what little corn there was by commissions from Britain and Europe.[1] A proclamation forbidding the export of corn to Europe—though not to England—had some easing effect on the situation even though it was not issued until 1729, a few years too late, and only then after much pleading.[2] The activities of engrossers whose aim was to secure a monopoly of the corn that remained in Ireland were another factor in intensifying scarcity and raising prices. Rioting against engrossers reached such a pitch in Dublin in 1729 that the congregations of all Roman catholic churches of the city were warned that all who took part in such demonstrations would be excommunicated.[3] It was to combat the engrossers that the bishops and landlords of the north, by now thoroughly alarmed at the extent of protestant emigration, subscribed £3,900 in 1729 to purchase corn wherever it was cheapest and sold it in the north of Ireland at or below the cost price.[4]

Three years of dearth had a terrible effect on a country whose powers of resistance had already been undermined. Negligible yields more than offset the artificial boost that famine had given to prices. Yields fell so much in parts of the north that some

---

coloured by the opposition of the landlords to the levying of tithes on grazing land (ibid., ii. 120, 150, 151, 171, 181).

[1] Lords justices to Carteret, 23 Nov. 1728 (P.C. 1/48); Boulter to Newcastle, 17 Dec. 1728 (*Boulter letters*, i. 216); Carteret to Ed. Southwell, 9 Dec. 1729 (B.M., Add.MS 38016). The price of wheat rose in England from 32s. 11d. at Lady-day 1727 to 49s. 2d. a year later. 1728 and 1729 were the only years in the first half of the eighteenth century when more wheat was imported into England than was exported (Tooke, *History of prices*, i. 40).

[2] Boulter to Carteret, 14 Dec. 1728 (*Boulter letters*, i. 214–5); same to Newcastle, 17 Dec. 1728 (ibid., i. 216).

[3] *Dublin Weekly Journal*, 19 Apr. 1729; Wyndham to—, 11 Jan. 1728/9 (T.S.P.I., T.659, pp. 64–6). Engrossers were active at other times during the century. Two sentences of a 'political litany' printed in 1766 read:
'From all Monopolisers, Forestallers, and Regulators . . . . .,
    Good Lord deliver us!
'That it may please Thee to bless our Magistrates and give them
    Grace to put the Laws into Execution against all Engrossers and
    Forestallers of Provisions,
    We beseech Thee to hear us, good Lord.'
                    (*Freeman's Journal*, Aug. 12).

[4] Representation, Irish Society to M.T. Co. 21 Feb. 1728/9 (M.T. Co. P. (T.), T.656, No. 48); Boulter to abp. of Canterbury, 13 Feb. 1728/9 (*Boulter letters*, i. 223–4).

farmers had not merely no surplus to sell but had to eat the oats they should have saved for the following year's sowing.[1] Bad seasons swept away those farmers whom high rents had condemned to live on the fringe of sufficiency. Severed from stability, they were swept into 'a scene of misery and desolation' with the landless poor who 'crowded along the roads, scarce able to walk, and infinite numbers starved in every ditch in the midst of rags, dirt, and nakedness'.[2]

Emigration agents could not have wished for a more promising field in which to work. Their 'artful insinuations' found attentive ears among a people whose home ties were already being loosened by necessity.[3] Though 'great numbers of labouring men and women [went] about the country, in a starving condition, begging to get meal alone for their labour', thousands were said to be leaving the north of Ireland for England in search of work.[4] This appears to have been one of the earliest movements from Ireland to Britain, whether for seasonal employment or for permanent settlement, and, six years later, a similar event was reported as a matter of some interest.[5] There was, therefore, a general spirit of restlessness abroad in the north, a preparedness to leave one's native townland and even one's native country. Thus was the agents' battle half won for them before they launched their attack. They were also aided by accounts sent by emigrants of previous years to the afflicted people of the north,

> inviting and encouraging them to transport themselves thither, and promising them liberty and ease as the reward of their honest industry, with a prospect of transmitting their acquisitions and privileges safe to their posterity, without the imposition of growing rents and other heavy burdens.[6]

The influence of such letters and the use made of them by agents who added their own highly coloured accounts of life in America were important factors in the emigration of the late 'twenties and of other times in the century when life was more than usually

---

[1] Boulter to Newcastle, 12 Mar. 1728/9 (*Boulter letters*, pp. 229–31).
[2] *Dublin Weekly Journal*, 5 July 1729.
[3] Lords justices to Carteret, 23 Nov. 1728 (P.C. 1/48).
[4] *Dublin Weekly Journal*, 7 June 1729.
[5] *F.D.J.*, 3 June 1735.
[6] Enclosure, lords justices to Carteret, 8 March 1728/9 (Latimer, 'Ulster emigration to America', in *R.S..A.I. Jn.*, series 5, xii. 389–92).

difficult in Ireland. Indeed, the north-western justices reported in 1729 that highly coloured accounts of life in America were, as a cause of emigration, even more important than hardship at home.[1]

Factors which, according to all shades of interested opinion, contributed to emigration during the 'twenties are indicated in the following table. A definite statement that a particular cause was operative is indicated by the word *yes* in the appropriate place; a specific denial by the word *no*; a blank indicates that the particular factor was not mentioned.

The feature of the table which would have most surprised a north Irishman of half a century later is the apparently slight connection between emigration and the linen trade. This trade was 'much decayed' in 1729[2] but only one of the six sources mentioned it as a major cause of emigration and a second merely referred to it casually at the end of a tirade against landlords and tithe farmers. Linen was of great importance to Ireland even in the early eighteenth century and the authorities expressed alarm at the effect on the trade of the heavy emigration of the 'twenties, but it was certainly not generally accepted that emigration was regarded as a consequence of the linen failure.[3] Later in the century the tide of emigration seemed to rise and fall as the linen trade declined and prospered. In the earlier years of the century, however, the north depended for a livelihood on the produce of the fields and was not so deeply committed to linen as it was to become by the 'seventies. The loss of even a subsidiary source of income must, of course, have had a serious effect while rents were high, crops poor and prices soaring.

The reference by emigrants to 'overpopulation' at a time when the north supported only a fraction of the population of a century later may seem ludicrous but, nevertheless, there were, indeed, local population problems even in the eighteenth century. For example, a Mr Browne established a settlement of north Irish

---

[1] Report to Carteret, enclosed in Carteret to Newcastle, 26 June 1729 (T.S.P.I., T.659, pp. 75–9). The north-eastern justices similarly reported on the circulation among the people of accounts of 'the great advantages they may expect from their removal [and] likewise of the prosperous condition those are in who some time ago went thither, and these accounts are. . . .artfully kept up and propagated on the part of the people of those colonies by their emissaries here . . .' (ibid., pp. 79–81).

[2] *Dublin Weekly Journal*, 7 June 1729.

[3] Lords justices to Carteret, 23 Nov. 1728 (P.C. 1/48).

Cause	Judges[1]	Presbyterian ministers[2]	Bishops[3]	Landowner[4]	Emigrants[5]	'A northerner'[6]
High rents	Yes	Yes	Yes	Yes	Yes	Yes
Short leases	Yes	Yes			Yes	
Famine	Yes	Yes	Yes		Yes	Yes
Luxuries of the rich				Yes	Yes	
Methods of tithe collection	Yes	Yes	No	Yes	Yes	Yes
Encouragement from America and emigration agents	Yes	Yes			Yes	Yes
Decay of linen trade	Yes				Yes	
Sacramental test		Yes	No			
Overpopulation					Yes	
Absentees and pensions				Yes	Yes	
Oppression by J.P.s.		Yes				
Poor circulation of coin					Yes	Yes	Yes
Too little tillage				Yes	Yes	
To avoid creditors	Yes					

[1] Reports, justices of the north-eastern and north-western circuits. Enclosure, Carteret to Newcastle, 26 June, 1729 (T.S.P.I., T.659, pp. 75–81).
[2] Iredell and Craghead to lords justices. Enclosure, lords justices to Carteret, 8 Mar. 1728/9 (Latimer, 'Ulster emigration to America', in R.S.A.I., Jn., series 5, xii. 389–92).
[3] Boulter to abp. of Canterbury, 24 Feb. 1727/8 (*Boulter letters*, i. 175–8); same to same, 13 Feb. 1728/9 (ibid., i. 223–4); same to Newcastle, 25 May 1728 (ibid., i. 193–4); same to same, 12 Mar. 1728/9 (ibid., i. 229–31); same to bp. of London, 13 Mar. 1728/9 (ibid., i. 231–6).
[4] Marmaduke Coghill to Southwell, 3 Oct. 1729 (B.M., Add.MS 21122). Judging from the Boulter letters that have been cited, the admission of the contributory effects of high rents was not general among landowners. Indeed, Coghill was not a typical landowner in that he drew much of his income from public appointments.
[5] *Dublin Weekly Journal*, 7 June 1729.
[6] A long letter dealing with emigration and signed 'A northerner' appeared in the *Dublin Weekly Journal* on 5 July 1729.

weavers at Monolla in county Mayo in 1732 and it was hoped that other gentlemen in the south of Ireland would do likewise 'since the northern counties are becoming so populous, that they are forced to send every year large colonies to America'.[1] Unfortunately, the districts from which the settlers went to Mayo are unknown. Possibly they were from the Lisburn vicinity, the region referred to in the table: possibly they were from county Londonderry where, in 1775, Arthur Young predicted serious consequences from overpopulation if emigration to America were not resumed.[2]

Famine was the basic cause of the heavy emigration of the 'twenties. Other factors were there but famine aggravated and developed them. Boulter believed that 'if it please God to send us a good harvest, things will gradually mend'.[3] His hopes with respect to the 1729 harvest were more than fulfilled. The price of corn in the north collapsed to less than half of what it had been in 1728[4] and Carteret turned some of his energies to the lifting of the embargo on the export of that commodity.[5] Boulter's expectations of the effect of a good harvest on the volume of emigration were also fulfilled, for the privy council in London reported that emigration had by 1730 declined to inconsiderable proportions as a consequence of good harvests and a fall in prices,[6] though the latter was no inducement to the ending of emigration among the farming class.

---

[1] *F.D.J.*, 5 Aug. 1732. The reason given two years later for establishing the settlement was 'want of room in the north' (ibid., 16 July, 1734).
[2] *Tour*, i. 189. In a letter to the lord lieutenant in 1768, T. Taylor wrote that 'several thousands of women could be spared from Ireland and they would readily export themselves if their freight was paid', 16 Jan. 1768 (Nat. Lib. Ire., Townshend MS No. 246).
[3] To Walpole, 31 Mar. 1729 (*Boulter letters*, pp. 236–7).
[4] The price of oatmeal was 12s. per cwt. in 1728 (*Dublin Weekly Journal*, Dec. 7); it was 4s. 2d. in 1730 (*F.D.J.*, July 4). The July and December prices of oatmeal were, in most years, approximately the same.
[5] Carteret to Southwell, 26 Feb. 1729/30 (B.M., Add.MS 38016).
[6] P.C. 2/91, pp. 192–5 (12 Mar. 1729/30).

CHAPTER IV

The Middle Years: 1731–1769

DEARTH of information is the chief reason for the selection of this comparatively long period as the third stage in the examination of emigration from Ulster to colonial America. Official correspondence concerning emigration was not profuse at any time in the eighteenth century but, except for dealings with promoters of American lands, that unsatisfying well was almost dry between 1731 and 1770. In previous periods, it was the attempts of the presbyterians to attach a religious significance to emigration that had evoked counter-explanations from King and Boulter. In the middle of the century, the established church lacked men of the stature of these great prelates and, in any case, the presbyterian church desisted from its fruitless efforts to link emigration and religious disabilities. Emigration had become a commonplace thing rather than a phenomenon that called for explanation. A similar silence with regard to north Irish emigration is unbroken in the reports of the governors of the colonies and of the port authorities, except at Charleston and New York for brief periods. Though the *Belfast News Letter* was first published in 1737 and has appeared regularly since then, the surviving pre-1760 issues are far from complete, whole years being unrepresented.[1] In the issues that do remain, the volume of information about north Irish affairs in general and emigration in particular is dwarfed by foreign dispatches and by advertisements dealing with subjects ranging from latin schools to stallions.

[1] See bibliography. The *B.N.L.* was the only north Irish newspaper till the *Londonderry Journal* began publication in 1772.

The Middle Years: 1731–1769

In each of the two periods already studied there was a clear mingling and accumulation of forces leading to a climax of emigration: in each, a wave of emigration was seen rising till it reached its crest and then falling. Years that are bound together by the negative unity of obscurity cannot have, of course, the sense of unity of the earlier periods nor can their examination follow the same pattern. In the pages that follow, the causes and extent of emigration will advance together through the varying circumstances of a changing period and, finally, an attempt will be made to estimate the approximate number of north Irish emigrants during these forty years.

The good harvests of 1729 and 1730 brought relief to Ireland but they were not an unmixed blessing to the rack-rented farmer. Prices collapsed in 1730 and generally remained low until 1740, lower than in the ten years before the dearth of 1727, despite the advances in rents during that time.[1] Competition for farms meant that rents still increased and expanding linen markets enabled those rents to be paid, but the rents were artificially high for they reflected the dearth of land rather than its productivity. The labouring class could bask in the luxury of cheap and plentiful food and settle down again to the life from which many of its members had been driven by famine: most farmers found low prices as great a burden as famine had been.

The chief feature of the 'thirties, from the point of view of emigration, was, moreover, one that appealed more to farmers in difficulties with rents than to labourers whose yardstick of contentment was the price of food. South Carolina, for long nervous of danger from Spanish and Indian invasions and negro insurrections, passed a law in 1731 imposing, for seven years, a duty on all negro slaves brought into the colony and applying the proceeds to aid the immigration of Europeans to settle in the townships that had been laid out on crown lands. In this way it was hoped to reduce the dangerous preponderance of slaves, the titheable number of whom was 20,000 in 1729 compared with 2,000 white men. Each immigrant, man, woman or child, was to be granted fifty acres of land free from rent for ten years and at a rent of 2s. 6d. per hundred acres thereafter. Of equal importance to the immigrant was the promise of assistance in the shape of provisions and tools. The

---

[1] Tooke, *Prices*, i. 41–2.

London authorities supported the efforts of the colonial assembly, and an influx of French and Swiss protestants followed.[1]

The number of Scotch-Irish who took advantage of the bounty is uncertain as both the governors' correspondence and the port returns of Charleston are silent on the matter though, had they been led by an organiser like John Peter Purry, the story of their part in the settlement of South Carolina at that time might have lived as vividly as that of the Swiss.[2] There is however evidence that the bounty induced substantial emigration from the north of Ireland. An eighteenth century historian of the colony wrote that accounts of the 'great privileges and indulgences' promised by South Carolina in 1731 were circulated through Ireland, and many who were 'oppressed by landlords and bishops, and unable by their utmost diligence to procure a comfortable subsistence' emigrated to the colony.[3] John Pringle and other protestants who had just arrived in the colony from Ireland petitioned the provincial council in 1732 that the expenses of their passage should be paid. The council agreed, allotted the township of Williamsburg to the settlers, and supplied them with tools and with provisions for a year.[4] Two vessels carried about 650 emigrants from Belfast to South Carolina in 1736 and 1737 and, in the latter year, it was

---

[1] A petition of the colony's house of assembly spoke of 'such vast numbers of enemies, as are the Spaniards on one side, the Indians on the other and a more dreadful one amongst ourselves, viz. such vast quantities of negroes to grapple with' (C.O. 5/360, 5 Apr.1728); *Commons' jn.*, xviii, 250; C.O. 5/361, ff. 22–3, Memorial, Geo. Barrington, agent of S.C. in London, to B.T., 28 July 1729; C.O. 5/361, ff. 78–9, Col. Johnston, governor, to B.T., 7 Mar. 1730/1; *Hist. account S.C.*, ii. 63; *Dublin News Letter*, 21 May 1737; E. E. Proper, *Colonial immigration laws*, p. 69; C.O. 5/383 *passim*; McCrady, *S.C. under royal govt.*, p. 121; London and Bristol merchants engaged in the slave trade petitioned against the bill (C.O. 5/361, f. 84, n.d.), but apparently no action was taken. It seems that it was not till 1756 that the instructions to the governors of the colony included the direction to refuse assent to any law imposing a duty on negroes or convicts (McCrady, op. cit., p. 378).
[2] H. L. Osgood, *The American colonies in the eighteenth century*, ii. 508.
[3] *Hist. account S.C.*, ii. 63.
[4] The tools included an axe and a broad and a narrow hoe to each man and a still mill to the company. The provisions consisted of Indian corn, wheaten flour, beef, pork, rum and salt. After great suffering, the settlers procured negro slaves on credit and prospered. The council also guaranteed that the people would be allowed to enjoy their own faith without intrusion and Williamsburg never became a parish. At no time, therefore, had its inhabitants to support the established church (McCrady, *S.C. under royal govt.*, pp. 51, 63; Bolton, *Scotch Irish pioneers*, pp. 288–91). A list of heads of families who emigrated from the north of Ireland to South Carolina between 1730 and 1734 is given in W. S. Fleming, 'Scotch Irish settlers in South Carolina, and their descendants in Maury country, Tennessee', in *Scotch-Ir. in Am.*, i. 202.

reported that twelve or thirteen vessels were expected off Portrush during the summer to carry emigrants thence.[1] South Carolina may have been the destination of many of those who were taking part in a heavy emigration during the middle 'thirties from Belfast. This emigration became sufficiently great to provoke the local landlords into making a strong though unavailing attempt to put a stop to it.[2] By 1737, however, the news reached Ireland that the bounty money had been exhausted by the success of the plan but, in spite of warnings printed in a Dublin newspaper, many persisted in emigrating and were forced to beg from door to door on their arrival in Charleston.[3]

Lest judgment of the extent of emigration in this period becomes unbalanced by talk of 'multitudes' embarking at the north Irish ports for South Carolina,[4] it is salutary to reflect that, in the forty years after 1724, the white population of South Carolina increased by only about 20,000.[5] To find what part of this total originated in the north of Ireland, one must deduct from it the contributions of natural increase and of immigration from other parts of Europe and from the land hungry colonies to the north. It must also be remembered that the part played by the north of Ireland in this increase was restricted to the bounty period of the middle 'thirties. Practically all issues of the *Belfast News Letter* between 1750 and 1761 survive and show that not a single vessel was advertised to leave a north Irish port for South Carolina in that period.[6]

Circumstances tended to make emigration to South Carolina a farming-class movement but it was, of course, not confined to that class. An adventurous or dissatisfied labourer could go to the province without capital and set up as a farmer on assistance given by the colonial authorities. A more direct stimulus to emigrate was provided by periods of local distress, despite the general cheapness of food. For example, distress due to a scarcity of provisions was reported in Coleraine in 1735[7] and it may have been

---

[1] D. Ramsay, *History of South Carolina*, i. 20.

[2] See Chapter IX.

[3] *Dublin News Letter*, 14 and 21 May 1737; Bolton, *Scotch Irish pioneers*, pp. 288–91.

[4] Proper, *Immigration laws*, p. 80.

[5] The white population increased from 14,000 in 1723 to between 30 and 40,000 in 1763 (*Hist. account S.C.*, i. 230, and B.M., Add.MS 29973, p. 24).

[6] See Appendix E.

[7] *Concise view of the Irish society*, p. 107.

a continuation of this scarcity that led to preparations for heavy emigration from Portrush in 1737.

The general respite of the poor from the tyranny of famine ended abruptly in 1740. The preceding winter had been one of the three most severe winters of the century and ruined the Irish potato crop.[1] Famine in its most acute form, not a mere shortage of provisions, followed and, though its visitation was a comparatively brief one, it left tens of thousands of dead in Ireland as a grim reminder of nature's uncertainty and of Ireland's helplessness.[2] The hardships and legacy of the terrible winter caused many to emigrate, but the numbers were small compared with the less severe times that had gone before.[3] The reason was twofold. Britain was engaged in a war in which enemy fleets and privateers were not without their successes.[4] This additional peril to the transatlantic adventure must have deterred many from emigrating, particularly as at least some of the vessels that sailed with emigrants were themselves privateers—the only advertisement for emigrants in the surviving copies of the *Belfast News Letter* between 1740 and 1746 was that of a privateer, the *William and Mary*, advertised to sail from Belfast and Larne to Philadelphia.[5] Additional risks may have led to an increase in the cost of a passage to America and emigrants who could not pay their fares may have been less welcome than hitherto unless the sale of indentures in America rose in price accordingly and immediately. The brevity of the famine of 1740 was a second reason for its comparative failure to provoke emigration. The price of bread in Dublin in April 1741 was higher than it had been for at least a quarter of a century—and higher than it was to be at any time till after 1775—but prices broke in all parts of Ireland during the following two months and by September returned to little above normal.[6] The 1739 emigration season was over by the time famine conditions appeared and famine prices had become but a memory by the time the 1741

[1] Tooke, *Prices*, i. 43. The river Foyle was frozen over and an ox roasted on the ice opposite the ship quay (Hempton John, ed. *The siege and history of Londonderry*, pp. 412–3).
[2] O'Brien, *Econ. hist. Ire. 18th cent.*, p. 104; Lecky, *Ire.*, i. 185–6; *Concise view of the Irish society*, p. 113.
[3] Myers, *Quaker emig.*, pp. 48–9.
[4] Representation, merchants and inhabitants of Philadelphia to house of representatives, 4 June 1741 (C.O. 5/1234, f. 125); *Lords' jn.*, xxvi. 43, 57–8.
[5] *B.N.L.*, 10 June 1746.
[6] *F.D.J.*, 7 Apr. and 22 Sept. 1741.

emigration season really got under way and so emigration as the direct result of this particular catastrophe was confined to a single year, though its memory and after-effects must have had repercussions on Irish emigration for some time after that.

Emigration between 1741 and 1760 was sporadic and local. Families who could not or would not pay higher rents than they were already paying emigrated as their leases expired. It may be said that these were, on the whole, years of moderate prices and prosperity,[1] though such a generalisation must be qualified in the light of the rapidity with which famine succeeded poverty in eighteenth century Ireland. For example, an Irish quaker described the winter of 1742–3 as 'a time of peace, health, and great plenty', but high prices and starvation were noted a few months later in county Londonderry and more grain had to be imported into Ireland in 1746 than in any other year in the first three-quarters of the century.[2] However, the only period in these two decades when the food position became really acute was the years between 1756 and 1759[3] when, as in 1739 and 1740, well-founded fears of privateers served to moderate any increased tendency to emigrate.[4]

Though Irish emigration during this period has left little mark on the page of recorded history, it did witness an important innovation. Ever since the early days of Scotch-Irish settlement in America, letters from north Irish emigrants influenced the direction and volume of succeeding emigrations. At this distance of time it is not possible to trace the effect of all these emigrant letters but, in their day, their influence upon the home population was as certain as is the erosion of the tides on a coastline. Most of the time the only apparent effect is the detachment of a few grains, but after a storm the attrition is clearly discernible. The importance of letters from settlers should not, therefore, be underestimated, especially in

---

[1] In 1751 the earl of Orrery wrote of the state of Ireland as being 'as flourishing as possible', no kingdom having been more improved in the space of eighteen years (In Macpherson, *Annals of commerce*, iii. 289).

[2] Mungo Bewley, quoted in Myers, *Quaker emig.*, pp. 48–9; John Lenox of Gracehill, co. Londonderry, to Wm. Lenox—[1743–5], (*P.R.O.N.I., rep. D.K. 1929*, p. 17); *Commons' jn. Ire.*, xvi. 253.

[3] *Concise view of the Irish society*, pp. 119–20; *B.N.L.*, 4 Jan., 1 Feb., 13 May 1757. Daniel Mussenden, a Belfast merchant, tried without success to purchase corn in the south of Ireland in 1757. His Waterford correspondent wrote on April 23 that the mob 'vow vengeance against any man that would attempt shipping any corn or meal' (P.R.O.N.I., Mussenden papers, uncalendared, D.354/293).

[4] *F.D.J.*, 9 Aug. and 1 Nov. 1757; *B.N.L.*, 23 Feb. and 10 Oct. 1758.

times of economic distress, but it was inevitable that, sooner or later, some of the more prosperous of these settlers should do more to encourage emigration than merely write letters. Those who acquired large tracts of land had to find settlers for them and their thoughts naturally turned to their native land: indeed, at least one person who was not an Irishman was attracted thither in his quest for settlers by the magnitude of north Irish emigration.[1] Three of the most prosperous of Ireland's former sons in the American colonies were Henry McCulloh, William Johnson and James Patton. McCulloh, a native of Ulster, had been agent to Lord Granville and had become surveyor, inspector, and controller of the revenues and grants of land in North Carolina. Using his official position to best advantage, he secured a pre-emption on over a million acres of land in the province and introduced settlers from the north of Ireland.[2] William Johnson, the Indian agent who originated in county Meath, settled an Irish colony of sixteen families at Fort Hamilton in New York in 1740. In the following year he transported sixty families from Ireland to Warrenbush, also in New York, and advertised lands in that province for settlement in the *Belfast News Letter* in 1754. This advertisement may not have attracted many emigrants as the terms of letting offered by Johnson ranged from fifty shillings per one hundred acres for a life or lives to £5 per hundred acres to be held in fee.[3] James Patton was granted 120,000 acres in Virginia in 1736 and is said to have planted a large number of people there from his native north-west of Ulster.[4] Patton's action is doubly significant

---

[1] Colonel Samuel Waldo. Details of the activities of Waldo and other important land promoters of the period will be found in Chapter VIII.

[2] Williamson, *History of North Carolina*, i. 65. McCulloh is said to have introduced between three and four thousand Scotch-Irish settlers into North Carolina in 1736 (C. H. Smith, *The history of education in North Carolina*, p. 22; P.R.O.N.I., T.342). This must be doubted as he did not receive his pre-emption till 1737, and, by 1767, only 322 people had settled on his lands. By a deed dated in April of the latter year, all McCulloh's pre-emption was forfeited to the crown except 64,400 acres, representing a firm grant of 200 acres for the introduction of each settler (Williamson, op. cit., i. 65). See also C.O. 5/297, ff. 10-20, 333-5. Memorials, McCulloh to B.T., 22 Feb. 1750/1 and n.d. (1756).

[3] R. J. Purcell, 'The Irish contribution to colonial New York' in *Studies*, xxix. 599, and ibid., xxx. 108; S. H. Sutherland, *Population distribution in colonial America*, p. 88; B.N.L., 12 Dec. 1754.

[4] H. J. O'Brien, 'Burke's Garden, Virginia', in *Amer.-Ire. Hist. Soc. Jn.*, xxvi. 59. O'Brien states that Patton, captain of a merchant vessel, crossed the Atlantic twenty-five times from Ireland and therefore carried about seven thousand emigrants to America. This estimate is valueless as it is merely a statement of the maximum

in the history of Irish emigration for it seems probable that one of those who went to his lands was Alexander McNutt who was to become the most ambitious of the promoters of American lands in Ireland.

In the years between 1731 and 1760 there were few peaks of north Irish emigration that can be discerned above the mists of time. Beneath that shroud, however, the westward movement to America continued. The shadow of war often lay across the path and at times dissuaded the timid and undecided, but the will to emigrate continued to be fostered by the seemingly inexorable advance of rents, periodic visitations of famine and growing contacts with the American colonies.

Life in the north of Ireland followed its normal course in the years between 1760 and 1770. Rents continued to mount[1] and plenty followed hard on the heels of shortage. The only time of acute distress was the winter of 1765–6 after the failure of the harvest, though heavy imports of grain helped to compensate for the fall in home production.[2] Three years before, the first concerted protest against rising rents and tithes had been made by the Oakboys in counties Tyrone, Fermanagh, Londonderry and Armagh[3] but prosperity in the linen trade in the second half of the decade[4] postponed for a few years a real trial of strength between privileged and underprivileged.

One hundred and ninety-four vessels were advertised to leave north Irish ports with emigrants to America during this decade, the peak years being, significantly, 1766 and 1767. One hundred and sixty-five of the vessels seem to have been engaged in normal Irish-American trade—over ninety per cent. of them sailed to either Philadelphia or New York—and generally advertised for

---

number of passengers that Patton's vessels *could* have carried on their twenty-five voyages.

[1] See Chapter V.

[2] *B.N.L.*, 11 Feb. and 14 Feb. 1765; *Freeman's Journal*, 22 May 1766; *Concise view of the Irish Society*, p. 123; *Commons' jn. Ire.*, xvi. 257. Exports of Irish oatmeal fell from 24,156 barrels in 1765 (financial year) to 278 barrels in 1766; imports of wheat rose in the same period from 14,130 cwt. to 39,456 cwt.

[3] *Charlemont MSS.*, pp. 21–2, 137; Minutes of Bangor presbytery, 9 Aug. 1763; Hamilton, *Earliest times*, pp. 319–21. The immediate cause of the outbreak was a dispute concerning the repair of roads.

[4] The average annual value of linen cloth exported from Ireland rose by over 27 per cent. in the period 1765–70 as compared with the previous five years. *Commons' jn. Ire.*, xvi. 405–8.

freight as well as for passengers. It has been possible to discover the number of emigrants in only seven of these vessels, the average being 146 passengers, the number declining in the last few years of the decade.[1] These vessels ranged in size from the smallest to the largest advertised during the period, but, as six of the seven sailed before 1766, the average passenger list of the 165 vessels engaged in this branch of the emigration trade may not have been much greater than one hundred.

Six vessels sailed to Nova Scotia between 1760 and 1769 under the direction of land promoters in that province, but comment on the extent of this movement will be reserved. South Carolina or Georgia was the destination of the remaining twenty-three vessels which sailed during the decade on other than normal trading voyages, thanks to the renewal of the bounty system which had attracted immigrants to South Carolina in the 1730s. By 1760, Indian attacks were causing 'distress and consternation' in South Carolina and, in order to increase the number of the white inhabitants of the colony, a duty was levied on the importation of negroes and the proceeds used to pay the passage money of protestant immigrants from Europe and to give forty shillings to each immigrant to purchase tools and provisions. Immigrants were to be exempt from taxes for ten years and the head of every family was to be granted one hundred acres of land, together with fifty acres for each member of his family.[2] The agents of at least one vessel, the *Falls*, added to the attraction of the bounty by offering a free passage, the royal bounty of land and money, and an annual wage of £5 to all who would indent for a period of four years.[3] These terms were much more generous than could have been

---

[1] The vessels and number of passengers were: *Providence*, Belfast—Philadelphia, 300 (*B.N.L.*, 14 Jan. 1763); *Marquis of Granby*, Belfast—Philadelphia and New York, 212 (ibid., 20 May 1763); *King of Prussia*, Newry—Philadelphia, 221 (ibid., 24 May 1763): *Venus*, Newry—New York, 22 (C.O. 5/1228, 24 Oct. 1763); *Prince of Wales*, Belfast—New York, 170 (C.O. 5/1228, 15 June 1764); *William*, Newry—Boston, 71 (Donovan, *Irish in Massachusetts*, p. 36); *Providence*, Portrush—New York, about 25 (*B.N.L.*, 3 Feb. 1769). The *William*, 140 tons, was the smallest vessel advertised during the decade and the *Providence*, 300 tons, among the largest. See Appendix C.
[2] Bull, governor of S.C., to B.T., 29 May 1760 (C.O. 5/377, f.20); same to same, 23 Sept. 1761 (C.O. 5/377, ff. 85–7); B.M., Add.MS 29973, pp. 26–7; McCardy, *S.C. under royal govt.*, p. 318; *Hist. account S.C.*, ii. 268. O'Brien, *Hidden phase*, p. 355. The bounty money offered was £4 sterling to all immigrants above twelve years of age, £2 to all between two and twelve years and £1 to all under two years.
[3] *B.N.L.*, 21 Oct. 1763. An account of the system of indentured labour will be found in Chapter VI.

secured by indentured servants in any other colony at the time. Despite news of attacks on north Irish settlements established during the first few years of the operation of the bounty,[1] the course of north Irish emigration was, in a measure, diverted for some years from the middle to the southern colonies. The surviving copies of the issues of the *Belfast News Letter* before 1762 do not reveal a single advertisement of passages on any ship bound for South Carolina. Between 1762 and 1767, the last year of the bounty, three vessels were stated to have sailed to Charleston at the request of passengers instead of to the north American port to which they had originally advertised sailings: in 1768 a vessel changed its destination from Charleston to Philadelphia for the same reason.[2] Nine vessels sailed with passengers from the north of Ireland to Charleston in 1767 but only three sailed to South Carolina and Georgia in 1768 and two of these were chartered by a Matthew Rea who had close personal contacts with the southern colonies.[3]

Fifteen of the twenty-three vessels that sailed to South Carolina and Georgia during the decade carried 2,472 emigrants.[4] These fifteen vessels represent a fair cross-section of emigrant shipping to South Carolina both in tonnage and in the years of sailing, the preponderance of statistics for the years 1765, 1766 and 1767 being an accurate reflection of the preponderance of those years in emigration to the southern colonies.[5] The average number of emigrants who sailed in each of the twenty-three vessels may, therefore, have been approximately 150, giving a total of between three and four thousand north Irish emigrants to South Carolina and Georgia in the decade reviewed. Scotch-Irish immigrants, both from Ireland and, more particularly, from North Carolina and Virginia have been given, with German immigrants, the credit for being mainly responsible for the doubling of South Carolina's white population to 70,000 in the period between 1763 and 1775.[6]

[1] *F.D.J.*, 24 Mar. 1764; *B.N.L.*, 30 Mar. 1764.
[2] *Sally*, 1765 (*B.N.L.*, May 14), *Belfast Pacquet*, 1760 (ibid., June 27) *Earl of Donegal*, 1767 and 1768 (ibid., Aug. 14 and June 28).
[3] See Appendix A and Chapter VIII. Two of the three advertised voyages to Charleston and Savannah in 1769 were sponsored by Rea.
[4] See Appendix C.
[5] Twelve of the fifteen vessels for which passenger statistics are available sailed between 1765 and 1767: fifteen of the twenty-three emigrant voyages advertised to South Carolina and Georgia between 1761 and 1769 were made in those three years.
[6] B.M., Add.MS 29973, p. 24; Sutherland, *Pop. distribution in col. Amer.*, p. 248.

The Middle Years: 1731–1769

From the evidence that has been cited it is reasonable to conclude that the number of emigrants who left the five north Irish ports in the 'sixties was in the region of 20,000 or slightly higher. The resulting yearly average is much lower than has been advanced hitherto. It has been stated, for example, that the number of emigrants from the north of Ireland to the American colonies rose from 3,000 to 6,000 per annum between the years 1725 and 1768.[1] In 1767 it was estimated, however, that a total of 4,000 people emigrated annually from all Irish ports during the 'sixties and the writer of this pamphlet would have tended to exaggerate rather than underestimate the extent of emigration, as his purpose was to draw attention to the great sums of money carried out of the country by absentee landlords, emigrants and others.[2] Arthur Young's statement that 2,000 people emigrated annually from Belfast in the 'sixties is of little value as his tour was spent among landlords who exaggerated the extent of emigration during the 'sixties in order to minimise the increase which took place in the early 'seventies. Young was persuaded that only a slight increase had taken place and that the increase was caused solely by the depressed state of the linen trade.[3]

Many estimates have been made of the extent of north Irish emigration during earlier parts of this long period of forty years. The most commonly accepted of these is that 12,000 people emigrated annually between 1729 and 1750 but the mode by which this estimate has been reached has not, unfortunately, been stated.[4] Its accuracy must be doubted as almost half the period was occupied by war, and emigration on such a scale would have dwarfed all previous emigrations from the north of Ireland. The emigration of 12,000 people would have involved the annual sailing of about sixty average vessels. Records, in whole or in part, of the *Belfast News Letter* exist for three years of the period. These show that one vessel was advertised to leave the north of Ireland with emigrants in 1739, one in 1746, and eleven in 1750.[5] In only one

[1] *Dublin University Magazine*, i (1832), 476–7.
[2] *A list of the absentees of Ireland* (1767), p. 12.
[3] *Tour*, i. p. 164.
[4] Proud, *History of Pennsylvania*, ii. 273–4; Lecky, *Ire.*, i. 247; W. D. Killen, *The ecclesiastical history of Ireland from the earliest period to the present times*, p. 261–2; O'Brien, *Hidden phase*, pp. 257–8; Latimer, *Hist. Ire. pres.*, p. 321; Ford, *Scotch-Irish*, p. 198.
[5] Surviving issues of the B.N.L. of 1746 are confined to the months of June, August and September. In later years, issues in these months included the bulk of emigration advertisements.

year during the early 'seventies, the greatest period of north Irish emigration prior to the outbreak of the American war, did the rate of emigration exceed 12,000 people.[1]

The estimate is further disproved by an analysis of the statement that about 50,000 emigrants from the north of Ireland arrived in Philadelphia between 1733 and 1750.[2] O'Brien based this estimate on the tonnage of the vessels that arrived at Philadelphia from the north of Ireland during these eighteen years, assuming that every vessel carried passengers equal in number to its tonnage. This was the mode of estimation adopted in 1773 with regard to the heavy emigration that was then taking place[3] but no attempt has been made to justify its extension to an earlier period. In 1773, vessel after vessel was noted as sailing 'full of passengers' from the north Irish ports but the comment does not appear in any of the available copies of Irish newspapers published between 1733 and 1750. The vessels that arrived in Philadelphia in this period probably did not carry more than half the number of passengers that they would have carried in the 'seventies. Assuming that this was so and that O'Brien's tonnage statistics are reliable[4] the total number of north Irish emigrants to all American ports in these eighteen years may have been between 30,000 and 40,000 as Philadelphia was the most popular destination at the time.[5]

The number of vessels that advertised passages to America from the north of Ireland averaged only about six in each year of the 'fifties.[6] Cursorily advertised and seldom announcing delays in their departure, these vessels probably carried fewer than 500 emigrants annually in a decade that was overshadowed by war.

Though it is impossible to ascertain with any degree of certainty the number of north Irish emigrants during the forty years reviewed in this chapter it is felt that, from the composite picture that has been drawn, an estimate of between 50,000 and 70,000 would not be unreasonable or grossly inaccurate.

[1] See Chapter V.
[2] O'Brien, *Washington's Irish assoc.*, p. 220.
[3] B.N.L., 6 April.
[4] The total tonnage of shipping that left north Irish ports may have been somewhat greater than that given by O'Brien. Many emigrant vessels from the north of Ireland called at Cork for provisions on the outward journey and the latter port was sometimes noted in American newspapers as the port of origin. See Chapter V.
[5] Nine of the thirteen vessels advertised in surviving copies of the *B.N.L.* prior to 1750 gave Philadelphia as their destination.
[6] See Appendix A.

CHAPTER V

The Climax: 1770–1775

THE emigrant trade subsided into a limited decline with the ending of the South Carolina bounty in 1767 but this decline was halted in 1770, and, in the following year, the trade boomed as never before and once more—as in the 'twenties—fears were expressed of 'pernicious consequences' should the drain of protestants from Ireland continue unchecked.[1]

Evidence by interested parties is always suspect and often contradictory and inconclusive. Emigration agents were interested parties in the emigration scene but their self-interest has served to give a rough guide to the fluctuations in the emigrant trade. That they undertook the expense of fitting out additional vessels for the passenger trade and advertising them more profusely in the 'seventies than ever before is an indication of the prosperity of their business. In the seven complete emigration seasons after the treaty of Paris, an average of 5,900 tons of emigrant shipping was advertised annually: in the four seasons prior to the outbreak of war in 1775, the average annual tonnage increased to 10,400.[2] The increase in the normal emigrant trade in the 'seventies was even greater than this comparison suggests for, between 1761 and 1767, many vessels which would not otherwise have been in the trade were attracted by the bounties offered to immigrants by South Carolina. This special factor ceased to operate after 1767 and

---

[1] M. Paterson, lord chief justice of Ireland, to—, 2 Nov. 1772, (National Library, Dublin, Townshend MS 394a).
[2] Details of the number and tonnage of emigrant vessels that were advertised in north Irish newspapers will be found in Appendix A.

the average emigrant tonnage advertised between 1768 and 1770 was only 4,200. The increased energies after 1770 of the promoters of the emigrant trade are a measure of the increased demand for their services.

Various estimates have been made of the volume of north Irish emigration in the years 1771–5. On the one hand, the historian of early nineteenth century emigration from Ireland has stated that the movement to colonial America reached a peak of about six thousand emigrants annually during the period:[1] on the other, the historian of the Celtic Irish in America has numbered the emigrants from the ports of Belfast, Londonderry, Newry, and Larne at 34,700 in the years 1771 and 1772.[2] One was pointing out —not unfairly—the 'very slight' volume of Irish emigration to colonial America and the other was stressing the part played by Irishmen in the revolution.

Much of the haze which surrounds the extent of emigration during the period would have been cleared away had port officials obeyed the instruction of the Irish customs commissioners that they should collect information on the number of people emigrating to America in 1772 and 1773.[3] Unfortunately, the minutes of subsequent meetings of the commissioners contain no further reference to the matter. Nevertheless, two factors enable a more accurate estimate to be made of the volume of emigration between 1771 and 1775 than in any other part of the century—not only do the complete copies of an interested newspaper span the years but evidence of the extent of emigration from Belfast and Londonderry during 1772 and 1773 was submitted to a committee of the Irish parliament.

According to a letter to this committee from representative linen drapers in county Londonderry, 6,000 emigrants left the port of Londonderry in 1772 and 1773. Evidence was given before the same committee that 3,541 emigrants had gone to America through the port of Belfast between October 1771 and October 1773[4]—that is, roughly, during the 1772 and 1773 emigrant seasons. Belfast and Londonderry accounted for 48½[5] of the 72

[1] Adams, *Irish emig. in 19th cent.*, p. 69.
[2] O'Brien, *Hidden phase*, p. 285.
[3] Customs, 1/125, p. 26 (19 Oct. 1773).
[4] *Commons' jn. Ire.*, xvi. 411, 413. The committee was set up to examine the extent and causes of the decline of the Irish linen trade.
[5] One vessel was advertised to call at both Belfast and Newry for emigrants.

vessels which advertised for emigrants from north Irish ports in these years. Assuming that the two statements presented to parliament were accurate and that the number of emigrants leaving each port was proportionate to the number of emigrant vessels which left that port, this evidence would suggest that about 15,000 people emigrated through the five north Irish ports in 1772 and 1773. Exaggeration of the extent of emigration would have been in the interests of the Londonderry linen merchants, who wished to impress on the government the urgent need of measures to aid their declining trade. Yet, as will be seen, their estimate was a reasonable one. The accuracy of the Belfast evidence is very doubtful, despite its apparently conclusive preciseness. It is known that each of eight vessels which left Belfast during the period carried an average of 230 emigrants:[1] if the statement presented to parliament was correct, the remaining 14½ vessels, including some of the largest which left the port, unaccountably carried an average of only 117 passengers. Even Arthur Young whose estimates of north Irish emigration during this period erred on the conservative side stated that 4,000 people had emigrated to America through Belfast in 1773.[2]

Contemporary newspapers supply a less obvious but broader and more reliable basis for measuring the volume of emigration during the early 'seventies. Advertisements in the *Belfast News Letter* and the *Londonderry Journal* give a well-nigh exhaustive list of the ships which sailed with emigrants to the American colonies in this period.[3] It was assumed by the *Belfast News Letter* that the number of emigrants from the north of Ireland to America in the early 'seventies was approximately equal to the total tonnage of the vessels as given in the advertisements.[4] If such an assumption could be proved sound, the adequacy of shipping records would permit the reliable estimation of the numbers who emigrated at this vital time.

A study of the available evidence shows that this guide can be

[1] Details of the number of emigrants carried in particular vessels will be found in Appendix C.
[2] *Tour*, i. 164. Young stated that no emigrants sailed from Belfast to America in 1775, but 480 sailed on board one vessel alone (*Prosperity*, B.N.L., 8 June 1775).
[3] The voyages of two emigrant vessels which sailed in these years without advertising are recorded in Irish newspapers. The *Rogers* sailed from Portaferry, co. Down, to Baltimore in 1775 (*B.N.L.*, 21 July 1775) and the *General Wolfe* from Londonderry to Philadelphia in 1772 (ibid., 15 Dec. 1772).
[4] Ibid., 6 April 1773.

accepted with little amendment. There is specific information, about the number of north Irish emigrants carried by forty vessels between 1771 and 1774. The following table, a summary of Appendix C, is a yearly synopsis of the relevant information available about these vessels.

Year	Tonnage of vessels concerned	No. of passengers carried	Average no. of passengers per ton
1771	600	500	.83
1772	4,400	4,796	1.09
1773	4,650	5,017	1.08
1774	3,150	2,103	.67
Totals	12,800	12,416	.97

The forty vessels listed were only one-third of the total number of vessels advertised to carry emigrants in these years and so it may be doubted if they represented a cross-section of the trade or were selected by the newspapers merely because the number of passengers each vessel carried was sufficiently great to attract public attention. Emigrant ships did sail, even in peak years, with relatively small numbers on board[1] but it would seem that these forty vessels did not alone reap the richest harvest of the emigrant trade. Many other vessels were stated to be carrying 'a great number of passengers' or were 'full of passengers' when they sailed. The diversity of the sources of the information shows that no special effort was made by the *Belfast News Letter*, despite its hostile attitude to emigration, to select a few extreme examples to stress the magnitude of the exodus. No notice of the numbers on board twelve of the vessels appeared in the *Belfast News Letter*, though the average number per ton in those vessels was as great as the average of those noted in that newspaper. Moreover, though in many cases the number of emigrants on board a vessel was included in the announcement that the vessel had sailed, American newspapers were often the source of the *Belfast News Letter*'s information. Had the ships which brought these newspapers to Belfast left America a few weeks

[1] The *Lord Chatham* found it so difficult to sign on passengers for Charleston at Belfast in 1773 that the vessel finally sailed to Barbados (*B.N.L.*, 16 Nov. 1773).

before or after they did, the appendix would not contain many of the names it now includes but would almost certainly contain equally striking evidence concerning other vessels.

About 40,000 tons of emigrant shipping left the north Irish ports between 1771 and 1774. It would, therefore, follow that the number of emigrants approached that total though it must be remembered that the table is weighted by the more complete returns of 1772 and 1773, years of intensive emigration. The annual proportion of passengers to tonnage would suggest that about 7,700 emigrated in 1771, 9,300 in 1772, 12,300 in 1773, and 8,300 in 1774.[1]

Widely different sources substantiate these estimates and justify the manner of compiling them. Robert Stephenson, inspector to the trustees of the linen manufacture in Ireland, in a report to a British parliamentary committee, based his estimate of the number of north Irish emigrants in 1771 and 1772 on the tonnage of the vessels concerned and believed that each ton of shipping represented one emigrant.[2] An American newspaper reported that 3,500 people left the port of Londonderry during the year ended mid-September 1773:[3] that period embraced part of 1772 and part of 1773 and the average annual emigrant tonnage from the port in those years was 3,700 tons. It was stated in the British house of commons that 30,000 people had emigrated from the north of Ireland between 1771 and April 1774.[4] In 1788, when the events of the 'seventies were sufficiently distant to be dispassionately reviewed yet sufficiently recent to be a memory and not a legend, the number of north Irish emigrants in 1771, 1772, and 1773 was reported as 28,650.[5]

Despite this confirmation of the *Belfast News Letter*'s estimate that the number of emigrants equalled the tonnage of the vessels concerned, it has been claimed that the number of emigrants was really double that tonnage. M. J. O'Brien has based this claim on

---

[1] Though 510 passengers left the north of Ireland for America in 1775 on board the vessels *Prosperity* and *John*, whose total tonnage was 950 (*B.N.L.*, 18, 23 and 25 Apr. 1775), it would be impossible to conclude that about 5,000 people emigrated on board the 9,150 tons of shipping advertised to sail from the north of Ireland to America in that year—the clouds of war were uninviting and, moreover, the linen trade had stabilised itself and rents had fallen in some parts of the north.
[2] *Commons' reports* (G.B.), iii. 107b.
[3] *Maryland Journal*, 16 Oct. 1773 (*B.N.L.*, 25 Jan. 1774).
[4] *Parliamentary Debates* (1771–4), xvii, 1145 (20 Apr. 1774).
[5] *F.D.J.*, 26 Apr. 1788.

the eighteenth century technical meaning of the term *passenger*[1] and has concluded that the newspaper did not include servants in its calculation. He has assumed that the number of those who emigrated as servants was equal to the number who paid their passage money and so has concluded that almost 35,000 emigrants left the four principal north Irish ports for America in the years 1771 and 1772. Some colour is given to O'Brien's distinction by the fact that the *Belfast News Letter*'s comment did suggest that each of the 17,400 emigrants it referred to paid £3. 5s. as passage money. Nevertheless, had 34,800 and not 17,400 people emigrated, it is inconceivable that the newspaper would have been so class conscious as to have omitted the number of servants, for the purpose of the comment was to stress the magnitude of emigration. Indeed, O'Brien accepted the statement that 'almost all' the north Irish emigrants in those years made the journey at their own expense. Moreover, a second conclusion by O'Brien illustrates his exaggeration of the volume of Irish emigration. He has stated that about 100,000 people emigrated between 1771 and 1773 because 18,000 were said to have emigrated in the first six months of 1773.[2] Such a statement ignores the fact that emigration was much greater in the first half of 1773 than in any other period of six months in the 'seventies.

A second factor which has not helped in arriving at an accurate estimate of the number of north Irish emigrants in the early 'seventies is an apparent exaggeration of the number who left Ireland as a whole. When one reads O'Brien's claim that 100,000 emigrated from Ireland to America in the period 1771–3, or that 150,000 did so in the early 'seventies,[3] and recalls the comment that 'these emigrations [were] from the protestant part of Ireland',[4] the impression must remain that the number of north Irish emigrants was little short of these figures.

---

[1] The term was used in advertisements to distinguish emigrants who paid for their passage from those who emigrated as indentured servants or redemptioners.

[2] *Hidden phase*, pp. 237, 285–9.

[3] Klett, *Pres. in Pa.*, p.22; MacLean, *Scot. highlanders*, p.45; Flood, 'Irish emigration to the American colonies', in *Amer.-Ir. Hist. Soc. Jn.*, xxvi., pp. 205–6. The only evidence Flood cites in support of his estimate is the statement that he made 'a careful study of the emigration returns published in the Dublin, Belfast, Cork, Galway, and Waterford papers'. I am not aware of the survival of any Galway newspapers of the period. I have not examined any Waterford newspapers, but no such returns were given in the Belfast, Dublin and Cork papers.

[4] *Parliamentary Debates* (1771–4), xvii. 1145 (17 May 1774).

Creating such an impression was not the purpose of the writers who have made these claims. O'Brien's estimate was accompanied by the claim that two-thirds of the emigrants were Roman catholics and hence, presumably, largely from the south of Ireland. Flood's figures would suggest that emigration from the north Irish ports between 1771 and 1773 was little more than three-quarters of that from Dublin, Cork and Waterford. The volume of south Irish emigration does not fall within the scope of this book but it is felt that an unchallenged acceptance of the estimates given by Flood and O'Brien would serve to give an exaggerated view of north Irish emigration and an acceptance of their comments would relegate that emigration to a wrongfully minor place in the Irish emigration scene of the eighteenth century.

Emigration from the south of Ireland to the American colonies in the 'seventies was certainly not unknown. One thousand families were said to have emigrated through Galway in the years 1772–3:[1] the appearance of 'several ships' seeking emigrants at Cork, Limerick and Galway was said to have caused 'great alarm' in 1773.[2] On the other hand, evidence of the dominantly southern nature of emigration in these years is singularly lacking. The total number of emigrants from Ireland was stated to have been not less than 30,000 in 1772 and 1773,[3] and, of these, the north Irish ports accounted for over 22,000. Young saw no evidence of emigration worthy of note till he arrived in the north of Ireland. An exhaustive search has not been made of all south Irish newspapers of the period but a cross-section of newspapers covering the entire period has been studied[4] and reveals two significant features. First, with few exceptions, comments on emigration originated in one of the northern ports. Second, comparatively few transatlantic shipping advertisements were printed in south Irish newspapers and none of these was backed by any but the most elementary organisation.[5] Vessels advertised in the northern

---

[1] *Commons' jn. Ire.*, xvi. 412. Letter from Loughgeorge, co. Galway, 11 Feb. 1774. Another correspondent estimated that about 800 people had emigrated from Galway and neighbourhood in the years 1772–3 (Andrew French, Galway, 11 Nov. 1773: ibid., p. 415).

[2] *F.D.J.*, 10 April 1773.

[3] *Commons' reports (G.B.)*, iii. col. 1076.

[4] 1771—*Dublin Chronicle, Limerick Chronicle*: 1772—*Public Journal*: 1773- *F.D.J.* and *C.E.P.*: 1774—*F.D.J.*: 1775—*F.D.J.*

[5] Of the eight vessels advertised in *F.D.J.* in 1773, two were to sail from Newry:

newspapers carried about two-thirds of the 6,222 passengers noted as landing at six north American ports in the period August – November, 1773.[1]

Flood and O'Brien estimated the number of immigrants entering America from Ireland as a whole on the basis of one immigrant per ton of shipping. Such a basis of estimation is unwarranted for it was originally made by the *Belfast News Letter* in respect of north Irish vessels and no attempt to justify the extension of its application to other ports has been made. The assumption is made even more inaccurate by the fact that many vessels from the north of Ireland called at Cork—generally for provisions—on the outward voyage and, as Cork was given in the American newspapers as the port of departure from Ireland, the passengers carried by such vessels have been claimed as southern Irish. For example, though the *Nedham* (or *Needham*) left Newry in May 1773 with 500 emigrants on board,[2] yet, because it called at Cork on the voyage to Newcastle and New York, it is claimed that these emigrants were from the Cork district.[3] Had between 60,000 and 70,000 Irish Roman catholics emigrated to America in the 'seventies, it is difficult to believe that John Adams would have said that 'a native who cannot read and write is as rare an appearance as a Jacobite or a Roman catholic, that is, as rare as a comet or earthquake'.[4] O'Brien's explanation that the majority of the Irish Roman catholics changed their religion in the colonies when surrounded by protestant settlements is both unconvincing in the light of Irish history and unjust to the people whose interests he defends.[5]

---

three of the seven vessels advertised in 1773 referred to Newry sailings and in none of these cases was a Dublin agent named.

[1] The six ports were New York, Philadelphia, Charleston, Halifax, Newport, and 'New Jersey' (*Gentleman's Magazine*, (July 1774), xliv. 332).

[2] *B.N.L.*, 21 May 1773.

[3] O'Brien, *Washington's Ir. assoc.*, p. 234. The danger of basing claims of the origins of Irish emigrants on the stated destinations or clearance ports of ships engaged in Irish-American trade is illustrated by O'Brien's quotation from the shipping news of the *Pa. Gazette* of 15 Aug. 1771 (O'Brien, *Hidden phase*, p. 277). Of the four vessels named as trading with south Irish ports, three—*Philadelphia*, *Wallworth* and *Newry Packet*—were at the time engaged in the north Irish emigrant trade. See Appendix D.

[4] *Works of John Adams*, iii. 456; Klett, *Pres. in Pa.*, p. 23.

[5] O'Brien, *Washington's Ir. assoc.*, pp. 2–3. The fantastic claim has been made that the number of 'keltic or catholic' Irish emigrants to colonial America was twenty times that of 'protestant Irish of possible Scotch descent' (T. H. Murray in *Boston Traveller*, 1 May 1895, in Green, *Scotch-Irish*, pp. 42–3). Only ignorance of the weakness of the Roman catholic element in colonial America could explain such a statement. Two

Little need be said of north Irish emigration in 1775. It would be misleading to place the number of emigrants in that year on a par with tonnage. Emigration declined by about one-third in 1774 and falling rents and a quickening in the recovery of the linen trade would have, of themselves, caused a continuation of this trend in 1775, but an additional factor caused its acceleration. While the burden of life in Ireland was becoming less oppressive, the dark clouds of war were gathering beyond a fickle Atlantic which had reaped a grim harvest from among those who had sailed from Newry in 1774.[1] Though many, such as those with family ties with America, were undaunted, the emigrant trade was less appealing than hitherto to the shipping interest. The falling-off of interest in emigration and the exclusion of Irish goods from America[2] turned the eyes of ship owners to other regions. The rebellious colonists invited the people of Ireland to emigrate to America where they were promised 'a safe asylum from poverty, and, in time, from oppression also',[3] but non-importation was no inducement to the shipping industry to provide facilities for a dwindling number of emigrants. In 1775 only one-tenth of the year's transatlantic vessels were advertised after the end of April, compared with over two-fifths in the previous two years. It was significant that, though the *Prosperity* left Belfast for Philadelphia with a full complement of 480 emigrants, the *John* left the same port four days later with only thirty emigrants on board for the lesser known Baltimore.[4] Families and friends were reuniting before the storm broke and it is probable that few left at this late hour for other reasons. North Irish emigration to pre-revolutionary America ended silently with the

---

informed Roman catholic observers may be cited to show that weakness. In a report in 1785 to Vergennes, the French foreign minister, the Marquis de Barbe-Marbois estimated the total Roman catholic population of the infant republic at about 32,500, excluding those in purely French districts (G. Bancroft, *History of the formation of the constitution of the United States of America*, i. 421). Dr Carroll, the first Roman catholic bishop in the United States, in a report to the Propaganda in 1785, estimated the Roman catholic population of the republic to be 26,000 (Maguire, *Irish in America*, p. 357). These estimates would probably have been even smaller had they been made in 1775 for, in the intervening decade, the number of Roman catholics in the thirteen states had increased (C. H. Metzger, *The Quebec act: a primary cause of the American revolution*, p. 7).

[1] *B.N.L.*, 30 Sept. 1774.
[2] Macpherson, *Merch. shipping*, iii. 421; *B.N.L.*, 5 May 1775.
[3] Address to the people of Ireland, 28 July 1775 (*Journal continental congress*, ii. 212–8).
[4] *B.N.L.*, 18 and 23 April 1775. The *Prosperity* and the *John* were approximately the same size: the advertised tonnages were 500 and 450 respectively.

departure of the *Waddell* for Madeira instead of Maryland[1] and the disappearance, one by one, of shipping advertisements before the vessels were due to depart on their transatlantic voyages.

The primary cause of the sharp increase in emigration during the first two years of the decade was the fact that rack-renting reached a crescendo in the north of Ireland in the late 'sixties and early 'seventies. The common people complained of the 'extravagant rents' there[2] and one of the most graphic descriptions of the tyranny of rents spoke of

the deplorable state to which oppression has brought us to, by reason of heavy rents which are become so great a burden to us that we are not scarcely able to bear . . . that one and all . . . . . are grevious to be born: so that betwixt landlord and rectors, the very marrow is screwed out of our bones, and our lives are even become so burdensome to us, by these uncharitable and unreasonable men, that we do not care whether we live or die; for they lay such burthen upon our shoulders that they cannot touch them with one of their fingers; they have reduced us to such a deplorable state by such grievious oppressions that the poor is turned black in the face, and the skin parched on their back, that they are rendered incapable to support their starving families with the common necessaries of life, that nature is but scarcely supported, that they have not even food, nor yet raiment to secure them from the extremities of the weather wither by day or night . . . . .[3]

The belief that rents were oppressive was not confined to the cottages of rebels but was held even in Dublin castle. Townshend denounced the northern landlords whose rents were 'stretched to the utmost' and Harcourt, his successor as lord lieutenant, wrote in similar vein of 'the unreasonable rise of lands' as the main cause of unrest in the north.[4]

Historians have accepted the fact that rents rose considerably but a detailed examination of rentals yields revelations that would

[1] Ibid., 12 May 1775.
[2] Proclamation of the Hearts of Steel, enclosed in Townshend to Rochford, 27 Mar. 1772 (S.P. 63/435, no. 63e).
[3] Proclamation of the Hearts of Steel, dated 23 Mar. 1772 (P.R.O.N.I., D. 654).
[4] Townshend to Rochford, 18 Mar. 1772 (S.P. 63/635, no. 45a); Harcourt to same, 18 July 1773 (S.P. 63/440, no. 50).

have startled even Francis Joseph Bigger, the most bitter critic of the Irish landlords of the eighteenth century.[1] The only concrete comparisons between north Irish rents of the 'seventies and those earlier in the century were made by Arthur Young but, unfortunately Young's comparisons concerned districts removed from the usual recruiting areas of the emigration ports.[2] Few rent-rolls of the period survive but it is possible to form an accurate picture of conditions in the north of county Down and in the south of county Londonderry, two regions of considerable emigration, from the estate office records of the Stewart family, the head of which became the first marquess of Londonderry towards the end of the century.

An examination of the leases of the Stewart lands in north Down shows that the average rent per acre of newly-leased land in each decade between the 1720s and the 1770s was as follows:

1720s	1730s	1740s	1750s	1760s	1770s
2s. 11d.	4s. 5d.	4s. 2d.	6s. 9d.	12s. 7d.	13s. 6d.

Reservations must, of course, be made in making generalisations from the data available for compiling this table. It would be impossible to state precisely the advance in rents unless a particular farm or complete townland were leased every decade, but the usual term of leases granted by the Stewarts and by the Colvilles, their predecessors, was three lives or thirty-one years, whichever was the longer. Land values vary from townland to townland, and even from farm to farm within a townland, but a survey of the incomplete leases of a whole estate cannot indicate such variations. On the other hand, such a number of townlands is embraced that a more accurate view of the average price of land is given than would be covered by the statistics of a single townland. The basis of the summary has also one great advantage over a succession of rent-rolls—all the rents included are on new leases and so the levelling tendency of unexpired leases is not carried through two or three decades as in the case of rent-rolls.

The accuracy of some details of the summary as an indication of what was happening on the estate as a whole may be doubted. For

[1] See *The Ulster land war of 1770*.
[2] *Tour*, i. 49, 236, 473.

example, few new leases were granted during the 'forties and so it would be unjustifiable to conclude that, as indicated by the table, rents fell in North Down during that decade though they may well have done so following the great famine of 1740.[1] It is intended to draw only two conclusions from the table, namely, that rents in north Down rose steeply in the 'sixties when the linen trade was extremely prosperous and that, by the 'seventies, rents were treble what they had been thirty or forty years before. In other words, to renew a lease which expired in the 'seventies entailed the trebling of the former rent. Evidence from adjacent parts of the county supports this generalisation. The rent of four townlands of the Saintfield estate of Francis Price rose from £279. 5s. 4½d. in 1751 to £583. 10s. 5d. in 1776, even though in the latter year some of the rents were the same as they had been in 1751 as the leases had not expired.[2] When nine farms in the townland of Drumlough were advertised for sale in 1769 it was advertised that their annual rental value had increased to £165. 10s. 1d. from £96. 15s. 7d. in 1758.[3]

County Down was not the only area in which rents were increasing in the 'seventies. Correspondence between Alexander Stewart and Thomas Bateson shows that the same thing was going on in the south of county Londonderry. Bateson had acquired a lease of part of the Salter's proportion in the Magherafelt area and Stewart purchased half of Bateson's interest in the proportion in 1754 and at the same time made the speculative purchase of half of any rent increases, these being expected to amount to £900 by 1772. By 1771 the rental of the estate had increased by £150; in 1772 there was a further advance of £1,500 and it was estimated that there would be a further increase of £250 in 1773. In other words, the actual increase in rents was £1,800 and not £900 as had been estimated in 1754. As the total rent of Bateson's original holding in the proportion was £4,128. 16s. 7d. in 1773, it follows that, when leases expired during the 1771–3 period, rents rose by at

---

[1] For the effects of this famine on the region, see Stevenson, *Two centuries of life in Down*, pp. 239–40. According to a pamphleteer of 1730, the average rental of Ireland was then 4s. 6d. per acre (*An appeal to Dean Swift, by way of a reply to the observer on seasonal remarks*, p. 124).

[2] The townlands were Carsons, Lisowen, Aghadarragh, and Ballyagharty.

[3] B.N.L., 12 Sept. 1769. The rental of Lord Dungannon's estate in county Down reveals a similar trend to the rentals of the estates of Stewart and Price (P.R.O.N.I., D. 162/85).

least two-thirds over what they had been twenty years before. The actual increase may have been greater as the 1773 rental probably included many farms held under pre-1754 leases.[1]

Coupled with Young's observations, the Stewart documents dealing with counties Down and Londonderry indicate that there was a swift upward surge of rents in the north of Ireland in the 'sixties and 'seventies. One reason for this was the method by which lettings were made. The system of 'canting' the tenancies of farms has drawn the fire of the critics,[2] but this system of auctioning is today accepted as normal and just over a wide compass of life. The real evil lay in the insistence on written bids for farms, coupled with the refusal to allow any person to bid a second time for a farm and the ignoring of the claims of the person in occupation. This system was becoming common about 1770, and more and more advertisements added postscripts such as 'No preference is promised nor will any be given, and as soon as a sufficient proposal is received the tenant will be declared. No second proposal will be received from the same person.'[3] Rents fixed by canting may have been unreasonably high because of the great demand for land but they became even more unreasonable under this system which ensured that the sitting tenant would if at all possible bid more than the land was worth in order not to risk losing his farm.

Another cause of mounting rents was the growing tendency of landlords to lease land in large areas. Such lettings were convenient to the landowner as they facilitated the collection of rents, but the divisions were too extensive for both the means and the needs of the majority of the people. The original lessees, known as middlemen or land-jobbers, divided the lands among tenants who, in turn, often sub-leased part of their holdings: it was alleged that as many as five intermediate lessees stood between the resident tenant and the landowner.[4] The profits on all the intermediate leases had ultimately to be borne by the tenant who worked the land and it was on estates which had been leased to middlemen that rack-renting was seen at its worst. The leases granted by Sir

---

[1] Londonderry Estate Office Papers (P.R.O.N.I., D. 654).
[2] See printed remonstrance signed 'Northern protestant draper', enclosed in Townshend to Rochford, 27 Mar. 1772 (S.P. 63/435, no. 63g).
[3] Advertisement of letting of lands of James Dawson, Tandragee, county Armagh (B.N.L., 3 Mar. 1769).
[4] Jas. Erskine, capt. in Ld. Drogheda's light dragoons, to John O'Neill, M.P. for Antrim, enclosed in Townshend to Rochford, 15 Apr. 1772 (S.P. 63/435, no. 82c).

The Climax: 1770–1775

George Saville on his Irish estate at Augher, county Tyrone, had let the land at between three shillings and five shillings per acre but, because of the 'claws of preying vultures', the resident tenants had to pay rent of between forty shillings and sixty shillings per acre.[1] The middlemen were vigorously condemned. Charlemont wrote of them as 'monopolising land-jobbers' and 'intermediate oppressors';[2] their activities were described in the British parliament as 'a new oppression under an Hebrew tribe, called . . . leasees . . . in the case of Ireland, grinding the hard-labouring man'.[3] It was this class that Young denounced most bitterly, describing its members as 'blood-suckers of the poor tenantry' and 'the most oppressive species of tyrant that ever lent assistance to the destruction of a nation'.[4]

The middleman was not a phenomenon peculiar to the 'seventies. For a century before that date, the London companies had leased their lands to men such as Jackson and the Colville and Stewart leases of the early eighteenth century often refer to under-tenants, even in farms of only twenty acres in area. The system reached its zenith in the north of Ireland in 1770, however, with the appearance of Thomas Greg and Waddell Cunningham, two Belfast merchants, as leading contenders for the leasing of entire estates.[5] It was the activities of these two men that fanned simmering discontent into insurrection, which, in turn, resulted in heavy emigration.

The most striking feature of the *Belfast News Letter* files of 1769 and 1770 is the unusually heavy amount of land advertised to be let. Some of the largest and most prosperous estates in the north of Ireland were involved in this abnormal turnover of leases. The ninety-six farms, covering over four thousand acres, advertised to be let by Clotworthy Upton included some of the best land on the main road from Belfast to the town of Antrim.[6] The two thousand acres, occupied by over one hundred tenants, advertised by Lord

---

[1] *Scots Magazine* (Nov. 1773), xxxv. 591.

[2] *Charlemont MSS.*, p. 21.

[3] *Parliamentary Debates* (1773-4), xvii. 1116–17 (20 Apr. 1774).

[4] *Tour*, ii. 97.

[5] John Greg, the father of Thomas Greg, was a middleman in the fifties, subletting the lands at exorbitant rents (Bigger, *Land war of 1770*, p. 28). The indignant tenants replied by wrecking his house (*B.N.L.*, 14 Dec. 1757). Cunningham had been a prosperous merchant in New York before he returned to his native Belfast in the early 'sixties and entered into partnership with Thos. Greg. It has been stated that Cunningham was concerned in the slave trade (*B.N.L.*, 2 July 1765).

[6] *B.N.L.*, 3 Jan. 1769.

Dungannon comprised equally good land in the neighbourhood of Larne.[1] Middlemen were expressly excluded by Dungannon's advertisement and no outrages were reported on his lands. Outrages in plenty followed on the estates of Upton and others. In the five years previous to 1769 only three references to disturbances caused by discontent over the land system appeared in the *Belfast News Letter*:[2] in the five years which followed, ninety-one such references appeared, forty-four of them in March and April 1772.[3]

Though there was indignation against both the landlords and the new lessees who had displaced the former tenants, the disturbances did not become widespread till the leases of the earl of Donegall's county Antrim estate expired in 1770. Donegall, preferring cash in hand to an increase in annual income, wished to relet the estate at its former rent and raise £100,000 in fines as compensation for this concession. This sum—which amounted to between three and four times the annual rental of the estate—was far beyond the means of most tenants who found a single year's rent an ample burden.[4] The tenants who could not raise sufficient money to pay their portion of the fines were evicted or their leases disposed of to Thomas Greg and Waddell Cunningham who raised the rents of some of the under-tenants and turned the remainder of the land over to pasture.[5] Outrages followed at once and the hough-

---

[1] Ibid., 19 Jan. 1770.
[2] Ibid., 21 Feb. and 12 June 1764, 17 Mar. 1767.
[3] Ibid., 6 June, 25 July, 5 Sept. 1769; 17 and 24 Apr. 22 May, 4 Sept., 30 Oct., 2 Nov, 1770; 4, 8, 18, 25 Jan., 5, 8, 12, 15, 22 Feb., 23 Aug., 3, 6, 13, 17 Sept., 12, 22 Nov., 31 Dec., 1771; 24 Jan., 13, 17, 24, 27, 31 Mar. 3, 7, 10, 14, 17, 21, 24, 28 Apr. 1, 5, 8, 12, 19, 22, 29 May, 9 June, 17, 21, 28 July, 25 Aug., 25, 29 Sept., 13, 17 Nov., 11 Dec., 1772; 8 Jan., 12 Mar. 1773. These references include reports of disturbances, advertisements offering rewards for the arrest of rioters, announcements of the formation of local associations to preserve peace, and 'admonitions' by various presbyteries addressed to those presbyterians who had taken part in the disturbances.
[4] Froude, *English in Ire.*, ii. 118–20; Lecky, *Ire. 18 cent.*, ii. 50; O'Brien, *Econ. hist. Ire. 18th cent.*, p. 83. Young estimated that Donegall's annual income from his county Antrim estate was £31,000 in 1776 (*Tour*, ii. 166). The income of the estate was £4,004 in 1715. (P.R.O.N.I., *rep. D.K. 1928*, p. 16). The development of Belfast accounted for part of the increase.
[5] The incident was thus described three years later:
A certain noble lord of very limited abilities, but extreme property . . . visited this country to let his lands. The method he pursued opened the way to tyranny and oppression. He either set a great scope to one man, or he took fines, by which means the poor industrious tenants, who occupied the land, unable to pay the demand of

ing of cattle became so prevalent that it was carried on 'even at noonday undisguised'.[1] During the next year the disturbances spread to other parts of county Antrim and into counties Down, Londonderry, Tyrone and Armagh. Generally under the name of Hearts of Steel, though little co-ordination existed among the bands of the various districts, the malcontents maintained 'a lawless, turbulent, and dangerous Spirit of Insurgency' throughout 1771 and 1772, their activities ranging from attempts to regulate rents to the fighting of pitched battles against the troops sent against them.[2]

Troops were dispatched to the north but Townshend's sympathies were with the Hearts of Steel. He stated bluntly that the disturbances were wholly due to the excessive rents charged for lands and believed that a display of leniency by the landowners, rather than the use of force, would restore peace. He saw that failure to ease the burden of rents would 'compel [the] wretched tenants to go to America, or any other part of the world where they can receive that reward which is honestly due to their labour'.[3] Excessive rents drove thousands in the years prior to the American revolution from 'the rich pastures of Ireland [where] many hungry parricides are fed, and grown strong to labour in its destruction',[4] to a land where as a shipping advertisement put it 'instead of Tenants they become Landlords .... and fully enjoy the fruits of their own labour in Freedom, Peace, and Plenty'.[5] The only

---

their landlord ... were obliged to leave their habitations or remain at a rack-rent. Nay, they were often turned off their farms, and those fertile fields, which produced bread for their inhabitants, were converted into pasturage, and the country, once populous wore, and still wears the face of depopulation and misery (*Public Journal*, 5 Aug. 1772).

1 Letter addressed to 'the inhabitants of a certain part of co. Antrim' (*B.N.L.*, 30 Oct. 1770).

2 Memorial, gentlemen of cos. Antrim, Down, Tyrone and Londonderry to Townshend and memorial, gentlemen and justices of co. Armagh to Townshend, enclosed in Townshend to Rochford, 11 Mar. 1772 (S.P. 63/435, no. 36c); Townshend to Rochford, 18 Mar. 1772 (S.P. 63/435, no. 45b); *Public Journal*, 22 Mar. 1772; *F.D.J.*, 2 Oct. 1773. Insurgents in the Lurgan, co. Armagh, neighbourhood were known as 'The Boys'.

3 Townshend to Rochford, 11 and 21 Mar. 1772 (S.P. 63/435, no 38a and 57). A view similar to that of Townshend was expressed in a letter from London printed in *F.D.J.*, 20 Sept. 1774.

4 Address to the people of Ireland, 28 July 1775 (*Continental congress journals*, ii. 212–8).

5 *Hopewell*, Londonderry to Nova Scotia (*B.N.L.*, 21 June 1771).

practical consequence of rioting and insurrection was an increase
in emigration. The formation of the Hearts of Steel had brought
the sufferings of people of the north of Ireland within the ken of
Townshend's sympathy but the accompanying disorders placed
them outside the law. As force gradually ended the disturbances,
fear of punishment under the trials act passed by an alarmed
parliament grew.[1] As soon as circumstances permitted, both the
privy council and Townshend recommended a general pardon in
order to avoid the 'pernicious consequences' of an 'emigration
proceeding from the Apprehensions of being taken and brought
to Tryal' and a proclamation of pardon was issued in November
1772.[2]

Arthur Young, whose tour of Ireland took place only a few years
after these disturbances, believed that both they and the emigration
which had taken place at the same time were caused by set-backs
in the linen trade and not by the harshness of landowners[3] but his
belief was not shared by the many others whose opinions were
expressed in parliament, in official dispatches from the Castle to
London, in the newspapers and in the addresses of presbyteries to
their congregations.[4]

Emigration during the early 'seventies is most accurately viewed
if 1772 is regarded as a bridge year between two periods of emigration rather than as the middle year of the single emigration period
into which the years 1770–4 are generally classified. The sudden
increase in the volume of emigration in 1771 cannot be accounted
for by a linen slump because that year was one of unprecedented
prosperity in the linen trade:[5] on the other hand, by 1773 the

---

[1] 11 and 12 Geo. III, c.5 (Ire.). 'An act for the more effectual punishment of wicked
and disorderly persons in Antrim, Down, Armagh, the city and county of Londonderry, and county Tyrone'. Many insurgents were drowned while attempting to
escape to Scotland in open boats (*Public Journal*, 15 Apr. 1772).
[2] Townshend to Rochford, 5 Nov. 1772 (S.P. 63/436, nos. 103a and b); Paterson to
Townshend, 6 Nov. 1772 (Nat. Lib. Ire., Townshend MSS, 394a). The trials act was
repealed at the end of 1773 by 13 and 14 Geo. III, c.4 (Ire.) but it was alleged that
several Hearts of Steel were condemned and executed after the repeal. If so, these
may have been listed among the exceptions named specifically in the repealing act.
[3] *Tour*, ii. 130.
[4] *Parliamentary Debates* (1773–4), xvii. 1152 (17 May 1774); Harcourt to Rochford,
18 July 1773 (S.P. 63/440, no. 50); letter signed 'Mercator' in B.N.L., 31 Mar. 1772;
address of presbytery of Templepatrick (B.N.L., 4 Jan. 1771). This address was
commended by Townshend to Rochford for its accuracy (S.P. 63/435, no. 38a).
[5] See the account of the value of linen cloth and linen yarn exported from Ireland
during each year from 1710 until 1773 printed in *Commons' jn. Ire.*, xvi. 405–8.

impetus of the advance of rents was spent for a time, thanks partly to disturbances, emigration and the decline of linen. Conversely, the years 1770–2 saw the climax of half a century of rack-renting and the years 1772 and 1773 saw a sudden and disastrous collapse in the linen trade. If rack-renting and linen slumps had the effect that contemporaries believed them to have had on emigration, it would appear logical to attribute emigration in the first part of the early 'seventies to the activities of the grasping landlords and emigration in the latter part of the period to an unexpected set-back in the linen trade.[1]

The foreign demand for Irish linens fell by almost half in 1771 and 1772. Superficially it would appear that the period of greatest depression was the year previous to March 1772, for linen exports fell by six million yards in that time, whereas the decline was little more than half that amount in the following year. The fall in exports during the former period had, however, little effect on the linen worker as the merchants continued to purchase as much linen as in the previous year.[2] Continued buying and the slow disposal of stocks in 1771 and 1772 resulted in a dangerous accumulation of linen in the hands of the merchants and it was inevitable that the spinners and weavers would soon feel the effects of the decline. The transfer of part of the burden from the shoulders of the merchants to those of the workers commenced at the end of 1772[3] and, in the year that followed, linen production declined by between one-third and one-half in most parts of the north of Ireland and linen prices declined by one-quarter in the same period. By 1773,

---

[1] When a New York newspaper of 1772 reported the arrival of a vessel with north Irish emigrants on board it stated that the causes of emigration at that time were high rents and expensive foodstuffs (*N.Y. Gazette*, June 22, in O'Brien, *Hidden phase*, p. 280).

[2] The number of looms employed in Belfast and in the neighbourhood of Lurgan, co. Armagh, was 1,939 in 1772 compared with 2,139 in 1771 (*Commons' jn. Ire.*, xvi. 409,411). This fall of less than ten per cent. compares with a fall of twenty per cent. in exports. The decrease in the number of looms employed was no greater than one would expect in view of the restlessness of the north, regardless of all other factors.

[3] Typical of newspaper comments during the winter of 1772/3 on the state of the linen trade was that of the *Londonderry Journal*, 6 Apr. 1773—'Trade was never more stagnant in the memory of living man'. Despite reduced purchases, the Irish merchants were left with £900,000 worth of linen on their hands—more than half the normal annual value of linen exports from Ireland (Memorial, trustees of the linen manufacture to Harcourt, enclosed in Harcourt to Rochford, 24 Apr. 1773, S.P. 63/439, no. 84b).

the Irish linen industry appeared to have collapsed into a 'drooping and almost ruined state'.[1]

To appreciate the consequences of the decline of the linen industry it must be remembered that linen held a unique position in the north of Ireland. The lack of demand for linen hit most families in districts such as the Lagan, Foyle and Bann valleys and led to a shortage of money and to a decline in all branches of trade.[2] The linen decline irritated the old wound of exorbitant rents, for those rents had been agreed to in the expectation of linen profits and had passed beyond what farming profits could support. Universal distress and widespread starvation were said to have taken possession of the north of Ireland in 1773,[3] their effect being so great that rents started to fall, a striking comment on the immensity of the linen catastrophe which thus succeeded where insurrection had failed.[4]

The breakdown of the linen trade had a great effect on emigration. Evidence was given before a committee of the British house of commons by Robert Stephenson, the inspector to the trustees of the linen manufacture, that almost every one of the thirty thousand people who were said to have emigrated from Ireland in 1772 and 1773 were linen workers.[5] Similar evidence was given before the Irish house of commons where it was stated that only a revival of the linen trade could prevent further emigration.[6] Arthur Young was no mean observer and, allowing for a natural bias and his lack of distinction between the earlier and later phases of the emigration of the 'seventies, his insistence on the close relationship between the linen trade and emigration must carry some weight:

> The spirit of emigrating in Ireland appeared to be confined to two circumstances, the presbyterian religion, and the linen manufacture. I heard of very few emigrants except among manufacturers

---

[1] *Commons' jn. Ire.*, xvi. 409 (report of conditions in Lurgan), 409–10 (Lisburn), 411 (Coleraine), 411 (Belfast), 413 (Antrim), 414 (Londonderry and Limavady, co. Londonderry); *Commons' reports* (G.B.), iii. 101ff; *Parliamentary Debates* (1773–4), xvii. 1150 (17 May 1774). According to Young, there was no decline in the industry in the south of co. Down (*Tour*, i. 161).

[2] *Commons' jn. Ire.*, xvi. 409–10.

[3] *Scots Magazine* (Oct. 1773), xxxv. 557.

[4] Young, *Tour*, i. 115, 149, 185, 191; B.N.L., 5 Sept. 1775; F.D.J., 16 Sept. 1775; *Commons' jn. Ire.*, xvi. 395.

[5] *Commons' reports* (G.B.), iii. 103ff.

[6] *Commons' jn. Ire.*, xvi. 409, 411.

of that persuasion . . . . . When the linen trade was low, the passenger trade was always high . . . . . . Some emigration always existed, and its increase depended on the fluctuations of linen.[1]

The hardships resulting from rack-renting and the linen depression were aggravated by a consistently high level of prices during the years 1770–4. The cost of bread rose from 1770 until 1773 when it approached the famine prices of 1741 and 1757. High prices of provisions were universal throughout the British Isles and, though they were attributed to many causes including the activities of engrossers, the increased consumption of distilleries, the breeding of horses and waste among the upper classes, the basic cause was a series of bad harvests.[2] The word *calamitous* was used to describe Ireland's food position in 1770, 1771 and 1772 and relief measures such as the purchase of corn and its resale at less than the cost price were undertaken in many districts.[3] The cries of the poor penetrated even into the halls of Dublin Castle and the sympathetic Townshend reported that, because of the scarcity of food, the Irish were 'the most wretched people on earth' and that they were 'in a state of poverty not to be described'.[4]

The increasing scarcity of food combined with the diminishing sales of linen reduced many to a level of poverty that they had not hitherto known and inevitably had an effect on the volume of emigration. Hunger was gnawing at the ties of home and kindred and all were not so thoroughly broken in spirit as the man who, when asked in 1773 how he lived, replied, '*Live*! Sir, we *bide* here'.[5] High prices naturally intensified the emigration of unemployed linen workers but, in the ordinary course of events, would not

---

[1] *Tour*, ii. 131.

[2] *F.D.J.*, 2 Mar. and 29 May 1772; *L.J.*, 6 June 1772 and 3 June 1773; *B.N.L.*, 22 May and 28 July 1772; *Scots Magazine* (Mar. 1772), xxxiv. 112-18; and ibid. (Dec. 1772), xxxiv. 665-7. It was stated categorically that 'THE SEVERITY OF THE SEASONS IS NOW AND HAS BEEN, THE ONLY CAUSE of the dearness of provisions' (*Scots Magazine* (Mar. 1772), xxxiv. 117).

[3] *B.N.L.*, 11 Sept. and 21 Dec. 1770 and 25 Jan. 21 May and 27 Sept. 1771; *Public Journal*, 1 Apr. 1772. *Concise view of the Irish Society*, p. 127. The poor of Dublin were supplied with money, waistcoats, breeches and night-caps in 1774 (*B.N.L.*, 18 Jan. 1774). See the Foster collection of pamphlets, vols. 45 and 46, in the library of the Queen's University of Belfast.

[4] To Weymouth, 23 Nov. 1770 (S.P. 63/432 no. 53); to Rochford, 18 Mar. 1772 (S.P. 63/435, no. 45a). No famine such as that of 1740 or near famine such as that of 1727-8 occurred in these years—there was a 'scantiness' rather than an absolute scarcity of food (*Scots Magazine* (March 1772), xxxiv. 115-8).

[5] F. Moore, *Considerations on the exorbitant price of provisions* (1773), p. 68.

have led to the emigration of the farming class or of those whose linen losses may have been balanced by increasing returns from the sale of produce. There is, however, no evidence to suggest that the profits of farming increased as much as prices or rents. Light crops, more than any other factor, caused the price increases of the 'seventies and any hope of increased farming returns when yields became more normal after the harvest of 1773 was negatived by the collapse of the linen trade. The consequent scarcity of money served to drag the prices of provisions down to their pre-1770 level, regardless of the great increase in rents that had since taken place.[1] Arthur Young believed that the sale of their new leases by many of Donegall's tenants for considerable sums during these years was proof that the fines levied when the leases were granted in 1770 had no effect on the volume of emigration.[2] Actually, the sale of the leases and the fall in the price of other lands during the 'seventies was an indication of the uneconomic level of rents that could not stand during what was, admittedly, a severe testing time of poor crops and unemployment. Emigration of the farming class did not end with the passing of the worst phase of rack-renting in 1772 but continued side by side with emigration of the landless class.

It may be concluded that it was the sum of these circumstances—together with the ever present factor of encouragement from America—that led to the north Irish emigration of the 'seventies, but it is to be desired that confirmation of this conclusion could be obtained from those who emigrated. Different men react differently to the same circumstances. The Americans believed that it was the bold, the 'living', who found and nurtured their country but it is also the bold who refuse to bow to circumstances and who try to turn them—as did the Hearts of Steel—rather than be forced into emigration, the conventional route of escape. Again it may be claimed that it was those who emigrated who resisted the circumstances to which those who remained at home had to bow. It is impossible to probe the minds of thirty thousand people who viewed thirty thousand different combinations of circumstances in thirty thousand different ways. A great deal of light would have been thrown on the motives of the north Irish emigrants had lists of emigrants from the Irish ports been compiled by the customs

[1] *Commons' jn. Ire.*, xvi. 410.
[2] *Tour*, ii. 131.

authorities between 1773 and 1775 as was done in Scotland and England.[1] These Scottish and English lists vary greatly in value, as most give no information about the causes of emigration; but the lists which do give this information are not valueless from the Irish point of view, for ominously familiar forces—rack-renting, high prices and unemployment—were active in Britain in those years.[2] For example, four vessels which sailed to Nova Scotia in 1774[3] carried 518 emigrants who gave the following reasons for emigrating, some naming two factors:

The scarcity and dearness of provisions	67 persons.
To seek a better livelihood and employment	298
Excessive rents	156
The engrossing of small farms	4
Various (to visit relations, to see the country, etc.)	19

Conditions in Ireland and Britain at the time were too similar to allow the Irish historian to ignore the overwhelming preponderance of emigrant voices raised in complaint against rack-renting, high prices and uncertain employment.

[1] Treasury 47/9–12.
[2] M.I. Adam, 'The highland emigration of 1770', in *Scot. Hist. Rev.*, xvi. 280–93; Selkirk, *Highland emigration*, pp. 57, 157; *Scots Magazine* (1772), xxiv. 115–18, 221, 665–7, 697–700; ibid. (1773), xxxv. 65, 173, 230' 557; *Commons' reports* (G.B.), iii. 101ff.
[3] Treasury 47/9–12; see Chapter I.

CHAPTER VI

The Emigrants

EIGHTEENTH-CENTURY emigrants from the north of Ireland to America were of two classes—those who went voluntarily and those who were sent as convicts. The system of transporting felons was envisaged as early as the sixteenth century,[1] but, although many were transported by royal order to the American colonies from soon after their establishment and Popish clergy were liable to transportation from the 1690s,[2] it was not until 1703 that a law authorising the transportation of criminals appeared on the Irish statute book. Thus did the government hope to rid the homeland of its undesirable citizens and, at the same time, provide the middle and southern colonies with much-needed white labour.

The authorities handed over the work of transporting convicts —or his majesty's seven-year passengers, as they were called—to 'merchants transporters' who were paid a sum of money, usually between three and five pounds, and had the right to indent the convicts and of disposing of the indentures in America.[3] The Irish counties paid almost £8,500 for the transportation of 1,890 convicts in the years 1737–1743[4] but it would appear that the merchants transporters received much less than this amount: a former high sheriff of county Dublin admitted to a parliamentary committee that, though he had received £5 per head for the

[1] 39 Eliz. c.4 (Eng.) enacted that 'dangerous rogues must be banished from the realm' (Hurd, *Law of freedom and bondage in U.S.*, i. 219 n).
[2] 9 Wm. III c. 1 (Ire.).
[3] 6 Anne c.11 (Ire.).
[4] *Commons' jn. Ire.*, vii. 557–630 *passim*.

transportation of convicts, he had paid the merchants transporters only £2. 10s. per head.[1] Merchants transporters, usually the same people who acted as agents for the normal passenger trade, were required to return a certificate within eighteen months to show that they had fulfilled their contract, but this law was, in most cases, ignored by both the merchants and the magistrates. On the other hand, a bond of £50 penalty for the transportation of each convict was insisted on even by those magistrates who did not insist on the certificate, in order to ensure that the felons were indeed transported.[2]

After indentures had been signed, the convicts were driven from jail to ship in open carts, often amid turbulent scenes caused by friends or by a sympathetic or contemptuous rabble.[3] Though very few masters and agents called for passengers, servants and convicts in the same advertisement, a comparison of sailing lists in Irish newspapers and notices of the arrival of convicts at southern ports makes it clear that many ships which advertised only for passengers and servants carried convicts as well. The experience of the passengers of the *Hero* in 1768 was certainly not unique. The vessel called at Dublin on its voyage from Whitehaven to Virginia with convicts, though the reference to convicts was contained in the port news of Dublin newspapers and not in the advertisement which appealed for passengers and servants to sail in the vessel. Those who responded found their surroundings no less unpleasant than they found their travelling companions, for the vessel was also carrying a cargo of coal.[4] Little wonder that many agents thought it advisable to assure prospective emigrants that the vessel for which they acted would not carry convicts.[5]

Not one emigrant vessel which left the north of Ireland in the third quarter of the eighteenth century advertised for convicts and on the only occasion when the *Belfast News Letter* stated that convicts had been brought to a north Irish port to be transported,

[1] Ibid., p. 559. The detailed accounts of a merchant transporter will be found in Treasury 1/500, 15 Feb. 1774.
[2] Evidence of John Langley, a Dublin merchant (*Commons' jn. Ire.*, vii. 558).
[3] *Dublin Chronicle*, 21 Oct. 1771; *Public Journal*, 6 Apr. 1772; *F.D.J.*, 23 Apr. and 20 Sept. 1774.
[4] *F.D.J.*, 8 Mar. and 17 May 1768. One of the few ships which advertised for passengers and convicts was the *Industry* which sailed from Limerick to New York in 1771 (*Limerick Chronicle*, Oct. 3).
[5] E.g. *Bourdeaux Yacht* and *Earl of Chatham*, both from Dublin to Philadelphia (*F.D.J.*, 1 July 1764 and 23 June 1768).

the agents of the vessel named in the report issued a prompt and indignant denial.[1]

Fortunately, lest one should conclude that this absence of canvassing meant that the Ulster emigrant was not embarrassed by the company of convicts for a few months, a single advertisement shows that the northern convicts journeyed in as sedate company as their fellow-unfortunates of the south. The *Newry Assistance,* as prim a vessel and with as good a record as any in the emigration trade, advertised with all the usual flourishes for passengers and servants in 1771 and sailed from Newry to Philadelphia in October of that year without any unusual event being noted. In the following June, however, the grand jury of Armagh offered a reward of £10 for the capture of each of six men who had been put on board the vessel to be transported but had escaped as the vessel sailed.[2]

Branded as 'thieves, burglars, pick-pockets, and cut-throats, and a herd of the most flagitious banditti upon Earth'[3] convicts were received in the colonies with a not unnatural lack of enthusiasm even though the harshness of the penal code led to the transportation of many who were luckless wretches rather than hardened criminals. The provincial assembly of Virginia led the way in the attempt to stop the importation of convicts by prohibiting their entry into the colony in 1670 because of the danger which would arise 'from the barbarous designs and felonious practices of such wicked villains'.[4] The assemblies of other colonies followed with laws placing restrictive duties on the importation of convicts or prohibiting such importation altogether. After 1717, most of these

---

[1] *B.N.L.,* 29 June and 3 July, 1739. The vessel was the *William and James,* bound from Belfast to the Carolinas.

[2] *B.N.L.,* 13 Aug. 1771 and 23 and 26 June, 1772.

[3] W. Smith, *A history of the province of New York, from its first discovery to the year MDCCXXXII,* p. 207. Benjamin Franklin forcibly expressed the American point of view, though his observations were undoubtedly influenced by the passage of troubled times: 'the former masters of this country were accustomed to discharge their jails of the vilest part of their subjects and to transport ship loads of wretches, too worthless for the old world, to taint and corrupt the infancy of the new' (*The American Museum or Universal Advertiser,* July–Dec. 1791, pp. 165–6, in Abbott, *Immigration; select documents,* p. 705).

[4] Minutes, Virginia assembly, 20 Apr. 1670 (Abbott, op. cit., p. 542). This act was confirmed in England through the influence of Lord Arlington and extended to the other continental colonies, but, by 1717, it was clear that the West Indies could not receive all those whom it was considered desirable to transport (C.O. 5/1269, f.141; Ballagh, *White servitude in Va.,* pp. 36–7).

laws were disallowed by the authorities in the colonies or in London but persistence brought its reward for, by 1770, Maryland was the only colony whose efforts to exclude convicts were not successful.[1] In any case, the demand for indentured convict labour diminished with the ever-increasing supply of free Irish and German immigrants.[2]

The number of convicts who went to the American colonies through the north Irish ports was comparatively small—probably only five or six hundred during the period. Records are available for only seven years and these show that exactly one-tenth of the 1,890 convicts transported from Ireland during the period 1737–1743 were sent from Antrim, Armagh, Down, Londonderry and Tyrone, the counties served by the northern ports.[3]

Convicts formed but a small minority of Irish emigrants to the American colonies and the next smallest group is to be found at the other end of the social scale—the emigrant with sufficient means to pay for his passage and enter an American port as a free man and master of his own destiny. Between these two extremes was a large class whose emigration was assisted by the exchange of a free passage in return for indenting for a period of service in America.

Almost all vessels which advertised in the north of Ireland for emigrants for the American colonies asked for both 'passengers'— that is, those who could pay the full passage money—and servants. All the exceptions were in years when the emigrant trade was at a low ebb. In these years, emigration advertisements, whose length generally reflected the volume of the trade, briefly asked for 'passengers and goods', though the term 'passenger' was probably used in a wide sense. Certainly, no north Irish vessel followed the example set by some southern advertisements which stated specifically that no servants would be carried on certain vessels.[4]

---

[1] E. I. McCormac, *White servitude in Maryland*, pp. 75, 97–104; Eddis, *Letters from America*, p. 66.

[2] 'So many volunteer servants come over, especially Irish, that [convict labour] is a commodity pretty well blown upon' ('A traveller in 1746', in Farnam, *Social legislation in U.S.*, p. 346).

[3] *Commons' jn. Ire.*, vii. 557–630 passim.

[4] A postscript to the advertisement of the *Earl of Chatham*, Dublin to Philadelphia, stated: 'Note: This vessel will take neither servants nor convicts' (*F.D.J.*, 23 June 1768). With a delicacy worthy of its name, the *Countess of Donegall*, Dublin to New York, advertised for passengers with the assurance that the 'state room and cabin are particularly well adapted for the accommodation of genteel passengers, and to make it more agreeable, no servants, except those belonging to the passengers will be admitted' (ibid., 20 Apr. 1774).

Few emigrant vessels from the north of Ireland to colonial America did not carry the man who had staked his passage money in the hope of winning a happier life and the man to whom happiness was worth four years of servitude, the only specie he could offer.

It is not easy to determine how much the independent passenger had to pay for his passage to America, for it was uncommon for a ship's advertisement to give more specific information than the assurance that the terms would be moderate. Moreover, the cost of passage naturally varied according to the type of vessel[1] and according to the port to which passage was desired.

Allowing for these fluctuations, it would seem that the cost of a passage to America decreased as the eighteenth century progressed. A passage from London to America at the end of the seventeenth and beginning of the eighteenth centuries cost about five or six pounds.[2] The cost from Ireland was about the same, for a receipt dated 1722 shows that when the Rev. Michael Jones emigrated to America with his wife and five children the amount paid for passage money was £33.[3] If all seven were 'full' passengers, the passage money for each was about £4. 14s., but, even if all the children were reckoned as 'half' passengers, the resulting 'full' fare of £7. 6. 8 was still much less than the estimate of £9 given by a Pennsylvania quaker in a letter to a friend in Ireland in 1729.[4] By 1773 the average cost of a 'full' passage from Ireland to America, was estimated by the *Belfast News Letter* to be £3. 5s.[5] and by the

---

[1] Just after the Napoleonic wars the cost of a passage from Ireland to Canada on a vessel engaged in the timber trade was between two and three pounds, the passenger supplying his own provisions. On board the even more uncomfortable vessels bound for the Newfoundland fisheries, the passage money was only ten shillings (H. I. Cowan. *British emigration to British North America 1783—1837*, pp. 131-2).

[2] Farnam, *Social legislation in U.S.*, p. 365. Osgood estimates that the cost of a passage from Britain to America in the first half of the eighteenth century ranged from £6 to £10 (*Amer. in 18th cent.*, ii. 484). In an account published by the New Jersey proprietors in 1682 for the information of prospective immigrants it was stated, 'The price is five pounds per head, as well master as servants, who are above ten years of age, all under ten and not children at the breast pay fifty shillings, sucking children nothing' (*A history of the new world called America as discovered by the Spaniards . . .* p. 107). The cost of transporting the Palatines from London to N.C. in 1709 was £5. 10s. per head (North Carolina colonial records, i. 986). All these figures include provisions during the voyage.

[3] King, *A great abp.*, p. 30.

[4] Myers, *Quaker emig.*, pp. 75, 91.

[5] B.N.L., 6 Apr. 1773. The *Betty Gregg*, Belfast to Charleston, advertised passages for £4 (ibid., 4 Oct. 1768): passage from Londonderry to Philadelphia in the *Phoenix* cost three guineas (ibid., 3 July 1770). The average cost of a passage from Sutherlandshire to America was £3. 10s. in 1773 (MacLean, *Highland settlements in Am.*, p. 421).

end of the century was stated by Phineas Bond to be between three pounds and three and a half guineas.[1] This gradual reduction in the cost of passage was due to the increase of trade between Ireland and North America and the resulting increase in the keenness of competition between agents and captains of emigrant vessels.

By no means all of those who paid for their passage set up on their own behalf when they arrived in America. To do so, the immigrant needed sufficient funds to transport him to the place of his intended settlement, to pay various fees to secure his grant,[2] to purchase the necessary seeds and the implements to clear and cultivate his land, and to subsist till at least the first harvest. These expenses were even greater than the cost of passage from Ireland. An emigrant who set out with an available capital of less than £10 would have been hard pressed to remain solvent until he reaped his first harvest, and £10 was no negligible sum, being a year's wages of an Irish labourer.[3] Because of this heavy expense, many who paid for their passage entered into service in America, thus gaining experience and the necessary additional funds while retaining their personal liberty.

Those who wished to emigrate to America but had not the means to pay for the journey had the choice between two ways of securing passages. The method most commonly adopted was to sign an indenture agreeing to serve the master of a ship or his assigns for an agreed period. On landing in America, the indenture would be sold by the master to the highest bidder. Alternatively, the emigrant could agree to pay the cost of passage within a short time after arrival in America, hoping to raise the necessary money either from friends or by indenting on the best terms he could secure. If the 'redemptioner' failed to raise, within the agreed time, the cost of his passage—which was probably greater than that of the paying passenger—his services were then sold by the ship's

---

[1] To Grenville, 10 Sept. 1791 (Abbott, *Immigration: select documents*, p. 222).
[2] These amounted to £2. 19s. 6d. proclamation currency per hundred acres in S.C. in 1731 (C.O. 5/362, f.125) or about 8s. 6d. sterling (C.O. 5/361, f.84). See also C.O. 5/362, ff.122–4; C.O. 5/363, ff.199–203; C.O. 5/297, f.45. The fees in S.C. in 1771 were stated to be £27 per hundred acres (B.L.N., 10 Jan. 1772) and $75, plus the cost of surveying, in N.Y. about the same time (MacLean, *Highland settlements in Am.*, p. 181). Both these sums were, presumably, in terms of local currency.
[3] A report to the Board of Trade in 1709 stated that £2 was necessary for the supply of necessary implements and £5 for subsistence during the first year (Farnam, *Social legislation in U.S.*, p. 45).

master to the highest bidder as in the case of the indentured servant.[1]

The advantages to both the poor and the colonies of the system of granting free passages in return for a period of servitude were realised in the earliest days of English colonisation. Sir George Peckham, a partner in Sir Humphrey Gilbert's colonising schemes, wrote in 1582 that 'there are at this day great numbers (God he knoweth) which liue in such penurie and want, as they could be contented to hazard their liues, and to serue one yeare for meat, drinke and apparell only, without wages, in hope thereby to amend their estates'.[2] Because of the immense quantities of land available in America, the system took early root in the British colonies with the blessing and encouragement of both the British and colonial authorities and continued throughout the seventeenth and eighteenth centuries.[3] Indentured servants continued to arrive in the United States from Ireland till the end of the century, though the trade from Britain had been prohibited in 1785.[4]

On occasions when no particular type of servant was required, an advertisement for 'passengers, servants and redemptioners' was inserted in the local newspapers but from time to time advertisements appealing to specific trades appeared. For example, Thomas Greg of Belfast advertised in 1760 that he had 'received a commission to send to New York sundry artificers—a gunsmith, house carpenter, blacksmith, cooper, brick layer, and a leather dresser' and two years later he advertised for two house carpenters and a skilful gardener who were willing to indent for service in South Carolina.[5] Sometimes an Irish merchant who was neither the owner nor the agent of a vessel advertised for servants, offering to pay the expenses of the passage to America in return for the signing of indentures.[6] Such indentures were then sold by agents in

[1] Farnam, *Social legislation in U.S.*, pp. 60-2.
[2] Ibid., p. 60.
[3] Adams, *Provincial society*, p. 317.
[4] 25 Geo. III, c.67 (Eng.). The Dublin newspapers, in 1792, attacked the continuation of the servant trade from Ireland to the United States of America, a trade by which people 'sell themselves as perpetual slaves as the price of their voyage to the *land of liberty*' (F.D.J., 25 Oct. 1792).
[5] B.N.L., 11 Mar. 1760 and 9 Nov. 1762. Those who responded were required to indent for four years.
[6] E.g., Robert Wilson, a Belfast merchant, offered to pay the passage money to America of servants who would sign indentures for four or five years. The trades he specified were 'smiths, tin-men, brasiers, or brass-founders, shoe-makers, taylors, carpenters or coopers, or good stout labouring young fellows' (B.N.L., 31 Mar. 1761).

America or by the Irish merchant if he personally accompanied the servants to America. The profits in this type of transaction were likely to be higher than the merchant would have secured had he merely acted as an agent for a ship's captain but much more complicated organisation was required and the sale of the indentures involved some risk, depending on the effects of the voyage on the servants and on the demand for the various classes of servants at the ports of disembarkation.

Some emigrants engaged indentured servants before leaving Ireland and thus secured cheap labour for their vital first few years in America or made a handsome profit by selling the indentures on landing. A method to combine these benefits was suggested in 1725 by a Pennsylvania quaker to a friend in Ireland urging a third to join him in America. 'I wod have him Procure 3 or 4 Lusty Servants', he wrote, 'and agree to pay their passage at this side he might sell 2 and pay the others passage with the money'.[1] The extent of such arrangements was sufficiently great to provoke unfavourable comment in 1772[2] but it is impossible to say if they were a common feature of the emigration trade from the north of Ireland as, by their nature, they were most likely to be made through personal contacts with intending emigrants rather than through advertisements or professional agents, though the services of the latter were sometimes used.[3]

The second party to an indenture was usually the captain of the vessel in which the servant sailed: this facilitated the taking out of indentures in Ireland and their sale in America though, in effect, the captain's role was that of an agent for his owners or for merchants in Ireland or America. Servants had to appear before a magistrate to be indentured before embarkation. Not only had indentures to be signed with the formality required by the law, but such appearance was necessary under statutes relating to apprentices and minors.[4] Though no reference to the procedure of indenting servants appeared in the *Belfast News Letter*, such references were common in advertisements in the newspapers of the south of Ireland. One of the most detailed and enlightening of these advertisements was that of the *Britannia*, bound from Dublin to

[1] Myers, *Quaker emig.*, p. 99.
[2] *Scots Magazine* (Append. 1772), xxxiv. 699.
[3] See advert. of Robert Wills of Belfast (*B.N.L.*, 8 June 1762) and that of James Crawford of Londonderry (*L.J.*, 6 Apr. 1773).
[4] 14 and 15 Car. II, c.19 (Ire).; 2 Geo. I, c.17 (Ire.).

Virginia in 1749. Intending applicants for passages were warned that no servants or apprentices would be taken without a proper discharge from their last employers or without the consent of their parents or relations or their husbands or wives. The examining and indenting of the servants was to take place in public before the lord mayor of Dublin.[1]

It was customary for servants to receive some clothing after their indentures had been signed. Such promises as 'servants will be completely outfitted and clothed' were often included in shipping advertisements and in one case it was promised that all servants should receive clothing worth forty shillings after they had signed their indentures.[2] In 1735, ten servants were secured in Belfast by John Lusks, master of the *Elizabeth and Catherine*, for John McEvers, of New York, owner of the vessel. The expense account of the vessel's stay in Belfast included the following items:

To 8 men and 2 women servants expnces. taking indentures	£0	3	7
To 4 hatts, 9 pairs shoos, & half Doz. course stockings do.	1	17	8
To Pᵈ Wm Charleys acct Dieting etc to do. servts.	0	17	11
To Pᵈ Saml. Catherwood cloating bᵗ for Ditto.	6	15	1
To Pᵈ the Taylor for making their Clouths	1	5	11
To pᵈ for Straw to servants Bedds		1	1
To Will Johnston Esq. for signing servts. Indentures at 2/8	1	7	1

It will be seen that, in this instance, about twenty-five shillings was spent on each servant before embarkation to cover the expenses of indenting, clothing, and lodging.[3]

When the servants landed, advertisements for their sale were inserted in the American newspapers. For example, the people of Charleston were informed as follows in 1734:

> Just imported and to be sold . . . Irish servants, men and women, of good trades, from the north of Ireland, Irish linen, household furniture, butter, cheese, chinaware and all sorts of dry goods . . .[4]

---

[1] *F.D.J.*, 21 Feb., 8 Apr. 1749. See also *Pue's Occurrences*, 18 May 1751; Memorial, earl of Seaforth to Suffolk, n.d. [1774] (S.P. 54/45 no. 167b); Eddis, *Letters from America*, p. 77; *Commons' jn. Ire.*, vii. 558.

[2] *B.N.L.*, 21 Oct. 1763 (*Falls*, Belfast to Charleston) and 5 Feb. 1771 (*Newry Packet*, Newry to Philadelphia).

[3] Daniel Mussenden to McEvers, 8 Apr. 1735 (P.R.O.N.I., D. 354/293).

[4] *Charleston Gazette*, 7 Dec. 1734, in McCrady, *S.C. under royal govt.*, p. 129 n.

Many contemporaries were horrified by this method of disposing of human beings and, in a letter to his father in Lisburn, an army officer described the arrival at Philadelphia of servants from the north of Ireland. 'They sell the servants here as they do their horses, and advertise them as they do their oatmeal and beef' he wrote.[1] The same scene was described at greater length in a report of the examination of Dr Williamson, an American colonist, by a committee of the British house of commons. A newspaper report of Williamson's evidence reads:

> . . . it appeared that a trade was carried on in human flesh between Pennsylvania and the province of Ulster. Such of the unhappy natives of that part of Ireland, as cannot find employment at home, sell themselves to the masters of vessels, or persons coming from America to deal in that species of merchandise. When they are brought to Philadelphia . . . they are either sold aboard the vessel or by public vendue, which sale on arrival there is public notice given of, either by hand-bill, or in the newspapers. They bring generally about fifteen pounds currency at market, are sold for the term of their indentures, which is from two to four years, and on its expiration, receive a suit of clothes, and implements of husbandry, consisting of a hoe, an axe, and a bill from their taskmasters. Several gentlemen in the committee expressed their abhorrence of such a barbarous traffic. . . Mr. Rose Fuller, resolving to have some information from him in order to estimate the comparative value between a man and other animals, asked him the price of a saddle horse, to which the doctor replied, from £25 to £40.[2]

The life of the servant after the disposal of his indenture has aroused equal horror. Intending emigrants were warned that servants were bound for a period of years to an imperious land-owner whose only object was 'to derive a profit from their misfortune, and to aggrandise himself at the expense of industry in distress'.[3] The lot of the servant was compared unfavourably with that of the convict and negro, and indentured servants were said to groan under a bondage that was worse than that suffered by the Israelites in Egypt.[4] Judged by modern standards, the bartering of a transatlantic passage for years of servitude is repre-

[1] *B.N.L.*, 1 Oct. 1773.
[2] *B.N.L.*, 22 Mar. 1774. This evidence is stated to have been given on Mar. 10.
[3] *Look before you leap* (Abbott, *Immigration: select documents*, p. 26).
[4] Eddis, *Letters from America*, p. 70.

hensible, but such servitude was the foundation on which many who endured it built a more successful life than would have been possible in Ireland. All did not rise to the eminence of Charles Thomson who left Maghera, county Londonderry, as an indentured servant and became secretary to the continental congress, but not a few became owners of holdings and became, in turn, masters of indentured servants.[1] Servitude in the hope of real freedom was preferable to the shackles of high rents and recurring depressions: temporary bondage in heaven was preferable to a false freedom in hell.

Despite the resemblance between the sale of the indenture of white servants and the sale of cattle or slaves, the indentured servant was not at the mercy of a colonial master whose whims and brutalities were outside the ken or interest of the law. For the most part the colonies welcomed the immigration of protestant servants[2] and, in an age when few classes benefited from official protection, the rights and interests of the servant were safeguarded by the colonial assemblies. The status of the servant, though varying from province to province and from time to time within each province, was fairly clearly established in law by the middle of the eighteenth century. Generally speaking, a servant could not be severely punished without the consent of a justice of the peace and could claim his independence if harshly treated. Other safeguards of vital concern to the servant were granted by laws such as a Virginia act of 1748. A master's duty to his servants and the period of service of a person without indenture were defined in this act which also prohibited the making of contracts between master and servant except in open court, forbade the discharge of sick or lame servants and stated that all servants were to receive 'freedom dues'. These freedom dues were payable to the servant on the expiration of his term of service and, in the seventeenth century, usually included about fifty acres of land as well as corn, clothing and a musket. By the eighteenth century, these dues were discharged by a money equivalent and gifts of clothing. In North

---

[1] O'Brien, *Hidden phase*, p. 274; J. Crimmins, *Irish American historical miscellany*, pp. 181ff.; J. Hurd, *Law of freedom and bondage in U.S.*, i. 220; H. T. Lefler, *North Carolina history told by contemporaries*, p. 29; *Hist. account S.C.*, ii. 129-30.

[2] Farnam, *Social legislation in U.S.*, p. 50; Adams, *Provincial society*, p.98; P. W. Bidwell and J. I. Falconer, *History of agriculture in the northern United States, 1620-1860*, p. 33; McCormac, *White servitude in Md.*, p. 30; U.B. Phillips, *Life and Labour in the Old South*, p. 29n.

Carolina, for example, they consisted of £3 proclamation money and one suit of clothes. The inclusion of lands among freedom dues had ceased by the beginning of the century in the more densely peopled colonies but continued till a later date in colonies such as North Carolina where they were included by law as late as 1737. In the decade before the American revolution, the proprietors of land in Nova Scotia promised a grant of fifty acres to immigrants for every servant introduced into the province, and also fifty acres to every such servant at the expiration of his term of service, thus repeating the tactics that had proved so effective in peopling the older colonies.[1]

Despite the benevolent eye of the colonial authorities, the life of the indentured servant was not an easy one nor was it free from exploitation at the hands of his master. The lot of the servant, especially in Maryland, was made more unpleasant by the intermingling of convicts and servants and the lack of differentiation between them in the public mind. The two modes of regulating the conduct of the servant and punishing his offences were corporal punishment and additions of time, usually one or two years but sometimes as many as seven years, to his term of servitude.[2] Whipping and branding and the parading of erring servants in chains were unenlightened punishments, but it must be remembered that the same unenlightened punishments were meted out to apprentices in Ireland, though the nature of settlement in America often gave the master greater freedom in the treatment of his servants than he would have possessed in the homeland.

There were two types of redemptioner—the comparatively few whose passage money was paid by friends who had prospered in America, and those who felt that they could persuade American farmers or merchants to pay the cost of their passage in return for the signing of indentures for comparatively short terms. Unfortunately for the latter, so many indentured servants were usually

1 Farnham, *Social Legislation in U.S.*, pp. 64, 365–6, 505; Hurd, *Law of freedom and bondage in U.S.*, i. 243, 267; Ballagh, *White servitude in Va.*, pp. 58, 62; J. S. Bassett, *Slavery and servitude in N.C.*, pp. 78, 84; Lefler, *N.C. history told by contemporaries*, p. 42; E. L. Whitney, *The government of the colony of S.C.*, p. 65; Adams, *Provincial society*, pp. 98–9; E. L. Bogart, *The economic history of the U.S.*, p. 82; *Scots magazine* (Sept. 1772), xxiv. 482; *B.N.L.*, 3 June 1766. A Maryland court defined dues in 1648 as, 'one cap or hatt, one cloake or frize suite, one shirt one pr shoes and stockins one axe one broad and one narrow hoe, 50 acres of Land, and 3 barrells Corne' (McCormac, *White servitude in Md.*, pp. 24–26).
2 McCormac, op. cit., pp. 44, 52, 56, 76. Eddis, *Letters from America*, p. 69.

available that it was more economical for the colonist to purchase an indenture than to bargain with a redemptioner except where the latter was a highly skilled craftsman.[1] Another circumstance which operated against the redemptioner was the frequent curtailment of the period of redemption agreed before the start of the voyage. The speedy disposal of redemptioners was to the advantage of ships' masters who had to proceed to other ports or who simply wished to end the expense of supplying provisions to redemptioners as soon as possible after arriving in port. This was particularly true of unskilled labourers who were suffering from the rigours of the transatlantic voyage, for such redemptioners were usually scorned by the colonists.[2]

The plight of the redemptioner was lamentable even in cases of fair treatment by shipmasters for, when he was finally allowed to land on the American shore, it was usually as an indentured servant, the class he had possibly despised at the beginning of the voyage. If the redemptioner failed to pay for his passage within the agreed time, he was sold into a period of servitude as stipulated in the agreement he had signed before leaving his native country. If such agreement did not include a definite period of servitude, he was sold for the term authorised by the particular colony for servants without indentures.[3]

All those who emigrated as servants were not unskilled labourers or persons in menial positions. An examination of advertisements in which the occupations of emigrant servants are detailed reveals a substantial proportion of skilled tradesmen. When the *Freemason* of Newry advertised for redemptioners and servants to go to Philadelphia in 1768, the following trades were named: carpenters, tailors, shoemakers, wheelwrights, millwrights, smiths, weavers, bricklayers, plasterers, millers, coopers, barbers, bakers, milliners, cabinet makers, hatters, turners, and tanners.[4] Schoolmasters and surgeons were also included among those who emigrated as servants.[5]

---

[1] Myers, *Quaker emig.*, p. 100.

[2] McCormac, *White servitude in Md.*, p. 43; G. Mittelberger, *Journey to Pennsylvania in the year 1750 and return to Germany in the year 1754* (Abbott, *Historical aspects of immigration*, p. 9); Eddis, *Letters from America*, pp. 74–5.

[3] Peter Brunnholtz, a German pastor, to—, 21 May 1750 (Abbott, *Immigration: select documents*, p. 12).

[4] *F.D.J.*, 4 Aug. 1768.

[5] O'Brien, *Pioneer Irish in New England*, p. 22; Donovan, *Pre-Revolutionary Irish in Mass.*, p. 42. The forty servants who sailed in the *Adventure* from Baltimore in Ireland

The relative value to shipowners of paying passengers and servants varied. The carriage of servants was more profitable when the demand in America for servants was great. The average selling price of a male servant indentured for four years was about £12 in the middle of the century and rather less for a female servant.[1] As the expense of clothing and indenting a servant amounted to a maximum of £2, a gross profit of £10 was made, at least twice the passage money of a paying passenger.

More risk was involved in the carriage of servants than in the carriage of passengers who paid for their passages before leaving Ireland, especially if the vessel were going to a port north of New York for there was little demand for indentured labour in New England.[2] The mortality rate during the voyage was often high and the selling price of the indentures of the servants who remained was often reduced by disease. A glut of servants naturally reduced the value of indentures during years when the emigration trade was busiest. On the other hand, sickness and lack of demand for servants were of little concern to the master who had already received the passage money in Ireland. Indeed, the death of a passenger, however regrettable, served to enhance the profits of the voyage by saving provisions. Paying passengers were a satisfactory cargo for the master who desired a handsome profit while running as little risk as possible: a core of paying passengers was an insurance against loss in a vessel which sought even greater profits by the addition of a leavening of servants.

Miss Glasgow has claimed that eighteenth century emigrants from the north of Ireland to America belonged to the paying-passenger class. Carrying 'not only the implements of their trade, but capital as well', they are carefully distinguished by Miss Glasgow from the 'destitute emigrants' who left Ireland after the famine of 1846.[3] There was indeed a reluctance on the part of many to emigrate to America unless they had the means to pay for their passage, particularly, it would seem, in the last few years of the

---

to Baltimore in Md. in 1774 included six schoolmasters and two surgeons (O'Brien, *Washington's Irish assoc.*, p. 221).

[1] Farnam, *Social legislation in U.S.*, pp. 369–70. The price was probably less in the southern colonies because of the relative cheapness of slaves (ibid.; McCrady, *S.C. under royal govt.*, p. 129; Bull to Hillsborough, 6 Dec. 1769, C.O. 5/379, ff.90–100; U.B. Phillipps, *Industrial society*, i. 374).

[2] Bidwell and Falconer, *Agric. in the northern U.S.*, p. 33.

[3] *Scotch Irish in Ire. and Am.*, p. 156.

period studied—committees of both the Irish and British parliaments were informed in 1774 that those who had sufficient money to emigrate had already done so, and many more would go if they had the money to pay for their passages.[1] In spite of this, it is clear that most of the emigrants from the north of Ireland to colonial America were people whose only hope of getting to America was to go as redemptioners or servants. The judges of both the northeastern and north-western circuits of Ireland reported in 1729 that several people who were not in needy circumstances had emigrated, but the north-eastern judges added that this class was 'the smallest in number of those who have left the kingdom'.[2] This gives credibility to Boulter's estimate in the previous year that only one emigrant in ten could pay for his passage.[3] According to the *Pennsylvania Gazette*, not one of the 1,155 immigrants who landed in 1729 at Philadelphia from Ireland was a servant,[4] but this remarkable and seemingly conclusive indication of the preponderance of paying passengers does not stand up to examination. James Logan was a tolerant man but the activities in Pennsylvania of his former countrymen often angered him and his uncomplimentary comment on the Irish influx into Philadelphia in 1729 was that 'few besides convicts are imported thither'.[5] It is inconceivable that over one thousand Irish convicts were landed at a single American port in 1729, as the number transported in that year did not attract particular attention and as, on average, only 270 convicts were transported annually from Ireland between 1737 and 1743.[6] Logan's statement may have been caused by a mixture of spleen and of the confusion that Eddis later reported in the colonial mind between convicts and indentured servants.[7] Further evidence to disprove the *Pennsylvania Gazette*'s assertion is provided by the passing of a law by the Pennsylvania assembly in 1729 placing a duty of twenty shillings on each immigrant servant landed in the colony.[8] The relevance of the law is obvious if the Irish immigrants

---

[1] *Commons' jn. Ire.*, xvi. 410; *Commons' reports* (G.B.), iii. 107.
[2] Enclosure, Carteret to Newcastle, 26 June 1729 (T.S.P.I., T.659, pp. 78, 80).
[3] To Newcastle, 23 Nov. 1728 (*Boulter letters*, i. 210).
[4] J. F. Watson, *Annals of Philadelphia and Pennsylvania*, ii. 266. The same was said of earlier Irish immigrants into New England (Lechmere to Winthrop, 27 July 1718, in Akagi, *Town proprietors of New England*, p. 261).
[5] Watson, op. cit., ii. 260.
[6] *Commons' jn. Ire.*, vii. 557–630.
[7] *Letters from America*, p. 69.
[8] 'An act laying a duty on persons convicted of heinous crimes and to prevent poor

were mainly convicts or servants as four-fifths of immigrants into Pennsylvania at the time were Irish: the law would have had little meaning if most Irish immigrants were paying passengers.

The year 1729 was one of famine and followed years of famine. It was natural that the proportion of indigent emigrants in such a period was much greater than it was in more prosperous times. The scene was very different in the 'seventies however, when rising rents and a slump in the linen trade were the chief forces that led to emigration. The decade before 1771 had been one of unprecedented prosperity in the linen trade and the fruits of those few years of relative plenty enabled many to sail to the west in pursuit of a departed prosperity. Reports to parliament in 1774 from Belfast, Lisburn and Newry were unanimous on one point—those who were emigrating were paying passengers of the middle class.[1] Laid low by a double blow, this class saved what it could from the ruins and invested part of the proceeds in the cost of a passage to the land of hope.

Little can be said of the relative numbers of paying passengers and servants in the half-century between the 'twenties and the 'seventies. True, the *Belfast News Letter* claimed on 6 April 1773 that, till the late 'sixties, it was 'the very meanest of the people that went off, mostly in the station of servants, and such as had become obnoxious to their mother country' and true, also, that the heaviest emigrations between 1729 and 1771 took place in years of scarcity and famine, circumstances that tended to uproot the labourer rather than the farmer, but rack-renting was not peculiar to any particular years of the eighteenth century and it is to be expected, therefore, that dispossessed farmers and others who had taken warning from the writing on the wall were to be found on board most emigrant vessels, side by side with 'the very meanest of the people'.

---

and impotent persons being imported into Pennsylvania' (C.O. 5/1269, f.142). Large numbers of indigent immigrants were unwelcome not merely because of their poverty but because of the effect on prices of such sudden increases in numbers (Bolton, *Scotch Irish pioneers*, p. 159).

[1] *Commons' jn. Ire.*, xvi. 410, 411, 413.

CHAPTER VII

Ports and Agents

THE majority of emigrants to colonial America left the north of Ireland through five ports—Newry in county Down, Belfast, Larne and Portrush in county Antrim, and Londonderry in the county of that name. Except for an occasional vessel which called at Ballycastle after its departure from Belfast or Larne, the advertisement and shipping lists in the *Belfast News Letter* during the period 1750-1775 named only one emigrant vessel—the *Rodgers* which sailed from Portaferry in county Down to Baltimore in 1775—which did not sail from one or other of these five ports.[1] Of the 442 vessels which advertised sailings from north Irish ports to America in the third quarter of the century, 143 (or 32·4%) left Belfast, 127½ (28·8%) left Londonderry, 84 (19·0%) left Newry, 57½ (13·0%) left Larne and 30 (6·8%) left Portrush.[2] Belfast had not as yet secured the supremacy in the American trade which she was to share with Dublin over the other Irish ports from the beginning of the nineteenth century. The lack of development of inland transport and the smallness of the vessels employed ensured for the minor ports a place which they have long since lost in transatlantic trade.

No part of the north east of Ireland was more than forty miles distant from one of these five ports and each port was backed by an obvious hinterland. The three chief river valleys, the Foyle, the Bann and the Lagan, looked out to Londonderry, Portrush and Belfast, respectively. Larne stood on the Antrim coast at the foot of

[1] B.N.L., 21 July 1775.
[2] Several vessels called at two or more ports for emigrants. See Appendices A and C.

the plateau, while behind Newry lay the district cut off from the rest of Ulster by the Mournes and the Armagh mountains.

If each port served almost exclusively a well-defined district, it would be possible, from the number of sailings from each port, to make a rough estimate of the contribution the various parts of the north of Ireland made to the total emigration from the whole area. For example, it would be a valuable pointer in the study of district emigration if it were possible to say that one-third of all north Irish emigrants were from the Lagan valley because one-third of all emigrant vessels sailed from Belfast.

The only conclusive way of deciding whether or not each port had a definite emigrant hinterland would be to examine the places of origin of emigrants who left the port. Unfortunately, such information is not available except for a few isolated instances such as when emigrants appointed committees to act on their behalf.[1] The only method of determining the hinterland of each port would appear to be to examine the location of the agents who acted on behalf of the emigrant vessels which left that port. The chief agents were, of course, in the port of departure; but additional agents were often appointed in other places where, presumably, it was hoped that emigrants who would be willing to go to that port might be found.

Surprisingly few out-agents were appointed to act on behalf of the 143 vessels advertised to sail with emigrants from Belfast during the period 1750–1775. The locations of these out-agents and the places visited during tours by captains or agents of vessels sailing from Belfast were as follows, the numbers stated in each case being the number of voyages in respect of which out-agents were appointed or tours were made:[2]

OUT-AGENTS:

10	Ballycastle
9	Drumbo (co. Down)
6 each	Ballymena (co. Antrim); Newry
5	Larne
4	Carrickfergus
3 each	Caledon (co. Tyrone); Loughbrickland (co. Down)

[1] For example, the committee appointed by Londonderry emigrants to Nova Scotia in 1761 was named in the *B.N.L.* of 11 Mar. 1762.
[2] This and similar information regarding the other ports has been compiled from advertisements in *B.N.L.*, *L.J.* and contemporary Dublin newspapers.

2 each Saintfield, Dromore (co. Down); Lurgan (co. Armagh)

1 each Killyleagh, Ballynahinch, Ballyreany, Banbridge, Newtownards, Portaferry, Magheralin (co. Down); Antrim,
Galgorm, Templepatrick, Ballymoran, Lisburn (co.
Antrim); Richhill, Portadown (co. Armagh); Dungannon (co. Tyrone); Coleraine (co. Londonderry); London
derry

PLACES VISITED DURING TOURS:

5   Dromore

4 each Ballymena, Ballynahinch; Lisburn

3 each Armagh, Lurgan

2 each Banbridge; Coleraine

1 each Garvagh, Magherafelt (co. Londonderry); Castleblaney
(co. Monaghan); Cookstown (co. Tyrone); Downpatrick, Newtownards (co. Down); Antrim; Portadown

It is rather surprising to find that out-agents for Belfast vessels
were appointed in the ports of Ballycastle, Larne, Newry, and
Londonderry. The obvious explanation is that the vessels concerned were intended to call at those ports on the outward voyage
or would do so if sufficient passengers were engaged to make such
a slight diversion profitable. For example, of the five vessels with
agents in Larne, two were later advertised to call at Larne, another
was advertised to sail from Carrickfergus, half-way between
Belfast and Larne, and a fourth sailed to Philadelphia in 1773, a
year in which no ship was advertised to sail from Larne to that port.
Again, on six of the ten occasions on which a Ballycastle out-agent
was appointed for a vessel leaving Belfast, the vessel was the
Philadelphia. The appearance of the Ballycastle agent's name in the
Philadelphia advertisement year after year, even when vessels left
the more convenient ports of Larne and Portrush for the same
destination, suggests that the *Philadelphia* called at Ballycastle on
her outward voyage each year.

Two conclusions may be drawn. In years when vessels left other
north Irish ports for both the central and southern colonies, the
majority of the emigrants who left through Belfast came from the
district enclosed by a line joining Carrickfergus, Ballymena,
Cookstown, Caledon, Armagh and Downpatrick. On the other
hand, vessels from Belfast often touched at the other ports of the
north of Ireland, often without being advertised to do so—that
information could be conveyed by the out-agents—and so it

would be inaccurate to suggest that all the emigrants who sailed in vessels that originally left Belfast were from the limited area defined.

Port authorities were required[1] in the early years of the nineteenth century to compile lists of all emigrants and an examination of the places of origin of emigrants who sailed from Belfast in the year following March 1803—the first year in which the port authorities made such returns[2]—confirms the approximate accuracy of this definition of the emigrant hinterland of Belfast. Of the 183 emigrants who sailed from Belfast in that year, 123 were from this area and 38 were from areas which cannot be identified or were broadly defined by counties.

Out-agents were appointed in the following centres to act on behalf of one or more of the 127½ emigrant vessels which left Londonderry during the period 1770–1775:

5   Coleraine
4   Maghera (co. Londonderry); Ballygawley (co. Tyrone);
     Rathmelton (co. Donegal)
3   Belfast
2 each Omagh, Strabane (co. Tyrone)
1 each Garrison (co. Fermanagh); Caledon, Carnteel, Eskra
     (co. Tyrone); Castledoe, Convoy, Fahan, Letterkenny,
     Raphoe (co. Donegal); Richhill (co. Armagh); Down-
     patrick (co. Down); Ballymoney (co. Antrim)

No tours by captains or agents in quest of passengers for any Londonderry emigrant vessel were advertised.

The appointment of agents in Belfast should not be taken as an indication that Londonderry looked to the Lagan valley for emigrants in normal times. One of the three agents was appointed by Alexander McNutt, the land promoter, after his failure to arouse sufficient interest in the Belfast area to justify the chartering of a vessel to sail from that port to Nova Scotia. The second was appointed in 1760, a year in which only a privateer advertised for emigrants from Belfast. The third agent was appointed to act on

[1] 43 Geo. III, c.56.
[2] B.M., Add.MS 35932. Four emigrant vessels left Belfast during this period, viz. the *Eagle* (two voyages), *George*, and *Lady Washington*. The distribution of agents named in newspaper advertisements is indicated on the map at p. 106. The places of origin of immigrants into New York between 1803 and 1811 are contained in lists printed in *The recorder: bulletin of the American Irish Historical Society*, iii. no. 5, pp. 2–23; iii. no. 6, pp. 20–1; iii. no. 7, pp. 25–9.

behalf of a Philadelphia vessel in 1761 after the last vessel of the year had sailed from Belfast to Philadelphia.

The location of the agents indicate that the Londonderry emigrant vessels looked for passengers to eastern Donegal, most parts of Tyrone and all parts of county Londonderry. Most of the agents were located near loughs Foyle and Swilly or in the valleys of the Foyle and Strule. These were the more protestant parts of the counties named and, on the evidence of Young, Boulter and others, it is to be expected that most of the Londonderry emigrants came from these parts. Portrush was a more convenient port for those who left eastern Londonderry but so few vessels left Portrush that emigrants who travelled there had little or no choice of either vessel or port of destination. Probably as many emigrants from the Bann valley sailed from Londonderry as sailed from Portrush.

Considering both the agents named in shipping advertisements and the earliest substantial number of places of origin that have been recorded it would appear that the Londonderry emigrant hinterland lay inside a line joining Dunfanaghy in county Donegal, Castlederg and the Clogher valley in county Tyrone, and the lower part of the Bann valley. Of the 423 emigrants who left Londonderry in the eight vessels that sailed between March 1803 and March 1804, 269 were from within this area, 60 from outside it and the origin of the remainder was either given as 'county Donegal' or cannot be traced.[1]

More out-agents were appointed to act on behalf of the 84 emigrant vessels which were advertised to sail from Newry to the American colonies than for vessels which left any of the other north Irish ports. Out-agents were appointed in the following centres:

13 Belfast
6 each Richhill (co. Armagh); Moneymore (co. Londonderry)
5 Cookstown (co. Tyrone)
4 each Caledon, Dungannon, Stewartstown (co. Tyrone)
3 each Lurgan (co. Armagh); Moyallon (co. Down)

[1] B.M., Add.MS 35932. The vessels were the *American* (two voyages), *Pennsylvania*, *Mohawk*, *Ardent*, *Serpent*, *Independence*, and *Stafford*. Those from outside the area defined came from Ballyshannon, Kilcar, Killybegs, Killaughter and Mount Charles in county Donegal (12); Enniskillen, Lisnaskea and 'county Fermanagh' (23); county Down (3); county Armagh (2); county Sligo (6); Carrickfergus (2); counties Monaghan and Cavan (11).

2 each Ballymena (co. Antrim); Armagh, Keady, Markethill
(co. Armagh)

1 each Banbridge, Bryansford, Clough, Loughbrickland (co.
Down); Blackwatertown, Portadown (co. Armagh);
Charlemont, Coagh, Coalisland (co. Tyrone); Ballyronan,
Castledawson, Londonderry (co. Londonderry); Larne,
Lisburn (co. Antrim); Ballybay, Monaghan (co. Mona-
ghan); Belturbet, Cootehill (co. Cavan)

The following towns and villages were visited during tours made
on behalf of emigrant vessels which sailed from Newry:

3   Armagh

2 each Dungannon, Stewartstown (co. Tyrone); Banbridge
(co. Down); Cootehill (co. Cavan)

1 each Belfast; Rathfriland (co. Down); Aughnacloy, Caledon
(co. Tyrone); Ballybay, Castleblayney, Monaghan,
Clones (co. Monaghan); Tandragee (co. Armagh)

From this it can be seen that the majority of out-agents and places
included in tours to stimulate emigration through the port of
Newry were located in county Armagh, the south and west of
county Down and—as they lay along the coach route from
Londonderry to Dublin which passed through Newry—the east
of county Tyrone and the south of county Londonderry. Most of
the Newry emigrants may have been from some distance inland as
the town was flanked by sparsely populated mountainous regions,
peopled largely by Roman catholics. One hundred and three
emigrants were noted in the report of the Newry port authorities
in 1803, and, of these, fifty-five were from the areas indicated,
sixteen were from outside those areas, the places of origin of the
others being mainly noted by counties.[1]

Larne's natural hinterland was mid-Antrim and so it is not
surprising to find that, of the sixty-two occasions on which out-
agents were appointed to act on behalf of the 57½ emigrant vessels
which were advertised to sail from Larne between 1750 and 1775,
on twenty-one occasions they were located in Ballymena. The

[1] See G. Taylor and A. Skinner, *The post chaise*, pp. 22–7, 31–2, B.M., Add.MS
35932. The vessels were the *Patty, Diana, Betty* and *Alexis*. Of the emigrants from
outside the area, seven were from Dundalk, seven from Belfast and two from Queen's
County. County Tyrone was given as the place of origin of ten emigrants and eighteen
were stated to have come from county Down.

remaining out-agents were centred in ports north and south of Larne—fourteen vessels were represented in Ballycastle to the north and four in Carrickfergus, eighteen in Belfast and five in Newry to the south. In the case of only one vessel were out-agents appointed in Ballycastle and also in ports to the south of Larne. This suggests that emigrants recruited at the out-centres were embarked at those centres, those at Ballycastle on ships sailing by the northern route and those at the other ports on ships sailing by the southern route. Unfortunately, no emigrant vessels sailed from Larne in 1803 nor is there any record of the arrival in New York of an emigrant vessel from Larne between 1804 and 1811.

The lack of a good harbour deprived Portrush of a substantial share of the emigrant trade. From accounts of the earlier phases of emigration such as that of McGregor in 1718 it would appear that vessels sailed from well within the Bann estuary to America, but with the increase in the size of transatlantic vessels as the eighteenth century progressed, the Skerries roads, a mile from Portrush, had to serve as the anchorage though the Coleraine merchants still controlled the trade. This natural handicap, together with the proximity of Portrush to the routes from Belfast, Larne, and Londonderry to America, normally restricted the transatlantic sailings from Portrush to one vessel a year. In fact, no vessel was advertised to sail from the port in 1773, the year of heaviest emigration from the north of Ireland to colonial America. Of the thirteen out-agents appointed to act on behalf of the thirty emigrant vessels advertised to leave Portrush between 1750 and 1775, eight were located in Ballymoney[1] and it is probable that Portrush sailings attracted few people from beyond Ballymoney, a dozen miles away, and the lower reaches of the Bann.

Reference has already been made to tours by captains or agents to attract passengers. Few such tours were advertised, though it could well be that tours were a much more common feature of the emigrant trade than the advertisement columns of the newspapers would suggest—when tours were made, towns and villages were invariably visited on market days[2] and it did not need any advertisement to attract people to markets. The tours which were

---

[1] The other out-agents were located at Ballymena (2), Larne (1), Moneymore (1) and Garvagh (1). No tours to attract emigrants were advertised on behalf of any Portrush vessels during the period.

[2] E.g., advertisement of the *New Hope* (B.N.L., 15 Mar. 1765).

MAP OF ULSTER

1. The broken lines show the catchment areas of the ports.

2. The position of the shading in the circles indicates which ports had emigration agents in the towns shown.

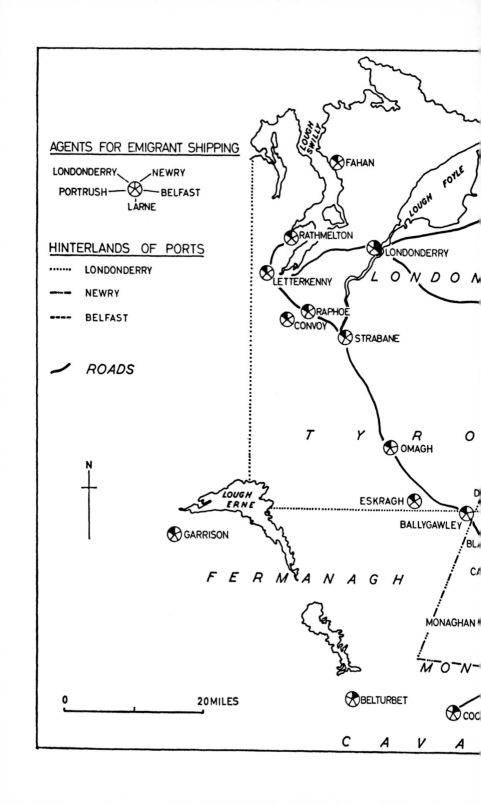

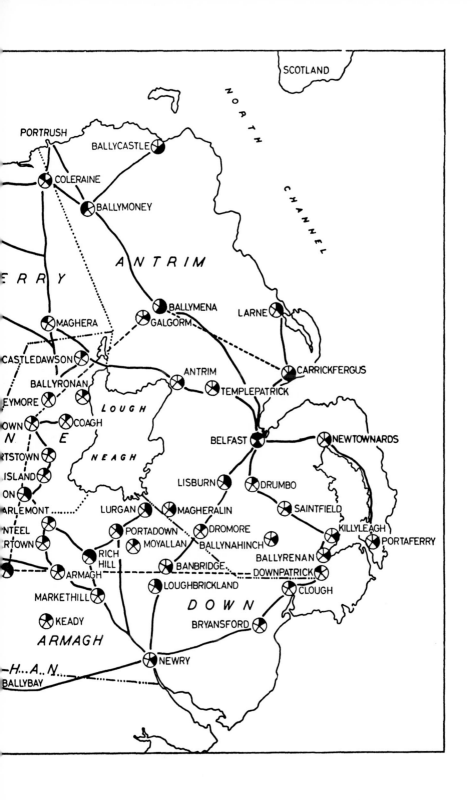

advertised were made by land promoters or in years of heavy emigration when competition among vessels was keen and when it was profitable to delay sailing for a time if a full complement of passengers was well-nigh assured.

Tours from the various ports were usually made within the respective hinterlands described above. For example, Charles McKenzie, master of the *Peace and Plenty*, Belfast to Philadelphia and New York, visited Ballynahinch, Lisburn and Ballymena in search of emigrants.[1] Again, the masters of the *Newry Assistance* and the *Minerva*, both bound from Newry to Philadelphia, visited, between them, Coalisland and Cookstown in county Tyrone, Banbridge, Rathfriland and Dromore in county Down and Castledawson in county Londonderry.[2] It may be that the places included in tours such as these, rather than the places where out-agents were appointed, are a more accurate indication of the region from which a particular port drew its emigrants. An agent may have been nominated because of personal or business connections with the main agent and not because emigrants habitually came from his locality to the port concerned. Unfortunately, so few tours were advertised that it is not possible to generalise in this respect.

The three vessels named above—the *Peace and Plenty*, *Newry Assistance* and *Minerva*—carried about a thousand emigrants when they sailed after the completion of the recruiting tours.[3] The *Needham* of Newry was the only other vessel whose captain was advertised to visit neighbouring towns in 1773 and a full complement of about five hundred passengers may have been a tribute to the persuasiveness of William Cheevers, the vessel's master.[4]

It is not difficult to picture the activities of a captain during these tours. Just as wandering tinkers harangued the market-day crowds and extolled their wares, so did the captain, proclaiming the virtues and attractions of a land of plenty beyond a sea that had terrors in store for all ships but his own. The report of the judges of the north-western circuit of Ireland in 1729 gives some indication of these market-day scenes:

As to the advantages expected in New England we find the people deluded and drawn into a belief of them, not only by letters and

[1] *B.N.L.*, 12 Apr., 1774.
[2] Ibid., 12 Mar., 1773.
[3] See Appendix C.
[4] *B.N.L.*, 26 Mar. See Appendix C.

emissaries from New England but by masters and owners of ships in this kingdom, who, for the profit of extraordinary freights which they get on this occasion, send agents to markets and fairs and public advertisements through the country to assemble the people together, where they assure them that in America they can get good land to them and their posterity for little or no rent, without either paying tithes or taxes, and amuse them with such accounts of these countries as they know will be most agreeable to them . . .[1]

A more detailed account of how the people were 'deluded' was given seven years later to the Irish house of commons by a committee appointed to inquire into the case of the *George*, a vessel which had been advertised to sail from Dublin to North Carolina but which, it was believed, the captain meant to 'knock on the head' in order to get the insurance. The committee reported that

> . . . some time in the month of August last [1735], Thomas Cumming, master of the ship *George*, of Dublin, intending to sail for North Carolina, sent Joseph Cumming and John McFarran to several parts of the counties of Monaghan, Cavan, and Meath, to get passengers for said voyage, that accordingly they dispersed public notice throughout the country . . . . . and said Cumming and McFarran represented to the emigrants, and others, the great advantages they would get by going to North Carolina, and among other arguments, that a common labourer would by easy labour gain £20 a year, and others would get fifty acres for nothing. And Thomas [Cumming] soon after following them to that country, at the public meeting-house, at Banbraghey, confirmed what had been so told them. [He told them] they might easier borrow £60 there than sixpence here, and that they might with less difficulty get credit for a cow in North Carolina, than for a hen in this country; he told some that they would be put into farms of which they would get half the profit for managing them; that their wives immediately upon landing would be put into dairies of as many cows as they could manage, and would have half the produce, as well of the calves, as butter and cheese, for their labour. He assured David Wright, that he might earn 40s. sterling a month by easy labour, and told Robert Oliver, who is a linen weaver, that he would get a guinea sterling for weaving a ten hundred piece of cloth, which according to the labour of a good workman in linen of that sort, would produce above £100 sterling a year. It was likewise represented as a most powerful and specious argument of per-

[1] T.S.P.I., T.659, pp. 75–9.

suasion, that they would have neither rent or tithes to pay in that country, and would live happily from the time they landed there.[1]

Provincial agents and touring captains were but the trappings of a trade which was firmly in the hands of the merchants of the ports. Attention has been drawn to the relatively small number of out-agents appointed for vessels leaving Belfast and the same was true of the other ports of the north of Ireland. Tours may have been made by masters or other emissaries without preliminary advertising but, even after reasonable allowance is made for such tours, the fact remains that at least half the vessels which left the north of Ireland with emigrants for America were represented by agents only at the ports of departure.

It was not till after Waterloo that offices devoted exclusively to the emigrant trade were opened in the north of Ireland,[2] though the existence of such offices in London and other English ports was mentioned as early as 1770.[3] In the eighteenth century the sale of a passage to America was regarded in the same light as the sale of household goods and both lines of business were transacted by the same merchant in the same shop. For example, a person could purchase, according to his inclination, a pound of garden seeds or a passage to America from McKedy and Elder at the sign of the Orange Tree in High Street, Belfast. The sale of flour or flaxseed brought over by a vessel was often advertised by a merchant as a postscript to his offer to sell passages to America in the same ship. Mussenden, Bateson and company, of Belfast, were active in the chartering of ships but were equally active in the sale of Scotch herrings.[4] A striking feature of the advertisements of eighteenth century merchants was the variety of the wares of each of them, few specialising in any branch of trade—not unusual was the advertisement of R. Caldwell of Londonderry who offered for sale 'flax, spirits, rum, brandy, soap, indigo, steel, almonds, gunpowder, tar, tea, porter, etc'.[5] If anything—including a passage to America—could be sold, then the eighteenth century merchant was prepared to offer it for sale.

The emigration agents in the ports were of three classes. Some

[1] *Commons' jn. Ire.*, vi. 635.
[2] Adams, *Ir. emig. in 19th cent.*, p. 71.
[3] W. Eddis, *Letters from America*, pp. 76–7.
[4] See Mussenden papers, P.R.O.N.I., D. 354/293.
[5] *L.J.*, 3 Oct. 1772.

acted merely as agents for the captain or owners of a vessel and were presumably paid by results. Others were themselves the owners of the vessels in whose interests they acted and their reward was the passage money and the proceeds of the sale in America of those carried as servants. The third class—by far the smallest—consisted of a few people, mostly merchants, who advertised for passengers and servants, chartered a vessel to carry them to America, and there sold the servants.

The distinction between the shipping and the mercantile interest was gaining a foothold by the middle of the eighteenth century. It is difficult to discover which of these interests was dominant in the north Irish emigrant trade, but the carriage of emigrants was an attractive proposition whether a vessel was owned by people whose main interest was in the sale of cargoes or in the profits of shipping. Dry goods, the general cargo from the north of Ireland to America, were of comparatively little bulk and so the conveyance of passengers was welcomed by both interests. In days when forwarding agents were unknown it was the captain's duty to secure as profitable a cargo as possible.[1] If his mind turned to emigrants, it was natural for him to seek to secure these through the merchant to whom he had brought a cargo or who was organising a cargo for him to carry on his return voyage. 'Passengers, redemptioners, servants and freight' was a recurring phase in the shipping advertisements of the time and the securing of these on behalf of an English or American captain was the beginning and end of the interest of many merchants in the emigration trade. This incidental interest explains why the majority of the merchants who acted as agents in the ports did so only occasionally. For example, of the twenty-three Belfast agents who acted on behalf of emigrant vessels advertised to sail from that port in the period 1770–5, ten did so once only and four acted as agents twice during the six years.

The second class of agent—the owners of vessels, who collected the full profits of any emigration they organised and not merely a commission—corresponds fairly closely with the Irish section of those engaged in the dying mercantile branch of the transatlantic

[1] C. E. Fayle, *A short history of the world's shipping industry*, pp. 201–6. Fayle quotes as typical the experiences of Samuel Kelly, master of a merchant vessel. Kelly waited 'on several manufacturers who were in the habit of sending goods to America to solicit their favours for the *John*'; he was given 'liberty from [his] owners to embrace a freight for any port most eligible'; when the freight markets were dull he was obliged 'to cruise the city for goods'.

trade. Their vessels brought them flaxseed and flour from America in the spring, often went to a European port in the early summer and then returned to the north of Ireland and sailed with linen and emigrants to America in time for the flaxseed market in November and December. Lack of direct evidence often makes it impossible to unravel the efforts of this class from the efforts of those who acted as agents from time to time for vessels which called occasionally at the north Irish ports in the course of normal trade or were attracted there by the prospect of securing a profitable complement of emigrants. To complicate matters further, these two classes of agents were not separate entities: a company which owned vessels in the transatlantic trade often acted on behalf of vessels which were obviously casual callers.

Newspaper advertisements give little direct help in determining the ownership of vessels for they seldom included that information. An analysis of these advertisements reveals, however, two points of significance. First, some advertisements named the master as an agent while others did not. Second, most of the vessels for which the masters did not act as agents made voyages in several years with emigrants, whereas most of the other vessels sailed with emigrants in only one year. One would expect the master of a vessel not locally owned to take an active part in recruiting emigrants: again, one could expect that vessels not locally owned made fewer voyages from a port than did vessels belonging to that port. It would not be unreasonable to assume, therefore, that merchants who represented a vessel which sailed year after year and for which the master was not named as an agent were the owners of the vessel. This is so in those cases where the owners of the vessels concerned are known; and, if true in other cases also, throws a revealing light on the organisation of the emigration trade.

The application of this test of ownership to Portrush and Larne shows that, in both cases, the bulk of the emigration trade was directly in the hands of the owners of the vessels. The *Providence* and the *Rainbow* accounted for sixteen of the twenty sailings from Portrush to the American colonies between 1762, when the vessels were built, and 1772, when the *Rainbow* made her last journey. It would seem that Alexander Laurence and the Galt family—William, John, James and Charles—of Coleraine were part owners of both vessels for they acted as agents on all sixteen occasions, together with Hugh Lyle and Andrew Ferguson in the case of the *Providence*. An additional indication of the local owner-ship of the vessels was that the *Providence* sailed annually to New York and the *Rainbow* to Philadelphia, but when the *Providence* was lost in 1768[1], the *Rainbow* was switched to the New York route. Two conclusions may be drawn from these facts—not only were most of the Portrush emigrants of the period 1762–72 carried in two vessels, but the bulk of the Portrush emigration trade was in the hands of a few Coleraine merchants *cum* shipowners *cum* emigration agents.[2]

Similar conclusions with regard to the organisation of the emigration trade from Larne are justified by an analysis of the sailings from that port. Seven of the vessels which sailed from Larne to North America between 1750 and 1775 after advertising for passengers account for forty-four sailings, nine other vessels sharing the remaining fifteen sailings. Each of the seven vessels which made the passage regularly had the same main agent on all occasions and in not one of the forty-four advertisements was the master of the vessel named as an agent. On the other hand, the master of each of the other vessels was always named as one of the agents for his vessel. It follows that about three-quarters of the voyages with emigrants from Larne were directly controlled by the merchants of the port. The proportion of emigrants carried by local vessels may have been even greater than this because of the natural preference for crossing the Atlantic in a Larne vessel rather than in an unknown one from England or America.[3]

It has been shown that the emigration trade from Portrush and Larne was mainly in the hands of local merchants who owned the

---

[1] *B.N.L.*, 6 Jan. and 3 Feb. 1769.
[2] Of the thirty advertised sailings from Portrush to America between 1750 and 1775, one or more of the Galts was agent on twenty-four occasions.
[3] The Larne merchants most concerned with the emigration trade, together with the number of occasions on which they acted as agents, were:

Jas. McVicker	— agent for 17 sailings, 12 of which were of the *James and Mary*, 1764–75.
Hugh Montgomery	— 11 sailings: 8 for *William and George*, 1754–62.
John Montgomery	— 11 sailings: 5 for *Jupiter*, 1770–4, and 4 for *Lord Dunluce*, 1772–5.
Robert Wilson	— 8 sailings: 3 for *Antrim*, 1752–4, and 4 for *Lord Dunluce*, 1756–9.
John Wilson	— 8 sailings: 7 for *Lord Dunluce*, 1756–63.
Jas. Agnew	— 4 sailings: 4 for *Antrim*, 1750–4.
Samuel Montgomery	— 4 sailings: 4 for *Betty*, 1772–5.

vessels they canvassed for and reaped the main profits of the trade they organised. The same was true of Londonderry. Of the 127½ voyages advertised from that port between 1750 and 1775, ninety-three were of vessels certainly or probably in local ownership.[1]

Though Portrush and Larne were the smallest of the north Irish transatlantic ports and Londonderry one of the most important, varying factors led to the continued operation from all three ports of locally-owned vessels whose primary task was to meet the trading needs of the merchants who owned them. Lack of harbour facilities in the case of Portrush and the absence of a large and distinctive hinterland behind Larne restricted the part played by those ports in the Atlantic trade in the eighteenth century and ended the participation of both ports in that trade in the nineteenth century. The few ocean-going vessels which were locally owned could cope with each port's transatlantic commerce and so other vessels did not often have cause to call there. Londonderry had both a good harbour and an extensive hinterland but was at the head of a deep inlet off the main summer Atlantic route and completely removed from the main winter route between Britain and America. Londonderry's trade with America tended, therefore, to be self-contained.

It is clear that the majority of emigrants from Newry and Belfast to colonial America sailed in English or American vessels which either called at those ports in the course of trade or were attracted there by heavy emigration. It follows that in the majority of emigrant voyages from both ports local merchants were merely sub-agents of the masters of the vessels. In the case of Newry, local ownership of vessels was indicated in only thirty-three of the eighty-four emigrant sailings advertised between 1750 and 1775 and no fewer than twenty-five of the forty-three vessels which advertised during that period did so on only one occasion.[2]

---

[1] Thirteen emigrant vessels were stated to be owned by Londonderry merchants. These vessels, and the number of voyages with emigrants that each advertised, were: *Diana* (1), *Hamilton Galley* (2), *City of Derry* (3), *Hopewell* (9), *Willey* (1), *Jupiter* (10), *Admiral Hawke* (7), *Henry* (1), *Alexander* (2), *Hellen* (1), *Mary* (1), *Minerva* (3), *Betty* (2). The first three vessels sailed in the 'fifties, years when the B.N.L. records are far from complete: the last six vessels commenced sailings in 1773 or 1774. Other vessels which were probably owned by Londonderry merchants were: *King George* (6), *Phœnix* (11), *Marquis of Granby* (8), *Rose* (7), *Hibernia* (3), *Wallworth* (5), *Prince of Wales* (6), *Hannah* (4).

[2] The ownership of six vessels was stated. These, with the number of sailings, were: *Free Mason* (4), *Robert* (5), *Nedham* (3), *Prosperity* (1), *Betty* (3), *Elliott* (1) (1774). Four

Portrush, the smallest of the north Irish ports, had the highest proportion of emigrant voyages which were locally directed: Belfast, the largest port, had the greatest proportion of voyages for which the port's merchants acted only as sub-agents. Of the 143 sailings from Belfast for which emigrants were advertised in the third quarter of the eighteenth century, local ownership of vessels was stated or indicated in only forty-three cases.[1] Of the eighty-seven vessels which called at Belfast in the same period after advertising for emigrants, no fewer than fifty-three did so on only one occasion. The growth of Belfast, its proximity to the Irish Sea shipping routes, and its hinterland which made it one of the most attractive ports in the British Isles for vessels in the flaxseed trade attracted vessels which went wherever cargoes were available.

The two types of agents studied—those who acted on behalf of their own vessels and those, sometimes the same people, who acted on behalf of visiting vessels—were the main media in the organisation of emigration but there is little evidence of methodical organisation. Each effort was made with one particular vessel and one particular voyage in mind. Occasionally the effort was forceful but more often it was unstimulating. On the whole, the organisers of emigration played a passive role, advertising for and thankfully accepting passengers, rather than actively encouraging emigration. Occasionally, particularly in years of heavy emigration, tours such as have been described were made. Part of the purpose of these, however, was to direct as well as to provoke emigration for, even in years of heavy emigration, the shipping available was more than ample to cope with the volume of people desiring

---

other vessels were probably locally owned: *Newry* (5), *Britannia* (4), *Newry Packet* (3), *Newry Assistance* (4).

[1] Ownership stated (with the number of emigrant voyages): *Lord Russell* (2), *Ross* (1), *Warren* (1), *Prince of Wales* (8), *Betty Gregg* (4), *Lord Chatham* (1), *Peace and Plenty* (1), *Liberty and Prosperity* (1), *Glorious Memory* (1). The last four vessels commenced sailings in 1773 or 1774. Ownership indicated: *Philadelphia* (8), *Belfast Packet* (3), *Countess of Donegall* (1), *Earl of Donegall* (3), *Friendship* (5), *Two Peggys* (3). The most prominent of the Belfast merchants in the emigration trade between 1765 and 1775 were Thomas and John Greg and Waddell Cunningham. Cunningham, in partnership with the Gregs till 1772 and usually in collaboration with them after that date, acted as agent for 22 emigrant vessels which made 26 voyages. Only one of these vessels was stated to belong to him but he may have owned others too. Cunningham and the Gregs are stated to have had four ships plying between New York and Dublin, Londonderry, Newry and Belfast (Purcell, 'The Irish contribution to colonial New York', in *Studies* (1941), xxx. 114).

transportation.[1] A similar stress on the means of travel rather than on the benefits of emigration was evident in the shipping advertisements. These sometimes included a hackneyed phrase such as 'For the flourishing and prosperous port of Baltimore', but most of the advertisements detailed the good treatment to be expected on the voyage rather than the blessings that awaited on the American shore. Similarly, though shipping advertisements tended to become longer as the volume of emigration increased, it was minute descriptions of vessels rather than stimulating accounts of America that caused the expansion. When emigration was heavy, the merchants marshalled sufficient shipping to deal with it; when it was light, they hopefully advertised for emigrants and continued, perhaps regretfully, with their normal trade.[2]

It is the third class of agents—those who deliberately and determinedly stimulated emigration—who have attracted most attention. The Rhenish states of Germany saw this type of agent in its most active form and the heavy emigration from those states was in no small measure due to the emissaries of Penn and, later, to the 'newlanders'. The latter acted as agents for both land speculators and the ship-owners of Rotterdam and, in quest of emigrants, travelled from place to place in gaudy dress and in beribboned wagons to the flourishes of trumpets. These 'soul traffickers', as their luckless dupes called them, were the cream of emigration organisers, the agents *par excellence* of the eighteenth century.[3]

Such intense campaigning was not necessary in a small region like the north of Ireland where no district was far from a port engaged in the American trade and where thoughts of a better life turned naturally to the British colonies. Yet so much wrath has

---

[1] In 1773, for example, the *Lord Chatham*, which had been advertised to sail from Belfast to Charleston (*B.N.L.*, 10 Aug. 1773), sailed instead to the Barbados after several vain appeals for passengers (ibid., 8 Oct. and 16 Nov.).

[2] There are, however, indications that the merchants might have adopted a more active policy in encouraging emigration had the American revolution not broken out in 1775. Because of the great success of the voyages of 1771–3, many large ships had been built for the passenger trade, e.g., *Prosperity* (500 tons) which left Belfast and *Liberty* (500 tons) which left Newry. As fewer people showed any inclination to emigrate after 1773, the owners of, or agents for, these vessels organised tours and spread their nets far and wide by appointing a great number of out-agents.

[3] W. A. Knittle, *The early eighteenth century Palatine emigration: a British Government redemptioner project to manufacture naval stores*, pp. 12, 22, 31; E. Abbott, *Immigration: select documents and case histories*, pp. 3, 11–13; E. Abbott, *Historical aspects of the immigration problem*, p. 9; Osgood, *Am. in the 18th cent.*, ii. 499; J. T. Adams, *Provincial society, 1690–1763*, pp. 175–8.

been poured upon the heads of this third class of agents that, at first glance, one is tempted to believe that they were the most influential and the most numerous of all the agents. These 'harpies, . . . these invaders of domestic happiness and improvers of popular discontent . . . the artful sycophants' who 'hovered like birds of prey' were denounced in a pamphlet published at the end of the eighteenth century[1] and Thomas Millar, the lord justice clerk of Scotland, had already spoken of 'so many emissaries from America who are employed in seducing our people'.[2] These denunciations do not dispose of the argument that the great majority of agents in Ireland—and in Britain, too—played a passive rather than an active part. Violent language proves nothing and the author of *Look before you leap* had in mind nothing more than the merchants who acted as agents in practically all the Irish ports. The absence of dynamic activity on the part of these agents was admitted in the statement that they 'hovered like birds of prey' while others, 'a kind of jackal', supplied these 'ravenous animals with prey'. Similarly, judgment of Miller's statement must be tempered by the event which had first attracted his attention to emigration, namely, the attempt of Thomas Desbrisay to secure settlers for Prince Edward Island. Desbrisay, whether in Scotland or Ireland, was certainly not a passive agent, but neither was he a typical agent. He was a land speculator, a class which had comparatively little success in Ireland.[3] The majority of agents, whether acting for their own vessels or on behalf of visiting vessels, watched and waited rather than campaigned and persuaded. As the board of trade observed, their role was 'to avail themselves' of the existence of a spirit of emigration and to direct that flow into the holds of their vessels.[4]

The only north Irish merchant of the time who is recorded as having gone on tour in search of emigrants was William Beatty of Belfast who, between 1763 and 1774, was concerned in ten emigrant voyages, eight of them to Charleston. After two unspectacular years as an orthodox agent, he joined in the promotion of the voyage of the *New Hope* to Charleston in association with Robert Wills who had long since decided that it was more profitable to

[1] *Look before you leap* (1797), in Abbott, *Immigration: select documents and case histories*, pp. 24–6.
[2] To Suffolk, 25 Apr. 1774 (S.P. 54/46, no. 164a).
[3] See Chapter VIII (iv).
[4] Representation to P.C., 8 Apr. 1762 (P.C. 1/48).

sell groceries than to teach the classics.[1] To further the venture, Beatty went on a tour embracing Lisburn, Ballynahinch, Lurgan and Dromore.[2] Beatty's interest in South Carolina continued and he left for that province on board the *Prince of Wales* in January 1766 after advertising that he

> hereby offers his assistance to such as incline to go with him as servants; and proposes to clothe them in a genteel manner, pay their passage, and take care to have them happily settled in that country, where industry is amply rewarded and poverty is a stranger: therefore all young girls and spirited lads that choose to accompany him under these circumstances are desired to apply to him without loss of time, that their clothing and other things may be properly provided to their liking.[3]

As the *Prince of Wales* was the only vessel which was advertised to leave the north of Ireland with emigrants for South Carolina in January 1766, it seems likely that the fifty-one 'poor protestants lately arrived from Ireland' who petitioned the provincial Council on 31 March 1766 for the bounty of five pounds per head and for grants of 5,550 acres of land in the townships of Boonesborough and Belfast were among the passengers on that vessel.[4]

In October 1766 Beatty chartered a vessel in Belfast and, in a long advertisement, called on people to 'embrace this favourable opportunity' of emigrating to South Carolina.[5] On the ending of the South Carolina bounty in 1768, he joined in the efforts of Matthew Rea and George Golphin[6] to stimulate emigration to Georgia but did not advertise any further tours, depending for a response on long advertisements and the appointment of an unusually large number of out-agents.

Visiting Americans or departing emigrants occasionally advertised for servants—for example, Charles Hamilton advertised for 'blacksmiths, taylors, coopers, shoemakers, and a genteel lad that understands waiting on a single person' and interviewed those interested on his journey from Enniskillen, in county Fermanagh,

---

[1] *B.N.L.*, 20 Mar. 1738/9.
[2] Ibid., 19 Feb. and 15 Mar. 1765.
[3] Ibid., 29 Oct. 1765.
[4] Revill, *S.C.*, pp. 56–8.
[5] *B.N.L.*, 7 Oct. 1766.
[6] See Chapter VIII. (v).

to Londonderry from which port he emigrated to Pennsylvania[1]—
and land promoters sometimes toured the country in quest of
servants, but, apart from these infrequent deviations, the organisation of emigration from the north of Ireland to pre-revolutionary
America followed a well-beaten and unexciting path. The organisation was, happily, unspectacular in other ways for the north of
Ireland was spared the depths of inhumanity which Scotland and
England witnessed from time to time. Two of the most evil ways
of securing a cargo of emigrants were the 'spiriting' of youths and
the abduction of adults. 'Spirits', kidnappers of youths who were
then sent to be sold into servitude in America,[2] were unknown in
the north of Ireland: a single instance of 'spiriting' would have
been a most powerful argument for the suppression or control of
the emigration trade, yet it was not mentioned once by magistrates,
landlords or clergy in their diverse reports and petitions.

The seizure of adults would likewise have been trumpeted from
mansion and pulpit had an instance of it been established. Such
seizures were unknown; but a sequel to a seizure in the island of
Harris in Scotland took place on the road from Bangor to Donaghadee in county Down in 1739 when men and women, with their
hands bound behind them, were to be seen running, hastened on
by the blows of the clubs and sticks of the seamen of the vessel
William of Donaghadee. Some of the one hundred and eleven
passengers in this ship had escaped when the vessel put in at
Donaghadee on her voyage to America and the manner by which
they had been recruited was described in a letter, based on the
evidence of the unfortunate passengers, from two local justices:

> Husbands were in the dead of and darkest time of the night torn by
> ruffians out of bed from their wives, wives from their husbands,
> mothers from their young children, and children from their mothers,
> and all dragged on board the ship; and in particular one woman
> was in the open day and in the face of the ship's crew dragged by
> the heels over rocks to the shore and exposed in the most shameful
> manner till she was brought on board the ship and confined there:
> others were seized on the roads and forced on board the ship, and
> some boys were sent as messengers with letters to be delivered to

[1] *L.J.*, 23 Feb. 1773. John Crawford, also an emigrant, offered to take redemptioners
and servants with him to Philadelphia in the vessel *Alexander* (ibid., 6 Apr. 1773).
[2] MacLean, *Highland settlements in Am.*, p. 39; J. C. Ballagh, *White servitude in the
colony of Virginia*, pp. 38-9.

persons in the ship and were immediately forced down into the hold and confined there . . . . .[1]

The villain of the piece was Norman McLeod of Berneray who chartered the vessel ostensibly to carry convicts.[2] Happy is the country without a history: fortunate was the north of Ireland that the organisation of the emigration trade was comparatively placid, that the emigration agents did not stray from the shallows of deception to the depths of kidnapping.

By the middle of the eighteenth century the great majority of north Irish emigration agents, though not of land speculators, had come to depend largely on newspaper advertisements to recruit passengers. An advertisement was inserted in one or both of the north Irish newspapers,[3] often before the arrival of the vessel in the port from which it was to sail. This was the main advertisement of the voyage and invariably appeared in every issue of the newspaper till the vessel sailed, the original advertisement being supplemented from time to time with additional details of the vessel's attractions or with postponements of the date of departure. The advertisements were of two main types, depending on whether or not the carrying of passengers was the main purpose of the voyage. A typical advertisement of a voyage in which the carriage of freight was as important as the carriage of passengers was that of the *Pitt* in 1763:

For NEW-CASTLE and NEW-YORK in AMERICA.
The Ship PITT, burthen 250 Tons, John Montgomery, Master, will be clear to sail from the Port of Larne about the 15th of July next. For Freight or passage apply to Mr Thomas Greg of Belfast, or to William Montgomery of Larne, or the Captain on Board. Larne 26th April.
N.B. Passengers may depend on being well treated, and servants will meet with good Encouragement.[4]

[1] To Michael Ward, circuit justice, 22 Nov. 1739 (T.S.P.I., T.827, pp. 85–6). Similar activities in Scotland were reported in 1773 by Miller who advised that the emigration trade be regulated so that all vessels left ports where customs officials could examine emigrants before departure (To Suffolk, 4 July 1774: S.P. 54/46, no. 168).
[2] T.S.P.I., T.827, p. 60.
[3] Some voyages from the northern ports, particularly from Newry, were also advertised in Dublin newspapers. For example, three of the thirteen vessels that were advertised in the *B.N.L.* to sail with emigrants from Newry in 1774 were also advertised in *F.D.J.* (*Hope*—24 Feb.; *Robert*—17 Mar.; *Renown*—24 Mar.). The name of a Dublin agent was sometimes added to the southern advertisement.
[4] *B.N.L.*, 29 Apr. 1763.

The second type of advertisement made no reference to freight and magnified the advantages of taking passage in the particular vessel advertised. Typical was the advertisement of the *Glorious Memory* in 1774:

> For NEWCASTLE, PHILADELPHIA, and BALTIMORE.
> The good Ship GLORIOUS MEMORY, Burthen 400 tons, William Stewart, Master, will be clear to sail from Belfast for the Ports aforesaid by the first of August next. Passengers, Redemptioners, or Servants, will meet with good Encouragement, by applying to the Owner, Jesse Taylor, who will take particular Care to have Plenty of the best Provisions and Water put on board for the Voyage, and will spar no Expense to have those who take their Passage in her agreeably and comfortably accommodated.
> The above Ship sails remarkably fast, and will be compleately fitted out, is near six Feet high between Decks, and in every other Respect as good a Ship as in the Trade; the Captain well experienced (having been for several Years first Mate with Capt. Malcom). As no more Passengers will be allowed to go on Board than can be accommodated with the greatest Ease, those who intend going with her had better give Ernest immediately, lest they should lose so good an Opportunity.[1]

As would be expected, the former type of advertisement predominated in years when comparatively few people wished to emigrate: the more laudatory type was frequent in years when the demand for passenger accommodation was heavy and when, consequently, competition among shipowners and masters for full complements of passengers was keenest. For example, of the twenty-one vessels which advertised for passengers before leaving north Irish ports in 1769, nineteen published brief advertisements along the lines of that of the *Pitt*, the remaining two being chartered by a land promoter to carry passengers to Georgia. On the other hand, thirty-six of the thirty-nine vessels which were advertised to sail in 1774 paraded their virtues before the public in the manner of the *Glorious Memory*.

The principal advertisement was seldom published less than a fortnight before the vessel was due to sail; usually about a month's notice was given and at times three months were to pass between the publication of the advertisement and the sailing of the vessel. There was no distinctive difference in the length of notice given of

[1] *B.N.L.*, 21 June, 1774.

voyages intended primarily for the carriage of emigrants and those intended primarily for the carriage of goods. The average notice given by the vessels which left Belfast in 1773, a peak year of emigration in which no reference to freight appeared in advertisements, was five weeks: five weeks' notice was also given by the vessels which left Belfast in 1765, a year in which all the vessels advertised for freight. The period of delay varied with the vessel rather than with the season but, as a general rule, the notice given by vessels advertising later than August was shorter than that given by vessels leaving earlier in the year. This was caused by a combination of respect for the elements, the knowledge that most of the season's linen and emigrants had already gone and the desire to be in time to join the flaxseed sailings from America in December.

William Beatty prefaced one of his advertisements with the self-denying assurance, 'I know well the oppression that abounds',[1] but he and all the other agents took part in the emigration trade for the profits that were to be derived from it and all the evidence suggests that the statement of the British consul in Philadelphia that 'in this sort of trade there is little risk and great profits' was as true in the earlier part of the eighteenth century as when it was made in 1789.[2] At the height of north Irish emigration in the 'seventies, a vessel advertised as of 300 tons carried about 300 emigrants who, according to an estimate made by the *Belfast News Letter* on 6 April 1773, paid about £1,050 for their passages. From this sum must be deducted expenses such as the wages of the crew and the cost of provisions during the voyages. A vessel of this size had a crew of about twelve[3] and as the average monthly wage of a seaman was slightly over one pound,[4] wages amounted to about £40 allowing for a stay of six weeks in port and a voyage of the same duration. The cost of provisioning the vessel for the crew during this period and for the passengers during the voyage was about £350 as the daily cost per head was probably between sixpence—an estimate of 1764 in connection with a German emigration project—and sevenpence-halfpenny—the allowance paid to a contractor for

---

[1] B.N.L., 6 Aug. 1773.
[2] Phineas Bond to F.O. (Abbott, *Historical aspects of the immigration problem*, p. 10).
[3] *John* and *Newry*, both advertised as of 300 tons, had each a crew of twelve on the voyage from Newry to New York in 1764 (B.N.L., 27 Mar. and 10 Aug. 1764; C.O. 5/1288, 26 July and 19 Nov. 1764).
[4] 2 Geo. II, c36 (Eng.); W. S. Lindsay, *History of merchant shipping and colonial commerce*, iii. 244.

transporting troops and their families from Dublin to the Isle of Wight in 1773.[1] Lesser expenses such as harbour dues and structural alterations may have brought the total expenses of the voyage up to about £500, leaving a net profit of over £500 on the voyage. The cost of building a vessel of 300 tons at the time was about £2,500,[2] so that the net proceeds of the voyage with emigrants represented a return of twenty per cent. on the cost of constructing the vessel. Satisfactory as this may appear from the shipowner's point of view, the actual return was probably above forty per cent. because the tonnage of a vessel seldom exceeded half the tonnage stated in the advertisement, so that the estimated cost of building the vessel must be reduced proportionately.[3]

No information has come to my notice of the scale of fees—if any—paid to out-agents or to merchants who acted merely as agents for visiting vessels. It is to be expected that the main or only payment to these agents was in the form of a commission as in the Rhine ports where the agents received between fourteen and twenty shillings for each emigrant they recruited.[4]

It must be added as a postscript to the activities of the north Irish emigration agents that they were assisted to a much lesser extent than their counterparts in Scotland by group emigration organised primarily from within the group itself. Naturally, many Irish emigrants did go in groups of relatives or neighbours and many people who might not otherwise have emigrated did so because of their ties with such groups but, apart from a very few cases such as the Aghadowey emigration of 1718, what group emigration there was from the north of Ireland in the eighteenth century was in small units and was organised through shipping agents and out-agents. In Scotland, however, especially in the 'seventies, strong local groups were sometimes formed. These groups or societies usually consisted of farmers with some capital who, before emigrating, collected funds and sent a few of their number to America to

[1] C.O. 217/20, no. M. 66 (1764); S.P. 63/440, no. 276. (1773).
[2] F. Moore, *Considerations on the exorbitant price of provisions*, p. 82n.
[3] The advertised tonnage of each of the following emigrant vessels in 1764 was 300 tons: *John* (B.N.L., Mar. 27), *Newry* (ibid., Aug. 10), *Pitt* (ibid., Aug. 10). The New York port returns stated that the tonnages of the vessels were respectively 80 (C.O. 5/1228, Jan. 27), 70 (C.O. 5/1228, Nov. 16), and 90 (C.O. 5/1228, Nov. 27). See Chapter X and Appendix B. For an examination of the profits of the emigration trade half a century later, see Adams, *Ir. emig. in 19th cent.*, p. 40.
[4] Farnam, *Social legislation in U.S.*, p. 347.

purchase land for the whole body.[1] The shipping agent entered the scene only when representatives of the society were sent to the ports to arrange for the voyage to America. In this group emigration, as distinct from mere associations of individuals, the shipping agents played a less significant part than did the agents at the north Irish ports.

Community emigration with its distinctive organisation did not arise in the north of Ireland for a number of reasons. The local outlook of the highlander, imposed by broad mountains and narrow valleys and by the strong though waning power of the clan system, was conducive to mass action. The proximity of all parts of the north of Ireland to an emigrant port contrasted with the isolation of highland villages to which the idea of emigration was largely new and somewhat forbidding despite local emigration after the 'Forty-five. Well-known paths and time-established methods led the Irish emigrant of the 'seventies to America just as they had led his countrymen for half a century before and as they were to lead succeeding generations until the coming of shipping offices and assisted emigration half a century later.

---

[1] In the *Scots Magazine* of April 1774 (xxxvi. 221) four such societies were noted as being in various stages of formation. The description of one of them may serve as a sample for the others.

'Cardross, near Stirling, April 7. A society, consisting mostly of farmers, is lately established at a village called Arnpyre in this country. They have already subscribed £500 for the purpose of purchasing land in America, to be divided among the subscribers. They have drawn up and printed a system of rules and regulations for their conduct, and are to send two of their number immediately to America, to choose a proper situation for them.'

The growth of these associations alarmed Miller, who wrote:

'Various associations have been formed for purchasing lands in the colonies upon a joint stock, to be afterwards divided amongst the contributors upon their arrival in America. And if this idea of acquiring land property, so natural to man, ... shall seize the minds of such of our people as can carry over money to purchase and clear the lands in America, it may in time effectually depopulate this country as the mines of Peru and Mexico depopulated Spain' (to Suffolk, 25 Apr. 1774; S.P. 54/46, no. 164a). See also Selkirk, *Highland emigration*, p. 143.

CHAPTER VIII

The Activities of Land Promoters

I: INTRODUCTION

THE blandishments of shipping agents were the normal means of encouraging emigration, but the monotony of their stereotyped methods was sometimes relieved by the appearance on the Irish scene of agents of a different stamp. Interested in securing settlers for American lands rather than in the profits of the emigration trade, these occasional visitants were colonising rather than shipping agents. The wares they offered were lands that ranged from the banks of the St Lawrence to the Floridas; the reward they sought was either a grant of land in proportion to the number of settlers secured or the difference between the quit-rent they paid to the crown and the rent the settlers could be induced to pay them. The land promoter had the advantage over the shipping agent of being able to offer emigrants leases of defined lands at a definite rent before they left Ireland; but, on the whole, he competed with the orthodox emigration agent under handicap. In most cases, his main interest was in the potential emigrant with sufficient capital to set up as a farmer and, where this was so, he had to ignore the much greater number of less substantial people whose thoughts were turning to America. Moreover, because of the terms of his grant, he had often to fight an up-hill battle at a time when comparatively few people wished to emigrate and fight it with the additional disadvantage of being able to offer only a very limited choice of land, while the parts of America from Halifax to Savannah were all within the orbit of the shipping agent. The subdued efforts of ever-wakeful merchants and shipmasters carried off many more emigrants than did the land promoters but the concentrated labours of a few of the latter class are much more striking and personal than the seemingly casual activities of men who thought in terms of indentures and cargoes of emigrants.

Contemporary newspapers are the main source of information about the colonising agents. The only occasions on which references to them appeared in official records were in relation to their affairs in America or when the extent of their activities in Ireland had so alarmed landlords and government authorities that censure was needed to halt a threatened large-scale emigration of protestant farmers tempted by the prospect of cheap land held on secure tenure. The efforts of Alexander McNutt and Thomas Desbrisay, two of the most vigorous of the land promoters, were prematurely ended by such intervention and official sources are silent on the activities of all the agents except these two. The silence of non-official contemporary sources is more surprising than the silence of eighteenth-century government departments. The persistence and the energy of the land promoters must have attracted notice in many parts of the north of Ireland, yet the minutes of synods and presbyteries contain no reference to this vociferous group and all but one[1] of the series of letters which have been examined are equally uninformative.

Newspaper advertisements and reports cannot give the full story of the land promoters but they do give the side of the story that is of most interest in a study of north Irish emigration. The nature and results of the activities of the land promoters can be discovered with a fair degree of accuracy from the *Belfast News Letter* which had become the recognised medium between the would-be emigrant and the new world by the middle of the eighteenth century. A reference was made in an advertisement to the distribution of handbills[2] but the day had not yet dawned when handbills appeared 'on every corner, tree, and pump, and public place', contrasting American prosperity with Irish poverty.[3] Through this reliance on newspaper contacts, the land promoters of the second half of the eighteenth century have left a detailed record of their movements and plans and even of their hopes and disappointments.

Efforts to secure settlers from the north of Ireland for lands in America, particularly in New England, had begun before the

[1] Dobbs papers, [P.R.O.N.I., D. 162].
[2] *B.N.L.*, 18 Mar. 1774: *Needham, Newry to Philadelphia.*
[3] Abbott, *Immigration; select documents and case histories,* p. 3.

The Activities of Land Promoters

Belfast News Letter was first published in 1737. Offers of cheap lands in the colonies attracted many people such as McGregor and his friends but a more typical example of land promotion at work was the attempt of the Lincolnshire proprietors of Massachusetts to secure Irish settlers. The proprietors made an agreement with a Robert Edwards, formerly of Castleburg (*sic*)[1] in Ireland, in 1720 to settle two townships. Edwards was to send fifty families to each of these townships, recruiting them with the aid of eight or ten influential people in Ireland. His reward on the successful completion of his task was to be 25,000 acres in each township. Each immigrant family was to receive 300 acres and the proprietors undertook to maintain a minister for two years and to erect block-houses for the protection of the settlement. Edwards's efforts seem to have produced little result.[2]

By 1734, two-thirds of the total interests of the Lincolnshire company had been acquired through gift and purchase by Samuel Waldo, adventurer and land speculator, and son of a leading Boston merchant of Swedish–Pomeranian ancestry.[3] While in Britain contesting the legality of the actions of David Dunbar, the surveyor-general of the woods, Waldo used the opportunity to distribute handbills in Ireland between 1733 and 1736 to attract settlers to his lands. By this time, however, Irish emigration had turned south to Pennsylvania, partly because of the hostile reception given to earlier immigrants by the authorities and people of New England, and so Waldo's efforts met with little success. He soon turned more hopefully to take advantage of the rising tide of emigration from Germany and, after 1746, from Scotland.[4]

With these minor exceptions, Ireland saw few attempts to promote American lands in the first half of the century but, during the following twenty-five years, proprietors and would-be proprietors of land in colonies from Nova Scotia to Florida competed in eulogies and enticements for the favour of the Irish emigrant.

---

[1] Probably Castlederg, county Tyrone.
[2] Akagi, *Town proprietors of New England*, p. 262.
[3] Osgood, *Amer. in 18th cent.*, ii. 510.
[4] Akagi, *Town proprietors of New England*, pp. 263–4. Waldo may have had some interest in the *Dove*, the *Eagle* and the *Britannia* which sailed from Portrush to Boston in 1750 (*B.N.L.*, 23 Feb. and 13 Mar.). These were the only vessels that were advertised to sail from Portrush to Boston between 1750 and 1775 and Waldo was active in Scotland at this time (Akagi, op. cit., p. 264). See also Chapter XI.

The Activities of Land Promoters

Arthur Dobbs was, socially, the most prominent of the organisers of Irish emigration to pre-revolutionary America. A large landowner in county Antrim, he was in turn high sheriff of the county, a member of the Irish parliament and engineer-in-chief and surveyor-general of Ireland. Though a bitter opponent of popular government during his term of office in North Carolina, he held enlightened views on the wisdom of reforming the Irish parliament. His *Essay on the trade and improvement of Ireland* won for him some fame as an economist and epitomised the evils of Irish land-tenure at the time. From 1730 he took an increasing interest in colonial affairs. Though at first he was mainly concerned with attacks on the Hudson Bay Company and with the discovery of the North-West passage, at various times he advocated the settlement of a supposed land off Peru, the pacification of the Indians by christianising them and the expulsion of France from her continental and inland possessions in America, and he anticipated by thirty years the main terms of the Quebec Act. Among the first of the promoters in Ireland of American lands, Dobbs set an example of moderation in his undertakings and of thought for the welfare of those whom he took to America—an example which was not followed by all his successors.[1] In 1745, Dobbs purchased a part interest in 400,000 acres in the present counties of Mecklenburg and Cabarrus in North Carolina from the McCulloch estate and, with McCulloch, was granted 60,000 acres in New Hanover county,[2] but during the next few years he took little interest in his American acquisitions. Rebellion and war occupied men's minds and, in addition, official duties and the fortunes of the 1746–7 attempt to discover the North-West passage concerned Dobbs too deeply to leave him time to do much about his lands in North Carolina. The details of the purchase were completed early in 1747 and, with the disposal of his posts under the crown, Dobbs's eyes turned westward. As he would have 'some leisure', he wrote to Matthew Rowan, the surveyor-general of North Carolina, he intended 'to take a trip to Carolina and take over some families . . . and servants to settle

---

[1] D.A.B., iii. 336–7; D.N.B., xv. 130–2; P.R.O.N.I., Dobbs papers, D. 162/21, 30, 42, 45.
[2] D.A.B., iii. 336; Sutherland, *Pop. distribution in col. Amer.*, p. 227. See Chapter IV (note 7).

them there and see the country'. He knew little about conditions in the province—he did not even know the exact location of his purchases—and so asked for advice as to the type of people he should endeavour to secure and the terms they were to be offered. Being a thorough and painstaking man, he inquired:

> which kind of artificers or servants I should take with me as most wanted there, such as carpenters, smiths, masons, and coopers— and what number would be proper at first or could be accommodated with provisions and necessaries to form a settlement, and what kind of goods, tools, etc., I should take over with them, for I think if I could take a trip and fix several it would induce many more to go from hence and help to increase that colony . . . [Advise me], if I agree with any here who can transport themselves, upon what terms I should agree with each family, the number of acres, term rent or produce, that I may know how to conduct myself in any bargains I shall make.[1]

At about this time, however, Dobbs's attention seems to have been diverted from North Carolina to a projected settlement on the Ohio west of the Appalachians.[2] Moreover, it soon became apparent that there was little urgency in securing settlers from Ireland, for great numbers were moving south from the interior regions of Pennsylvania and Virginia 'and set down on any place they fancy, plant away, they expect some owner will claim and they then intend to purchase'.[3]

Dobbs had certainly not been to Carolina, nor had he dispatched settlers, before February 1750 when a William Faris, who sought Dobbs's influence to secure him the post of collector in the colony, wrote from Wilmington advising Dobbs not to pay his first visit to the colony in that year. Should Dobbs wish to send colonists to his lands, Faris advised him to send only a few at first—and these, if possible, to be frugal Germans and not Irish. These pioneer settlers would be able to provide provisions for a greater number

[1] Draft letter—May 1747 (P.R.O.N.I., D. 162, no. 46).

[2] Copy letter—Smith, London, to J. Hanbury, 24 June 1749 (ibid., D. 162, no. 47a). The writer suggested that an attempt should be made to divert to the new settlement the stream of protestant Irish emigrants who sailed yearly to New England and Pennsylvania. He concluded by stating that he was going to Ireland to consult Dobbs about the scheme. Samuel Smith, a Belfast merchant, was one of the agents for the *Elizabeth*, Dobbs's emigrant ship of 1753 (B.N.L., 29 May 1753).

[3] Copy letter, John Campbell, N.C., to—, n.d. (ibid., D. 162, no. 47b). As this letter is copied on the same sheet of paper as D. 162, no. 47a, it probably belongs to 1749.

in a few years but, if a considerable settlement were attempted at the beginning, the immigrants would be disappointed as the present settlers kept prices very high and took all possible advantage of strangers. It was recommended that the Irish emigrants should take with them coarse blankets and coarse bed-ticks, low priced house furniture such as pots and pans, coarse shoes, brogues with stockings, and hats. If a large settlement were attempted, Faris advised that the immigrants should guard against the resulting rise in the price of provisions in the neighbourhood of the settlement by carrying over plenty of oatmeal from Ireland with them.[1]

The first Irish tenants for Dobbs's lands sailed in April 1751 in a Dublin vessel, probably chartered at Dobbs's expense.[2] With them, Dobbs sent a covering letter to Rowan in which the emigrants were described as 'my tenants and their neighbours and friends'. Dobbs may have advertised for settlers—no copies of the *Belfast News Letter* published in 1751 survive—but it is more probable that, in accordance with Faris's advice, no extensive plans were made to encourage large numbers of settlers and that the emigration was privately arranged between Dobbs and some of his tenants in county Antrim. That the numbers were small is indicated by Dobbs's description of the emigrants by phrases such as 'several . . . . . of my tenants', and 'some families'. Dobbs regarded these settlers as the forerunners of many more from Carrickfergus and asked that they should be befriended and assisted in every way as 'according to their report of the country, you may expect a further trade to be opened from hence and the north of Ireland'.[3]

If Dobbs continued to be guided by Faris's advice, he sent no settlers from Ireland in 1752. In this year, too, the *Belfast News Letter* files unfortunately provide no assistance,[4] but Dobbs seems to have spent much of the year in securing for himself a governorship in North America. By December he was able to announce his impending appointment as governor of North Carolina and the appointment was confirmed in the following January.[5] In a letter

---

[1] 18 Feb. 1749/50 (P.R.O.N.I., D. 162/48).
[2] Draft letter,—, N.C. to S[amuel] S[mith], 19 Sept. 1751 (ibid., D. 162/57).
[3] To Rowan, n.d. (ibid., D. 162/52).
[4] The only available 1752 issues are for December.
[5] Draft letter, Dobbs to Andrew Stone, n.d. (ibid., D. 162/63); draft letter, same to the earl of Halifax, n.d. (ibid., D. 162/65); Dobbs to Conway Dobbs, 16 Dec. 1752 (ibid., D. 162/64); C.O. 5/297, f.102.

full of plans for the future, he showed that he intended to take his duties seriously and to use his high position to put into practice the ideas he had long advanced. 'I must take up house there and begin the world anew,' he wrote. Plans were outlined, ranging from the settlement of French protestants to the conversion of the Indians by Moravian missionaries, and from that to the introduction of camels and silkworms into the province. Significantly, the most restrained part of the letter concerned possible Irish emigration to his lands. 'If I find any choose to go from Ireland with me', he wrote, 'I will engage a ship from Liverpool well appointed to carry them over.'[1] In other words, he would take over with him those who had made up their minds to go but he did not intend to indulge in any land-pushing schemes. Part of the reason was that his own lands were being rapidly settled by migration from the more northerly colonies.[2] His motive may have been deeper than that for he now regarded himself as the governor of a colony and not merely the proprietor of colonial lands. He had already witnessed and deplored the emigration of Irish protestants[3] and, believing in a protestant God who 'in many remarkable instances had defeated all popish schemes',[4] he had no wish to cause a further weakening of the protestant interest in Ireland. Such an explanation would be true to Dobbs's character for, though a man of bitter prejudices, he showed in everything he did that he was a man of high principle.

The 'ship from Liverpool' was the *Elizabeth* which arrived in Belfast lough at the end of June 1753, to 'take over the people and servants who are sent to the captain or are recommended to him by Arthur Dobbs, Esq.'. Advertised for Newbern, the vessel was to carry over the retinue and baggage of the governor and intending passengers were to apply to either of two Belfast merchants, to

[1] To Conway Dobbs, 16 Dec. 1752 (P.R.O.N.I., D. 162/64).
[2] Draft letter,—to S[amuel] S[mith], 19 Sept. 1751 (ibid., D. 162/57).
[3] *An essay on the trade and improvement of Ireland*, pp. 335, 417, 482 in second volume of *A collection of tracts and treatises*.
[4] His religious views were expressed with some force in a message to the assembly of North Carolina in December 1754. The French, he declared, had proselytised the Indians by 'their hellish Jesuitical missionaries . . . ., not to the true christian religion . . . but to the pomps and outward trappings of the popish hierarchy'. His views on the relationship between the Roman catholic church and the spiritual world were defined in his account of the French plan to subjugate the British colonies, the 'rope of sand', a plan that was 'hatched in hell, and supported by the court of Rome' (C.O. 5/297, ff.173-4).

Dobbs himself, or to the captain. As was usual, the climate and the soil of the province were praised and a special appeal was made for tradesmen—house carpenters, joiners, smiths, shoemakers, tailors and millwrights. The *Elizabeth* was a small vessel—130 or 140 tons—and it was stated that not more than half the number of passengers usually carried by such a vessel were expected. The date of departure was not extended beyond July 10, the original date, and the vessel arrived safely in North Carolina after an uneventful passage of five weeks from Cork.[1] A total of two advertisements, the narrowness of the field of appeal and the prompt departure of the emigrant ship would have struck a McNutt or a Desbrisay as a quaint way to organise a mass emigration, but the stimulation of mass emigration was not Dobbs's intention.

It seemed for a time in 1754 that Dobbs was going to run more true to form as an organiser of emigration. On 6 June 1754, two letters regarding North Carolina were printed in the *Belfast News Letter*. One was from Alexander Stewart, Dobbs's chaplain. Fulfilling a promise he had made to friends in Lisburn prior to sailing in the *Elizabeth* in 1753, Stewart gave examples of tradesmen's wages in North Carolina. The comparative opulence of these wages must have impressed many people for even a labourer earned one shilling and sixpence a day, twice what he would earn in the north of Ireland. The other letter shows, however, that Dobbs had not suddenly decided on a policy of encouragement to wholesale emigration. This letter was from Dobbs himself and was addressed to those who intended to settle in North Carolina, advising them to sail in a vessel belonging to John Sampson, a North Carolina merchant. Dobbs did not promise a new heaven and a new earth. The limits of his promises were good land, freedom of conscience and such treatment as 'the character, ingenuity, and industry' of the immigrants should deserve. Dobbs's obvious purpose in the letter was not to incite emigration but to direct into a decent vessel those who wished to follow friends or who had already decided to emigrate to the province. Stewart's letter would not in itself have been sufficient to induce people to emigrate but it may have induced some who had already decided to emigrate to go to North Carolina rather than to another province. Sampson's vessel, the *Vaughan*, was later advertised to to sail on 1 September, but did not arrive at Belfast till the beginning

[1] *B.N.L.*, 4 June 1754.

of October[1] and sailed for North Carolina about the middle of that month. Dobbs's recommendation of the vessel was underlined in the advertisements by the promise that, though the vessel could accommodate 250 people, not more than one hundred would be taken and that each passenger would receive one-third more provisions and water than was usual on the Atlantic voyage.

The *Vaughan* was not the only ship which sailed from the north of Ireland to North Carolina in 1754 for the *Dobbs Galley* was advertised to sail about the middle of September.[2] The vessel's purpose was stated to be to convey Dobbs's tenants to America, but little time was given to the passengers to prepare for the journey as the vessel was to sail from Belfast to Portrush two days after the advertisement appeared and was to lie off Portrush for ten days before proceeding to North Carolina. Despite the association suggested by its name, the *Dobbs Galley* had not the backing of either Dobbs or his usual Irish representatives—his son Conway and Samuel Smith, a Belfast merchant. The *Dobbs Galley* was a new Liverpool vessel and, as few ships from that port were engaged in the Irish emigration trade at this time, it is possible that it belonged to the owners of the *Elizabeth* which had carried over Dobbs's tenants in 1753. It was not unnatural that Dobbs should employ a North Carolina vessel in 1754 or that a Liverpool owner should seek to repeat the success of the *Elizabeth*'s voyage of 1753, taking advantage of the late arrival of the *Vaughan* in Belfast. Therefore, though two vessels were advertised to leave with Dobbs's tenants in 1754 and though facilities were now offered to emigrants from the north of Antrim, these facts do not prove that Dobbs changed his intentions of a very limited emigration or that a large number of people sailed from the north of Ireland for North Carolina in 1754.

The *Dobbs Galley* reappeared in 1755, being advertised to sail in July from Belfast lough to North Carolina. Though Smith was an agent for the vessel, it would seem that the voyage had not the direct blessing of Dobbs as neither he nor his tenants were mentioned. In September, on the other hand, it was advertised above the name of Conway Dobbs that the *Merrimack* had arrived at Carrickfergus, 'having called in to take over some people for governor Dobbs'. This advertisement appeared in only one issue

[1] Ibid., 19 July and 8 Oct. 1754.
[2] Ibid., 10 Sept. 1754.

of the *Belfast News Letter* and the *Merrimack* was advertised to sail three days later. Once again, the owners of the *Dobbs Galley* seem to have stepped in to trade on the name of their vessel.[1]

Dobbs toured his lands in North Carolina in 1755 and his report to the board of trade in August of that year confirms the assertion that he took comparatively few emigrants from the north of Ireland. Of the seventy-five families who had settled on his lands, between thirty and forty were Scotch-Irish families who had moved south from Pennsylvania and twenty-two others were German or Swiss. It follows that a maximum of about eighteen families had arrived in North Carolina from the north of Ireland by the summer of 1755 to become Dobbs's tenants. This number may have been increased when the *Merrimack* arrived later in the year, but the colony received no further settlers direct from the north of Ireland until thirteen years later, chiefly because of the lack of trade between the two places.[2]

In one way, Arthur Dobbs stood alone among those who played any part in promoting north Irish emigration during the eighteenth century. Personally known to most of the settlers who accompanied him, he showed a consideration and a moderation which made him a strange bed-fellow of a man such as Alexander McNutt.

III: ALEXANDER MCNUTT

The Acadians were expelled from Nova Scotia in 1755 and vigorous attempts followed to settle the peninsula with less recalcitrant subjects. Both episodes were intended to utilise the great strategic importance of a region which could serve not only to guard the northern flank of the British possessions in America but to menace those of the French by partially controlling the southern entrance to the St Lawrence and partially nullifying the importance of Louisbourg. The settlement of loyal subjects in the peninsula had progressed very slowly since the treaty of Utrecht. By 1755 the only inhabitants, other than French and Indians, were a summer colony of New England fishermen at Canso, a German settlement at Lunenburg and the military settlements at Annapolis

---

[1] Ibid., 30 May and 26 Sept. 1755.
[2] C.O. 5/297, ff.279–84; Dobbs to B.T., 4 Jan. 1755 (C.O. 5/297, ff.227–30). See also Appendix E. In the *B.N.L.* of 17 Oct. 1755 the *Friends Goodwill* was advertised to sail from Belfast to North Carolina three days later but only one person, a tanner, was asked for.

and Halifax.[1] The prospect of settling on the inferior lands uninhabited by the Acadians was no adequate compensation for the savagery of the Indians and the hostility of ten thousand French, a not insignificant fraction of the total French population of North America. From available evidence it seems certain that no vessel carrying settlers to Nova Scotia left any port in the north of Ireland before the transportation of the Acadians.[2]

With the approach of the last phase of the Anglo-French struggle for dominion in north America, the Acadians were expelled and the board of trade, until now indifferent as to the settling of the peninsula, regarded 'the peopling of the colony and filling it with hardy and industrious settlers' as 'an object of the utmost importance' and Charles Lawrence, the governor, was instructed to secure settlers for the vacated lands as rapidly as possible. More pressing matters occupied Lawrence's attention for the next two years but with the fall of Louisbourg he began his quest for immigrants by issuing a proclamation inviting the settlement of the lands vacated by the Acadians. As this proclamation was in the most general terms, another which detailed the terms on which land would be granted to settlers soon followed. The head of each immigrant family was to receive one hundred acres with fifty acres more for each member of his family. An annual quit-rent of one shilling per fifty acres was to commence after ten years by which time a third of the land granted had to be cleared for cultivation. The remainder of the land was to be cleared or enclosed within a further period of twenty years.[3]

Substantial immigration from the continental colonies followed almost at once. One factor which led to the success of Lawrence's efforts was the cheapness of the Nova Scotia lands. The quit-rent was little different from what it was elsewhere in America but the lands were partly cleared—though they had lain derelict for some

[1] T. C. Haliburton, *A historical and statistical account of Nova Scotia*, pp. 136–8; A. B. Warburton, *A history of Prince Edward Island*, p. 85; N. Macdonald, *Canada, 1763–1841. Immigration and settlement: the administration of the imperial land regulations*, pp. 41–2; Mackintosh, *Settlements and churches in N.S.*, p. 6.

[2] Some north Irish families had emigrated earlier in the century to Maine but, being obliged by the New England council to remove from thence, were in 1730 granted land on the eastern side of the Kennebec in Nova Scotia (P.C. 2/90, pp. 462, 479–80; P.C. 2/91, pp. 376–7).

[3] B. T. to Lawrence, 8 July 1756 (C.O. 391/63); W. O. Raymond, 'Colonel Alexander McNutt and the pre-loyalist settlements of Nova Scotia', in *Proc. and Trans. Roy. Soc. Can.*, 3rd series, v. 34–5; enclosure in memorial, McNutt to B.T., 17 Apr. 1766 (C.O. 217/21, no. N.64); P.C. to B.T., 2 Sept. 1766 (C.O. 217/21, no. N.108).

years—and were in the coastal region, an inducement which none of the other colonies except those in the extreme south could offer. The London authorities saw the strength of the appeal of these attractions in 'such of the neighbouring colonies as abound in inhabitants and whose cleared lands are already taken up'. A second factor which contributed to immigration from the other American colonies was the assistance given to new settlers by the British government through the Nova Scotia authorities, over £5,000 being spent in 1760 for the transportation and provisioning of new settlers.[1] The recruitment of these immigrants was done through continental agents, the chief of whom was Thomas Hancock, a Boston merchant.[2] The leading agent appointed by Hancock to tour the colonies in quest of settlers was Alexander McNutt.

McNutt was a native of Londonderry and had emigrated to America about 1750, settling at Staunton in Virginia.[3] In the French wars he raised three hundred men and as a colonel of militia had been present at the siege of Louisbourg. He was in Nova Scotia at the time of Lawrence's proclamations and after some experience as an agent under Hancock he acted on his own behalf and later claimed that he had persuaded about one thousand families to emigrate in 1760 to Nova Scotia from New Hampshire, Massachusetts, Rhode Island, Connecticut, New York, Pennsylvania and Virginia.[4] This success so inspired McNutt and impressed Lawrence that McNutt sought and was granted reservations totalling 817,000 acres in the province. The terms under which the reservations were made were that six hundred families were to be

B.T. to P.C., 20 Dec. 1759 (C.O. 391/66, f.305); abstract of the state of the civil establishment of N.S., 1760 (C.O. 217/18, no. L.77).
[2] Abstract of the state and expense on account of the new settlements, 10 Dec. 1760 (C.O. 217/18, no. L.19). The amount due to Hancock for his services was £2,400. Thomas Hancock was the uncle of John Hancock whose signature was to be the first on the declaration of independence (*D.A.B.*, xii. 155. The biographical details of McNutt are from the same source).
[3] See *ante*, ch. IV, p. 55.
[4] Memorial, McNutt to B.T., read 19 Jan. 1763 (C.O. 217/19, no. L.144). In 1761, however, McNutt's estimate of the number of people he had brought into the province in 1760 was 600 (B.T. to P.C., 5 Mar. 1761: C.O. 218/6, f.59). On the other hand, a committee of the provincial council reported in 1766 that, though McNutt had produced a list of 600 people who had agreed to settle in the province in 1760, only fifty families had actually settled and they had to be supported out of public funds for two years (Enclosure, Michael Franklin, lieut.- gov. of N.S., to B.T., 2 Sept. 1766: C.O. 217/21, no. N. 108).

settled on the lands within four years, each family receiving five hundred acres. McNutt's reward would have been over half a million acres—the remainder of the reserved lands—had his plans been successful. Free of military duties by November 1760, McNutt informed the Nova Scotia council and Jonathan Belcher, the lieutenant-governor, that, because of the encouragement offered to him by Lawrence, since dead, he was proceeding to the northern part of Ireland, there to direct the rising tide of emigration to the shores of the province.[1]

No one was better qualified than McNutt to undertake such a mission. Irishman, emigrant and emigration agent, he possessed a tireless energy and a dauntless persistence that were not crushed by a succession of blows in the years which followed. His three outstanding characteristics were his optimism, his belief in his own abilities and his persuasiveness. All three shine through his dealings with Lawrence and the London authorities: all three were to shine in Ireland but they were to dazzle the Irish peasant less than they had dazzled the statesmen of Halifax and Whitehall.

Before proceeding to Ireland, McNutt wisely went to London to secure the backing of the board of trade. Lawrence had never been authorised to grant lands on the conditions he had agreed with McNutt and, as the latter's schemes would be costly, he wanted to have them confirmed before he launched them. The plan he submitted in London in February 1761 wisely differed from the one which Lawrence had approved. Instead of asking for a large grant of land and undertaking to plant part of it with an agreed number of settlers, McNutt asked that his reward should be one hundred acres for every five hundred acres granted to the settlers he introduced, the latter receiving land according to the terms of the proclamation of 1759. He also asked that the board of trade should provide a vessel capable of transporting four hundred people from Londonderry as soon as possible. McNutt promised to repay at the end of three years the expenses in which the board would thus be involved, 'leaving to their Lordships at the end of the term to consider the services [he] may have rendered'.[2]

---

[1] Memorial, McNutt to B.T., 17 Apr. 1766 (C.O. 217/20, no. N.64); B.T. to P.C., recvd. 7 Mar. 1761 (P.C. 1/50); Raymond, 'McNutt and . . . N.S.', in *Proc. and Trans. Roy. Soc. Can.*, 3rd series, v. 64 and vi. 213.

[2] Proposals, McNutt to B.T., recvd. 24 Feb. 1761 (C.O. 217/8, ff.143-4, 148-57). Among other proposals he made were (a) an assurance that the sacramental test would not be imposed in Nova Scotia and (b) an alteration in the terms of settlement.

McNutt's foresight in including these two points in his proposal was rewarded with a most cordial endorsement of the plan by the board of trade. The two chief obstacles to the rapid peopling of the colonies in the eighteenth century were the granting of huge tracts of land to individuals who took little trouble to develop them, and the parsimony of a government which was not prepared to advance sufficient and sustained financial support to secure an end it ardently desired.[1] McNutt's plan was attractive because it involved the government in no ultimate expense and because McNutt asked that deeds and not promises should be rewarded. Never again did approval beam down upon McNutt as it did in the first few days of March 1761. His proposals were held up as an example of the ideal in one of the periodic lamentations of the board of trade about the expense of the new settlements, and the whole scheme was recommended for the approval of the privy council in terms of unusual warmth. Unstinted praise was given to McNutt's proposal for his own reward for, 'in cases of this sort, no species of reward can be so fit to be granted as that which, being contrived to depend on the performance of the undertaking, will be more or less considerable in exact proportion to the benefit which the public will derive from it'.[2]

McNutt then proceeded to Ireland. He appointed agents to act for him in what he anticipated would be the most fruitful districts and then publicly launched his campaign in a letter-advertisement written from his native Londonderry. The letter, unlike some written by later land promoters, did not concern itself with trivial details of geography and topography but simply told the people why they should go to Nova Scotia and how they could get there. 'Having received a generous grant of any of the choicest lands [in Nova Scotia] which he shall think fit to settle upon', McNutt stated that he had come to Ireland to procure settlers and to invite his fellow countrymen to 'a grand outlet and relief for all such indus-

---

The suggested amendment was that three acres in every fifty should be cleared within three years of the date of the grant or, if the soil were barren, that three 'neat cattle' or six hogs should be settled on each fifty acres at the end of that time.

[1] See Belcher to B.T., 11 Jan. 1762 (C.O. 217/18, no. L. 68). A notable exception was the expenditure of over £415,000 in grants to the Halifax settlement between 1749 and 1755 (Haliburton, *Account of N.S.*, p. 142n.).

[2] B.T. to Belcher, 3 Mar. 1761 (C.O. 218/6, ff.23–58; C.O. 341/68, f.157); same to P.C., 5 Mar. 1761 (C.O. 218/6, ff.59–64). This approval did not, however, make McNutt a mere 'agent of the British government' (Green, *Scotch-Irish in Am.*, p. 14).

trious farmers and useful mechanics as may find themselves in difficulties in the mother country'. The head of each family would receive two hundred acres and also fifty acres for each member of his family, the only rent being a quit-rent of one shilling per fifty acres, free of all tithes. The advertisement referred readers who wished to know more about Nova Scotia to a 'printed account' which had been distributed by McNutt. McNutt's hopes lay in the north-west of Ulster for the agents he had engaged to work on his behalf lay in a broad semicircle round Londonderry.[1] As yet, no indication was given of when or, indeed, from which port, the emigrants would sail. McNutt had informed Belcher in the previous November that he had already sent a vessel for that purpose to Londonderry[2] but, as his plans had been accepted in their entirety by the board of trade, he had every reason to expect that a vessel would be sent to Londonderry to transport his settlers to Nova Scotia at no immediate expense to himself. He was soon to learn that the adage 'out of sight, out of mind' was all too true of the board of trade.

McNutt had every reason to be optimistic about the outcome of his venture. The advertisement presented to people a picture of an ideally honest broker whose profits from the undertaking were not to be borne by his followers as the Nova Scotia land was to be held directly from the crown, the most favourable of all land tenancies. The proposed rent of approximately one farthing per acre was a small fraction of contemporary rents in Ireland—a small fraction, indeed, of the rents at which American lands had already been offered in Ireland.[3] The advertisement committed the sin of omission in two respects. No reference was made of the fact that

[1] *B.N.L.*, 21 Apr. 1761. The quit-rent named was as McNutt had agreed with the B.T. (Instructions to gov. of N.S., 20 May 1763: C.O. 324/40, f.360), but, according to the second proclamation of Lawrence, the head of each family was to receive only one hundred acres (Report, P.C. to B.T., 2 Sept. 1766: C.O. 217/21, no. N.108). Eleven of the twelve agents appointed—in Londonderry, Castledoe, Rathmelton, Letterkenny, Fahan, Raphoe, Convoy, Strabane, Omagh, and Maghera—lay in the emigration hinterland of the port of Londonderry: the other was in Castleblaney in co. Monaghan, far outside that hinterland. The appointment of the Castleblaney agent may have been caused by the desire to take advantage of a rising emigration fever in nearby Ballybay from which place 300 people emigrated in 1763 (see below, Section (vi)).

[2] Raymond, 'McNutt and . . . N.S.', in *Proc. and Trans. Roy. Soc. Can.*, 3rd series, v. 64.

[3] Sir Wm. Johnston's lands in the Mohawk valley had been advertised at 50s. per hundred acres under lease or £5 per hundred acres held in fee simple (*B.N.L.*, 12 Nov. 1754).

the lands were mostly in a state of nature and so the obvious comparison with Irish rents was a misleading one. Moreover, much of the 'choicest lands' were already settled or granted and so were excluded from the reservations made to McNutt. Considered as a whole, however, the advertisement was a truthful and modest display of the wares on offer.

As became usual in such cases, the advertisement reappeared three weeks later, urging haste and recommending that, if a family could not go immediately, then it should send one of its number to take possession forthwith and prepare for the ultimate arrival of the remainder of the family.[1] The integrity of such advice may be questioned as lands were to be granted *per capita* on arrival and a mere promise of future settlement would not have obtained land for a family before its arrival in the province.[2] Equally misleading was the promise that servants would receive a grant of fifty acres each on completion of their period of servitude. McNutt's agreement with the board of trade specified a grant of fifty acres to any immigrant for each servant he brought to Nova Scotia but no provision was made for a subsequent grant to the servant.[3] Such a grant would depend on the success of the freed servant's application for land at the end of his term of servitude and not on any promise made by McNutt. These two deviations from the spirit of strict honesty suggest that the response to the earlier advertisement had not been as great as had been hoped, partly because of the inability of families to settle their affairs at a few weeks' notice. As yet, the volume of response was not great enough to fix a date for the voyage and the width of appeal was extended to include counties Down and Antrim. People living in those areas were invited to get in touch with Thomas Greg, the Belfast merchant, and were informed that, if the response should justify it, a vessel would be engaged to take the passengers on board at the most convenient port.

The response from Down and Antrim did not induce McNutt

---

[1] *B.N.L.*, 12 May 1761.
[2] Reservations could, of course, be made as was done in the case of a Robert Smith who petitioned the N.S. assembly on behalf of himself and twenty-three other people who were resident in Ireland (Copy, minutes of assembly of N.S., 27 Feb. 1762: C.O. 217/19, no. L.140). The N.S. council complained in 1766 that McNutt had 'obstinately insisted from time to time upon terms of settlement that the government were . . . forbid [*sic*] to grant' (C.O. 217/21, no. H.106).
[3] Proposals, McNutt to B.T., recvd. 24 Feb. 1761 (C.O. 217/18, no. L.26).

to charter a special vessel for that area. Those who did intend to go from the Belfast area were instructed to meet McNutt there on 6 June and to embark with the Londonderry emigrants on the *Jupiter* at Londonderry on 1 July. Intending tenants from the Londonderry vicinity were instructed by the same advertisement to meet McNutt and 'give earnest at the appointed sundry times and places'. The *Jupiter*, advertised as of 250 tons, was neither the vessel that McNutt had claimed seven months earlier to have engaged nor was it the vessel the board of trade had agreed to provide. Belonging to two Londonderry merchants, Arthur Vance and William Caldwell, the vessel was chartered by McNutt at the rate of £3. 5s. per day.[1]

A week before the intended departure it was advertised that the voyage was postponed till 9 July at the request of passengers who wished to have more time to prepare for the journey.[2] Such a brief delay was unusual and suggests that a satisfactory number of passengers had been engaged for the voyage. This seems to be borne out by the fact that the *Jupiter* sailed on or very soon after the revised date of departure. Indeed, when McNutt gave notice of the brief postponement of the *Jupiter*, he announced that a second vessel would sail with his tenants and servants to Nova Scotia from Londonderry. A special appeal for servants was made in the advertisement. These, he stated, would receive two hundred acres of land instead of the fifty acres already promised and would be given ample time to pay for their passage 'as he comes not to Ireland to buy and sell his countrymen'. Presumably the difference between the promised grant and the official grant was to be made good by McNutt out of his own lands.

The second vessel was named a month later. The *Hopewell*, advertised as of 250 tons, was, like the *Jupiter*, chartered from Vance and Caldwell at the rate of £3. 2s. 6d. per day.[3] The *Hope-well* was a regular sailer from Londonderry to Philadelphia and was probably unloading in port at this time in the course of its

---

[1] B.N.L., 2 June 1761; enclosure in memorial, McNutt to B.T., 17 Apr. 1763 (C.O. 217/21, no. N.64). Vance and Caldwell made a general agreement with McNutt in April 1761 to supply the necessary vessels (Memorial, Vance and Caldwell to Belcher, 28 Aug. 1761: C.O. 217/18, no. L.63).
[2] B.N.L., 26 June 1761.
[3] B.N.L., 28 July 1761; enclosure in memorial, McNutt to B.T., 17 Apr. 1763 (C.O. 217/21, no. N.64).

normal trade.[1] Except for his abortive Belfast plan, McNutt had never indicated that he had contemplated employing two vessels and so, presumably, his success in the north-west must have been greater than he had expected and induced him to organise hurriedly the sailing of the *Hopewell*. The vessel sailed about the middle of August with McNutt and his remaining tenants on board. McNutt informed the public in his message of farewell that another vessel would sail from Londonderry to Nova Scotia at the end of the month provided a sufficient number of passengers applied to Vance and Caldwell.[2] Despite his success in sending two vessels with settlers to Nova Scotia, his hope that a third vessel would sail was not fulfilled for even the *Hopewell* had to sail with seventy fewer passengers than McNutt had expected.[3]

The last of the north Irish emigrants to Nova Scotia in 1761 arrived in October. Estimates of their total number vary between 'upward of two hundred people' to 'near four hundred'.[4] The former is more likely to be accurate being the figure given by a witness who was unprejudiced at the time he reported the arrival of the settlers. This witness, Jonathan Belcher, was well pleased with the new arrivals and reported to the board of trade that, 'Though not of substance, [they] have recommendations for industry and sobriety . . . They have shewn their industrious dispositions by engaging in common labour upon far more moderate and exemplary terms than the poorer sort from New England . . .' The immigrants appointed a committee to report on the lands reserved for them at Cobequid and Chubenacadie, on the basin of Minas. Though the committee reported favourably and the immigrants expressed 'their great satisfaction in the conduct of Mr McNutt', the lateness of their arrival made it impossible for them to settle on their lands till the following

---

[1] The *Hopewell* sailed with emigrants from Londonderry to Philadelphia in 1760, 1762, 1763, and 1764 (B.N.L., 18 Apr. 1760, 20 June 1762, 25 June 1763, 20 Apr. 1764).

[2] B.N.L., 14 Aug. 1761.

[3] Enclosure in memorial, McNutt to B.T., 17 Apr. 1763 (C.O. 217/21, no. N.64). This enclosure—McNutt's account with Vance and Caldwell—also shows that McNutt did not charter a third vessel in 1761.

[4] Franklin to B.T., 2 Sept. 1766 (C.O. 217/21, no. N.106); Belcher to same., 3 Nov. 1761 (C.O. 217/18, no. L.62); McNutt to same., 23 Mar. 1763 (C.O. 217/20, no. M.5). A year previously McNutt had stated the number to be three hundred (to B.T., 11 Mar. 1762: C.O. 217/18, no. L.87; C.O. 218/6, ff.153–60; C.O. 391/69, ff.81–3), as had Vance and Caldwell in their memorial to Belcher (C.O. 217/18, no. L.63).

spring. As they were 'indigent people, without means of subsistence', most of them had to remain in Halifax during the winter, depending on the charity of the citizens and on provisions supplied by the provincial government and by McNutt who had, in turn, borrowed them from the government. A vessel was chartered in the spring of 1762 by the Nova Scotia council and the principal citizens of Halifax to carry the immigrants who had arrived in the *Jupiter* and *Hopewell* to the Cobequid district and supplies of provisions, seed corn, tools and building materials were granted to them.[1]

From this unexpected burden on public funds developed the opposition of Belcher and the majority of the council of Nova Scotia, an opposition which reached its climax when McNutt arrived in November 1762, with another shipload of indigent Irish immigrants. For a time, though, McNutt's liberal assurances of repayment of all official help given to the immigrants and the acquisition of such a number of citizens made Belcher temporarily unmindful of the board of trade's economy injunctions and he reported enthusiastically to the board that McNutt had 'contracted for 10,000 tons of shipping, 5,000 bushels of wheat, 5,000 bushels of potatoes, 3,000 bushels of flax-seed, 300 bushels of hemp-seed, with other seeds in proportion for the use of the Irish settlers in Nova Scotia in the ensuing spring'. Such promises indicated neither poverty nor parsimony, and the prospect of securing the large number of settlers that these preparations indicated was not the least of Belcher's reasons for declaring that 'the zeal and resolution of Mr McNutt cannot be sufficiently recommended'.[2] But when Belcher realised that McNutt was a man whose zeal and resolution were more impressive in prospect than were their results in practice, his opinion changed and he was to give McNutt's settlers of 1762 a very different reception from that which had greeted their predecessors.

The autumn storm was still afar off when, in the spring of 1762, McNutt was called to the board of trade where Belcher's enthusiastic reports of his plans for the year in Ireland had been received.[3]

[1] C.O. 217/18, no. L.62 (3 Nov. 1761); B.N.L., 11 Mar. 1762; B.T. to P.C., 8 Apr. 1762 (C.O. 218/6, ff.153–60); Franklin to B.T., 2 Sept. 1766 (C.O. 217/21, no. N.106).
[2] Belcher to B.T., 3 Nov. 1761 (C.O. 217/18, no. L.62); *Boston Gazette*, 26 Oct. 1761 (A. W. H. Eaton, 'The settling of Colchester county, Nova Scotia, by New England puritans and Ulster Scotsmen', in *Proc. and Trans. Roy. Soc. Can.*, 3rd series, vi. 255).
[3] C.O. 391/69, f.77 (10 Mar. 1762).

This summons did not act as a warning to McNutt that, possibly, all was not well. Instead of minimising his schemes—he was not a man to let his efforts go unheralded and unsung—he confirmed what Belcher had written. He informed the board that he had entered into contracts with Londonderry merchants, involving over £26,000, to charter ten thousand tons of shipping to transport seven or eight thousand people to Nova Scotia from the north of Ireland during the approaching summer. He stressed his ability to carry out this heavy task and asked the board not to think of him as one of 'the schemers who may have without foundation or abilities undertaken such a work'. He was so confident of the board's approval of the plan—which he described as 'so laudable and which has been so much the object of your lordships'—that he did not think it necessary to ask for a renewal of official approval or for a reaffirmation of the decision of 1761 with regard to land grants. His memorial consisted of a long series of requests for concessions and privileges which he obviously felt the grateful authorities would be only too willing to grant.[1] Unfortunately for McNutt, the prospect of any increase in emigration from the protestant parts of Ireland so alarmed the government that instructions were given that no further grants of land in Nova Scotia were to be made to immigrants from Ireland.[2]

McNutt had some grounds for grievance over this *volte face*. The board of trade stated that McNutt's plans would not have been approved in 1761 but for their limited nature and McNutt's request for a vessel to transport four hundred people in 1761 may have served to support this view. On the other hand, his declared intention of directing Irish emigration to Nova Scotia should have indicated an operation of less limited scope and he had specifically stated to the board of trade that he planned to complete the settlement of his reservations with Irish immigrants. As the

---

[1] Memorials, McNutt to B.T., 16 Mar. and 8 Apr. 1762 (C.O. 217/18, no. L.83; C.O. 218/6, ff.153–60). The main purpose of the privileges McNutt sought was to reduce his expenses. For example, he asked that he should be given the contract for road-making in Nova Scotia so that his settlers could earn their own living while waiting to be taken to their lands, and asked, also, for the contract for transporting the French from the province in order that the vessels that brought his Irish settlers would not have to go further afield in search of return cargoes.

[2] B.T. to P.C., 8 Apr. 1762 (C.O. 218/6, ff.153–60; C.O. 391/69, f.47; P.C. 1/50); P.C. to B.T., 29 Apr. 1762 (C.O. 217/18, no. L.87); B.T. to Henry Ellis, governor of N.S., 27 Apr. 1763 (C.O. 218/6, f.202). For a fuller account of the official attitude to McNutt in 1762 see Chapter IX.

average amount which each family would get under the terms of the proclamation of 1759 was about 300 acres, about two thousand families would have been required to people McNutt's grant. He had stated that six hundred settlers had been brought to his lands in 1760 so that the deficiency—which he had said he hoped to make good in Ireland—was about nine thousand souls. McNutt's hope of transporting between seven and eight thousand people from Ireland to Nova Scotia in 1762 had, therefore, been indicated indirectly a year before and had been approved.[1]

McNutt had not waited for official blessing before opening his 1762 campaign for settlers in Ireland. Official wheels turned slowly and those of the emigration trade did likewise so McNutt determined that these unavoidable handicaps would be partially offset if both sets of wheels were put in motion at the same time. His first advertisement of the new emigration season was printed in the *Belfast News Letter* on the day he appeared before the board of trade.[2] The method he adopted to launch the drive for emigrants was to become a common feature of the emigrant trade in later years. A laudatory letter from the emigrants of the previous year was printed instead of an advertisement inviting people to settle on his lands. This letter, signed by the committee appointed by the emigrants to view the allotted lands, painted a glowing picture of Nova Scotia where, it was stated, the lands inspected fully lived up to the description McNutt had circulated. Fully half the letter stressed specifically the features in which Nova Scotia was said to excel Pennsylvania: the soil was more fertile and the lands available were adjacent to markets, whereas all land available for settlement in Pennsylvania was more than two hundred miles inland. Philadelphia had a virtual monopoly of the Londonderry emigrant trade at the time,[3] so this detailed insistence on the superiority of Nova Scotia seems an obvious attempt to end the prejudice in favour of that port, a prejudice which McNutt realised threatened the success of his plans. It was to the benefit of McNutt rather than of the

---

[1] B.T. to P.C., 5 Mar. 1761 (C.O. 218/6, ff.59–64; P.C. 1/50); P.C. to B.T., 29 Apr. 1762 (C.O. 217/18, no. L.87). The average emigrant family probably consisted of five or six persons. McNutt's reservations totalled over 800,000 acres, but only five-sixths of this land had to be settled to fulfil the terms agreed on by the board of trade, the remainder being McNutt's reward. If each family got 300 acres, the settlement of 1,900 families would have been necessary to qualify McNutt for the maximum grant.
[2] 11 Mar. 1762.
[3] Appendix E.

settlers—their friends would tend to follow them to Nova Scotia—that future emigrants should be turned from Pennsylvania and so it is clear that, if McNutt's hand did not write the letter, his head and influence certainly inspired its contents. This prelude to McNutt's activities in 1762 had been foreshadowed eight months before by Vance and Caldwell, who had written that thousands of people would emigrate to Nova Scotia provided favourable reports were sent back to Ireland by the emigrants of 1761.[1] McNutt's prompt and skilful opening of the 1762 emigration season promised a drive for settlers on a scale that Ireland had never before witnessed.

The campaign soon fizzled out. Aware of the government's disapproval of his plans, McNutt arrived in Londonderry on 5 June and published a rather peremptory notice lacking his usual finesse. Readers were informed that, 'as his stay will be short, any persons who incline to proceed with him to Nova Scotia must be speedy in their application, as the season is far advanced'. Vessels would take emigrants on board at the most convenient ports.[2] McNutt must have been busy recruiting emigrants in the next few months but his activities lacked the fire and drive that had characterised them in 1761. Through his next advertisement—and it was the last he ever published under his own name in Ireland—shine the disappointment and failure of a discouraged man. Intending emigrants were to be in Londonderry on August 20, only three days after the publication of the advertisement.[3] Two hundred emigrants[4] sailed in two vessels, the *Nancy* and the *Hopewell*, both chartered from Vance and Caldwell.[5] The emigrants arrived in November and were ungraciously received by Belcher who was informed by McNutt that they would proceed to Philadelphia unless a sum of money was advanced for their provisions. Belcher acceded to this demand, feeling that it was in the best interests of the province to do so, but bitterly complained to London of 'the impracticability of [McNutt's] schemes for accomplishing any

[1] Memorial to Belcher, 28 Aug. 1761 (C.O. 217/18, no. L.63).
[2] *B.N.L.*, 29 June 1762 (dated at Londonderry, June 5).
[3] *B.N.L.*, 17 Aug. 1762.
[4] Various members of the N.S. council to Ellis, 13 Nov. 1762 (C.O. 217/20, no. M.12). The minutes of the N.S. council state that the number was 170 (5 Nov. 1762, in B. Murdock, *A history of Nova Scotia, or Acadie*, ii. 423). According to Franklin, only 150 immigrants arrived from Ireland in 1762 (to B.T., 2 Sept. 1766; C.O. 217/21, no. N.106).
[5] Enclosure in memorial, McNutt to B.T., 17 Apr. 1766 (C.O. 217/21, no. N.64). Only one vessel, unnamed, was mentioned in the *B.N.L.* advertisement of Aug. 17.

settlements in the province'. He wrote at the same time that he had delivered to McNutt an ultimatum that must have sounded strange to a body which had already issued instructions for an order to be prepared forbidding the grant of Nova Scotian land to Irish immigrants. 'McNutt having involved the government in his two transportations hither in the expense of near £500, I thought it high time to give him notice that unless his plan could be better supported in point of expence it could not possibly be carried further without peremptory orders from the King's minister and a public fund alloted for that purpose.' The settlers were carried to New Dublin township in Lunenburg county and provisions were voted by the council for one hundred of them for four months, the remainder being able to provide for themselves.[1]

McNutt never again publicly sponsored emigration schemes in Ireland[2] but his restless shadow fell across the Londonderry area in 1763 and 1765. He chartered the *Hopewell* to sail to Nova Scotia in 1763 but no attempt was made to recruit passengers through the *Belfast News Letter*. If the vessel actually sailed with emigrants, her passenger list was probably both short and confined to the friends and relations of the emigrants of the previous years.[3] Fifty persons 'chiefly belonging to families before introduced and settled by Colonel McNutt' sailed in the *Admiral Hawke* in 1765 in response to an advertisement for settlers inserted on behalf of McNutt by Caldwell, Vance and Caldwell, the successors of Vance and Caldwell.[4] McNutt, together with various associates including Arthur Vance, had once more succeeded in securing large reservations in Nova Scotia. One and three quarter million acres were reserved on condition that 8,625 settlers should be planted on

---

[1] Belcher to B.T., 24 Jan. 1763 (C.O. 391/70, f.11); Franklin to B.T., 2 Sept. 1766 (C.O. 217/21, no. 106).

[2] McNutt's main energies after 1762 were devoted to stimulating emigration from the other American colonies to Nova Scotia and to encouraging the immigration of French protestants into South Carolina (C.O. 217/20, no. M.52; C.O. 217/21, no. N.64; C.O. 5/377, 3 Aug. 1763; Raymond, 'McNutt and ... N.S.', in *Proc. and Trans. Roy. Soc. Can.*, 3rd series, v. 80–3).

[3] McNutt was debited by Vance and Caldwell with £218. 15s., for the demurrage of the *Hopewell* for two months and ten days (Enclosure in memorial, McNutt to B.T., 17 Apr. 1766; C.O. 217/21, no. N.64). The *Hopewell* advertisement of 1766 referred to emigration to Novia Scotia in 1761, 1762 and 1765, making no mention of 1763 (*B.N.L.*, Mar. 25).

[4] Franklin to B.T., 2 Sept. 1766 (C.O. 217/21, no. 106); Enclosure in memorial, McNutt to B.T., 17 Apr. 1766 (C.O. 217/21, no. N.64).

the lands by 1769.[1] Caldwell, Vance and Caldwell advertised the *Hopewell* to sail in 1766, referring to 'the blessings of freedom, peace and plenty' enjoyed by earlier emigrants from the north of Ireland to Nova Scotia. The response was sufficient to induce the dispatch of a second vessel, the *Falls*, advertised as of 250 tons, in the same year. Both vessels sailed from Londonderry.[2]

The reopening of the link between Londonderry and Nova Scotia promised by these renewed activities did not materialise. The London authorities intervened once more and instructed the governor of Nova Scotia that no land grants were to be made to Irish immigrants. Unlike the similar instruction of 1763, this instruction was enforced after some delay during which the *Hopewell* sailed from Londonderry to Nova Scotia in 1767.[3]

The effect of McNutt's 'indefatigable labour day and night through the different parts of the country' in 1761 and 1762 was to persuade between four hundred and five hundred people to emigrate from Ireland to Nova Scotia.[4] Two things indicate the districts from which these followers had come—the places of residence of the agents employed in the movement and the places of origin of the members of the committee appointed by the settlers of 1761 to view the lands in Nova Scotia. Ten of the thirteen agents resided in north-eastern Donegal, in the Foyle valley, or in north-western Tyrone: the other three lived at Belfast, Maghera (in the south-east of county Londonderry) and Castleblaney (in county Monaghan). The places of origin of the members of the land-viewing committee coincide fairly closely with the districts served by the agents. Though the long voyage across the Atlantic would tend to break down the exclusiveness of district prejudices, the comparatively large committee of sixteen members no doubt included representa-

---

[1] Abstract, McNutt's application for lands, 1 May 1765 (C.O. 217/43); return of state of the late grants of townships, n.d. (C.O. 217/44, ff.27-8); Memorial, McNutt to B.T., recvd. 18 June 1766 (C.O. 217/21, no. N.92); heads of proposals, McNutt to B.T., read 29 Apr. 1766 (C.O. 217/21, no. N.72).

[2] *B.N.L.*, 3 June 1766. The *Falls* was a vessel of one hundred tons according to the Halifax and Charleston port returns (C.O. 217/4, pp. 368-9; C.O. 5/511, 10 Mar. 1766).

[3] P.C. 2/111, p. 650 (5 June 1766); *B.N.L.*, 30 June 1767. See also Chapter IX.

[4] Memorial, Vance and Caldwell to Belcher, 28 Aug. 1761 (C.O. 217/18, no. L.63). It was stated that Nova Scotia's population of 13,374 on 1 Jan. 1767 included 2,165 Irish (Franklin to B.T., 16 Dec. 1767: C.O. 217/45, f.20), but the great majority of the 'Irish' must have been Scotch-Irish who had come in great numbers from Pennsylvania and New England (Raymond, 'McNutt and . . . N.S.' in *Proc. and Trans. Roy. Soc. Can.*, 3rd series, v. 26-114 *passim*, and vi. 201-15 *passim*; Eaton, 'Settling of Colchester county', in ibid., vi. 221-65 *passim*).

tives of all substantial parties among the emigrants. Thirteen of the members had emigrated from north-eastern Donegal and the vicinity of the town of Londonderry, the remaining three from the region of the lower Bann.[1] The indications are, therefore, that a negligible number emigrated from the Belfast and Monaghan regions. Considering both the agents appointed by McNutt and the committee elected by the emigrants, it would seem that at least four-fifths of McNutt's settlers were from the Foyle and Swilly districts and that most of the remainder were from the valley of the lower Bann.

One of the most striking features of McNutt's activities is not that he induced as many as five hundred people to emigrate to Nova Scotia but that the number was not greater. The years 1761 and 1762 were restless ones in counties Londonderry and Tyrone[2] and this should have swollen the number of aspiring emigrants. The spirit of emigration had certainly not died in the district, for a total of thirteen emigrant vessels left Londonderry for the American colonies in 1761 and 1762.[3] Yet only four of these ships were chartered for McNutt's tenants despite the very favourable terms offered by him—better than those of any other promoter of lands in colonial America. Part of the explanation may have been that a large proportion of McNutt's emigrants were representatives who went out to prepare the way for the settlement of complete households in later years. This was the explanation McNutt advanced, rather apologetically, to the board of trade; but the board was probably nearer the truth when, a year earlier, it had informed the privy council with regard to McNutt that, 'It is our duty to observe that the eager disposition which appears to the inhabitants of the north of Ireland to emigrate into the American colonies has not been particularly excited by the prosecution of this plan'.[4]

When McNutt applied for compensation for the losses in which

---

[1] *B.N.L.*, 21 Apr. and 2 June 1761. The places of origin of the members of the viewing committee were—
Fahan, Rathmullan, Mavagh (2), Rosses, Rathmelton, Clandahorky, Tollaghbegley, Letterkenny and Lake, all in county Donegal; Faughanvale, Tullyachnish, Drummacose, Tamlaughtfinleggan and Ballyrashane in co. Londonderry; Derrykeighan in county Antrim (*B.N.L.*, 11 Mar. 1762).
[2] *Charlemont MSS*, i. 21–2, 137. The disturbances were widespread over the north of Ireland. See minutes of presbytery of Bangor, 9 Aug. 1763.
[3] See Appendix A.
[4] McNutt to B.T., read 23 Mar. 1763 (C.O. 217/20, no. M.5); C.O. 218/6, ff. 153–60 (8 Apr. 1762).

his Irish schemes had involved him, he attributed his failure partly to the unfavourable decision of the authorities in 1762 at the time when he was preparing for the harvesting of the main emigrant crop. It would have been unwise to develop such a theme and so he alleged that the ultimate cause of his failure to establish a great Irish settlement in Nova Scotia lay with the machinations of 'a number of sycophants', to wit, Belcher and the Nova Scotia Council.[1] In reality, he defeated his own scheme by his failure to anticipate the attitude of the English authorities and his failure to understand the real nature of Irish emigration of the time. McNutt was a man in a hurry, a man who seemed to expect to hear the first notes of the last trumpet sound at any moment and was determined to accomplish his work before that dread event. To secure eight thousand emigrants in Ireland was no impracticable dream, but to organise and dispatch that number during the summer months of one year to a little known peninsula was an impossible task. Not only was it impossible, but to dream of it was disastrous because it aroused the opposition rather than the admiration of the authorities. Emigration from the north of Ireland was an unpleasant reality which the government felt it could do little about: a move to incite and expand that spirit of emigration was another matter and one which the authorities had no intention of abetting. The settlement of Nova Scotia was a cause worthy of support but not if it was to be accomplished by draining away the mainstay of the protestant interest in Ireland. The thought of ten thousand tons of emigrant shipping plying between Ireland and Halifax was one of McNutt's choicest dreams; to the government, such a thought was a nightmare.

McNutt's failure is not fully accounted for by official displeasure; even with the approval of Whitehall, his plans could not have succeeded. According to his own statement, the purpose of all his Irish activities was to divert emigration from the continental colonies to Nova Scotia[2] and he failed to accomplish even this. Thirteen emigrant vessels were advertised to sail from Londonderry in 1761 and 1762, four being chartered by McNutt and nine being bound for Philadelphia. As was pointed out many times in the century, emigration had become a habit: people emigrated

[1] McNutt to B.T., read 19 Jan. 1763 (C.O. 217/19, no. L.144); same to same, read 12 Apr. 1763 (C.O. 217/20, no. M.12).
[2] Memorial, McNutt to B.T., read 23 Mar. 1763 (C.O. 217/20, no. M.5).

because their acquaintances had done so to escape the same difficulties and they usually emigrated to the same places as those who had gone before. Philadelphia was the American port best known to Londonderry emigrants and so to Philadelphia the bulk of them went, despite the inducements held out by McNutt. Economic necessity as well as a conservative nature made them turn a deaf ear to McNutt's temptations. Farms of two hundred acres and more must have sounded like heaven itself in an area where farms consisted of a few small fields and where over-population and rack-renting had raised the rent of a single acre to what the rent of about seven hundred acres would be in Nova Scotia. Unfortunately, to most people it was an unattainable Utopia that McNutt described. Few of the emigrants could have paid the passage money for themselves and their families and purchased winter provisions and stock and seed for their new lands. True, assistance was given to the emigrants when they reached Nova Scotia, but the prospect of such assistance had been unknown in Ireland when the voyage commenced. Servants and redemptioners were encouraged by McNutt and it is obvious from the letters of Belcher and Franklin that many of those he carried over to Nova Scotia had not the means to set themselves up as farmers. Doubtless, some of these were indentured to better-class emigrants, but there was little in McNutt's offer to attract an industrious poor person to Halifax. The servant's prospects must have seemed much brighter in Pennsylvania, the stronghold of the white servant system, than in a young, poor and thinly-populated province, despite the promise of cheap land at the end of the period of servitude. The indentured servant had become a seemingly indispensable part of the Pennsylvanian labour system and so the emigrant with little capital went to Philadelphia where there was a certain market for his labour and where he would be among many of his own countrymen. When South Carolina offered not only a free passage to immigrants but seeds and the implements of labour, the preference for the middle colonies was shaken for a time, but McNutt could offer none of these things and so his proposals were uninviting to the class that formed a large proportion of the Irish emigrants.

Colonel Alexander McNutt was an energetic and ambitious man. His energies accomplished much but his accomplishments have been dwarfed in history by the magnitude of his ambitions.

When his restless nature responded to the call of revolution even the fruits of his energies were blasted and all that remained were the disappointed dreams of a bitter man.[1]

IV: THOMAS DESBRISAY

The difference of opinion among emigration agents as to the exact location in America of the new Eldorado must have been very confusing to their prospective clients. Philadelphia was usually named as the golden gate, though a bounty was at times sufficient to move the gate six hundred miles to the south. The mere fact that St John's Island (Prince Edward Island), Thomas Desbrisay's Utopia of the early 1770s, was really an outpost of that of Alexander McNutt must have sufficed in itself to provide reminiscences of McNutt's activities a decade before. The prophets as well as the Utopias were alike in some ways. The zeal and persistence of these two men were unsurpassed by any of their contemporaries in the same field of activity.

History records little of the life of Thomas Desbrisay but sufficient to indicate that he belonged to that not uncommon class of the eighteenth century, the soldier-cum-land-promoter. The board of trade referred to him as a captain of artillery though Desbrisay was careful to point out in Ireland that his regiment was the Royal Irish Regiment of Artillery.[2] He was not one of the original grantees among whom St John's Island had been divided in 1767 but purchased tracts near Charlottetown. Desbrisay was appointed lieutenant-governor of the island in 1769 and, though the post carried no salary, his services were repaid by the apparent authority which his office gave his search for settlers for his newly purchased lands. His services were, indeed, more than repaid, for he had not appeared in the island by 1775.[3]

---

[1] For accounts of McNutt's activities after 1762 and of the history of the north Irish settlers in Nova Scotia, see Eaton, 'The settling of Colchester . . .' in *Proc. and Trans. Roy. Soc. Can.*, 3rd series, vi. 234ff; Raymond, 'McNutt and . . . N.S.', in ibid., v. 80–91 and vi. 201–15; *Laing MSS*, ii. 406. McNutt is referred to in this collection as 'McWatt'.

[2] C.O. 391/77, f.2 (3 Jan. 1770); B.N.L., 2 Mar. 1770. Desbrisay stated that he had been an officer in the army since 1746 and a captain of artillery since 1762 (Petition to B.T., 1773; C.O. 226/1, f.159).

[3] C.O. 391/74, ff.256–62 (23 July 1767); A. B. Warburton, *A history of Prince Edward Island, 1534–1831*, p. 179. In an account of the state of the quit-rents in 1775 Desbrisay was named as the proprietor of three—numbers 14, 31, 33—of the island's 67 lots, each of which contained about 20,000 acres (C.O. 226/1, ff.190–1).

Circumstances lessened the attractions of what Desbrisay had to offer. McNutt was able to offer lands held directly from the crown but the all too familiar landlord and tenant relationship existed in St John, thanks to the granting away of the entire island on a single day in 1767.[1] The prejudice against settling on lands unless held in free soccage from the crown was to prove a stumbling block to Desbrisay's plans and hindered the settlement of the island for generations.[2] The average quit-rent of Desbrisay's lands, as fixed by the terms of original grant, was over five shillings per hundred acres,[3] double that in Nova Scotia. The difference in actual rent became even more unfavourable to the settler on St John when the proprietor's profit rents were added. Moreover, though officially prohibited, emigration from the north of Ireland to Nova Scotia took place in the 'seventies[4] and so Desbrisay had to compete with the attractions of adjacent Nova Scotia as well as with the prejudice in favour of the older colonies.

The laxity which marked the enforcement of the law in the eighteenth century is well illustrated by Desbrisay's emigration activities in Scotland and Ireland. McNutt's schemes had been brought to their abrupt close partly by the order in council forbidding the granting of lands in Nova Scotia to emigrants from Great Britain and Ireland; Desbrisay's schemes were illegal from the very beginning. One of the conditions of the St John grants was that the settlers to be introduced should be 'protestants, from such parts of Europe as are not within his Majesty's dominions; or such persons as have resided within his Majesty's dominions in America for two years antecedent to the date of the grants'.[5] Yet it was not till Thomas Miller, the lord justice clerk of Scotland, and a number of Scottish landlords had protested in 1773 against the ill-effects of the emigration incited by Desbrisay that official displeasure descended on the latter's head.

Desbrisay publicly opened his career as a land promoter in Ireland through a newspaper advertisement dated from Wexford in January 1770.[6] Like McNutt, he emphasised his connections

[1] C.O. 391/74, ff.256–62 (23 July 1767).
[2] J. McGregor, *Historical and descriptive sketches of the maritime colonies of British North America*, p. 89.
[3] C.O. 391/74, f.214 (8 July 1767). The quit-rents of lots 14, 31 and 33 were six shillings, six shillings and four shillings, respectively, per hundred acres.
[4] *B.N.L.*, 21 June 1771, 20 Apr. 1773.
[5] C.O. 391/74, f.218 (8 July 1767).
[6] *B.N.L.*, 2 Mar. 1770.

with Ireland though, being unable to claim Irish ancestry, he had to fall back on references to his captaincy in an Irish regiment. His advertisement mentioned his appointment as lieutenant-governor of St John and announced that he intended to let some of the large tracts of land which he had purchased adjoining the 'Metropolis and Seat of Government'. The fertility and attractions of the island were richly detailed. Desbrisay was looking for people who could not merely pay their passage money but also pay rents for their new lands and so applications were invited only from 'Young Gentlemen and Farmers, of small Fortunes, with or without Families'. Desbrisay himself would agree with prospective tenants in the neighbourhood of Dublin and agents were appointed in Wexford, Enniscorthy and Belfast to deal with inquiries in those regions. No port of departure was named, readers being merely informed that Desbrisay, together with his family and tenants, would embark for America on or about 10 April. Desbrisay naturally intended to decide on the port of departure in the light of the response to his advertisement.

The response must have been disappointing for a change of plan was announced in a second advertisement issued from Dublin on 26 March. The same agents as before were named but the date of departure was postponed till the latter end of May.[1] Postponements such as this were often caused by delays in the arrival of vessels chartered for the journey, but the continued omission of the port of departure suggests that such was not the explanation in this case. Indeed, after an exhaustive study of all available Irish newspapers of 1770, it would seem that no vessel sailed to St John at the latter end of May—or at any other time in 1770—with tenants engaged by Desbrisay or by anyone else. When Desbrisay advertised in the following year he again announced that he planned to take his family to St John and, in a letter from Charlottetown in the autumn of 1771, Walter Patterson, governor of the island, referred to the settlers from Ireland who had arrived that autumn and said that they would 'make a good beginning'.[2]

Desbrisay encountered the same obstacle in 1770 that had been mainly responsible for McNutt's failure. His was but a single voice proclaiming the virtues of a part of America little known to the

[1] Ibid., 6 Apr. 1770.
[2] Ibid., 29 Jan. and 31 Dec. 1771. No mention of Irish immigration was made in a detailed report of the arrival of settlers in 1770 by John Dupont, the chief justice (to Hillsborough, 23 Apr. 1771: C.O. 226/4, ff.81–4).

people of Ireland. The position of St John, 'in the Gulph of the St Laurence', damned it in the eyes of most people as a likely bone of contention with the French. Though Desbrisay's glowing description of the potentialities of the island was little exaggerated[1] and though the majority of the former inhabitants had been expelled, the probable proximity of French-settled lands did not promise security of tenure, one of the mainsprings of the emigration movement. At any rate, the hold of the regular agents was too firmly established to be shaken by a hurried campaign lacking in both vigour and precision.

The most surprising feature of Desbrisay's opening gambit was his choice of agents. His net was a widespread one, covering most of the east coast of Ireland. Both the government instruction that immigrants were to be protestants and the obvious predominance of the north of Ireland over the south as a centre of emigration, particularly of the class desired by Desbrisay, should have suggested the north as the most likely region for recruiting settlers. Desbrisay's eyes were clearly on the south and not the north of Ireland, for four of the five agents he appointed were in the south-east counties. However great his knowledge of Irish artillery regiments might have been, his knowledge of Irish emigration was surprisingly meagre.

Disappointment did not discourage Desbrisay and when he advertised in January 1771 he showed that he had profited from his failure of the previous year. This advertisement, though substantially the same as that of a year before, contained a number of significant changes. Except for Desbrisay who was available for consultation in Dublin, the agents appointed were confined to Londonderry and Belfast. By now the most promising area had been determined and the south-east of Ireland, which had previously figured so largely in Desbrisay's plans, was replaced by the north-east. The new advertisement was also more precise than those of 1770 as it stated not only the ports of departure but the terms of settlement. A vessel would leave Londonderry with Desbrisay and his family and tenants and would call at Belfast on the way to St John. Instead of vague assurances of 'the greatest encouragement', the terms of tenancy were specifically stated. Perpetual leases would be granted—a powerful inducement in itself—

---

1 Dupont noted that the soil of the island was very good 'and will plentifully reward industrious husbandman for his labour' (ibid.).

and rents would be moderate, rising from two pence per acre in the first year to a maximum of two shillings per acre in the sixth and subsequent years. This rental explains Desbrisay's anxiety to attract settlers for it represented, after the sixth year, more than sixty times the quit-rent. Had Desbrisay succeeded in settling his land, his profits—though less than this because he was not an original grantee—would have more than adequately rewarded his endeavours. No wonder he now offered a free passage to all who would accompany him! Finally, the advertisement painted much more fully than those of 1770 the attractions of St John, an island so blessed by nature that a man could supply the needs of his family by fishing and shooting during his leisure hours.[1]

The voyage was successively postponed from 16 May to 20 May, early June, 10 July, and 'exactly the 16th of July'.[2] The explanation given for the delays was Desbrisay's inability to wind up his affairs in Dublin and not the scarcity of emigrants. In the meantime, Desbrisay's agents in Belfast—William Beattie, the merchant, and Francis Joy, publisher of the *Belfast News Letter*—had issued leases and when Desbrisay at last arrived in Belfast at the beginning of July he apologised for his delay and offered to take back any lease if a tenant so desired.[3]

Instead of sailing from Belfast, as Desbrisay had promised in all his advertisements, the emigrants from the Belfast region set out by road for Londonderry 'in high spirits' on 25 July to join a vessel which was to sail for St John on 1 August. The emigrants sailed on the *Hopewell* in the second week of August. They were stated to have been mostly presbyterians, of 'remarkably decent and orderly appearance', and to have embarked at Londonderry in high spirits. The hope was expressed that this would be the beginning of settling 'so fruitful, healthy, and convenient a part' of the empire.[4]

Desbrisay was little more successful in 1771 than he had been in 1770. The *Hopewell* had not been chartered exclusively for the voyage to St John. The vessel's main destination was Halifax with tenants sent out by Caldwell, Vance and Caldwell, and the passengers included only nine families bound for Desbrisay's

[1] *B.N.L.*, 29 Jan. 1771.
[2] Ibid., 3 and 31 May, 18 June and 5 July 1771.
[3] Ibid., 5 July 1771.
[4] Ibid., 26 July and 13 Aug. 1771.

lands[1]— a very small number in a year when emigration from the districts covered by Desbrisay was greater in volume than at any time for at least thirty years. The limited nature of Desbrisay's appeal and the unwillingness to emigrate other than to the well-known provinces had, once more, laid his plans low.

Frustration may lead to despair, but in Desbrisay's case it led to a determination to beat down the prejudice against St John. Two glowing accounts of life on the island were published in the *Belfast News Letter* during the winter of 1771-2, a season when all emigration activities were normally at a standstill. The letters were from the two people whose opinions would most influence intending settlers—an immigrant newly arrived in St John and the governor of the island. The letter from the settler, a farmer from Berkshire, appeared in the *Scots Magazine* in October[2] and in the *Belfast News Letter* on 8 November. It may not have been a mere coincidence that Desbrisay was in Dublin in the latter month,[3] not having sailed in the *Hopewell*, or that he extended his search for settlers in 1772 to Scotland to take advantage of the fairly heavy emigration from thence to St John in the preceeding years.[4] Francis Joy, proprietor of the *Belfast News Letter*, had been agent for Desbrisay in 1771—the only occasion on which he acted as an emigration agent before the American revolution—and so had more than a passing interest in Desbrisay's plans. It certainly seems that something more than the hand of chance guided to Britain and Ireland the letters of both immigrant and governor.

The Berkshire farmer's letter repeated the well-known inducements. An island where the necessaries of life were produced with little effort under the kindest and most paternal of landlords was but a variation of an old theme. Only doctors were advised to keep away from the island as they would surely starve if they attempted to follow their profession. Whether the cards were being dealt from Charlottetown or Dublin, yet another ace, longevity, had appeared in Desbrisay's hand.

---

[1] Ibid., 21 June and 31 Dec. 1771; Dupont to Hillsborough, 15 Oct. 1771 (C.O. 226/4, f.185). The *B.N.L.* account of the *Hopewell*'s departure described Desbrisay's tenants as 'a number of families' (Aug. 13). Two hundred had been expected (*Scots Magazine* (July 1771), xxxiii. 379).
[2] Vol. xxxiii. 551.
[3] *B.N.L.*, 7 Feb: 1772.
[4] Dupont reported the arrival of a party of five hundred Scottish settlers in 1771 (to Hillsborough, 3 Sept. 1771: C.O. 226/4, ff.169-71).

Despite governor Patterson's Irish ancestry—his father had emigrated from Foxhall in county Donegal—it is surprising that his letter to the island's agents in London should have specially mentioned the arrival of Desbrisay's nine families rather than, say, the arrival of the one hundred and twenty families brought over from Scotland by a Mr Montgomery in the same year.[1] That the letter was really an open letter to the people of Ireland is made even more obvious from the three main topics it discussed—the thriving state of the island's potatoes, the proposed change of the name of the island to New Ireland and the expected substantial immigration from Ireland in 1772. Intended for such widespread publicity, it is natural that the letter did not repeat Patterson's complaints to Hillsborough that it had taken him seven weeks to furnish a house to keep out the cold.[2]

The publication of these letters marked the preliminaries of Desbrisay's most active season in Ireland. His main appeal of 1772 appeared in the *Belfast News Letter* of 7 February. Descriptions of the fertility of the soil, the abundance of game and fish and the details of rentals were all repeated as in 1771. Competing agents may have been circulating accounts derogatory to the island for Desbrisay offered £200 to anyone who could show that his printed description of St John did not agree with the survey of the board of trade. No longer was a free passage offered but the smallness of the passage money—one guinea for all above seven years of age, with free water, though passengers had to provide their own food—was in itself an inducement to join Desbrisay. Incidentally, this appears to have been the only occasion on which north Irish emigrants were required to provide their own food during the period. Moreover, if the tenant were disappointed with the island when he arrived there, the terms of his lease would leave him at liberty to go to the mainland. Desbrisay's project was most invitingly and disarmingly presented. Even the terrors of the sea were stilled by his pen which reduced the journey from Cork to St John to twelve days. Those who responded to the advertisement must have thought little of their vessel, the *John and James*,

[1] Warburton, *History of P.E.I.*, p. 151.
[2] 25 Oct. 1770 (C.O. 226/1, ff.13–7). Patterson was, however, really impressed by the fertility of the soil (to Hillsborough, 18 Oct. 1771: C.O. 226/4, ff.189–90).

which actually took ten and a half weeks to complete the voyage from Belfast.[1]

Desbrisay's only agent in the north of Ireland in 1770 had been in Belfast: a Londonderry agent was added in 1771 and an attempt was to be made in 1772 to secure settlers in a district hitherto untapped by Desbrisay as well as in these centres. North Antrim and east Londonderry were to be the main regions of activity as four agents were appointed there—in Ballymena, Ballymoney, Coleraine and Limavady—and a fifth was later appointed at Randalstown.[2] These agents were not merchants but were inn-keepers in every case, an original feature in the organisation of the north Irish emigration trade. They were empowered to contract for land in Desbrisay's name and were supplied with 'printed descriptions and maps' of St John. Vessels would leave Belfast and Londonderry for the island in April, the month recommended by Patterson.

Desbrisay arrived in Belfast on 11 February—five months earlier than in the previous year—to perfect the leases granted there by his agent, Mr Blakeley of the Donegall Arms. Ten days later he set out for Ballymena where he proposed to remain a week and then proceed through Belfast to Newry where he would stay for a time to deal with inquiries in that region as no agent had been appointed there.[3]

An average of three advertisements a month from February to May kept Desbrisay and St John in the public mind. The advertisements usually gave notice of Desbrisay's movements and included yet another long description of the island from 'Boston in New England, to a gentleman in London'. It appeared at the beginning of March, the best psychological moment for that was the time when people were deciding whether to emigrate or not and when many of those who had decided to do so were still undecided in their choice of destination. In the advertisement accompanying the letter and as an additional encouragement at a time so vital to his project, Desbrisay assured prospective tenants that they would not only receive a free grant of four acres but that he would take care to provide, at a reasonable rate, sufficient

[1] *F.D.J.*, 7 Jan. 1773.
[2] *B.N.L.*, 20 Mar. 1772.
[3] Ibid., 21 Feb. and 3 Mar. 1772.

provisions for their use to tide them over their first winter in St John.[1]

Despite this most active campaigning, Desbrisay's hopes were rapidly deflated. The original plan to charter vessels to sail from both Belfast and Londonderry had dwindled by the beginning of April to the advertisement of a single sailing from Belfast.[2] Desbrisay might appeal and parade the virtues of St John, but emigrants still sailed to the better-known parts of America.

Definite arrangements were announced at the beginning of May for the shipping of Desbrisay's tenants. The *John and James* was to leave Belfast on 7 May and call at Newry but would then depart immediately for St John. The vessel left Belfast on 19 May and the voyage from Newry started on 30 May. On board were two clergymen, a merchant, a surgeon—who, assuming that he had read the letter from the Berkshire farmer, presumably intended to become either a farmer or a fisherman—and 184 other people. All were in high spirits and went off 'with great decency and in good order'.[3]

The vessel was overcrowded, being advertised as of only 150 tons, and enthusiasm evaporated during an unusually long voyage of ten weeks and four days. By the time the *John and James* arrived at St John's Island the passengers had used up all their provisions and it was with consternation that they found that no provisions were to be had in spite of Desbrisay's promises and all the high sounding letters they had read about the island. They pleaded with John Baker, the master, to be taken on to Nova Scotia, a right Desbrisay had promised them, and offered to bind themselves as indentured servants but 'the cries and tears of the poor creatures could not prevail, so they were left there to starve'.[4]

It is impossible to trace Desbrisay's activities in Ireland in 1773

[1] Ibid., 3 Mar. 1772.

[2] Ibid., 3 Apr. 1772. In the *B.N.L.* of 15 May 1772 Desbrisay's long advertisement of 20 Nov. 1771 reappeared with the additional note that vessels would sail on April 1 (1772) from Belfast and Newry to St John both calling at Londonderry on their way thence. An unnamed vessel was advertised in the *B.N.L.* of 2 June 1772 to sail from Londonderry to St John on 25 June. It is improbable that Desbrisay was a party to this advertisement as it mentioned neither him nor his tenants. Certainly no record of the sailing of a vessel to St John from Londonderry appeared in the sailing lists of the *Londonderry Journal* in 1772.

[3] *B.N.L.*, 1 May and 29 May 1772; *F.D.J.*, 17 June 1772.

[4] Extracts of a letter from one of the passengers on the *John and James* (*F.D.J.*, 7 Jan. 1773).

with the same precision as in the two previous years. The only person who advertised in the *Belfast News Letter* in 1773 for tenants for St John was William Rogers of Carnmoney near Belfast.[1] Rogers's methods were so different from Desbrisay's that it is clear that it was indeed he and not Desbrisay who was behind this scheme. Though, naturally, he printed—at much shorter length than Desbrisay—a favourable description of the island and the prospects of settlers there, no details of rents were given and no network of agents was set up. Furthermore, Rogers finally appealed strongly to those without means to go out as servants, a thing Desbrisay never did even when he must have been very disappointed with the response of the more privileged class.

The only evidence that Desbrisay attempted to secure settlers in 1773 comes from Scottish sources. Emigration from Scotland to St John had taken place prior to 1773. For example, 170 settlers had sailed to the island from Campbelltown alone in 1770 and 1771.[2] When Desbrisay commenced a drive for settlers in Ayrshire in 1773 the attention of Thomas Miller, the lord justice clerk of Scotland, was drawn to his activities. Miller wrote to the earl of Suffolk, secretary for the southern department, enclosing a paper, 'copys of which had been dispersed over Ireland and this part of Scotland', and expressed alarm at the possible effects should such schemes be allowed to continue unchecked.[3] The paper, a single printed sheet, was the same advertisement Desbrisay had published in the *Belfast News Letter* in 1771 with the exception of the list of agents. Eight agents were named in the circular enclosed by Miller and six of these, including Desbrisay in Dublin, were in Ireland. The other five Irish agents, four of them innkeepers, were at Londonderry, Larne, Belfast, Donaghadee and Newry. Though the majority of the agents appointed were in Ireland, the two vessels Desbrisay intended to send were advertised to sail from the Scottish ports of Campbelltown and Lamlash, no mention being made of any proposed sailing from Ireland. Linked with the fact that all the Irish agents were in seaports in regular communication

---

1 B.N.L., 20 Apr. 1773. Desbrisay stated in a letter to John Pownall, secretary to the board of trade, that the only advertisement he inserted in 1773 was in a Londonderry newspaper (22 Nov. 1773; C.O. 226/5, ff.147-9). No such advertisement has been traced.
2 Report, collector and comptroller of Campbelltown to Miller, 1774 (S.P. 54/45, no. 167c).
3 S.P. 54/46, no. 89a, b (27 Oct. 1773).

with Scotland, the absence of any reference to sailings from Irish ports suggests that any emigrants secured by the Irish agents were required to journey to Scotland to join Desbrisay's vessels or to one of the named ports where they would await the vessels' arrival. It is not likely that many Irish people accepted either condition, especially the former. More emigrant vessels left the north Irish ports in 1773 than in any previous year and so more direct methods were open to the intending emigrant than going first to Scotland and there hungering or wasting his capital in the probable interval between the advertised and actual dates of departure.

Desbrisay was mentioned in only one advertisement in the *Belfast News Letter* in 1773. Rogers had engaged the *Yaward*, an unusually large vessel advertised as of 350 tons, to transport his settlers to St John. The response to his advertisement was not good and on the day the vessel was scheduled to sail he announced that the *Yaward* would carry over Desbrisay's tenants as well as his own. Desbrisay's tenants—if any—must have agreed some time before, possibly in 1772, or in response to a circular such as that which Miller sent to London, or were sailing to join relatives who had already sailed to St John. Desbrisay inserted no advertisement and gave no indication that he intended to be in Belfast to grant leases before the *Yaward* sailed. Desbrisay was a man of flourishes, not of postscripts, and a mere line at the end of another person's advertisement was not his method of conducting a serious campaign. The vessel left less than a week later carrying fifty heads of families, together with women and children.[1]

The experiences of the passengers of the *John and James* and other uncomplimentary reports of St John deterred large scale emigration from Ireland to the island in 1773. When the *Yaward* was advertised to sail it was found necessary to denounce the 'lies' that had been spread about the island. In reply to this, extracts of two letters from St John were printed in the *Belfast News Letter* on the same day as Desbrisay was mentioned in the postscript to Roger's advertisement. In the first letter it was admitted that the lands in the island were fertile but this advantage was more than offset by a harsh climate which made provisions scarce and expensive. The second extract was much more scathing. St John, it was bluntly stated, was not fit for any christian to live in because

[1] B.N.L., 20 and 30 Apr. and 7 May 1773.

for half the year the ground was covered with snow and frost and, in the other half, mice as big as rats ate all the crops. This was not an unfair exaggeration of a minor pest—Patterson informed Hillsborough that the mice, which were in size 'something between our mice and rats in England', were so numerous that they had devoured what little was attempted to be raised.[1] The writer announced his intention of going to Philadelphia 'if God spares us' and pleaded 'for God's sake do not send my babies here to starve with hunger'. His final words did not cheer the friends of those who had gone in the *John and James* for he believed that all who had arrived in that vessel were doomed to starvation. The experiences of the emigrants of 1772, together with these extracts—and other letters in similar vein that almost certainly circulated though they did not find their way into print—effectively ended emigration from the north of Ireland to St John and no vessels after the *Yaward* made the journey till after the American revolution. Emigrants went to America because they believed it to be a land of promise: the wrath of God in St John was in no way preferable to the wrath of man in Ireland.

It was the unusually firm action of the authorities following Miller's protest which put an end to the recruitment of settlers by Desbrisay in Britain and Ireland[2] but the writing had appeared on the wall long before and even Desbrisay saw it, for he all but abandoned his Irish activities after the summer of 1772. He had not encountered many of the difficulties which had beset McNutt. The fear of privateers no longer dissuaded the timorous; the volume of spontaneous emigration was much greater in the early 'seventies than it had been a decade before; the government did not intervene to check emigration to St John before Desbrisay's hopes were on the wane. Yet Desbrisay had no more success than McNutt. Nine families in 1771, 188 people in 1772 and a few in 1773 were numbers that were not commensurate with either Desbrisay's energies or with the volume of emigration in those years. Popular prejudice against any new region of settlement and Desbrisay's lack of interest in the poorer class were the chief factors which brought his schemes to all but naught. The unfortunate voyage of the *John and James*, the hardships her passengers endured in St John and the resulting revelation of conditions

---

[1] 21 Oct. 1770 (C.O. 226/4, ff. 51–6).
[2] See Chapter IX.

there confirmed the conservative doubts of intending emigrants and sealed the fate of Desbrisay's plans.

The methods of McNutt and Desbrisay were similar in many respects but, of the two men, McNutt shows up to advantage. He was an unpractical enthusiast but his dealings with the board of trade and with the Nova Scotia authorities show that he felt some responsibility for the welfare of those he took to Nova Scotia. Desbrisay had no such qualms of conscience for his tenants. He described Charlottetown as 'the metropolis and seat of government' though Patterson was complaining at the time that the tiny settlement had not even a barn to use for public worship.[1] Desbrisay's description was misleading but it was one of the least of his misrepresentations. Soon after he acquired his lands in St John's Island he mortgaged them to a Dublin merchant named Drummond and, according to Patterson, those who purchased deeds from Desbrisay had not only to pay exorbitant rents but eventually lost both their lands and their money.[2] Desbrisay and Dobbs may be grouped in the same general class as land promoters but their aims were poles apart.

V: MATTHEW REA

The trumpetings of McNutt and Desbrisay echoed over the north of Ireland but they failed to arouse the response evoked by the subdued but prolonged efforts of Matthew Rea. Being neither a king nor a prince among emigration organisers—nor even a captain of artillery—little can be told of Rea's background. He lived near the village of Drumbo in county Down, a fact he stated in all his advertisements, but nothing is recorded of his mode of life or his social position. He was probably either a small landowner or substantial farmer: he had the means to undertake several tours of the surrounding countryside in furtherance of his emigration plans, but was not sufficiently important to be on the grand jury of his county. He had apparently never been to America and never publicly expressed any desire to go there. Moreover, though his efforts were spread over eleven years, they were spasmodic and

---

[1] To Hillsborough, 25 Oct. 1770 (C.O. 226/4, ff.65–71).

[2] To—, 20 Aug. 1774 (C.O. 226/6, ff. 59–61). This may, however, have applied to only one of Desbrisay's three lots. In a memorial from the proprietors of St John's Island to the B.T. (recvd. 20 Jan. 1774) Drummond was noted as the proprietor of lot 31 (C.O. 226/1, ff.171–3).

lacked the intensity and urgency that had characterised the activities of McNutt. The latter's methods showed interesting signs of development; Rea's wooing of prospective emigrants showed few variations during its long duration.

The difference is easily explained. McNutt was a principal whereas Rea was but a middleman in the emigration trade. It was on behalf of his brother that Matthew Rea became an emigration agent and it was on his behalf that Matthew Rea's energies were directed for ten of his eleven years in that role. John Rea had emigrated from Maghrenock, near Ballynahinch in county Down, to South Carolina in 1729 or 1730, and, through Matthew, advertised for servants in 1763. Six or eight labourers and two dairymaids were required. In return for becoming indentured servants for four years, each would be paid £5 sterling per year and receive the colony's bounty of £4 and one hundred acres of land at the end of the period of service. These servants were to sail on the *Falls* or the *Prince of Wales* from Belfast to Charleston.[1] Emigration to South Carolina was heavy at the time because of the bounty and the appeal of serving under a north of Ireland man at such favourable conditions no doubt attracted a sufficient number of applicants.

His connections with the north of Ireland and the considerable numbers emigrating from there to South Carolina were two of the main factors which prompted John Rea to apply for a grant of land in Georgia. The Georgia council lent a very ready ear to such requests, provided there was any likelihood of the land being settled. This attitude is demonstrated by an act of June 1766 by which the council promised a township to any group of forty or more protestant families—an act which was disallowed in England because of the additional encouragement it would give to emigration from Great Britain and Ireland.[2] Rea's request was granted and he was allotted 50,000 acres on the Ogeechee River, in Queensborough county (now Burke county), about forty miles from Augusta. He stated that the lands had been granted 'for any of my

[1] *B.N.L.*, 21 Oct. 1763. When the South Carolina council met on 13 Jan. 1764 it considered a petition submitted by 26 persons, 'members of a protestant congregation' lately arrived from Ireland in the ship *Falls*. The Council instructed the acting commissary that 'he should endeavour to get Masters for as many of those people as should want them and do everything in his power to prevent their being cheated or imposed upon' (Revill, *S.C.*, p. 9). One hundred and seventy emigrants sailed on board the *Prince of Wales* from Belfast to Charleston in November 1763 (*B.N.L.*, 27 Mar. 1764).

[2] P.C. 2/112, pp. 390, 413, 429.

friends and countrymen that have a mind to come over to this country and bring their families with them'.[1] The statement may have been designed merely to stress his interest in Ireland but the Georgia council would have been only too pleased to co-operate in diverting the route of Irish emigrants still further south than South Carolina.

Two letters from John Rea asking for settlers appeared in the *Belfast News Letter* in 1765. The first, printed in May, was in very general terms but the second, four months later, was detailed and persuasive, dealing with every topic about which the intending emigrant might desire information. The location, climate and rents of the proposed settlement were described in flattering terms but the difficulties were also presented with convincing candour. It was admitted that Georgia was a young and poor colony: persons comfortably settled in Ireland were advised not to emigrate to the new settlement for they would miss the pleasures of society and the comforts of divine service there. Rea would lose nothing by such reservations for very few who were content in Ireland would be likely to emigrate to Georgia or anywhere else. The thorns served to enhance the appeal of the rose to the people whom Rea really expected to leave Ireland; the light clouds he painted on the American horizon were more convincing than the monotonous blue of the usual emigration canvas. The pleasures of society were of less interest to small farmers and tradesmen than the loaded table Rea promised. The general tenor of the letter was that an ordinary, honest Ulsterman who had prospered in America—he was sending £100 to educate the children of his dead brother— was inviting his fellow countrymen to share his good fortune. In a postscript to this letter, Matthew Rea added the guarantee that the settlers would be given the free use of cows and horses for five years.[2]

The Georgia act relating to new townships was not passed till June 1766, but lands must have been granted by the Georgia council before that date on terms which anticipated the act. Only such an explanation would make Rea's activities logical, for the only rent the new settlers were to pay was the official quit-rent of two shillings per hundred acres. As will be seen, John Rea was not a philanthropist whatever else he was. The 1766 act would have

[1] *B.N.L.*, 3 Sept. 1765.
[2] Ibid., 17 May and 3 Sept. 1765.

obliged him to settle forty families on his lands and, assuming that the average family of the time consisted of six persons, the settlers would have been entitled to 14,000 acres,[1] thus leaving Rea 36,000 acres for profitable settlement, or approximately 150 acres in respect of each settler introduced, compared with the two hundred acres promised to McNutt. If the assumption that the terms of the 1766 act were not anticipated before that date is incorrect, it was a remarkable coincidence that the terms offered by Rea should be almost exactly repeated by George Galphin before the act was passed. Galphin, who had emigrated from Armagh to South Carolina about the year 1750, specified the colour of the cows he would lend his settlers and offered to let land at three shillings per hundred acres.[2] Clearly, he did not intend to let all his lands at this rent as the resulting profit would not have been commensurate with the expenses involved in establishing the settlement.

Matthew Rea announced the arrangements for the emigrants' voyage a few days before the publication of his brother's second letter. The *Prince of Wales* was to sail in November from Belfast to Charleston with passengers, including those who had agreed with Rea.[3] Savannah was a more suitable port for Rea's tenants and the choice of Charleston seems to have been guided by three main factors: trade between Georgia and the north of Ireland was, apparently, non-existent before 1768;[4] the year was so advanced that the *Prince of Wales* was the only vessel available, being the last emigrant vessel advertised to sail from Belfast in 1765; the cost of chartering the *Prince of Wales* would have been very high as the vessel, by making the voyage to Savannah, would forgo the prospect of securing the South Carolina bounty on a heavy complement of passengers. John Rea presumably engaged transport to carry his tenants to Savannah, as Galphin had arranged for his tenants in 1766.[5]

The *Prince of Wales* had sailed from Belfast to South Carolina in February 1765 and it was not till October 24 that the vessel returned

---

[1] Each settler was to receive 50 acres, and the head of a family an additional 50 acres (ibid., 3 Sept. 1765).
[2] Ibid., 4 Mar. 1766 and 10 June 1768.
[3] Ibid., 30 Aug. 1765.
[4] The *Prince George*, chartered by Matthew Rea, sailed from Belfast to Savannah in 1768 and was the first vessel that was advertised in the *B.N.L.* to sail from a north Irish port to Georgia (ibid., 26 July 1768).
[5] Ibid., 4 Mar. 1766.

by way of Philadelphia. The departure for Charleston was scheduled for a month later but was delayed by the sudden appearance of William Beatty, the Belfast merchant, who initiated a drive to persuade servants to go to South Carolina 'where industry is amply rewarded and poverty is a stranger'. A shortage of potatoes for use during the voyage and the passengers' desire to spend Christmas in Ireland caused further delays and it was not till 19 January 1766 that the vessel sailed.[1] During the interval of four months between the publication of John Rea's letter and the departure of the vessel, Matthew Rea made no move to promote his enterprise, possibly because he had secured the number of emigrants his brother had asked for.

Matthew Rea's energies were turned in 1766 to the securing of settlers for his brother's lands in South Carolina. As it was believed that the South Carolina bounty was to cease at the end of that year, the re-direction of Rea's activities may have indicated a desire to recruit settlers for South Carolina while conditions were most propitious rather than that a sufficient number of settlers had gone to the Queensborough lands in the *Prince of Wales* at the beginning of the year. The emigrants secured by Rea in 1765 had sailed to Charleston because, unless a vessel were specially chartered for the voyage to Savannah, Charleston was the most convenient port to the Georgia lands, but the final destination of the emigrants recruited by Rea in 1766 was South Carolina. Not only was a vessel which was originally advertised to sail to Philadelphia chartered by Rea to sail to Charleston instead, but the emigrants were told to bring certificates with them to prove that they were protestants in order to secure the bounty. No special appeals were issued, apart from the assurance that the friendless would receive a welcome from John Rea; but Matthew Rea, for the first time, made a short tour in the parts of county Down where he and his family were known—to Lisburn, Ballynahinch, and Dromore. The *Belfast Packet* sailed with seventy-eight emigrants in August, just a fortnight after the advertised date of departure.[2]

This did not complete Rea's efforts to foster emigration in 1766. In December of that year he was active in conjunction with Beatty in securing emigrants for the *Prince of Wales*. The vessel arrived at

---

[1] *B.N.L.*, 25 and 29 Oct. and 10 and 24 Dec. 1765; 3, 17, and 21 Jan. 1766.
[2] Ibid., 17 and 27 June, 8 July and 26 Dec. 1766; C.O. 5/511, 24 Oct. 1766.

Charleston in the following May with 210 passengers on board.[1] No mention was made of John Rea's lands in the advertisements relating to the sailing and so it seems that in this episode Matthew Rea was acting as an emigration agent rather than as a land promoter.

The South Carolina bounty came to an end in December 1767 and, in 1768, Matthew Rea again drew public attention to his brother's settlement at Queensborough. In conjunction with Beatty he advertised the advantages of settling in Georgia under John Rea or George Galphin on the same terms of tenure as in 1765. Not more than two hundred 'decent healthy people' were required and the passage money from Belfast to Savannah was to be only one guinea per person. Three months' notice of sailing was given but the advertisement was really a straw in the wind to see if the response would justify the chartering of a vessel. As the South Carolina bounty had now ceased, sailings to the southern colonies dwindled and Philadelphia again became the chief attraction for emigrants. Had a suitable vessel been sailing to Charleston the additional expense of conveying settlers to Savannah would not have been great, but diverting a ship from Philadelphia was a different matter. The response to the initial advertisement was so good that the *Prince George*, already advertised to sail to Philadelphia, was chartered by Rea who made a short tour of central Down and north Armagh while William Beatty visited Ballymena to interview prospective settlers. The *Prince George* sailed to Savannah in October with 170 settlers for Queensborough on board.[2]

Matthew Rea's activities on behalf of the Queensborough township continued in 1769 and his association with the skilled campaigner William Beatty once more gave Rea's notices a polish which his earlier advertisements had lacked. The safe arrival of the emigrants of 1768 and their deep satisfaction with their lands and their treatment by John Rea and George Galphin were described in detail: Georgia's products were catalogued to show that the province was 'one of the most fertile and fruitful . . . in America'; the grant of lands to persons above sixteen years was raised from 50 to 100 acres. Rea promised that a vessel would leave Belfast for

[1] *B.N.L.*, 30 Dec. 1767; C.O. 5/511, 27 May 1767.
[2] *B.N.L.*, 18 Mar., 10 June and 26 July 1768 and 7 July 1769: O'Brien, *Hidden phase*, p. 369.

Savannah at the end of August if a sufficient number of people came forward. He visited Belfast and Lisburn to interview applicants, and, though the previous year's offer of a guinea passage was not repeated, not only did a sufficient number apply for the *Hopewell* to be chartered, but rumours were spread that she was overcrowded when she sailed on 5 October. Rea's future success in similar enterprises would have been jeopardised had such rumours remained unanswered. In a deposition before Stephen Haver, the sovereign of Belfast, Rea swore that only 166 'full' passengers had sailed in the vessel.[1] He did not state whether this number excluded 'half' passengers—generally those under sixteen years—or included them, reckoning two as a 'full' passenger.

This embarrassing tribute was not the only evidence of Rea's success in the 1769 emigration season. 'As sundry families were disappointed of a passage' in the *Hopewell*, the *Two Peggys* was chartered to sail from Belfast to Savannah at the end of November. This vessel had already been advertised in 1769 to sail from Belfast to South Carolina. As it was the only vessel advertised to make that journey in that year, it had a considerable cargo and the original advertisement had limited the number of passengers the vessel would carry to Charleston to forty. Not surprisingly, therefore, despite Rea's statement that the vessel would sail to Savannah, the *Two Peggys* sailed to Charleston where arrangements were made to complete the journey in a smaller craft.[2]

The first published letter from an emigrant sent to Georgia by Matthew Rea appeared in 1770 and certainly had a great effect on emigration to Georgia in the next few years—four fat years for the emigration trade. It was letters such as this, not the descriptions of land promoters, that really decided the success or failure of the latter's efforts. The writer had sailed in the *Hopewell* in 1769 and bluntly gave his views on John Rea and Georgia. Savannah was described as 'a woeful place . . . a poor hole . . . that accursed place', full of pride and wickedness, the home of high prices, inhabited by a few Irish and some runaways from all parts of America, and the settlers in Queensborough ran true to form—eighteen of them were being tried at the time of the writer's arrival for stealing cows and horses. John Rea, 'that old jockey', both a liar and a cheat, was more concerned with erecting a 'hedge'

[1] *B.N.L.*, 7 July, 11 Aug. and 12 and 24 Oct. 1769.
[2] Ibid., 15 Aug., 10 Oct. and 8 Dec. 1769 and 11 May 1770.

between himself and the Indians than with promoting the happiness of his settlers. The best that the writer could say about Matthew Rea was that he was probably not a knowing party to the evil design and was merely a dupe.[1]

Matthew Rea printed no defence of his brother. The letter was so damning that only a denial and not an explanation would have been adequate: it was so convincingly detailed that a denial from a person who had never been to Savannah would have been ludicrous. Rea confined his activities in 1770 to announcing that he had been requested by 'sundry men . . . from Ballyshannon, and other distant parts' to send a vessel to Savannah and stated that he would arrange for a vessel to leave Belfast or Newry—both rather inconvenient ports for Ballyshannon emigrants.[2] The *Hopewell*, on which Rea's critic had sailed the previous year, was the only vessel advertised to sail from the north of Ireland to Charleston in 1770[3] and none sailed to Savannah. Though Rea advertised no further particulars he may have sent settlers on the *Hopewell* for he later claimed that some people had left Belfast in 1770 to settle in Queensborough.[4]

Matthew Rea returned to the scene with renewed vigour during the period of heavy emigration in the early 'seventies. The passage of a year had, by 1771, dulled the memory of the attack on John Rea and Georgia. Moreover, the cheap lands of Georgia were no less attractive to those emigrants who possessed some capital than they were to thousands of the inhabitants of the more densely populated colonies.

In each of the three years, 1771–3, a vessel left Belfast for Savannah with tenants engaged by Matthew Rea whose organisation followed his customary pattern. The same quantities of land were promised as in 1769. Tours were made embracing Belfast, Lisburn, Banbridge, Ballynahinch, Armagh and Castleblaney, and in 1771 an agent was appointed in Newry. The radius of Rea's activities from Drumbo was little greater than in less rewarding years and his advertising was no more intense than before. A total of about 390 emigrants sailed in 1771 and 1772 in vessels chartered by Rea, the *Britannia* and the *Elizabeth*. Sufficient numbers were engaged

---

[1] Ibid., 27 Apr. 1770.
[2] Ibid., 3 June 1770.
[3] Ibid., 22 Oct. 1770.
[4] Ibid., 6 Aug. 1771.

in 1773 to charter the *Waddell*, advertised as of over 400 tons. This vessel was diverted to Savannah from her original destination and the *Lord Bangor*, advertised as of only 200 tons, sailed in its place to North Carolina. The chartering of a vessel of the size of the *Waddell* indicates that the 1773 season was a most successful one for Rea.[1]

With the sailing of the *Waddell* in November 1773, Matthew Rea's activities on behalf of Georgia and his brother came to an end. This sudden closure was unexpected, for Rea had advertised earlier in 1773 that settlers were required for three million acres in the vicinity of Augusta.[2] The renewal of Indian attacks caused the temporary abandonment of the Queensborough settlement in 1774, however, and many of the immigrants who arrived from the north of Ireland in the previous year had to seek relief from the provincial assembly.[3]

Matthew Rea made his last appearance as an emigration agent in 1774 in partnership with Waddell Cunningham. Rea's farewell was out of keeping with the nature of his activities in the preceding eleven years for in 1774 he acted on behalf of a vessel whose destination was neither Savannah nor Charleston but Philadelphia and New York.[4]

The reference in Rea's main advertisement of 1773 to vast quantities of unoccupied lands in Georgia may have been bait stretched out to land-hungry Irishmen. On the other hand, it may have indicated that Rea was contemplating extending his activities from being merely an agent on his brother's behalf to the more direct interest of a shipping agent, an interest in passage money rather than in settlers. The transformation did not produce any startling results. In place of the active organiser appeared the stationary agent, one among scores of others. The *Peace and Plenty*, the vessel for which Rea acted as agent in 1774, sailed with 400 emigrants on board. Though Rea who was now a well-known figure in the trade may have secured some of these, the vessel's

---

[1] Ibid., 6 Aug. and 1 Nov. 1771, 14 Aug. and 20 Nov. 1772, and 20 July, 14 Sept. and 23 Nov. 1773.
[2] Ibid., 14 Sept. 1773. This may have been the land between the Oconee and Savannah rivers purchased from the Indians in 1773 by James Wright, governor of Georgia, who took immediate steps to settle it (P. Calhoun, 'Scotch-Irish in Georgia', in *Scotch-Ir. in Amer.*, iv. 142).
[3] *Scots Magazine* (May 1774), xxxvi. 263; B.N.L., 10 June 1774.
[4] B.N.L., 14 Feb. 1774.

great success was due mostly to the efforts of its master, Charles McKenzie, who toured the region between Ballynahinch and Ballymena in search of emigrants.[1]

Matthew Rea stood unique among emigration organisers in that he had no clear financial interest in the settling of American lands except possibly in 1774. This may explain the comparative nonchalance and the comparative success of his activities. Land promoters were attracted to the north of Ireland by the apparent readiness of the people there to emigrate, but few of them could have been satisfied with their achievements. Rea was on the spot and understood the inclinations and prejudices of the people. Moreover, he could offer a hundred acres of land for the same rent at the same time as Desbrisay was offering one acre. A hundred acres in a district owned by a native of Ballynahinch and partly settled by people from the north of Down and Armagh was much more attractive than an acre in a little known island among strangers, some of them French Roman catholics. The efforts of McNutt and Desbrisay produced much foliage but little fruit: Rea's organisation was comparatively elementary but its results were more striking.

VI: OTHER LAND PROMOTERS

As well as the four chief land promoters whose activities have been detailed and a few whose more humble efforts have been referred to, several other people canvassed the north of Ireland for settlers for lands in America. All the land promoters who remain to be studied were active between 1763 and 1775 and most of them were interested in the province of New York. A multiplicity of reasons, chief among which were the threat of a French advance down the Hudson and the granting of land in huge blocks, had so retarded the settlement of the province that, with the official cessation of westward expansion in 1763, New York had more unsettled and even ungranted lands than any other colony north of South Carolina.[2] The defeat of the French was followed by a spate of grants to members of the council and others in the province in, unfortunately, as large units as was customary in the past and by

[1] Ibid., 12 Apr. and 15 Sept. 1774.
[2] Minutes, N.Y. council, 9 July 1754 (*Annals of New York*, ii. 610); Sutherland, *Pop. distribution in col. Amer.*, p. 80; Mackinnon, *Settlements and churches in N.S.*, p. 39.

grants to soldiers who often peddled their lands and disposed of them to the highest bidders.[1]

William Gilliland, a New York merchant, acquired lands to the west of lake Champlain from British soldiers and over 60,000 acres between Ticonderoga and Crown Point from the provincial authorities who were assured that the lands would be settled by Irish immigrants.[2] Four months before the grant was made in August 1763, Gilliland advertised in Ireland for settlers for the lands.[3] Gilliland did not himself come to Ireland but appointed John Eccles, a Newry merchant, as his agent and Eccles in turn appointed sub-agents in Newry and in Keady. The usual encouragements of cheap land and good treatment were offered and any who wished to 'embrace this favourable opportunity of being most happily settled, and rescued from misery and oppression' were to be sent to New York in vessels commanded by 'proper sea captains'. With the ending of the war and the rise of discontent that culminated in the Oakboy troubles in Armagh among other places, the emigrant trade was now recovering from a slump period.[4] The *Venus*, a Newry vessel advertised as of 140 tons, was engaged by Eccles and sailed from that port in the middle of July. The venture was not a particularly successful one for Gilliland as it brought him only twenty-two tenants.[5]

Eccles had sailed in the *Venus* and when he returned to Newry in 1764 he brought with him a Peter Vandervort who advertised that he had come to Ireland to seek tenants for estates he had acquired in the Hudson valley. The *John*, of 300 tons, on which Eccles and Vandervort had arrived, was engaged for the return passage. The same Newry agents were appointed as for the *Venus* in 1763 and the *John* presumably sailed about the beginning of May as advertised.[6]

At this point Eccles seems to have ended his career as an agent

---

[1] Farnam, *Social legislation in U.S.*, pp. 32–3; MacLean, *Highland settlements in Amer.*, p. 188; Bidwell and Falconer, *Agric. in the northern U.S.*, p. 73.

[2] O'Brien, *Hidden phase*, p. 297; O'Brien, 'Early Irish settlements in the Champlain valley', in *Jn. Am. Ir. Hist. Soc.*, 1927, p. 150.

[3] *B.N.L.*, 26 Apr. 1763.

[4] A vessel, the *Newry* sailed with 221 emigrants from Newry to Philadelphia in May 1763, two months before the advertised date of departure (*B.N.L.*, 22 Mar. and 13 Sept. 1763).

[5] Ibid., 10 July 1763; C.O. 5/1228, 24 Oct. 1763.

[6] *B.N.L.*, 27 Mar. 1764; *F.D.J.*, 31 Mar. 1764.

for the direct promotion of American lands. Though he chartered the *Buchannon* in 1765 and the *Britannia* in 1766 to sail from Newry to New York and though he announced his intention to travel in each of the vessels, his advertisements merely asked for passengers, servants and freight. Neither Gilliland nor Vandervort was named and no mention was made of cheap lands to be had in New York.[1] Both Gilliland and Vandervort may have secured settlers from the emigrants on these vessels, but Eccles's main purpose was obviously to dispose of his passengers at the greatest profit regardless of land promoters.

A special appeal was made to the people of the Antrim district by David Waugh in 1765. Waugh, a native of Antrim, had secured lands near Albany which he promised to let cheaply. It is impossible to tell how many people responded to his advertisement. He had to return to New York in 1766 and nominated no agent other than his father who, it was stated, would describe the land to inquirers. Waugh advised any who were inclined to become his tenants to follow him in the spring of 1766 but no vessel sailed from Belfast to New York in that year. The advertisement did not reappear but emigrants from Antrim in later years may have been attracted to Waugh's lands.[2]

An attempt was made in 1774 by Henry Caldwell, a retired major and a member of a prominent Londonderry landed family, to secure settlers for large tracts of land he had secured on the Richelieu in Quebec and in adjoining parts of New York province. Quantities of land ranging from one hundred to 2,000 acres were to be leased for ever to settlers at a rent of less than threepence per acre, payment to begin five years after the date of the lease. It was bluntly stated, that except for a few labourers for Caldwell's own lands,

> ... no person need apply that has not a sufficiency to pay the usual passage to America, to set themselves up in a little way as farmers, and maintain them for a year after their arrival, as before that time they will not be able to grow as much grain and potatoes as will support them; which will require a capital to each family of from £30 to £40 ...... Major Caldwell would not, on any account, wish to bring indigent people over there, as he cannot afford to give other encouragement but in the cheapness of his lands; and both

[1] *B.N.L.*, 29 Mar. 1765 and 6 May 1766; *Freeman's Journal*, 6 May 1766.
[2] *B.N.L.*, 13 Sept. 1765.

time and industry will be required before the new settlers can maintain themselves.[1]

Agents were appointed at Londonderry, Strabane, Garrison and Downpatrick but, though the advertisement stated that if sufficient numbers came forward a vessel would leave Londonderry in April, no record can be found to show that a vessel did leave Londonderry for New York in 1774 or 1775. Caldwell's hopes were disappointed by the lessening pace of emigration, the limited class to whom he appealed and by the unusual frankness of his advertisement.

The last attempt to be backed by an organisation reminiscent of McNutt or Desbrisay to secure settlers in Ireland for the American colonies prior to 1775 was that of William Smith, jnr., a member of the New York Council. Smith had secured grants to the north of Albany in the counties of Albany and Cumberland in New York province and proposed, in 1768, to sell lands in these grants at an average of six or eight shillings per acre. This was one of the very few occasions on which lands in colonial America were advertised in the north of Ireland to be sold rather than leased. Only those already in comfortable circumstances could have responded to Smith's advertisement and, as John Rea had already recognised, cheap American lands were not a sufficiently powerful inducement to persuade this class to emigrate. Therefore, despite Smith's assurance that it was 'to farmers of some substance that this is a situation superior to other countries', few had both the means and inclination to respond to the advertisement.[2]

Smith's name reappeared in Ireland at the height of the emigration boom in 1773 and the alternative was given of leasing the lands at sixpence per acre or purchasing them at six shillings per acre. The superiority of New York over other provinces was expounded in detail and an assurance was given that the settlers would receive a hearty welcome from the people already in the district—including assistance to build a house in a single day! Emigrants were advised to sail from Newry to New York on the *Needham* and, 'in the street called Broadway, ask for Hon. William Smith, Esq.'.[3]

[1] Ibid., 11 Feb. 1774.
[2] C.O. 391/76, f.163; *B.N.L.*, 1 July 1768.
[3] *B.N.L.*, 12 Mar. 1773.

A name of much greater significance in Ireland than William Smith, esquire, appeared in Smith's advertisements both in 1768 and 1773 and probably contributed more to Smith's success in the latter year than the attractive description of New York. Added to the advertisement of 1768 was a note of recommendation from Thomas Clark, minister and physician, who described Smith's account as 'a very modest, genuine and true one', and special mention was made in the 1773 advertisement to the success of Clark's settlement near to the vacant lands. Clark, a Scotsman, had been the very influential antiburgher presbyterian minister of Ballybay (Cahans) in county Monaghan from 1751 till 1764 and was well known as an itinerant preacher over a wide area in counties Monaghan, Tyrone, Armagh and Down. He left Newry for New York with three hundred presbyterian emigrants in May 1764 and settled at Stillwater (Salem).[1] Clark's name and reputation were well known in the southern counties of Ulster and so William Cheevers, the *Needham*'s master, went on an extensive tour through the region. The towns of Monaghan, Castleblaney, Clones, Cootehill, Ballybay, Caledon, Armagh, Stewartstown and Dungannon were all visited and the enterprise met with such success that when the vessel sailed about five hundred emigrants were on board. Smith's settlement did not benefit by this number, however, for about half disembarked at Newcastle on the Delaware before the vessel proceeded to New York.[2] Smith did not publish any advertisement in 1774 but some of the three hundred emigrants who sailed in the *Needham* from Newry in that year may have gone to his settlements. A 'printed paper' advertising American lands had been distributed by the owners of the vessel and, though the *Needham*'s destination was Philadelphia, Smith's advertisement of 1773 had stated that the passage from thence to New York was only 4s. 8d.[3]

[1] Reid, *Pres. ch. Ire.*, iii. 343-9; Witherow, *Presbyterian memorials*, ii. 85-98. Purcell, 'Irish contribution to colonial N.Y.', in *Studies* (1941), xxx. 110; MacLean, *Highland settlements in Amer.*, pp. 47-8. Witherow states that the emigrants sailed on May 10. If they did so, they probably crossed on the *John*, Vandervort's vessel, as it was advertised to leave on May 1 and the only other emigrant vessel of the year from Newry, the *Newry*, did not advertise till Aug. 10.

[2] *B.N.L.*, 26 Mar. 1773; O'Brien, *Washington's Irish assoc.*, p. 234. Newspaper reports of the number of passengers carried by the *Needham* vary: *B.N.L.*, 21 May 1773—'near 500'; ibid., 14 Sept. 1773—'500 passengers'; ibid., 18 Mar. 1774—'upwards of 400'; *C.E.P.*, 23 Sept. 1773—a letter of thanks to Cheevers for treatment during voyage, signed by 509 men and women.

[3] *B.N.L.*, 18 Mar. and 27 Sept. 1774.

Only one other attempt to secure tenants in the north of Ireland for American lands in the period under consideration remains to be mentioned. Lands to be leased in West Florida were advertised in 1773 by 'Moses Park and Company'.[1] Moses Park's name had never before appeared in Ireland as an emigration agent but the 'Company' may have included no less a person than Thomas Desbrisay, for a claim by Park, Desbrisay and Peter Fowler for a grant of land in West Florida was considered by the privy council in 1770,[2] though privy council records do not show whether the claim was successful. Desbrisay's stock was not too high in Ireland in 1773 and so the omission of his name from Park's advertisement does not prove that he was not interested in this attempt to secure settlers for West Florida. The terms offered by Park were unattractive: not only had the passage money of four pounds to be paid by servant and tenant alike but rents commenced in the second year and rose to 2s. 6d. per acre after five years, the highest rents at which American lands had so far been advertised. It would have taken much more persuasive terms than these to induce emigrants to settle in a little known region where, to their minds, popery and the inquisition had been entrenched till a short time before. Agents were appointed in Dublin, Newry, Antrim, Ballymoney, Richhill and Tandragee, but no further advertisements appeared in the *Belfast News Letter* on behalf of the enterprise. The departure of the first vessel to sail from the north of Ireland to Florida[3] would have been an event of some importance, but no reference to such a sailing appeared in the Belfast, Londonderry or Dublin newspapers of 1773. The meagre immigration into Florida during the period of British rule[4] probably included very few, if any, settlers direct from the north of Ireland.

VII: CONCLUSION

The most noticeable feature about these land promotion schemes was their failure to secure emigrants in proportion to the amount

---

[1] Ibid., 19 Mar. 1773. Conditions for settlement in West Florida were the same as in East Florida—immigrants were to be 'foreign protestants or persons that shall be brought from his Majesty's other colonies in America' (*Cal. acts privy council (col.)*, v.589, 593).

[2] *Cal. acts privy council (col.)*, v.594.

[3] Farnam, *Social legislation in U.S.*, p. 111.

[4] The arrival of 200 settlers from Ireland at Pensacola in Florida was noted, however, in 1766 (*N.Y. Gazette*, 3 Mar. 1766, in O'Brien, *Hidden phrase*, p. 302).

of effort and publicity that backed them. The total number of settlers attracted could be counted in hundreds rather than in thousands and was possibly fewer than the number which left Londonderry for Philadelphia on a single day in 1773,[1] though the latter were secured by much less effort.

Despite various promises of a cheap passage, the friendship of established settlers and the use of livestock, none of these schemes had anything to offer to those who had not the means to subsist for at least a year and the capital to purchase seeds and implements. This expense was made all the more prohibitive by the fact that a greater proportion of settlers brought their families with them than did those who emigrated as servants.[2]

The majority of even this more fortunate class ignored the pleas and temptings of the land promoters. Most emigrants preferred to go to those parts of America where their kith and kin were already settled. Most of the land promoters realised this and stressed, where possible, the presence and success of Scotch-Irish settlers on or near the advertised lands. But even this could not break the preference for, say, South Carolina to which thousands had been attracted from the north of Ireland in the 1760s by the bounty and the prospect of lands as cheap as any in North America. It is significant that the advertisements of Matthew and John Rea always stated the distance of the Queensborough settlement in Georgia from Charleston but seldom mentioned its distance from Savannah even when a vessel was chartered to sail to the latter port.[3]

The promotion of lands in colonies such as Quebec and Florida could have made little progress against this prejudice; but sustained efforts such as those of McNutt and Desbrisay on behalf of less outlandish places might have attracted progressively increasing numbers of settlers as Nova Scotia and St John became more and more familiar places to prospective emigrants. The unfortunate voyage of the *John and James* and the despair of her passengers when they saw their bleak destination ended Desbrisay's chances of success in the north of Ireland, for no land promoter could prosper after such a misfortune. The elements had, however, only anticipated the voice of authority, a voice which had already shattered

[1] The *Alexander, Hannah, Wallworth* and *Jupiter* sailed on 7 June 1773 with about 2,000 emigrants on board (Appendix C).
[2] Selkirk, *Highland emig.* p. 57.
[3] E.g., *B.N.L.*, 10 June 1768 and 25 July 1769.

McNutt's hopes. The latter's ambitions were too great to be fulfilled, but he did succeed in the difficult task of sending to Nova
Scotia the first settlers who went to that province direct from
Ireland. It is rather unfortunate that the government put a stop to
McNutt's Irish schemes for these were the most strongly pressed
of all attempts at land promotion there before the American
revolution. Had his activities remained unhindered it would have
been possible to see more clearly whether or not the obstacles
which faced the land promoters could have been overcome by
energy and persistence.

The failure of colonising schemes was not peculiar to the
eighteenth century, for the same fate awaited similar undertakings
in the century that followed. In the latter period, failure was due
not so much to lack of numbers but to inability to secure the right
type of settler. Increasing poverty, a deepening knowledge of the
colonies and assistance by home and colonial governments and
private charities provided the incentive and often the means to
emigrate. The failure, as colonists, of the broken-spirited and
poverty stricken people that these schemes attracted was sealed
by the provision of either too much or too little outside help.[1]
Philanthropic colonisers and assisted emigration, except for inter-
mittent bounties, were phenomena unknown in Ireland in the
eighteenth century. This partly accounted for the smallness of the
number of people who responded to the call of the land promoter
but it also contributed to the success of most of the settlements that
were established, for the emigrants could not have gone had they
been poverty stricken and would not have gone had their spirits
been broken.[2]

---

[1] S. C. Johnson, *History of emigration from the United Kingdom to North America, 1763–1912*, pp. 250–4.
[2] Eaton, 'Settling of Colchester county', in *Proc. and Trans. Roy. Soc. Can.*, vi. 234; McCrady, *S.C. under royal govt.*, ii. 132–5; *Hist. account of S.C.*, ii. 63–4. See also the works of the Irish and Scotch-Irish historians, particularly W. F. Dunaway, *The Scotch-Irish of colonial Pennsylvania*.

CHAPTER IX

The Official Attitude to Emigration

THE days when Peel was to advocate emigration as a remedy for Irish misery were still hidden in the mists of the future, separated from the eighteenth century by the industrial revolution, Malthusian theories and a new concept of empire.

Except in a few special cases, authority was hostile to emigration prior to the revolt of the American colonies. For one thing, it believed that 'the increase of people is a means of advancing the wealth and strength of a nation'[1] and so it followed that any reduction in population must inevitably lead to loss of power and influence. Thus foreign immigration into the American colonies was encouraged and sometimes subsidised[2] but convicts were the only British subjects deemed sufficiently unworthy to be spared from the homeland. This attitude was not, of course, peculiar to Britain, and practically every European country—including the Swiss cantons[3]—enacted anti-emigration laws. Again, the Government viewed colonies with a purely mercantilist eye. When Hillsborough was in charge of colonial affairs he named as the principal advantages to be derived from America 'the proper encouragement of the fishery, the production of naval stores, and the supply of the Sugar Islands with lumber and provisions'. As such advantages could be obtained from coastal settlements which 'could be kept

---

[1] Preamble of 7 Anne c. 5 (Eng.).
[2] For example, Thos, Lowndes, provost-marshal, etc. of S.C. to—, 25 Sept. 1728 (C.O. 5/360, ff 167–8); Pownall to 'Messrs Ditts, Damasle and comrades', 24 July 1764 (C.O. 218/6, 460).
[3] Adams, *Provincial society*, p. 173.

in subjection to the home government', he concluded that nothing was to be obtained from settlements in the interior. This partiality for maritime colonies was strengthened by the removal of the French danger from the American mainland and the rising spirit of unrest in the colonies there, but it was natural at all times to a country with strong mercantilist views and a powerful navy. Thus, on the few occasions in the eighteenth century when the government specifically approved of emigration from the British Isles, the regions involved were on the northern and southern flanks of the north American possessions, territories which were vital to the defence of the entire eastern seaboard.[1] Even in such cases, approval rarely amounted to little more than a recognition of the existence of emigration, a recognition that was both lukewarm and uncertain—lukewarm because expediency led to no real reformation of opinion and uncertain because the factors that led to the compromise with expediency were themselves uncertain.

The official attitude to emigration was hostile, but few steps were taken to curb the westward traffic. Opposition was latent rather than obvious and required the over-enthusiasm of a land promoter or the persistent proddings of an unusually zealous official to rouse it to the stage of articulation. Even when it was roused, feeling subsided as soon as the crisis passed and none of the few long-term prohibitive measures which were considered got beyond the proposal stage. Very limited action was occasionally taken to end the activities of land speculators such as Desbrisay and McNutt, but such action left the bulk of the emigration trade untouched, concerned few parts of the American continent and was soon forgotten by the government and ignored by the trade.

Being at the wrong end of the mercantilist stick, the Irish government was little concerned with theories of trade and population and condemned north Irish emigration on two strictly practical grounds. First, it weakened the protestant element, the loyal element, of the population. Second, heavy emigration would lead to lower rents by reducing competition for land. To some degree, these views were shared by the British government with memories of a bloody Ireland in the Bloodless Revolution, and with the promptings of the absentees in its ear. The effect of emigration uppermost in the minds of both the London and Dublin

[1] W. B. Stevens, *A history of Georgia from its first discovery*, i. 276; Haliburton, *Account of N.S.*, pp. 137–42.

governments during the first half of the eighteenth century was the weakening of the protestant minority in Ireland. As the ascendancy of that minority became more firmly established and as fears of the Stuarts faded, religious disquiet gave way to fears of declining trade and falling rents. It would be wrong to suggest, however, that such fears were consistently pressing: it will be seen, for example, that the demand for curbing emigration in the early 'seventies came from Scotland, not from Ireland. In brief, despite the disagreeable effects of the emigration trade on Irish life, Dublin's active interest in the trade was as transitory as that of London.

A twofold cause underlies this apparent indifference. With the death of Boulter, Ireland lacked a man who possessed his stature of mind, his influence with the English government[1] and his conviction that emigration was an evil which proper treatment could check. Moreover, Boulter's successors could not but remember the failure of the attempt with which he had been associated to persuade the English authorities to permit the introduction in the Irish parliament of legislation to prohibit emigration. That failure, together with the fact that emigration was becoming more and more common with the passing of the years, would have discouraged most people from fighting the inevitable.

In 1718, before Boulter's translation to Ireland, the lords justices had reported to the duke of Bolton, the lord lieutenant, that many people 'well affected to his Majestie's person and Government' were emigrating, but had confessed their failure to find any remedy.[2] Emigration had so increased ten years later that this resigned attitude had to give way to positive action. Carteret, the lord lieutenant, suggested in 1728 that the aid of presbyterian ministers should be sought to dissuade their people from emigrating.[3] The call for intervention on the part of the presbyterian ministers may have had some effect as emigration was not in the interests of presbyterianism, but it also had the unwelcome effect—unwelcome, that is, to the Irish bishops, though not to the English officials in Ireland—of giving the presbyterians a chance to air their

---

[1] J. L. McCracken, *The undertakers in Ireland and their relations with the lords lieutenant, 1724–1771*, p. 54.
[2] Latimer, 'Ulster emigration to America', in *R.S.A.I. Jn.*, series 5, xii. 387. The lords justices were the duke of Grafton and the earl of Galway.
[3] Ibid., p. 388.

views on the test act to a sympathetic government in London. Quite apart from this, it was soon seen that more direct methods were necessary to produce an appreciable result, so the lords justices instructed the law officers of Ireland to consider 'what laws are in force for preventing the subjects of this Kingdom from Transporting themselves, and carrying away their Money and Effects abroad, and to Report . . . what Method is to be taken upon the said Laws, or in any other legal maner to prevent the same'.[1] The law officers reported that the emigration of all save 'the Lords and other great men of the Realm and true and notable Merchants, and the King's Soldiers' was already prohibited under an act of the reign of Richard II.[2] By this act, any person, other than the classes named, who left the realm or who carried gold or silver abroad forfeited all his goods and the warders and searchers of the ports were to forfeit their offices and suffer imprisonment for a year if they permitted anything to be done contrary to the act. The law officers were therefore of the opinion that a proclamation forbidding emigration without a licence could be issued, a proclamation that would be enforced by the port officials. At the same time as these proposals were made, pressure was exerted on the lords justices by the landowning class who presented a memorial stressing the probable evil consequences of emigration on the protestant interest in Ireland. The lords justices sent Carteret this memorial together with their own proposal that proclamations should be issued prohibiting the exportation of corn, the carrying of bullion or money out of the country, and emigration.[3]

At least one of the lords justices was unenthusiastic about the proposed prohibition of emigration. Boulter had little respect for the conduct of the landlords in the matter and, on the day on which the lords justices made their recommendations to Carteret, wrote of his doubts of the wisdom of employing extreme measures.[4] Boulter was more deeply and more honestly concerned with the effects of emigration on the protestant interest in Ireland than were

[1] Report, law officers of Ire. to lords justices, 2 Nov. 1728 (P.C. 1/48). The lords justices were Abp. Boulter, Thos. Wyndham (lord chancellor), and Wm. Connolly (speaker); the law officers were Henry Singleton (prime sergeant at law), Thos. Marley (attorney general) and Robt. Jocelyn (solicitor general).
[2] Richard II, c.2 (Eng.). Thanks to Poynings' Law, this this act was binding in Ireland. Special permission to emigrate was contained in the charters of the early English companies in America (Proper, *Immigration laws*, p. 73).
[3] P.C. 2/90, p. 401; P.C. 1/48, 23 Nov. 1728; Klett, *Pres. in Pa.*, p. 21.
[4] To Newcastle, 23 Nov. 1728 (*Boulter letters*, i. 209–11).

most of the landlords whose lip service to religious anxieties hid other and less worthy motives. Compassion moved him to plead the cruelty of forcing people to remain in a country where neither work nor food was to be obtained,[1] so anticipating by three-quarters of a century the spirit of the earl of Selkirk's belief that restrictions on emigration entailed obligations to those retained in the homeland against their wishes.[2] Boulter did not disassociate himself from the proposals to which he, as a lord justice, had subscribed but he liked the remedy little better than he liked the disease. Failing the co-operation of the landowners, he looked for a solution to the mercy of the God of the harvest rather than to the vigilance of the customs officials of the ports.[3]

Boulter had the ear of both Walpole and Newcastle and his doubts did not go unheeded. The committee of the privy council to which the recommendations of the lords justices were referred approved of an embargo on the exportation of corn but it added that it was not sufficiently informed of the circumstances of Irish emigration to express an opinion on the advisability of prohibiting either emigration or the carrying of bullion or money out of the country.[4] This reluctance to approve of extreme measures against emigration in general remained the policy of the London authorities for half a century.

The measures proposed by the Irish authorities had been intended to provide an effective weapon to combat an expected heavy emigration in 1729, and, as the harvest of 1728 was a poor one, the lords justices soon renewed their appeal to London for adequate powers and backed their appeal with detailed information about the problem. They asked that the granting of lands in America to Irish immigrants should be forbidden unless those immigrants produced licences permitting their removal from Ireland, thus seeking to invoke the law of Richard II having failed in their attempt to secure a proclamation prohibiting emigration. This proposal may have been one of the various proposals and

---

1 To same, 13 Mar. 1728/9 (ibid., i.229–31). A fine tribute was paid to Boulter as a landlord and a friend of the poor in a Dublin newspaper in 1729 (*Dublin Weekly Journal*, June 7).
2 *Highland emigration*, pp. 88–99, 110.
3 Boulter to Newcastle, 23 Nov. 1728 (*Boulter letters*, i. 209–11); same to same, 13 Mar. 1728/9 (ibid., i.229–31); same to Walpole, 31 Mar. 1729 (ibid., i.236–7); same to Carteret, 11 June 1729 (P.R.O.N.I., T.659, p. 73).
4 P.C. 2/90, p. 409 (11 Dec. 1728).

reports regarding Irish affairs which were considered by the privy council in July, 1729, but, if so, it received scant attention as the council acknowledged that the existing laws in Ireland were not sufficient to put a stop to emigration but recommended merely that no action should be taken by the English authorities till after the Irish parliament had met, when, it was anticipated, effective laws would be passed.[1]

The delay in the consideration of letters and petitions that had been received over a period of more than three months indicates a reluctance on the part of the English authorities to approve effective anti-emigration measures. Newcastle's personal attention had been privately called to the seriousness of the effects of emigration and to the proposed measures to check it.[2] But, though a legal check that could be applied at any time would have suited the Irish landlords, the English government's concern was the immediate problem and, as in all matters, it had no desire to take steps which were not absolutely necessary, which would cause alarm or which might soon be unnecessary. The biennial meeting of the Irish parliament was in the offing and by the time it met the harvest prospects of 1729 would be known and appropriate legislation in the light of that knowledge could then be adopted in Ireland. Thanks to the political restraints on Ireland, such measures would be sent to England for the sanction of the English government. Thus both Dublin and London were given time for second thoughts and any necessary action could be based on parliamentary statute rather than on proclamations and broad powers derived from ancient laws.

The Irish government decided to act; but, knowing that a strong general measure stood little chance of approval, the proposed bill —*an act to prevent persons from clandestinely transporting themselves to America in order to defraud their creditors*—was, ostensibly, merely intended to check an evil which it was the duty of any government

---

[1] Lords justices to Carteret, 23 Nov. 1728. (P.C. 2/90, p. 401; P.C. 1/48); and 26 Mar. 1729 (P.C.2/90,p. 458); Boulter to Newcastle,13 Mar. 1728/9(*Boulter letters*, i.229–31); P.C. 2/91, p. 22 (2 July 1729). The communications considered by the privy council were: letter, lords justices to Carteret, recvd. 29 Mar. 1729; letter, lords justices to Carteret, 11 June 1729; letter, Carteret to lords justices, 26 June 1729; report, St. Leger and Ward to lords justices, n.d.; report, dissenting ministers to lords justices, n.d.

[2] Philip Yorke, 1st Earl of Hardwicke, to Newcastle, 14 Apr. 1729 (P.R.O.N.I., T.659, p. 70).

to check. The privy council committee which considered the bill summarised its provisions as follows:

> That after the 1st day of May 1730, no Person or Persons who have been Inhabitants of Ireland for Seven Years shall Transport themselves or be taken or suffered to go on board any Ship to America (Except only the Crew of such Ship, the Merchants or their Super Cargoes) without a Licence under the hand of the Collector or Chief Officer of the Port from whence the Ship should Depart. That such Licence shall be granted to such Persons only who shall produce a Certificate under the Hands and Seals of two Justices of the Peace of the County where they have resided, that they are Persons of full Age or have the leave of their Parents or Masters to remove out of the Kingdom and they are not Indebted to any one to the Knowledge and belief of such Justices.
>
> That no Justice shall give any such Certificate unless the Party shall appear at some Generall Quarter Sessions of the Peace in the County where they reside at least two Months before their intended Embarkation and shall by Petition to the Bench desire such Licence and sett forth the Place to which they intend to Transport themselves and the Port where they intend to Embark.
>
> That the Clerk of the Peace at such Sessions is to Post on the Door or some publick Place in the Court House, and likewise to send to the Collector or Chief Officer of the Port where such Persons intend to Embark a List of their Names additions and Places of abode, and if any two Justices of any County shall Certify to the Collector of the Port where such Persons intend to embark that it has appeared to them upon Oath that such Persons are under the age of twenty one Years or are apprentices and have not the Consent of their Parents or Masters or that such Persons are in Debt, or in case such oath be made before the Collector or Chief Officer then the said Collector or Chief Officer is to refuse a Licence and prevent such Persons from being Transported.
>
> But no Persons are to be prevented from Transporting themselves who shall obtain a Licence from the Secretary of the Chief Governors of Ireland.[1]

The purpose of the bill was obvious in spite of its title and it would have imposed a legal stranglehold on emigration had it become law, as the administration of the act would have been principally in the hands of the magistrates who, being landowners, were opposed to emigration. A wilfully biased enforcement of

[1] P.C. 2/91, p. 153 (2 Feb. 1729/30) and 193 (12 Mar. 1729/30).

the prohibition of the emigration of minors would not only have secured the co-operation of many parents but would have stopped the emigration of thousands of people of full age who were not debtors for, even where presbyterian baptismal records existed, they were of questionable legality. The holders of unexpired leases would also have been caught in the net because, by leaving their lands, they were guilty of a breach of contract and were debtors in law. Till now, a comparatively unheralded departure and a freedom of movement had enabled them to emigrate, despite their leases, but the end of such secrecy and freedom appeared to be in sight. The emigration of those who had not transgressed any law and could prove that they were of full age could be delayed or even prevented by deliberate delays in the issue of licences until a certain vessel—or all the season's emigrant vessels—had left a particular port. Of no less importance was the fact that the measure could be used to prevent impetuous emigration, for a person's mind may change if he has to wait at least two months between making and carrying out a decision. It is true of many people that real doubts assail when a decision has been taken. During the waiting period, ties of home and of friendships, ties which emigration would sever, would appear more dear and grow even more powerful. Reflection would deepen the determination of many but it would certainly turn many others from leaving what they had grown to value during two months as they had never done before. In brief, the purpose of the bill was to force people to secure elusive certificates before they could emigrate rather than to deny certificates to debtors.

The powers which the bill proposed to give justices of the peace shocked the examining committee of the privy council. The bill's real purpose was apparent and the privy council considered and condemned it on its merits as a measure to control emigration in general rather than as an attempt to stop the emigration of debtors. The 'unreasonable restraint' on the king's subjects and the 'absolute authority' the measure proposed to grant justices were censured, but the chief reason for the rejection of the bill was that Irish emigration was on the wane. The good harvest that Boulter had prayed for and in anticipation of which the privy council had delayed action early in 1729 had arrived, bringing with it cheap food. It was principally because of the decline in the volume of emigration that the rejection of the bill 'of this extraordinary nature' was proposed by the committee. The recommendation was accepted by the privy council and the bill was not returned to Ireland.[1]

So ended the first and only attempt of the Irish authorities to secure the sanction of the British government for measures to place legal obstacles in the emigrant's path. Distrust of extremes and distaste of any form of interference in any aspect of life underlay London's hesitation in taking action. Much more to official liking than the prohibition—either direct or indirect—of emigration would have been the removal of as many as possible of its causes and it was no coincidence that pressure from London on the Irish government to give satisfaction to the presbyterians in the matter of the test act now increased.[2]

Despair of English approval of prohibitory legislation forced the Irish parliament and gentry to make the best possible use of laws already on the statute book. Disappointment and better harvests led to little attention being paid to emigration for a time after 1729 but the ill-treatment of emigrants on board the vessel *George*, bound from Dublin to North Carolina, focused attention on the trade once more in 1735 and 1736 and the parliamentary committee which examined the affair took full advantage of it to paint a garish picture of the emigration trade. The committee's report broadened illogically into an attack on emigration and its promoters who were described as the enemies of both the government and the Irish protestant interest. Significantly, the report looked to the zeal of magistrates and justices and not to new laws for the prevention and suppression of the trade and the punishment of its sponsors.[3]

This advice did not go unheeded for, within a few weeks, landowners in the Belfast area decided to test the effectiveness of existing laws in the checking of emigration. According to John Stewart, a Dublin sea captain, the owners and masters of vessels that advertised for emigrants to sail from Belfast to America, together with the printers of the advertisements—presumably hand-bills—were arrested. They were given the choice of being

[1] Ibid., p. 193 (12 Mar. 1729/30) and 209 (16 Mar. 1729/30).
[2] Walpole to the duke of Dorset, lord lieutenant, 30 Dec. 1731 (*Stopford—Sackville MSS*, i.147); Beckett, *Prot. dissent in Ire.*, pp. 90–2.
[3] *Commons' jn. Ire.*, vi. 631–7 (3 Mar. 1735/6).

remanded in 'loathsome gaols' or on bonds of £1,000 to appear at the Carrickfergus assizes. However, they were discharged by the assize judge despite the opposition of the local magistrates.[1]

The only account of this episode gives no details of the court proceedings but evidence from another source is available of what Stewart went on to describe as 'a yet more hellish contrivance' on the part of the landlords to stop emigration from Belfast. With the acquittal of the ship-masters at Carrickfergus, the vessels at Belfast made ready to sail with between 1,700 and 1,800 emigrants, but clearance papers were refused by George Macartney, the collector of the port of Belfast. Macartney justified his action on one of the statutes forbidding the export of wool from Ireland, the wool in this case being the blankets provided for the emigrants. This unexpected move threatened serious loss to the shipowners. The Carrickfergus proceedings had already cost them both time and money and, at the time of Stewart's writing to Penn, Macartney had detained the vessels for a further period of almost three weeks. The two incidents reduced the ship masters to a state of supplication. Explaining that they were strangers to Ireland and so had not been aware of the feeling against the emigration trade, they petitioned that they should be allowed to proceed to America. They undertook to ensure that their passengers included no apprentices, servants, minors or debtors or other fugitives from justice. They also undertook to supply Macartney with accurate lists of all passengers and agreed to cancel their engagements with any emigrants whom Macartney or any justice believed to belong to one of the above categories. Finally, they promised that they would never again be concerned in the emigration trade except with the consent of the lord lieutenant and parliament of Ireland. No record has been found to show how the affair ended but the interests opposed to emigration won a partial victory as the experiences of the ship masters were not such as would have induced them or others to remain in or join the Irish emigration trade.[2]

The landlords, defeated at Carrickfergus, were behind Macart-

[1] To Wm. Penn, proprietor of Pa., [April] 1736 (Myers, *Quaker emig.*, pp. 90–2; Ford, *Scotch-Irish in Amer.*, pp. 196–8). Stewart regarded the terms *landlords* and *justices* as synonymous.

[2] Myers, *Quaker emig.*, pp. 90–2; Ford, *Scotch-Irish in Amer.*, pp. 196–8; 10 Wm. III, c.5 (Ire.); petition, nine shipmasters (named) to Macartney, 19 Apr. 1736 (P.R.O.N.I., Mussenden papers, T.649/4.).

ney's action. The commissioners of the Irish customs issued no instructions to him concerning emigration, either in general or specific terms nor did Macartney report his action to them.[1] Indeed, the Irish customs commissioners had issued instructions a few years before for the immediate release of the *Sally*, an emigrant vessel sailing from Larne, which had been detained on the charge of having wool on board. The only wool that the commissioners had considered should not be exported in that case was a roll of seventy-four yards seized from a passenger before he boarded the vessel. No reference was made to blankets.[2] The nine masters whose vessels Macartney detained may have been, as they claimed, strangers to Ireland but even they recognised the figures behind Macartney. Their petition explained that they had been 'ignorant that the gentlemen of this kingdom were offended at such trade' and they concluded by hoping that their proposals 'will give satisfaction to the gentlemen of this kingdom', no mention being made of any desired effect on Macartney's superiors, the customs commissioners.[3]

At this point the attempts of the Irish government and landlords to curb emigration ended abruptly and were not renewed until 1773. However, events elsewhere resulted in a change in London's attitude to emigration. The government there had not been in favour of the earlier emigration from Ireland, but while France remained a power in America such emigration was not entirely disadvantageous. The defeat of France and growing unrest in the British colonies inevitably influenced the attitude of London to further emigration.

Alexander McNutt was the first to feel the effects of the resulting reorientation of policy. Considering Whitehall's interest in the settlement of Nova Scotia and his own whole-hearted attempts to recruit settlers for the province in 1761, McNutt anticipated nothing but praise and commendation for his plan to transport 7,000 Irish emigrants to the province in 1762.[4] Praise he did get for the 'able and faithful manner' in which he had carried out all he had hitherto undertaken to do, but, while agreeing that the settlement of Nova Scotia was very desirable, the board of trade

---

[1] See Minutes, Irish customs commissioners, March–May, 1736 (Customs 1/27, pp. 418–99).
[2] Customs 1/23, p. 128 (6 July 1731).
[3] P.R.O.N.I., Mussenden papers, T.649/4.
[4] See Chapter VIII (iii).

expressed alarm at the prospect of the emigration of 'such great numbers of the most loyal and useful subjects' of Ireland. Nevertheless, because of the expense to which McNutt was already committed, his failure to excite much interest in Ireland in 1761, and the probability that if McNutt's plan were vetoed his prospective followers would emigrate elsewhere, the board of trade recommended that he should be allowed to honour his existing obligations.[1] This recommendation was rejected by the privy council who decided that

> However desirable an object the settling of Nova Scotia may be, yet the migration from Ireland of such great numbers of his majesty's subjects must be attended with dangerous consequences to that kingdom, [so we] do therefore order that the said Lord Commissioners for Trade and Plantations do prepare a draught of an instruction for his majesty's governor in Nova Scotia requiring him not to grant lands to or permit any of his majesty's subjects from Ireland to become settlers in that province except such as have been resident in Nova Scotia or some part of his majesty's colonies in America for the space of five years.[2]

This decision was indicative of an attitude of mind rather than notable as the deliberate launching of a new colonial policy or the beginning of a new drive against emigration. Indeed, even in the narrower field, it would appear that no instruction was issued— certainly not in 1762—prohibiting land grants in Nova Scotia to Irish immigrants. When governor Belcher refused to grant lands to the Irish who landed in 1762 he did so on the grounds that the grants of 1761 to McNutt had never been confirmed and not for the more positive reason that grants to Irish immigrants had been expressly forbidden by the London authorities.[3] Three years later, when conditions for the granting of land in Nova Scotia were sent to the governor, no reference was made to the disqualification of Irish immigrants.[4] Consideration of the huge reservations made for McNutt and various associates in 1765 recalled McNutt's previous exploits in the north of Ireland where, the board of trade noted, the ill-effects of emigration had been severely felt. It was

[1] Representation, B.T. to P.C., 8 Apr. 1762 (C.O. 218/6, ff. 153–60, and P.C. 1/50).
[2] P.C. to B.T., 29 Apr. 1762 (C.O. 217/18, no. L87).
[3] B.T. to P.C., 21 Jan. 1763 (C.O. 218/6, ff. 188–90); B.T. to Ellis, 27 Apr. 1763 (C.O. 218/6, f. 202); Franklin to B.T., 2 Sept. 1766 (C.O. 217/21, no. N108).
[4] C.O. 218/6, ff. 422–6 (5 June 1764).

therefore recommended that immigration into Nova Scotia should be confined to protestants from continental Europe and from the continental colonies.[1] For a time, this second suggested prohibition seemed destined to follow its predecessor into oblivion. A blank page and a half appear after a marginal reference purporting to be the title of an order in council approving the board of trade's report,[2] and a vessel, the *Hopewell*, carried emigrants from Londonderry to Halifax in 1767.[3] The recommendation of the board of trade was then enforced and Lord William Campbell, governor of Nova Scotia, protested that the exclusion of immigrants from England and Ireland was hindering the settlement of the colony.[4] No vessel was advertised to sail from a north Irish port to Nova Scotia between 1768 and 1772 but British immigrants poured into the colony in the 'seventies in greater numbers than ever before.[5]

Something similar happened at the extreme south of the British American colonies. Prior to 1767, land in East and West Florida could be granted to 'protestant white inhabitants , but in that year grants were restricted to 'foreign protestants or person that shall be brought from his majesty's other colonies in America'.[6] This did not deter Moses Park from advertising in the north of Ireland for settlers for lands in West Florida.[7] It is irrelevant that few—if, indeed, any—responded to his appeal, for it was preference for the better-known colonies and not land laws that worked against the settlement of the Floridas during the period of British rule.

The government's uneasiness over emigration, its readiness to strike at it and its desire to limit that intervention to particular instances or to the insertion of restrictive clauses in land grants may be illustrated by two outstanding cases in the 'seventies. In 1771, two natives of the island of Skye petitioned for a grant of 40,000 acres of land in North Carolina, naïvely stating that they had engaged servants to go there. The board of trade was naturally even less sympathetic than it would have been had the petition referred to Nova Scotia and commented that the plan, 'instead of meriting the encouragement, ought rather to receive the dis-

[1] P.C. 2/111, pp. 647–50 (5 June 1766).
[2] Ibid., pp. 673–4 (17 June 1766).
[3] *B.N.L.*, 30 June 1767.
[4] C.O. 217/22, no. O.45 (8 April 1768).
[5] Treasury 47/9–12 *passim*.
[6] *Acts privy council (col.)*, v. 589, 593.
[7] *B.N.L.*, 19 Mar. 1773.

countenance of government'. This judgment was based on the opinion that 'the emigration of inhabitants of Great Britain and Ireland to the American colonies is a circumstance which . . . cannot fail to lessen the strength and security and to prejudice the landed interest and manufactures of these kingdoms and the great extent to which this emigration hath of late years prevailed renders it an object well deserving of the serious attention of the government'. The board of trade reminded the privy council that, because of this consideration, one of the conditions which had been inserted in land grants in recent years was the limitation of settlement to foreign or American protestants and recommended, therefore, that the petition should be dismissed. The privy council acted accordingly.[1]

Two years later, the attention of London was again drawn to the ill-effects of emigration and this time the complaint concerned a man who was well known in Ireland. In October 1773, Thomas Miller, the lord justice clerk of Scotland, drew the attention of the earl of Suffolk, secretary for the southern department, to the activities of Thomas Desbrisay in Ayrshire and enclosed with his letter one of Desbrisay's advertisements which referred to his Irish as well as his Scottish quest for emigrants.[2] Within a few days of the receipt of this letter, Desbrisay was reminded that he had already been warned by Pownall that emigration from Great Britain and Ireland was regarded with ill-favour by the authorities. He had chosen to ignore that informal warning and so the government's attitude was made clear to him in the most unambiguous terms. He was told that advertisements had been published

> from which it appears that you have not only held out encouragements to emigration, as proprietor of lands in the Island of St John, but that you have unwarrantably presumed to recite in the preamble of those advertisements, the offices which you hold under the King's Royal Commission, evidently with the design to give the greatest colour of authority to your proposals.
>
> I am commanded, therefore, by the Earl of Dartmouth, to acquaint you that all such publications must be immediately suppressed, and that, if it shall appear that any of the King's subjects in Great Britain or Ireland shall have emigrated from these kingdoms in consequence

[1] C.O. 391/78, ff. 172, 177 (20 and 21 June 1771); P.C. 2/115, p. 276, and P.C. 2/116, pp. 298, 319.
[2] S.P. 54/46, no. 89a, b (27 Oct. 1773).

of any encouragement you may have offered, you must expect to receive the strongest marks of His Majesty's displeasure.[1]

There was some justice in Desbrisay's complaint, in reply to this letter, that it was hard that only he should be debarred from organising emigration from the British Isles to America.[2] Other proprietors had brought settlers from Scotland to St John's Island during the years when Desbrisay was active but the government had not even expressed its displeasure even though it had been informed of what was going on. For example, Captain John MacDonald of Glenade had organised the emigration of three hundred highlanders to St John's Island in the previous year and yet he had not been censured despite the fact that not only had he done what Desbrisay was trying to do but had broken a second land-grant condition in that all his settlers were Roman catholics.[3] The uncertainty of the government's reaction to emigration is shown by the fact that the only apparent reason in these cases for the difference between silence and rebuke was that Desbrisay's activities were presented as a disservice to Scotland and Ireland while MacDonald's activities were commended by the colonial authorities as of benefit to St John's Island.

However, there were already signs that a more consistent policy was in the offing. The board of trade felt in 1772 that emigration was 'an object well deserving of the serious attention of Government'.[4] Such attention followed Miller's report on Desbrisay in 1773. Suffolk sent Miller's views to the earl of Dartmouth, the secretary of the colonial department, and in his covering letter indicated that he felt that the time had come to take effective measures against emigration. 'Every check', he wrote, 'within the power of government, should be given to plans which tend, so fatally, to depopulate a considerable part of [the king's] dominions.'[5] The qualifying phrase, 'within the power of government' and the reference of the correspondence to Dartmouth indicate that the checks contemplated by the government concerned the discouragement of settlement in America rather than the direct prohibition of emigration from the British Isles.

[1] C.O. 226/5, ff. 69–71 (9 Nov. 1773).
[2] To Pownall, 22 Nov. 1773 (ibid., ff. 147–9).
[3] Warburton, *History of P.E.I.*, pp. 168–9; Campbell, *History of P.E.I.*, p. 23.
[4] Report, B.T. to P.C., considered 19 June 1772 (P.C. 2/116, p. 298).
[5] C.O. 5/138, pt. 2, f. 741 (4 Nov. 1773).

Desbrisay's efforts violated the terms of the St John's Island grants so their termination was obviously 'within the power of government' and Desbrisay was the first to feel the edge of the new policy. But the government had embarked on a more thorough project than the mere plugging of holes. Comprehensive measures were envisaged and so it was necessary to obtain an accurate view of the extent and nature of emigration. To obtain this, the customs commissioners were instructed to

> give Instructions to the several officers of the Customs within your department, to order the respective Officers in each port under them, to use every proper means in their power to obtain an account of all persons who shall take their passage on Board any ship or vessel, to go out of this Kingdom with a description of their Age, Quality, Occupation, Employment or former Residence and an Account of what port or place they propose to go, And on what Account, and for what purposes they leave this Country together with such other remarks and information as they may be able to obtain therein. And that you order such officers to make a weekly return thereof to your Board . . . .[1]

At least one periodical believed these instructions to be the prelude to parliamentary action in 1774.[2] A letter from the collectors at Wigtown suggests that they had received at about the same time some indication of the revival of the statute prohibiting the exportation of coin, 'excepting with his Majesty's special licence, and what is reasonable for personal charges to the person going forth of the kingdom'.[3] An examination of treasury records has not revealed that such a revival was devised in London and many instances of emigrants carrying off large sums of money were noted in 1774.[4]

Weekly returns were submitted by the collectors in London and

---

[1] John Robinson, secretary to the treasury, to the commissioners of the customs, 9 Dec. 1773 (Treasury 11/30, p. 450).
[2] *Scots magazine* (Dec. 1773), xxxv. 667.
[3] J. McCulloch and Wm. McConnel to 'Hon. sirs', 6 Jan. 1774 (Treasury 1/500, 2nd enclosure). Guidance as to what was a 'reasonable' sum that could be carried out of the country was sought.
[4] One emigrant on board the *Prince George*, bound from Yorkshire to Nova Scotia in 1774, found solace in the company of his thirteen children and £2,200 in cash (*Scots Magazine* (Apr. 1774), xxxvi. 217).

the out-ports during the following eighteen months[1] but no sweeping measure against emigration followed. Suffolk and Miller, the men mainly responsible for the investigation, expressed surprised pleasure when the customs returns showed that emigration was on a much smaller scale than they had feared and anxieties were allayed sufficiently to induce the government to abandon any idea of embarking on an energetic policy which was foreign to its natural inclinations. Official attention had not focused on the problem till emigration had reached its peak and, as the movement waned, so did the government's sense of obligation to take distasteful steps to counter it. It was also felt that any unnecessarily drastic measure at this time would have served only to revive a dying evil. It was this consideration that decided Suffolk against stationing troops in Skye. No suggestion had been made that these should have attempted to control any form of emigration other than the kidnapping of boys and servants by the masters of American vessels but Suffolk felt that any sign of forcible opposition to emigration would increase rather than diminish it.[2] But, regardless of the fortuitous decline in the number of emigrants, the fundamental deterrent to downright prohibition of emigration remained the same as in 1731. Miller favoured going to greater lengths to limit emigration than did Whitehall but even he recognised how difficult it would be for the government 'to enterpose, by any restraint upon the subjects to remove themselves from one part of his majesty's dominions to another'.[3]

Relief at the diminished scale of emigration did not cause Miller to abandon his quest for measures short of prohibition to curb emigration, which could again become a serious problem at any time. One of the suggestions he made was that regulations should be introduced to ensure that all emigrant vessels would leave ports staffed by customs officials so that a more accurate view of the emigrant trade could be obtained and many would be discouraged from emigrating because of the longer journey to the port of em-

[1] Treasury 47/9–12. Many references to these lists are to be found in Treasury 29/43 *passim*. The lists—those relating to Scotland will be found in S.P. 54/46, no. 168—are incomplete as many vessels 'had no business at the custom house and left for distant parts ... without our knowing anything of them but by report.' (Rod. Mackenzie and Alex. Watson, collectors at Inverness, to Wm. Nelthorpe, secretary to the commissioners of the customs in Scotland, 3 Jan. 1774: Treasury 1/500, 1st enclosure).
[2] Suffolk to the earl of Seaforth, 2 June 1774 (S.P. 54/45, no. 167e; Treasury 29/43, f. 390).
[3] Miller to (Suffolk), 4 July 1774 (S.P. 54/45, no. 168).

barkation. As a complement to this proposal he asked that the vessels should be inspected with regard to the space and provisions available for passengers during the voyage.[1] Such inspection would have required legislation, enacted a quarter of a century later,[2] defining minimum standards of accommodation and provisions. Needless to say, the suggestion was ignored as, by 1774, the problem of emigration was less serious than before and was becoming overshadowed by even darker clouds over America. Another method suggested by Miller for reducing emigration was the payment by the government of the passages back to Britain of a few hundred disillusioned emigrants who could counteract the widespread and carefully nurtured belief that America was a land where hardship and poverty were unknown. This suggestion was adopted 'in some measure' in Scotland and was also advanced in the Irish house of commons in February 1774 as an effective antidote to the spread of emigration. What a far cry such measures were from the deliberate preparations at the end of 1773 for an effective attack on emigration! What a comment on fruitless labour was the official statement that emigration was 'a matter that shall be considered' as the powder smoke rose over Lexington![3]

The reaction of the Irish ruling classes to emigration in the early 'seventies was a close, though apparently unconscious, parallel to that in England. It was not till 1773, when emigration reached its highest level for at least half a century and when authority was no longer distracted by disturbances, that signs of active concern were evident in Dublin. During the closing months of the year, it seemed that bold measures were to be adopted against the trade but the promise of action died in its infancy.

[1] Miller to Suffolk, 30 May 1774 (S.P. 54/45, no. 165). Miller was still complaining in 1775 of the 'licentious manner' in which emigrant vessels sailed from remote bays and creeks (to same, 14 Aug. 1775: S.P. 54/47, no. 168).

[2] 43 Geo. III, c. 56.

[3] Miller to Suffolk, 25 Apr. 1774 and Suffolk to Miller, 13 May 1774 (S.P. 54/45, nos. 164a and 165); same to Henry Dundas, lord advocate of Scotland, 13 Sept. 1775 (*Cal. H.O. papers*, p. 405); *Commons' jn. Ire*, xvi. 416;—to Miller, 31 Aug. 1775 (*Cal. H.O. papers*, 1773-5, p. 379). When action was finally taken in Scotland to stop emigration to the revolting colonies it was done by Dundas who wrote to the customs and port authorities and to the sheriffs to refuse clearance to any vessel which had more than the usual complement of hands on board. These 'seasonable and effective means' were approved with 'pleasure' by the London authorities (Dundas to Suffolk, 4 Sept. 1775: ibid., p. 405; and Suffolk to Dundas, 13 Sept. 1775: ibid., p. 405). Proper states that an act was passed by the English parliament in 1774 obliging all emigrants from Britain to America to pay £50 (*Immigration Laws*, pp. 75-6). I have been unable to trace such an act in the *Statutes at large*.

The reawakening of government interest in emigration was due to landowners who were, according to emigrants, 'truly alarmed at their tenants continuing to desert their lands'.[1] Many of the gentry formed an association to help to remove the causes of the trouble by letting land at moderate rents and in workable proportions, so excluding middlemen. The leading members of the association were the earls of Hillsborough and Hertford, both 'improving' landlords and two of the finest of their class. As a long-term policy this would have gone far to reduce the volume of emigration but, as a more immediate stop-gap, the association was believed to be in favour of a law to prevent emigration.[2]

Official intervention in the Irish emigration trade was to be preceded, as in Britain, by an investigation of the depredations of the trade in the immediate past. In October 1773, the Irish customs commissioners were instructed by a committee of the Irish house of commons to write to the port officials for 'an account from the best evidence they can obtain of the number of persons who have left their respective ports for his majesty's plantations in America for the last two years ended at Michaelmas; and if they cannot point out the number of persons who have sailed, they are at least to report the number of ships, their tonnage, and the number of voyages they have made, and the ports to which they were respectively outvoiced'.[3] Ten weeks later, in December, a committee of the commons was set up to inquire into the causes of emigration.[4]

At long last it seemed that emigration was to be systematically studied and effective action taken. It is surprising, therefore, to find that the records of the commissioners of the Irish customs between October 1773 and the outbreak of the American revolution contain neither directions concerning emigration to the port officials nor other than the most casual references to the trade by

---

[1] *South Carolina and American General Magazine*, 13–20 Aug. 1773 (C.O. 5/380).

[2] *Gentleman's Magazine* (Sept. 1773), xliii. 467–8; *Scots Magazine* (Nov. 1773), xxxv. 591; Gill, *Rise of the Irish linen industry*, p. 28; Young, *Tour*, i. 149. Benjamin Franklin stated that Hillsborough's chief characteristics were wrongheadedness, conceit, obstinacy and passion (J. B. Nolan, *Benjamin Franklin in Scotland and Ireland, 1759 and 1771*, p. 162), but Hillsborough was also the patron of Goldsmith and so tended his estate—a model for all Ireland in Young's opinion—that he was beloved by his tenants.

[3] Customs 1/125, p. 26. This instruction was probably given by the committee appointed a few days before to examine the state of the Irish linen trade (*Commons' jn. Ire.*, xvi. 14). See also *Lords' jn. Ire.*, iv. 694, 698.

[4] *Commons' jn. Ire.*, xvi. 305.

those officials in their reports to the board.[1] It was the British revenue commissioners who had initiated the system of weekly returns of emigrants from London and the outports, but their correspondence with their Irish counterparts between 1773 and 1775 includes not a single reference to emigration.[2]

Many factors lay behind this surprising and—from the present point of view—disappointing silence. As in England, the reduced volume of emigration after the 1773 season resulted in a disinclination to meddle with a problem which seemed to be resolving itself. Moreover, only a section of the landlord class had shown real concern over emigration. Donegall and others like him had got their middlemen and fines to protect them from the draught of emigration; the landlords who had contemplated action against the spread of the contagion regarded the removal of its basic causes as more effective than the negative solution of prohibition. With the decline in emigration after 1773 the need for action became less pressing and, had the desire for such a policy remained, the abandonment in London of strong measures would have served as a brake on the over-enthusiastic in Dublin. Hillsborough and his friends knew that disinclination to enact legislation in England meant equal disinclination to sanction legislation in Ireland and that attempts to secure the passage of such laws would meet with the same fate as in 1730.

Taking the period as a whole, emigration from the north of Ireland proceeded uninterrupted by official intervention and, indeed, generally without apparent official consciousness. When interest was aroused, intervention was contemplated but on only one occasion, at Belfast in 1736, did direct intervention against emigration become a reality. Dislike of emigration and fear of its consequences were seldom sufficiently strong to incline the government to consider the imposition of restrictions akin to serfdom on the movement of subjects.

[1] Customs 1/125–7.
[2] Treasury 29/43–4.

CHAPTER X

The Voyage to America

THE sensational is more striking than the commonplace and usually outlives it. The emigrant whose greatest hardships on the transatlantic voyage had been boredom and discomfort was less likely to record his experiences than was the emigrant whose most constant companions had been terror and death. The best-known accounts of voyages to colonial America are those recorded by German emigrants[1] whose experiences were often unbelievably horrible but were rarely shared by emigrants from Ulster. History has, as in the slave trade and slavery, recorded the memorable rather than the typical: death has enlivened the accounts of conditions on west-bound ships and stamped the entire traffic with its mark.

The realities of the normal emigrant voyage need no embellishments to make it surprising that so many people emigrated. Not even lavish advertisements, unblemished by doubts but appearing side by side with accounts of disasters at sea, could conceal the dangers entailed in a transatlantic voyage in an emigrant vessel. The mysteries of the deep, together with the vagaries of storms and calms over a period of weeks or months, lay ahead of all vessels. For many, man-made hardships were added to the caprice of nature. The brutalities of ship masters, the appearance of pirates and privateers, and shortages of water and food turned emigrant ships into floating islands of despair; disease and pestilence, always a grim possibility that was all too often nurtured by overcrowding, turned them into floating lazar-houses.

[1] E.g. Abbott, *Immigration: select documents*, pp. 11–3; Adams, *Provincial society*, pp. 108, 175–7; J. L. Rosenberger, *The Pennsylvania Germans*, pp. 17–23; Knittle, *Palatine emigration*, p. 147; Farnam, *Social Legislation in U.S.*, p. 63.

The trials of the emigrant often began before he set foot on the vessel that was to carry him to America. It was most unusual for an emigrant vessel from the north of Ireland to sail on the advertised sailing date. For example, only two of the eleven vessels that were advertised to leave Belfast with emigrants in 1774 did not publish notices of postponement.[1] The reasons given by the shipping agents for such delays ranged from the lateness of the harvests to the captain's poor state of health.[2] The most common excuse was that the delay was really a magnanimous and self-sacrificing concession to benefit intending passengers who had asked for further time in which to settle their affairs in Ireland. In some cases, the real reason was simply that the original advertisement had been inserted before the arrival of the vessel in harbour and, when the advertised date of departure arrived, the vessel had either not reached port or was discharging cargo. For example, ten weeks' notice of the departure of the *Pitt* from Larne to Newcastle and New York was given in 1763 but on July 19, four days after the original sailing date, it was announced that the vessel would not leave until 15 August as it had just arrived from Norway.[3] Vessels that advertised for freight as well as passengers sometimes postponed their departure for America for a longer period than did vessels that advertised for passengers only. On the whole, however, the latter vessels delayed their departure more often and for longer periods than did vessels that were not solely interested in passengers. On average, vessels bound from the north Irish ports to America in 1764 and 1765—years when few people emigrated and when all vessels advertised mainly for freight—started on their voyages less than a fortnight after the advertised date of sailing. Most of the advertisements warned that departure would not be postponed 'as the vessel is not intended to wait for passengers'.[4] The picture was very different in 1773 and 1774 when no apparent effort was made to secure freight and the average period of delay doubled to three and a half weeks.[5] This increase

---

[1] Appendix D.
[2] B.N.L., 2 Oct. 1771 (*Hopewell*, Belfast to Charleston and Savannah) and 5 July 1774 (*Liberty*, Belfast to Philadelphia and New York).
[3] Ibid., 29 Apr. and 19 July 1763. See also following vessels in appendix D: 1771— *Betty*; 1772—*Britannia, Pennsylvania Farmer, Nancy, James and Mary*; 1773—*Betty, Jupiter*; 1774—*Betty* (Belfast), *Jupiter, Liberty and Property, Glorious Memory. Minerva, Needham, Freemason, Lord Dunluce, Betty* (Larne); 1775—*Charlotte, Peace and Plenty*.
[4] E.g. *Hopewell*, B.N.L., 23 Mar. 1764.
[5] See Appendix D.

was due partly to the temptation to wait for a full complement of passengers—and keen competition made it difficult to secure a full complement of passengers, even in 1773—and partly to an increasing tendency to advertise before the vessel arrived in port in order to get into the lists before intending emigrants committed themselves to sail in other vessels. 1773 had been a very successful year for the passenger trade but the failure of the *Lord Chatham* to secure passengers after advertising in August—comparatively late in the emigration season—had shown that success was not assured even in bumper years. The same mistake was not made in 1774. Advertisements in respect of six of the twelve emigrant vessels due to leave Belfast and of five of the six vessels due to leave Larne were published before the vessels arrived in port. Indeed, the *Peggy* was wrecked on the voyage to Belfast weeks after the publication of an advertisement of her departure for America.

The consequences of such delays were often serious. The servant was probably given his allowance of food from the time he signed his indenture or from the advertised date of departure of the vessel on which he was to sail. The paying passenger was less fortunate, especially if the port was some distance from his former home, for he had to support himself till the vessel sailed. In so doing he used part or all of the money with which he had intended to pay his passage or which he had hoped would enable him to secure a footing in America. Indeed, it has been suggested that unprincipled shipmasters deliberately engineered delays in order to reduce emigrants to penury—many people who had arrived at the ports with sufficient to pay their passage money were obliged to become indentured servants or else return home penniless.[1] A paying passenger who had booked a passage on one vessel was, of course, free to travel on any other vessel which happened to be preparing to sail but this would have meant sacrificing the earnest money— usually a guinea—and paying a similar sum to book a passage on another vessel the actual departure date of which was probably equally uncertain.

The hardships caused by the unpunctual departure of ships would have been lessened had there been any regularity in the length of the period of postponement as there was in the early nineteenth century. In the latter period, vessels from the north

[1] Adams, *Provincial society*, pp. 175-7; cf. Adams, *Ir. emig. in 19th cent.*, pp. 79-82, and Cowan, *Brit. emig. to N. Amer.*, p. 134.

Irish ports normally left harbour about a month after the advertised sailing time but such postponement caused little hardship as the agents inserted final notices of clearance about a week before actual departure.[1] This was not so in the eighteenth century when intending passengers could not be sure that a notice of a change in the date of departure of a vessel would be published. Two extreme cases of this uncertainty happened in 1772. The last notice of the *Elizabeth* stated that the vessel would sail from Belfast for Savannah on 25 October, but the vessel was still in Belfast lough in the second half of November with 190 passengers on board.[2] On the other hand, the *Pennsylvania Farmer* was advertised to leave Belfast for Charleston on 23 October and left for Philadelphia a week before that date.[3]

'Final' notices were, indeed, often inserted but these were as unreliable as the notices that had preceded them. Intending passengers who arrived in Londonderry in response to a notice that the *Betty* would 'positively' sail on 1 August 1771 witnessed the arrival and unloading of the vessel and were informed that 'at the request of a number of passengers', the voyage to North Carolina was postponed till 20 August.[4] Similar examples abound, but one of the worst cases of misrepresentation of the date of departure was that of the *Hopewell* which was advertised to sail from Belfast to Charleston on 15 August 1772. The sailing was thoughtfully delayed, 'at the request of several passengers', till 28 August, the vessel in the meantime being 'daily expected' from Baltimore and England. After a further delay till 15 September, the vessel arrived from Norway. The transatlantic voyage started in the third week of October after the appearance of two further 'final' notices stating that the vessel would leave on 1 October and 5 October.[5]

In a few isolated cases the public was offered not merely the assurance that a vessel would sail on a particular date but that the agents were 'willing to enter into engagements for the punctual sailing of the vessel', or that, should the sailing have to be postponed, passengers would be taken on board on the advertised date

---

[1] Adams, *Ir. emig. in 19th cent.*, p. 82.
[2] *B.N.L.*, 6 Oct. and 13, 17, and 20 Nov. 1772.
[3] Ibid., 6 and 16 Oct. 1772.
[4] Ibid., 9 July and 2 Aug. 1771.
[5] Ibid., 16 June, 4 and 18 Aug., 15 and 18 Sept. and 20 Oct. 1772.

of departure and receive their full allowance of provisions.[1] That such promises were made shows that it was the practice not to supply provisions till the voyage began. It was not till 1835 that any attempt was made to protect the emigrant from the ill-effects on his capital of delays in the sailing of vessels.[2]

A speedy passage was ardently hoped for by all emigrants and was as ardently promised by the agents of all vessels. As the voyage lengthened, rations were reduced, adding to the dangers and discomforts that all emigrants had to face. The average duration of the transatlantic voyage remained fairly constant in the eighteenth century and in the following century till the advent of steam power. Given favourable conditions, the voyage lasted for eight to ten weeks in 1729 and for six to eight weeks in 1847.[3] The duration of thirty-eight emigrant voyages between 1771 and 1775 from the north of Ireland to the continental colonies in America has been recorded in Irish newspapers.[4] These passages were a fair cross-section of the entire trade during those years—some were short passages of which shipping agents boasted when inserting advertisements in respect of other vessels; others were long passages of which emigrants wrote in disgust or which had been made newsworthy by starvation; most were ordinary passages, details of which were copied by Irish newspapers from the shipping columns of their American counterparts. On average, it took each of these thirty-eight vessels seven weeks and four days to cross the Atlantic, the shortest voyage lasting twenty-seven days[5] and the longest seventeen weeks,[6] both voyages being from Londonderry to Philadelphia. Naturally, the voyage to Charleston and Savannah was of longer duration than the voyage to the more northerly ports. Whereas the average voyage to the latter ports lasted just over seven weeks, nine weeks were required before the average north of Ireland vessel arrived at the southern ports.

The stay on board an emigrant vessel sometimes did not end

[1] Ibid., 12 July 1765 (*Prosperity*, Belfast to Charleston) and 10 June 1769 and 29 July 1772 (*Newry Assistance*, Newry to Philadelphia).
[2] 5 and 6 Wm. IV, c.53. Passengers were to receive their allowance of provisions from the advertised date of sailing whether or not the vessel actually sailed then.
[3] Klett, *Pres. in Pa.*, p. 26; J. F. Maguire, *The Irish in America*, p. 135.
[4] See Appendix D. The sailing of one of the 38 vessels, the *General Wolfe*, was not advertised. For account of voyage of this vessel, see *B.N.L.*, 12 Jan. 1773.
[5] *Jupiter* (*B.N.L.*, 7 Aug. 1772).
[6] *General Wolfe* (ibid., 13 Jan. 1773).

with the entry into an American port. Any vessel on which fever had broken out during the voyage had to ride in quarantine until the danger of infection had passed.[1] The *James and Mary* sailed from Larne to Charleston in seven weeks and three days in 1772 but the passengers were not allowed to land for more than seven weeks after the arrival of the vessel.[2] Another Larne vessel, the *Lord Dunluce*, was quarantined in Charleston for the same reason, though for only fifteen days, thanks (it was claimed) to the influence of the ship's master.[3]

One of the factors that determined the profit of an emigrant voyage to its promoters was the amount of food consumed during the passage, an amount that depended mainly on the duration of the voyage. Profits were so limited in the nineteenth century by acts regulating the number of passengers that ships could carry and the amount of provisions that had to be supplied to each passenger that shipmasters preferred to secure a definite sum for the cost of passage only rather than to include provisions in the agreement with the emigrant.[4] This was not so during the colonial period when it was customary for those who promoted the passage to supply provisions to the emigrants.[5]

All vessels that advertised passages from the north of Ireland to America before 1775 stressed the abundance of provisions that would be supplied to emigrants, but only a few advertisements gave details of what emigrants might expect. One of these stated that beef and pork were among the provisions on board and that James Hunter, the master, was 'remarkable for his bountiful distribution of these'.[6] In only one case did an advertisement detail the quantities of provisions which passengers could expect. The *Britannia*, about to sail from Newry to Philadelphia in 1775, advertised:

These are to certify to all people that choose to take their passage on board the *Britannia* . . . the following allowance of provisions and water will be, per week, faithfully given to each passenger viz. Six pounds of good beef (which was put on board said ship at Cork),

[1] See *Jn. Mass. house of repres.*, ii. 172–3 (4 Nov. 1719) and ix. 98–9 ff. (20 Sept. 1729).
[2] *The journal of Alexander Chesney*, ed. E. A. Jones, pp. 2–3.
[3] B.N.L., 8 June 1773.
[4] Adams, *Ir. emig. in 19th cent.*, p. 79.
[5] See, however, the reference to Desbrisay's vessel, the *John and James* on p. 158.
[6] B.N.L., 1 Feb. 1774.

six pounds of good ship bread (brought from Philadelphia in said Ship) or six pounds of good oatmeal, as the passengers may choose to take; one pound of butter, or a pint of treacle or molasses, and fourteen quarts of water.[1]

On at least one occasion—and there is no reason to believe that it was the only occasion—the sponsors of a voyage entered into a written agreement with emigrants defining the scale of provisions during the voyage. The 'full' passengers on board the *Nancy* which sailed from Belfast to Charleston in 1767 were each promised seven pounds of beef, seven pounds of bread, one pound of butter and fourteen quarts of water weekly. 'Half' passengers, those aged between two and twelve years, were to receive half these amounts.[2]

These quantities compare favourably with the amounts prescribed in later passenger acts[3] and with the usual allowances to seamen in merchant vessels,[4] but they cannot be considered as normal in the eighteenth century emigration trade. The sponsors of a voyage were not likely to minimise the provisions they supplied and the most obvious reason for publishing the appendix to the *Britannia* advertisement was that the provisions promised were more generous than was common in emigrant ships. Moreover, abnormal inducements were needed to attract passengers in 1775, a year when the expectation of revolution in America reduced the already waning flow of emigrants from Ulster.

Provisions other than meat and breadstuffs were carried; among those named in advertisements and in letters from emigrants were potatoes—'large, not washed, but dried in the sun and not cut in the digging[5]—and rum which was sold on board many emigrant

---

[1] Ibid., 2 May 1775.
[2] Petition, Robert Wills (Willis) and William Ray, Belfast merchants, to Hillsborough, n.d. [1768] (C.O. 5/114).
[3] The first passenger act (43 Geo III, c.56) laid down a minimum of 3½ lb. beef or pork weekly for each passenger, though the Highland Society believed that 7 lb. was 'absolutely necessary for a passenger'. Meat was omitted in the requirements of the 1828 act (9 Geo IV, c.21) but a weekly allowance, per passenger, of 5 lb. bread, biscuit or oatmeal, and 5 gallons of water was required. The allowance of breadstuffs was raised in 1836 (5 and 6 Wm. IV., c.53) to 7 lb. per week (Selkirk, *Highland emig.*, p. 150; Cowan, *Brit. emig. to N. Amer.*, pp. 25ff; Macdonald, *Canada: immig. & settlement*, pp. 13–14).
[4] Lindsay, *History of merchant shipping*, ii. 501–2.
[5] B.N.L., 25 Sept. 1763 (*Prince of Wales*, Belfast to Charleston); ibid., 8 Mar. 1765 (*New Hope*, Belfast to Philadelphia); ibid., 23 Sept. 1768 (*Earl of Donegal*, Belfast to Charleston).

vessels in the 'seventies at 3s. 9½d. per gallon.[1]

Emigrants were never fed on a princely scale during the voyage but actual starvation was the lot of but few who sailed from the north of Ireland to colonial America. When starvation was experienced, it was caused by one of two things—either culpable neglect to ship a reasonable quantity of provisions, or a passage of inordinate duration.

However grasping the masters and owners of vessels may have been, it would be unjust to say that, as a class, they deliberately put on board less provisions than would have fed at subsistence level the emigrants who had agreed to sail in the vessel. On the other hand, many emigrants sought passages just before the vessel was about to sail and these were taken on board though the sailing was not delayed to take on additional provisions. The vessel sailed, the master hoping that the additional mouths would be offset by a speedy passage and usually the only effect was a meagre allowance of food during the voyage.[2] In a few cases, advertisements announced that provisions sufficient for a voyage of four months or longer had been put on board,[3] or that only a stated number of passengers would be carried.[4] Whether these statements were truthful or were merely inducements to attract passengers is, of course, another matter.

Avarice led to hunger, but starvation and thirst were usually due to calms and westerly gales. The worst examples of starvation on the voyage from the north of Ireland to colonial America show the havoc that overcrowding and calms or storms could cause. In 1729, 175 people died on two vessels during the crossing.[5] Six of the forty-six people who died on the *Seaflower* on the voyage from

---

[1] E.g. *B.N.L.*, 12 May 1772 (*Philadelphia*, Belfast to Philadelphia) and 7 May 1773 (*Waddell*, Belfast to Savannah). German immigrants who arrived in Philadelphia in 1805 on board the *General Wayne* had been promised meat, pease, fish, vinegar, potatoes, tobacco, and 'a dram in the morning' (Abbott, *Historical aspects of the immigration problem*, pp. 11-3).

[2] The agents of the *Philadelphia*, Belfast to Philadelphia, urged intending passengers to give ample notice and reminded them of 'several instances of passenger vessels being in distress for want of provisions . . . . . occasioned by people crowding on them at the time of sailing' (*B.N.L.*, 15 Mar. 1766.)

[3] E.g. *F.D.J.*, 3 June (*Phoenix*, Dublin to Philadelphia) and 17 June 1729 (*Mary*, same voyage). No vessel that advertised for passengers in the *B.N.L.* was so specific.

[4] E.g. *B.N.L.*, 16 Oct. 1774 (*Marquis of Granby*, Belfast to New York); ibid., 4 Oct. 1768 (*Betty Gregg*, Belfast to Charleston).

[5] *Pennsylvania Gazette*, 17-20 Nov. 1729 and 10-13 Feb. 1729/30 (Klett, *Pres. in Pa.*, p. 26).

Belfast to Philadelphia in 1741 were consumed by the sixty survivors.[1] Sixty-four deaths took place on board the *Sally*, Belfast to Philadelphia, in 1762,[2] and, of the 300 emigrants who set out from Londonderry to Hampton Roads in the *General Wolfe* in 1772, eighty died and the remainder landed 'mere skeletons, so weak they could hardly walk or stand'.[3]

An examination of the circumstances of the disasters reveals two significant points. First, four of the five voyages were made during periods of heavy emigration when most vessels carried full complements of emigrants. Second, all the voyages were of unusual length. The troubles of the emigrants on board the *Seaflower* started after the vessel had sprung her mast, and the other voyages were spread over twenty weeks, twenty-two weeks, fourteen weeks and five days, and seventeen weeks respectively. In at least three of these cases the allowance of provisions to each passenger was not reduced till it was obvious that the voyages were to be of unusual duration. The provisions that remained at the end of the voyage of one of the 1729 vessels consisted of twenty-five biscuits; the allowance on board the *Sally* was not reduced till a fortnight of storms had driven the vessel off its course; a full allowance was continued on the *General Wolfe* for the surprisingly long period of eight weeks, though the vessel was by then only in mid-Atlantic. Though no record has been found of the deliberate paring of provisions to starvation level in the case of the north Irish emigrant vessels, the experience of some English emigrants in 1774 was probably shared by others who sailed from Ireland. An English emigrant alleged when he arrived in Baltimore that as soon as the vessel had left Land's End the master 'used the passengers in a most cruel manner' and reduced the daily allowance of food to one and a half biscuits, three small potatoes and two ounces of salt beef, six spoonfuls of pea soup being substituted for potatoes and beef on Tuesdays and Fridays. The emigrant also alleged that passengers who complained were put in irons, lashed to the shrouds and flogged.[4]

For some degree of comfort and for the preservation of health the emigrant needed adequate provisions and a reasonable amount of

[1] J. D. Crimmins, *Irish American historical miscellany*, p. 149; Ford, *Scotch-Irish in America*, p. 207.
[2] *B.N.L.*, 13 May 1763. An account of this voyage will be found in Appendix F.
[3] Ibid., 15 Dec. 1772.
[4] Ibid., 15 July 1774.

living space during the voyage. The latter he rarely got, especially during periods of heavy emigration. So many emigrants were crammed into vessels that were seldom devised for the carriage of passengers that it is remarkable that the rate of mortality during the voyage was not even greater than it was.

It has been seen that the number of passengers carried in emigrant vessels during the early 'seventies was approximately equal to the advertised tonnage of the vessels. In actual fact, the average number of emigrants in peak years may have far exceeded the true tonnage of the vessels. The unreliability of advertised tonnages is shown by the advertisements themselves. Many instances could be cited,[1] but two manipulations in which John Montgomery, the Larne merchant, played a part will suffice to illustrate the point. He advertised the sailing of the *Lord Dunluce*, 'a vessel of about 200 tons' in 1761, but, either because appearances were against the vessel or because of his bad memory, the tonnage shrank to 'about 160 tons' in the following year. He remedied the defect a decade later when a stroke of the pen added fifty tons to the stature of a new *Lord Dunluce* between 1774 and 1775.[2] An even more blatant misrepresentation was that of the Belfast merchants, Greg and Cunningham, in respect of the *Hibernia*. Prior to a voyage to New York in 1767, the vessel was advertised as of 200 tons. When it was offered for sale, after its return to Belfast, its tonnage was given as 170.[3] Prospective purchasers were not as gullible as prospective emigrants.

These cases may, indeed, be but a faint indication of the real state of overcrowding on emigrant vessels. The average advertised tonnage of emigrant vessels during the period 1771 to 1775 was over 310 tons; but according to the returns of the port officials in America, the average tonnage of vessels that arrived there from Ireland between January 1768 and January 1771 was 94 tons.[4] A comparison between the advertised and the official tonnages of particular vessels shows as wide a discrepancy. In no case was the official tonnage more than half the advertised tonnage and in most cases it was only about one-third. Emigration agents had cause to exaggerate the size of the vessels they represented and port

[1] For a list of discrepancies in advertised tonnages and between advertised tonnages and official tonnages, see Appendix B.
[2] *B.N.L.*, 5 June 1761, 2 July 1762, 18 May 1774 and 14 Mar. 1775.
[3] Ibid., 17 Apr. 1767 and 18 Mar. 1768.
[4] Customs 16/1.

officials had no reason to minimise the tonnage of the vessels that entered the American ports, but part of the difference may have been due to the absence till 1773 of any enforced method of ascertaining the burthen of merchant vessels and of registering that tonnage.[1] On the whole, it seems likely that the feat of a nineteenth century ship in doubling her tonnage to attract emigrants[2] was emulated in the north of Ireland at least fifty years before.

Disease thrives on overcrowding; but even from the point of view of mere physical discomfort the effects of overcrowding were of grave consequence to the emigrant. When an act of 1828[3] limited the number of passengers that could be carried in an emigrant vessel to three to every four tons burthen, the comment of a Cork merchant was that it would legalise the most excessive numbers the trade had ever known. He stated that the law would permit the carrying of one passenger to every $20\frac{1}{2}$ square inches of deck space and believed that 'there was nothing in the annals of the slave trade equal to this'. The deck of a vessel which sailed with emigrants from Bristol during the time the act was in force was stated to be so crowded that 'when one passenger attempted to cross from one end of the vessel to the other the remaining portion were compelled to crowd themselves into one dense mass, many of them being obliged to clamber on top of the chests'.[4] The opinion that overcrowding under the 1828 act would surpass anything that the emigrant trade had previously seen was, however, incorrect: the space occupied by three of the emigrants on the Bristol vessel sufficed for five emigrants in the hey-day of the north Irish emigration sixty years before.

It was not only above deck that emigrant vessels were crowded during the busy years of the trade. Sometimes for days and even weeks the emigrants had to remain below deck because of the weather or the whim of their nautical overlords.[5] Conditions there may be judged from shipping advertisements. We may assume that agents boasted of conditions only when these were more attractive than was usual in the trade, yet only three of the emigrant vessels which sailed from the north Irish ports to colonial America

[1] 13 Geo. III, c. 74 (Eng.). amended by 26 Geo. III, c.60 (Eng.). See Macpherson, *Annals of commerce*, iii. 544, and iv. 107; Lindsay, *History of merchant shipping*, ii. 245,
[2] Adams, *Ir. emig. in 19th cent.*, pp. 81–2.
[3] 9 Geo. IV, c.21.
[4] Cowan, *Brit. emig. to N. Amer.*, p. 211–2.
[5] Lindsay, *Merchant shipping*, iii. 330.

announced that single berths would be provided for passengers.[1] On one occasion the *Belfast News Letter* referred, without apparent surprise and certainly without reproof, to an emigrant vessel of 1769 in which an average of twelve people occupied every seven berths, each of which measured five feet ten inches long and eighteen inches wide.[2]

No restrictions were laid by the Irish or British parliaments during the eighteenth century on the number of passengers in relation to berth-space, but overcrowding on board vessels led to the spread of disease in the ports of entry and so provincial authorities took action. In 1749 the assembly of Pennsylvania forbade the importation in any vessel of a greater number of passengers than could be suitably accommodated. The maximum permitted number of passengers was to be determined not by the tonnage of a vessel—as in the later British passenger acts— but by insisting on a minimum amount of berth-space for each passenger. This, it was ordered, was to be six feet long and eighteen inches broad, though such space could be used to accommodate two passengers who were less than fourteen years of age. Unfortunately, the act had little effect as it did not specify what height was to be left between a berth and the one above it. This defect was remedied in 1765 when the Pennsylvania assembly fixed the minimum height of berth-space at two feet nine inches.[3] The Ulster emigrants of the 'seventies were not to reap the benefits of this act for it was vetoed by the English authorities.[4] Except for a Massachusetts act of 1751, similar to the Pennsylvania act of 1749,[5] no other official attempt was made in the eighteenth century, on either side of the Atlantic, to ensure that an emigrant

---

[1] *Pennsylvania Farmer*, Belfast to Charleston (*B.N.L.*, 28 Aug. 1772); *Renown*, Newry to Philadelphia (ibid., 10 Feb. 1775); *Britannia*, same voyage (ibid., 7 Apr. 1775). The last vessel announced that 'separate rooms for the conveniency of each passenger' would be provided.

[2] *B.N.L.*, 20 Oct. 1769. The vessel was advertised as being of 450 tons and carried 517 emigrants.

[3] C.O. 5/1273, 11 Nov. 1750; Farnam, *Social legislation in U.S.*, p. 63.

[4] P.C. 2/111 pp. 657–60 (18 June 1766); Jernegan, *Laboring and dependent classes*, p. 51. The two acts mentioned were inspired partly by humanitarian motives and partly by the desire of the assembly to reduce German and Irish immigration. A bill to regulate conditions on board immigrant vessels was vetoed by the provincial governor in 1755 as it would have placed 'an absolute prohibition on Germans which might not look well at home nor be for the interest of the province' (Proper, *Immigration laws*, pp. 52–3).

[5] Abbott, *Historical aspects of the immigration problem*, pp. 6–7.

got the barest minimum of accommodation essential for his health and comfort.

Had the Pennsylvania act of 1765 become operative, many of the vessels which left the north Irish ports for Philadelphia during the following decade would have carried very many fewer emigrants than actually sailed in them. Except in a few vessels which were built specially for the passenger trade, all emigrants were accommodated in the space between decks. The Pennsylvania act would have made it illegal for more than two depths of berths to be built in the great majority of emigrant vessels, as the height between decks seldom exceeded five feet six inches. Indeed, no advertisement prior to 1774 claimed a height in excess of five feet. The *Sally* advertised in 1765, with obvious pride and as an inducement to emigrants, that the height between her decks was four feet six inches[1] and, in 1766, the *William* claimed to be a 'roomy' vessel as the height between decks was four feet nine inches.[2] These vessels were among the larger of the emigrant vessels, each being advertised as of 250 tons. An advertisement relating to a vessel of that tonnage informed emigrants as late as 1773 that the height between her decks had been increased at great expense to five feet, 'which must be very comfortable for passengers'.[3]

In the years of heaviest emigration and most intensive advertising, only seven north Irish emigrant vessels to the American colonies claimed that the height between their decks exceeded five feet six inches and all these were stated to have been built specially for the passenger trade and were advertised to sail in 1774 or 1775.[4] It is clear that this height could not be offered as an attraction by the remaining vessels. It is instructive to note in this respect that in a vessel of 270 tons carrying 400 emigrants to America in 1791 the berths were triple-tiered and were eighteen inches wide and two feet high.[5]

Only two north Irish emigrant vessels advertised accommoda-

[1] B.N.L., 7 May 1765.
[2] Ibid., 1 Apr. 1766.
[3] *Betty*, Belfast to Philadelphia (ibid., 20 Aug. 1773).
[4] *Liberty* (6': ibid., 3 Apr. 1774); *Alexander* (6': ibid., 8 Apr. 1774); *Needham* (near 6': ibid., 18 Mar. 1774); *Glorious Memory* (near 6': ibid., 21 June 1774); *Recovery* (near 7': ibid., 14 Mar. 1775); *Duke of Leinster* (6' 3": ibid., 14 Apr. 1775); *Britannia* (6': ibid., 7 Apr. 1775).
[5] Cowan, *Brit, emig. to N. Amer.*, p. 25. Cowan also cites a voyage of 1773 in which a vessel of 300 tons sailed with 450 emigrants to N.C. At first, 25 of the emigrants had no berths but everyone found accommodation when 23 passengers died.

tion other than in the space between decks. The *Minerva*, London-derry to Philadelphia was stated to have been built at great expense for the passenger trade and advertised for three classes of passengers who would be accommodated respectively in the cabin which was eight feet high, in the steerage, seven feet high, and between decks, six feet high.[1] The *Britannia*, Newry to Philadelphia, boasted of 'a large cabin, six state rooms, with air ports to each state room, large quarter galleries, with everything elegantly complete as a London trader' in addition to a space of six feet between decks.[2]

Port-holes to provide ventilation and light in the often over-crowded space between decks were usually non-existent in emi-grant vessels of the period. Surprising as it may seem, the first north of Ireland vessel which mentioned these did so in 1774 and many emigrant vessels were not fitted with means of ventilation even half a century later.[3] The only reference to ventilation in an advertisement prior to 1774 appeared in 1763 when the owners of the *Venus* claimed that the vessel's 'three hatchways would ensure an abundance of fresh air'.[4] Six vessels boasted of port-holes in 1774 and 1775,[5] stressing their hygienic value in such terms as to show that portholes were an innovation in the passenger trade. The *Liberty*, Belfast to Philadelphia, claimed that the port-holes would 'let out the foul, and in the fresh, air, for want of which disorders frequently happen on board passenger vessels'.[6] The *Hannah*, Londonderry to Philadelphia, was stated to have 'a sufficient number of air ports between decks in order to give a thorough circulation of fresh air, which contributes much to the health of passengers'.[7] Five of the six vessels fitted with port-holes were new and unusually large vessels, the smallest of them being advertised as being of 450 tons. The sixth vessel, the *Charlotte*, belonged to the more common 250-ton class and acquired port-holes to compete with the newer and larger vessels, the advertise-ment claiming that 'in order to preserve the health of the passengers in the summer season, the captain got twelve air ports cut in the

---

[1] *B.N.L.*, 19 Apr. 1774.
[2] Ibid., 7 Apr. 1765.
[3] Cowan, *Brit. emig. to N. Amer.*, p. 130.
[4] *B.N.L.*, 10 July 1763.
[5] *Charlotte* (ibid., 5 May 1775), *Liberty* (ibid., 8 Apr. 1774), *Hannah* (ibid., 11 Mar. 1774), *Recovery* (ibid., 14 Mar. 1775), *Britannia* (ibid., 14 Apr. 1775).
[6] *B.N.L.*, 8 Apr. 1774.
[7] Ibid., 11 Mar. 1774.

ship's side, which every judge must allow will be of infinite service during the passage'.[1]

Not only did emigrants sleep between decks: there they ate and washed in bad weather, sang and wept, chafed under and obeyed the petty tyrants in their midst, and rejoiced for the newly-born and mourned for the dead. According to one emigrant battened below decks during a storm, 'there were some sleeping, some damning, some blasting their legs and thighs, some their liver, lungs, lights, and eyes and for to make the scene the odder, some cursed father, mother, sister and brother'.[2]

A high rate of mortality was almost inevitable on these vessels but north Irish emigrants fared much better, on the whole, than did their European counterparts. Vessels carrying German emigrants in the early part of the eighteenth century were so often ravaged by typhus that that disease was known as 'Palatine fever' in the emigration trade from that time. On one such vessel, eighty people died before the transatlantic voyage began and, on another, 330 people were suffering from typhus at one time during the voyage.[3] The blackest picture of a black trade was painted by a German emigrant of 1750:

... during the voyage there is on board these ships terrible misery, stench, fumes, horror, vomiting, many kinds of seasickness, fever, dysentery, headache, heat, constipation, boils, scurvy, cancer, mouth-rot, and the like, all of which come from old and sharply salted food and meat, also from very bad and foul water, so that many die miserably. Add to this want of provisions, hunger, thirst, frost, heat, dampness, anxiety, want, afflictions and lamentations, together with other trouble as, for example, the lice abound so frightfully, especially on sick people, that they can be scraped off the body. The misery reaches the climax when a gale rages for two or three nights and days, so that everyone believes that the ship will go to the bottom with all human beings on board. In such a visitation the people cry and pray most piteously. ..... the ship is constantly tossed from side to side by the storm and waves, so that no one can either walk, or sit, or lie, and the closely packed people in the berths are thereby tumbled over each other, both the sick and

---

[1] Ibid., 5 May 1775.
[2] Jernagan, *Laboring and dependent classes*, p. 51. For a medical account of life on board vessels engaged on long voyages in the latter part of the eighteenth century, see J. A. Nixon, 'Health and Sickness', in *The trade winds* (ed. C. N. Parkinson), pp. 121–38.
[3] Knittle, *Palatine emigration*, p. 147; Adams, *Provincial society*, pp. 175–7.

the well—it will be readily understood that many of these people, none of whom had been prepared for hardships, suffer so terrible that they do not survive it.

. . . . . many hundred people necessarily die and perish in such misery, and must be cast into the sea, which drives their relatives. . . to such despair that it is almost impossible to pacify and console them. In a word, the sighing and crying and lamenting on board the ship continues night and day, so as to cause the hearts even of the most hardened to bleed when they hear it.[1]

The emigration agents of the north of Ireland painted a very different picture of the transatlantic voyage. The accounts of voyages they caused to be printed seldom mentioned sickness or death. One of these advertisements concerned the voyage of the *Jupiter* from Larne to Charleston in 1772 and had a more convincing ring about it than the others. Sixty-one emigrants signed the following tribute to Robert Shutter, the master of the vessel:

You may believe us that it is not in our power to express or set forth his character according to his good treatment; we are fully persuaded it would surprise you had you been witness to the humane care he took of every person on board: we thank God we had little or no sickness on board; there was only three children died during the passage, and as many born; and if either man, woman or child happened to be disordered, he was still ready with his cordials, of which he was very well supplied.[2]

It has already been stressed that death was a more frequent visitant to vessels carrying German emigrants than to those which sailed from the north of Ireland. The Pennsylvania act of 1765 which required every vessel carrying immigrants to that province to provide a surgeon for the free use of passengers was mainly the result of the efforts of the active German Society of Pennsylvania.[3] This was not a period of heavy emigration from the north of Ireland to Pennsylvania but German vessels had continued to be overcrowded after the abortive attempt of the provincial assembly in 1755 to limit the number of passengers that vessels could carry.

[1] Abbott, *Historical aspects of the immigration problem*, pp. 7–9.
[2] *B.N.L.*, 15 Sept. 1772.
[3] Farnam, *Social legislation in U.S.*, p. 63.

German rather than Irish suffering had also been responsible for the latter bill in which the Germans were the only race named.[1] Fever breeds on overcrowding, and conditions on north Irish vessels during years of heavy emigration sometimes approached those on vessels carrying European emigrants. Famine led to heavy emigration from the north of Ireland about 1740. In 1741 George Thomas, governor of Pennsylvania, asked the provincial assembly to provide a hospital or a pest-house to accommodate sick immigrants. Both he and the assembly specified Irish and German immigrants, in that order, as being in most need of such attention.[2] Reports of fever on north Irish emigrant vessels were renewed in the 'seventies. Smallpox broke out on at least two of the four vessels that sailed from Larne with emigrants in 1772.[3] The emigrants who sailed in two Newry vessels in 1774 were reported to have been 'remarkably sickly' during the voyage to Charleston and a 'very considerable' number died during the crossing.[4]

Children were the easiest prey to disease. It has been asserted that, in German vessels, children under seven years rarely survived the transatlantic voyage and that mortality in childbirth was so high that the bodies of mother and child were generally thrown overboard together.[5] There were many instances of a high death rate of children on other than German vessels. Only one of the fifty children aged under four years who sailed on a vessel from Sutherland to America in 1774 survived the passage and, of the seven women who were delivered during the voyage, six died, as did all seven infants.[6] There is an absence of references to epidemics on north Irish emigrant vessels of the eighteenth century except in the busiest years of the trade, but in those years a proportionately high death rate among children was reported in several ships. The three passengers who died on board the *Jupiter* in 1771 were all children; when small pox broke out in the *Lord Dunluce* in 1772, it 'occasioned the death of some children'; two emigrants, Samuel

---

[1] Proper, *Immigration laws*, pp. 52–3; Abbott, *Immigration: select documents*, p. 551. On the other hand, only the Irish were named when a bill was introduced in the Massachusetts house of representatives in 1739 to check the spread of 'fevers and other infectious distempers' (*Jn. Mass. house of repres.*, ix. 198).
[2] Abbott, op. cit., pp. 547–8.
[3] *Lord Dunluce* (*B.N.L.*, 8 June 1773) and *James and Mary* (*Journal of Alexander Chesney*, p. 3).
[4] *B.N.L.*, 30 Sept. 1774.
[5] Adams, *Provincial society*, pp. 175–7; Jernegan, *Laboring and dependent classes*, p. 51.
[6] *Scots Magazine* (Mar. 1774), xxxvi. 157–8.

McCulloch and Alexander Chesney, reported the deaths of children belonging to their own family circles.[1] This evidence is suggestive of the higher death rate among children than among adults, but it falls far short of proving that the rate of child mortality in Irish emigrant vessels even approached the rate in German vessels. Had the survival of a child been a rare occurrence, it is to be expected that, of the many letters to the *Belfast News Letter* deploring emigration and pointing out the dangers to which emigrants subjected themselves, at least one would have drawn the attention of intending emigrants to this sobering fact. Without exception, the letters were silent on the point.

Storms and shipwrecks claimed a heavy toll among eighteenth century transatlantic vessels, but north Irish emigrants were singularly fortunate in that they seldom experienced the greater of these dangers. Shipwrecks there were, of course, and intending emigrants became even more conscious of the dangers of the sea when a vessel foundered on the eastward passage to Ireland after preliminary notices had appeared advertising for passengers on its behalf. For example, two vessels bound from north America to Newry were lost in 1773, one of them, the *Phebe and Peggy*, having carried four hundred emigrants from Newry to Philadelphia in 1772.[2] The *Hopewell*, another vessel well-known in the emigration trade, lost all her sails on the voyage from New York to Newry in 1773 and was fortunate to reach Cork.[3] Of course it was not only on the eastward journeys that vessels ran into gales. The *Earl of Donegal*, bound from Belfast to Philadelphia in 1768, was blown to Antigua, arriving there in great distress.[4] The *Glorious Memory*, sailing from Belfast to Philadelphia in 1774, was fortunate in being able to put into Plymouth with only four fatal casualties after she had sprung her mast and the cargo had shifted.[5] But only two reports of the actual shipwreck of vessels with north Irish emigrants

[1] B N.L., 10 Jan. 1772, 8 June 1773 and 3 May 1774; *Journal of Alexander Chesney*, p. 3.
[2] *Phebe and Peggy*, Philadelphia to Newry, (*L.J.*, 12 Feb. 1773), and *Britannia*, Maryland to Newry (*F.D.J.*, 8 Apr. 1773). See also the *Betty* (*B.N.L.*, 15 Feb. and 15 Apr. 1774), and *B.N.L.*, 12 Mar. 1773: *New York Journal*, 10 Sept. 1772.
[3] *F.D.J.*, 6 Mar. 1773.
[4] B.N.L., 10 Mar. 1769. Similar incidents, though not concerning north Irish emigrant vessels, are recorded in Dupont to Hillsborough, 23 Apr. 1771 (C.O. 226/4, ff.81-4) and *Boston Chronicle*, 14-21 Mar. 1768 (J. R. Commons, U. B. Phillips, E. A. Gilmore, H. L. Sumner, J. B. Anderson (eds.), *A documentary history of American industrial society*, i. 372-3).
[5] B.N.L., 14 Oct. 1774.

on board were printed in the Irish newspapers between 1750 and 1775. The *Edinburgh*, bound from Newry to Philadelphia with forty passengers in 1755, ran aground near Cape May in New Jersey but all the passengers were saved.[1] The *Providence* ran into a heavy gale a fortnight after leaving Portrush for New York on 27 August 1768. The ship sprang a leak and only thirteen of the thirty-six souls on board were saved after spending a fortnight in the long boat, employing a large part of that time in prayer.[2] There was more news-value in such disasters than in the hundreds of accounts of disasters involving cargo vessels, so it would appear that the *Edinburgh* and *Providence* were the only vessels which were ship-wrecked with north Irish emigrants on board in the quarter-century before 1775.[3]

The published details of the loss of the *Providence* illustrate the slender chance of survival the passengers of a crowded emigrant vessel would have had in the event of the vessel foundering. The only alternative that the passengers of the *Providence* had to remaining on board the vessel and drowning was to take to the long boat and yawl and these, unfortunately, could accommodate only seventeen people. It is unlikely that precautions to help ensure the safety of a greater number would have been taken had the vessel been more crowded—it would have been physically impossible, for example, to ship lifeboats on vessels in which the passengers had barely room enough to move. Moreover, shipowners felt under no obligation to provide for the safety of passengers as the latter were regarded merely as a type of freight. A long boat and a yawl were carried on all vessels of the ocean class for the convenience and safety of the crew. When it was clear that the *Providence* was doomed, it was the captain and crew who took to the long boat, despite the pleas of those—including a woman and her two children—who were abandoned.[4]

Another of the hazards which faced emigrants was the possibility of capture by pirates or privateers. This danger was so great that transatlantic vessels generally sailed under convoy from Cork, even in the second quarter of the eighteenth century.[5] Though the

[1] Ibid., 2 Jan. 1756.
[2] Ibid., 6 Jan. and 3 Feb. 1769.
[3] About 100 emigrants were drowned when a Dublin vessel was wrecked off Cape Cod in 1729 (Purcell, 'Irish contribution to colonial N.Y.', in *Studies* (1941), xxx. 107).
[4] B.N.L., 3 Feb. 1769.
[5] W. O'Sullivan, *The economic history of Cork city from the earliest days to the act of union*, p. 148.

American coast had been cleared by 1728 of most of the pirates who had swept it from Newfoundland to South America, marauders were sentenced to death in Philadelphia as late as 1731 and commissions for the trial of pirates were issued for all the British colonies in America in 1762.[1] There is no record of the capture of a north Irish emigrant vessel by pirates, but a Dublin newspaper reported—and denied in the same issue—the capture by a French privateer of an unnamed vessel bound from Belfast to New York in 1757.[2] That this was the only reported capture is a tribute to the luck of the Irish rather than an indication of the inactivity of French and Spanish privateers whose exploits on the Atlantic shipping routes were frequently described in the Irish newspapers and provoked alarm in the colonies and in London.[3]

On the whole, the north Irish emigrant was more fortunate than his German comrade but he knew that before him, too, lay 'all the Tryles, Hardships, and Dangers of the Seas, by Storms, Shipwrecks, Turks and Pyrates, to be starved, or cast away by the Villany of Ship Masters . . .'[4]

S. C. Hughson, *The Carolina pirates and colonial commerce*, pp. 56, 59, 65–6, 69, 85 131–3; *Hist. account S.C.*, i.141, 207–8, 235; Bolton, *Scotch Irish pioneers*, pp. 18, 323; minutes, court of vice-admiralty, Philadelphia, 15 Oct. 1731 (C.O. 5/1234, ff.39–44, 46. One of the pirate vessels was stated to have sailed from Limerick); Admiralty 1/3679, p. 326.
[2] *F.D.J.*, 1 Nov. 1757.
[3] E.g. List of the ships taken by the Spaniards between the peace of Utrecht and 20 June 1728 (C.O. 5/383, ff.114–7); Representation, merchants and inhabitants of Philadelphia to the house of representatives of Pennsylvania, 4 June 1741 (C.O. 5/1234, f.125); B.N.L., 25 Feb. and 10 Oct. 1758; *F.D.J.*, 9 Aug. and 1 Nov. 1757, 26 May 1761, 15 June 1762.
[4] *Dublin Weekly Journal*, 7 June 1729.

CHAPTER XI

Arrival in America

VERY few people emigrated from the north Irish ports in the eighteenth century other than those bound for the American continental colonies. Comments by King and Boulter have led to the assertion that a not inconsiderable number emigrated to the West Indies but this ignores the broad and inclusive use of the term West Indies at the time those comments were made.[1] Certainly, some north Irish emigrants may have gone to the West Indies, but the invariable description of the Irish who landed there as Roman catholics[2] suggests that most of the Irish immigrants into the islands were from the south of Ireland. The same suggestion is conveyed by the almost invariable designation as Roman catholics of the Irish who landed in Newfoundland during the century, particularly as most of the Irish trade with the island was carried on by vessels which sailed from Cork and Waterford.[3]

Apparent religious affinity attracted to New England most north Irish emigrants at the beginning of the period of heavy

[1] Ford, *Scotch-Irish in Amer.*, p. 194; King to abp. of Canterbury, 6 Feb. 1717/8: '. . . last year some Thousands of Families are gone to the West Indies. (King, *A great abp. of Dublin*, p. 208); Boulter to Newcastle, 28 Nov. 1728: '. . . above 4200 men, women, and children have been shipped off from hence for the *West Indies*' (*Boulter letters*, i. 210); Part of the title of a book published in Belfast in the first half of the eighteenth century reads: . . . *With a view of the dominion of the crown in the West Indies, namely Newfoundland, New England, New York* . . .

[2] Robt. Hunter, gov. of Jamaica, to Newcastle, 8 Oct. 1731 (*Cal. S.P. Am. & W. Ind.*, 1731, no. 433); Francis Fane, B.T. solicitor, to B.T., 23 Dec. 1731 (ibid., no. 571).

[3] Geo. Clinton, gov. of Newfoundland, to—, 1 Oct. 1731 (ibid., 1731, no. 422, 422 ii(m)); same to Popple, 30 Mar. 1732 (ibid., 1732, no. 148); *Journal commissioners of trade and plantations*, 1741–9, p. 279 (14 Apr. 1748); A. H. McLintock, *The establishment of constitutional government in Newfoundland*, 1783–1832, p.88; B.N.L., 27 July 1762.

emigration after 1715; but, within little more than a decade, the movement was almost completely diverted elsewhere. Three factors were responsible for this virtual cessation of emigration to New England. First, ungranted lands of good quality became increasingly scarce in the region after about 1725 and it was so scarce by 1732 that the provincial house of representatives reported that great numbers of inhabitants had been forced to move to the south in search of accommodation.[1] Second, the family unit economy of New England could not induce any considerable immigration of the servant class. Third, not only was the policy of religious domination galling to the spirit of the presbyterian—for that, rather than religious affinity, was what awaited him—but he soon found that if he did not accept that domination he stood little chance of getting any land, thanks to the absolute control of the provincial legislature over land grants.[2] Moreover, the experiences of the early Scotch-Irish settlers were not conducive to any further immigration by their compatriots. While the great emigration of the late 'twenties was taking place from Ireland, the Irish settlers already in New England, faced by the 'inveteracy' of the provincial authorities, 'perplexed by various lawsuits' and 'violently persecuted', were preparing for the growing threat of a military expedition to dislodge them.[3] When Irish immigration into Massachusetts recommenced in the 'thirties on a comparatively small scale it occasioned a crowning example of New England exclusiveness—the requirement that ship-masters should enter into a bond for every Irish person landed at the port.[4] By that time, however, the eyes of most Ulster emigrants had turned elsewhere.

Some of the earliest of the north Irish immigrants into America

---

[1] Sutherland, *Pop. distribution in col. Amer.*, pp. 41–3; and Bidwell Falconer, *Agric. in the northern U.S.*, pp. 69–70; *Jn. Mass. house of repres.*, xi. 31 (14 June 1732).

[2] Proper, *Immigration laws*, pp. 17–23. This did not, of course, prevent grants by bodies such as the Lincolnshire proprietors to Irish presbyterians. For refusal of grant of Nutfield to McGregor and his associates, see *Jn. Mass. house of repres.*, iii.134 (10 June 1719) and 318 (1 Dec. 1720).

[3] Dunbar, surveyor of the woods, to Popple, 15 Sept. 1730 (C.O. 5/872, f.3); Petition, inhabitants of Londonderry (N.H.) to Dunbar, enclosed in Dunbar to Popple, 2 May 1730 (C.O. 5/871, f.188); Petition proprietors of Londonderry and Kingstown (N.H.) to Dunbar, enclosed in same (C.O. 5/871, f.190); B.T. to Newcastle, 11 Nov. 1730 (C.O. 5/916, pp. 393–4). Dunbar to John Scrope, 24 Apr. 1729 (*Cal. treas. bks. & papers*, 1729–30, p. 54); Order in council, 12 Nov. 1730 (P.C. 2/91, p. 283); Dunbar to Popple 17 Nov. 1730 (C.O. 217/6, f.8); Petition, John North and others praying for relief, considered 10 July 1739 (P.C. 2/95, p. 261).

[4] T. H. Maginnis, jnr., *The Irish contribution to America's independence*, p. 46.

had settled in Maryland[1] and in New York province:[2] but it was to Philadelphia and to Newcastle in Delaware that most emigrants after 1720 went, and continued to go, for the next half-century. The three factors that had operated against the continuation of emigration to New England were reversed in the case of the middle colonies, particularly Pennsylvania. Good land was to be had in these colonies for decades after all suitable land in New England had been occupied or granted.[3] Moreover, the middle colonies, flanked on the north by free labour and on the south by slavery, were the stronghold of the system of indentured labour, and so attracted those Irish emigrants who were unable to pay the cost of their passages to America and to whom the prospect of employment was of more immediate concern than the prospect of cheap land. To all Irish emigrants—presbyterian and episcopalian, rich and poor, free and servant—the broad toleration granted by the Pennsylvania charter of privileges of 1701 provided an additional inducement. In very few other parts of the world in the eighteenth century was any and every person who acknowledged God as the creator, upholder and ruler of the world free from religious persecution or prejudice and free from any obligation to attend or maintain any place of worship.[4]

There were times when it seemed that the Pennsylvania authorities were going to curb Irish immigration with as heavy a hand as had been used in New England. The 'bold and indigent strangers from Ireland' roused the ire of the proprietor's officials by squatting on land without troubling to approach the provincial land office for a title, and on at least one occasion they had to be dispossessed by force.[5] The provincial assembly, too, made moves against immigration by indirectly limiting the number of passengers vessels could carry and by imposing discouraging duties on the importation of servants.[6] Fortunately, the efforts of the two branches of government were neither concerted nor untroubled by doubts. The proprietor was opposed to land-squatting, not to immigration,

---

[1] John Mart, lieut-governor of Maryland, to B.T., 25 Aug. 1720 (*Cal. S.P. Amer. & W. Ind.*, 1720–1, no. 214).
[2] B.T. to P.C., 8 Sept. 1721 (ibid., no. 656, p. 417).
[3] Bidwell and Falconer, *Agric. in the northern U.S.*, p. 72.
[4] Klett, *Pres. in Pa.*, p. 29; Proper, *Immigration laws*, p. 44.
[5] Klett, op. cit., p. 235; Bidwell and Falconer, *Agric. in the Northern U.S.*, pp. 72–3; Watsons, *Annals of Pa.*, ii. 260.
[6] See Chapters VI and X.

so the governor vetoed the assembly's attempt of 1755 to restrict immigration. The assembly was opposed to an overwhelming influx of Germans and Irish and not, because of the Indian danger, to immigration in general. When the proprietor doubled the quit-rent to be paid for lands granted after 1732, a movement from Pennsylvania to Maryland and Virginia followed and the assembly protested against the action that had led to this weakening of the border region.[1]

Despite their rather lukewarm reception, most north Irish emigrants to colonial America sailed to Philadelphia. They had arrived in such numbers that, on the eve of the Revolution, Benjamin Franklin estimated that they and their descendants comprised about one-third of Pennsylvania's 350,000 inhabitants, and stated that north Irish immigrants and their descendants occupied more than half the seats in the assembly of the colony.[2]

The pre-eminence of Philadelphia over the other American ports as the destination of north Irish emigrants can be clearly seen by comparing the number of emigrant vessels advertised to sail to each American port between 1750 and 1775—so few copies of the *Belfast News Letter* issued before 1750 survive that a lengthening of this period would not be justified. The following table of advertised destinations is a synopsis of Appendix E. Where a vessel was advertised to sail to ports in two or more provinces, the voyage has been divided between those provinces:[3] where a vessel was advertised to call at two or more north Irish ports for emigrants, the voyage has been divided between those ports.

The most óbvious explanation of the supremacy of Philadelphia and New York is that most emigrants wanted to go there. But this is only a half-truth. Just as important as the wishes of the emigrants were the wishes of the owners of the vessels concerned. During the greater part of the period from 1750 to 1775, though emigrants were a welcome addition to normal trade, they were not a profitable substitute for it and in the ports of Philadelphia and New York about four-fifths of continental America's exports to Ireland

[1] Sutherland, *Pop. distribution in col. Amer.*, pp. 142–4; Klett, *Pres. in Pa.*, p. 35.
[2] Nolan, *Benj. Franklin in Scotland and Ire.*, p. 159.
[3] Except in voyages advertised to Newcastle and Philadelphia, in which case the destination has been given as Pennsylvania. Many emigrants did, indeed, disembark at Newcastle in earlier years (see Chap III), but advertisements made it clear that Philadelphia was the main destination. Most of these advertisements (a) printed *Philadelphia* in capitals or (b) announced the voyage as to 'Newcastle and the flourishing city of Philadelphia' or (c) described the attractions of Pennsylvania.

awaited shipment.[1] It is significant that, with the exception of vessels chartered by land promoters and those diverted to Charleston because of the numbers of emigrants who wished to take advantage of the South Carolina bounty, no vessel before 1771 gave notice of a change in its original destination.

Port of Departure	Destination									
	N.S.& P.E.I.	Mass.	N.Y.	Pa.	Del.	Md.	Va.	N.C.	S.C.	Ga.
Belfast	$2\frac{1}{3}$	$\frac{1}{3}$	$23\frac{3}{4}$	$64\frac{3}{4}$	$\frac{1}{2}$	13	$2\frac{1}{2}$	$6\frac{1}{2}$	$20\frac{5}{6}$	6
L'Derry	$9\frac{1}{2}$	0	$2\frac{1}{2}$	99	0	$2\frac{1}{2}$	0	$3\frac{1}{2}$	10	$\frac{1}{2}$
Newry	$\frac{3}{4}$	$\frac{3}{4}$	$23\frac{1}{4}$	$42\frac{3}{4}$	1	6	0	$2\frac{1}{2}$	$6\frac{1}{2}$	$\frac{1}{2}$
Larne	1	0	20	$18\frac{1}{4}$	$2\frac{3}{4}$	$3\frac{1}{2}$	0	0	12	0
Portrush	0	$3\frac{1}{2}$	$12\frac{1}{4}$	$11\frac{1}{2}$	$2\frac{1}{4}$	0	0	$\frac{1}{2}$	0	0
Totals	$13\frac{7}{12}$	$4\frac{7}{12}$	$81\frac{3}{4}$	$236\frac{1}{4}$	$6\frac{1}{2}$	25	$2\frac{1}{2}$	13	$49\frac{1}{3}$	7
% of whole	3·1	1·1	18·5	53·5	1·5	5·7	0·6	3·0	11·2	1·7

A more accurate view of the pre-eminence of Philadelphia and New York as the ports of reception of north Irish immigrants in normal years is to be obtained by dividing the quarter-century reviewed into two parts—years of light emigration and the periods 1763–7 and 1771–5 when the South Carolina bounty or hardship in Ireland provoked heavy emigration. During periods of heavy emigration, 67·2 per cent. of the emigrant vessels sailed to either Philadelphia or New York; during the remaining fifteen years of the quarter-century, the percentage of voyages to these two ports was 87·6.

Significantly, while the percentage of vessels sailing to Philadelphia in the years of heavy emigration fell by only one-sixth compared with the percentage of vessels that sailed there in normal years, the percentage sailing to New York fell by two-fifths.[2] The

[1] B.M., Add.MS 15485, pp. 8, 30–2, 35; Customs 16/1 *passim*: E. R. Johnson, T. W. van Metre, G. G. Huebner, D. S. Hanchett, *History of domestic and foreign commerce of the United States*, i. 118–9; Clark, *Manufactures in the U.S.*, p. 82.

[2] The corresponding percentages were:
Philadelphia : 61·6 falling to 51·5.
New York : 26·0 falling to 15·7.

obstacle put in the way of rapid settlement of New York by the granting of land in large tracts has been pointed out already. A discouragement of equal gravity to many Ulster people who might otherwise have settled there was the rigorous enforcement of the church establishment by many of the governors of the province.[1] It was natural, therefore, that New York's relative share in the emigration trade fell more than that of Philadelphia at times when emigrants had more say in deciding the destination of vessels.

The partial diversion of Irish emigration from Pennsylvania and New York in the decade before the outbreak of the American revolution was partly due to increasing scarcity of accessible land held directly under the proprietor or the crown in those provinces.[2] The middle colonies remained attractive to the servant class but, as the century progressed, many of the immigrants who had landed at Philadelphia moved inland and then turned to the south, moving parallel to the Blue Ridge mountains along valleys such as the Shenandoah, into Virginia and the Carolinas.[3]

Few emigrant vessels sailed direct from the north of Ireland to Virginia and, as the narrow religious policy of the council did not encourage presbyterian settlement,[4] most of the north Irish inhabitants of that province at the time of the American revolution were probably confined to remote western districts. As in the case of Virginia, there was little direct trade between the north of Ireland and North Carolina or Georgia and what emigration there was to these colonies was due to the efforts of men such as Dobbs and Rea.

South Carolina was in a different category. Here again, there was little trade between the north of Ireland and the colony in normal times but the bounties of the 1730s and 1760s certainly attracted large numbers of Scotch-Irish immigrants and—certainly in the 'sixties, at least—Charleston displaced New York as the second most important port of destination of north Irish emigrant vessels. While the percentage of shipping sailing from the north of Ireland to New York fell from 26·0 in periods of light emigration to 15·7

---

[1] W. Reid, *The Scot in America and the Ulster Scot*, pp. 30–1; *Hist. account of S.C.*, ii.182.
[2] Wilmot to B.T., 30 Apr. 1765 (C.O. 217/43).
[3] J. Campbell to—, n.d. [1749] (P.R.O.N.I., D. 162, no. 47b); F. J. Turner, *The frontier in American history*, pp. 104–5; Green, *Scotch-Irish*, p. 18.
[4] Proper, *Immigration laws*, p. 17; Osgood, *Amer. in 18th cent.*, ii. 522; see Chapter VIII (ii); Dobbs to B.T., 4 Jan. 1755 (C.O. 5/297, ff. 227–30).

per cent. in periods of heavy emigration, South Carolina's share rose from 2·0 to 16·0 per cent.

It is obvious that most of those who sailed from the north of Ireland to colonial America landed in Pennsylvania and that New York and South Carolina received most of the remainder but to trace where the immigrants went after disembarking is a task for American historians. In whatever colonies they settled, they fought with distinction and won honour in the conflict which was soon to result in the birth of the United States of America. Writers have not been slow to remind America of the debt which it owes to Scotch-Irish settlers. The existence of a debt would not have been acknowledged by the settlers themselves—their ardour in the Revolution was a thanksgiving to a land which had received them in their distress. They had heard America's greeting and had obeyed her command:

> Welcome to my shores. . .; bless the hour in which thou didst see my verdent fields, my navigable rivers, and my green mountains! —If thou wilt work, I have bread for thee; if thou wilt be honest, sober, and industrious, I have greater rewards to confer on thee— ease and independence. I will give thee fields to feed and clothe thee; a comfortable fireside to sit by, and tell thy children by what means thou hast prospered; and a decent bed to repose on. . . . . Go thou and work and till; thou shalt prosper. . .[1]

Provincial authorities might frown but west of the ports lay a land full of challenge and hope.

[1] H.St.J. de Crevecoeur, *Letters from an American farmer* [1782], pp. 67–8 (Everyman's ed.).

Place name abbreviations used in Appendices (except Appendix D)

An.–Annapolis
B.–Belfast
Ba.–Baltimore
Bar.–Barbados
Bo.–Boston
C.F.–Cape Fear
Ch.–Charleston
Ct.–Charlottetown
D.–Londonderry
De.–Delaware
Ga.–Georgia
Ge.–Georgetown
Ha.–Halifax
Ja.–Jamaica
L.–Larne
Mas.–Massachusetts
Md.–Maryland
N.–Newry
N.C.–North Carolina
Ne.–Newcastle
N.S.–Nova Scotia
N.Y.–New York
P.–Portrush
Pa.–Pennsylvania
P.E.I.–Prince Edward Island
Ph.–Philadelphia
Qu.–Quebec
Sa.–Savannah
S.C.–South Carolina
Va.–Virginia
Wi.–Wilmington

APPENDIX A

The Number and Tonnage of Emigrant Vessels Advertised to Leave North Irish Ports for Colonial America, 1750–1775

IN the few cases in which the tonnage of a vessel is not stated in the advertisement, the tonnage is assumed to be

(a) where applicable, the same as in other years when the vessel was advertised, or

(b) the average of other emigrant vessels in the particular year.

Where the advertisement stated that a vessel would call at two ports for emigrants, half the vessel and half its tonnage is included in the columns relating to each of the ports concerned. Where this occurred and is not obvious, the facts are footnoted.

Number of Emigrant Vessels Advertised and (Advertised Tonnage)

Year	Belfast	L'derry	Newry	Larne	Portrush	Total
1750	3(600)	3(660)	—	1 (200)	4(500)	11(1960)
1751	No copies of B.N.L.					
1752	1½(300)	—	—	1½(400)	1(160)	4(860)
1753	3(730)	2(550)	—	1(200)	1(160)	7(1640)
1754	2¼(475)	1(200)	2(300)	2(450)	1½(255)	9(1680)
1755	3(600)	—	—	1(250)	1(350)	5(1200)
1756	—	1(250)	1(300)	2(400)	—	4(950)
1757	3(600)	3(700)	—	2(400)	1(250)	9(1950)
1758	5(1000)	—	—	1(200)	1(250)	7(1450)
1759	—	—	—	3(700)	—	3(700)
1760	1(300)	3(770)	1(250)	4(950)	1(150)	10(2420)
1761[a]	4(880)	6(1550)	—	3(650)	—	13(3080)
1762	4½(985)	7(1980)	1(200)	1½(285)	2(550)	16(4000)
1763	5½(1275)	6(1730)	4(870)	3(800)	1½(425)	20(5100)

229

Appendix A

Year	Belfast	L'derry	Newry	Larne	Portrush	Total
1764	6½(1525)	4(1050)	2(600)	1½(425)	2(450)	16(4050)
1765[b]	10½(2570)	5(1350)	3(700)	½(125)	2(550)	21(5295)
1766[c]	9½(2615)	10(2650)	3(800)	2½(675)	2(550)	27(7290)
1767[b]	12(3150)	7(2000)	5½(1490)	2½(625)	2(525)	29(7790)
1768	7(1950)	5(1350)	7(1950)	1(250)	1(300)	21(5800)
1769	8(1960)	5(1500)	7(1830)	—	1(250)	21(5540)
1770	7(1880)	8(2100)	2(600)	3(780)	1(250)	21(5610)
1771	7(1800)	14(4050)	10(2950)	2(500)	1(250)	34(9550)
1772[d]	8(2250)	11½(3275)	6½(1925)	4(1100)	1(250)	31(8800)
1773	14(3590)	15(4250)	8(2550)	4(1150)	—	41(11540)
1774	10½(3725)	8(2850)	13(4200)	6½(1825)	1(250)	39(12850)
1775	7(2810)	3(1150)	8(3600)	4(1400)	1(300)	23(9260)
Totals	143(37570)	127½(35965)	84(25115)	57½(14740)	30(6975)	442(120365)
% of whole	32·4(31·2)	28·8(29·9)	19·0(20·9)	13·0(12·2)	6·8(5·8)	

(a) Two vessels sailed from both Belfast and Larne
(b) Two vessels sailed from both Belfast and Portrush
(c) One vessel sailed from both Belfast and Portrush; Newry and Larne; and Newry and Portrush
(d) One vessel sailed from both Belfast and Londonderry; and Belfast and Newry

APPENDIX B

Discrepancies in Tonnage

TABLE showing discrepancies between the advertised tonnage of emigrant vessels and
   (i) the tonnage recorded in port returns; and
   (ii) the tonnage of the same vessel in different advertisements.

The purpose of exaggerating the tonnage of vessels in advertisements and of minimising it for official purposes is obvious. But, in all cases where both figures are available, the difference is so great that it is clear that, whereas the customs authorities based their dues on the net register tonnage, the advertised figure was based on the highest justifiable tonnage, such as deadweight or displacement. It has not been possible to trace any of the vessels concerned in the printed registers of shipping at Lloyd's, possibly owing to the incomplete nature of the information available, but also possibly because – as an official of that society has suggested – only vessels holding classes were recorded in the registers.

No details have been paired except in cases where there cannot be the slightest doubt that the details relate to the same vessel.

Vessel	Voyage	Tonnage	Sources (B.N.L unless otherwise stated)	
Elizabeth	B.-N.C.	130/140	22 Jun. 53	29 May 53
William & George	L.-Ph.	200/250	30 Apr. 54	27 May 57
Antrim	L.-N.Y.&Ph.	200/60	17 May 54	C.O. 5/1227, 19 Nov. 54
Annabella	N.-Ph.	200/100	16 Jul. 54	C.O. 5/1227, 23 Jan. 55
Dobbs Galley	B.-N.C.	250/200	10 Oct. 54	30 May 55
Admiral Hawke	D.-Ph.	250/300	7 May 62	15 Mar. 71

Vessel	Voyage	Tonnage		Sources (B.N.L unless otherwise stated)
Lord Dunluce	L.-N.Y.	c.200/c.160	5 Jun. 62	2 Jul. 62
Orangefield	B.-N.Y.	230/100	14 Sep. 62	C.O. 5/1228 29 Jan. 63
Marquis of Granby	B.-Ph.&N.Y.	250/80	25 Mar. 63	C.O. 5/1228 5 Mar. 63
Prince of Wales	B.-Ch.	240/110	12 Aug. 63 30 Aug. 65 12 Dec. 66	C.O. 5/511, 20 Jan. 64, 29 Mar. 66 (100 tons), 27 May 67
Prince of Wales	B.-N.Y.	240/100	16 Mar. 64	C.O. 5/1228 15 Jun. 64
Falls	B.-Ch.	200/100	12 Aug. 63	C.O. 5/511, 9 Jan. 64
Venus	N.-N.Y.	140/80	6 May 63	C.O. 5/1228, 24 Oct. 63
King of Prussia	N.-Ph.	250/80	5 Apr. 63	C.O. 5/1228, 17 Feb. 63
Pitt	L.-Ne.&N.Y.	300/90	29 Apr. 63 10 Aug. 64	C.O. 5/1228, 7 Jan. 63, 27 Nov. 64
Culloden	B.-Ph.	350/150	24 May 63	C.O. 5/1228, 9 Jan. 64
Lord Dunluce	L.-Ph.	200/50	10 Jun. 63	C.O. 5/1228, 8 Nov. 63
Providence	P.-Ne.&N.Y.	300/150	27 May 63	C.O. 5/1228, 28 Feb. 63, 26 Nov. 64
Boscawen	B.-Ph.	200/60	29 Jun. 64	C.O. 5/1228, 6 Jan. 65
James & Mary	B.&L.-N.Y.	250/80	31 Jul. 64	C.O. 5/1228, 7 Dec. 64
John	N.-N.Y.	300/80	27 Mar. 64	C.O. 5/1228, 27 Jan. 64
Newry	N.-N.Y.	300/70	10 Aug. 64	C.O. 5/1228, 19 Nov. 64
Admiral Hawke	D.-N.S.	250/100	31 May 65	C.O. 221/31, p. 308
Belfast Pacquet	B.-Ph.	250/100	17 Jun. 66	C.O. 5/511, 24 Oct. 66
Hopewell	D.-N.S.	250/100	25 Mar. 66	C.O. 217/44 29 Sep. 66
Falls	D.-N.S.	250/100	12 Aug. 66	C.O. 217/44, 8 Nov. 66

Vessel	Voyage	Tonnage		Sources (B.N.L unless otherwise stated)
Nancy	B.-Ch.	300/80	30 Dec. 66	C.O. 5/511, 25 Jun. 67
Hibernia	B.&P.-Ne. & N.Y.	200/170	17 Apr. 67	18 Mar. 68
Britannia	N.-Ch.	300/70	13 Mar. 67	C.O. 5/511, 31 Aug. 67
Lord Dungannon	B.-Ch.	200/180	8 Sep. 67	10 Mar. 69
Earl of Hillsborough	B.-N.Y.	200/90	20 Nov. 67	C.O. 5/511, 27 Feb. 67
Friendship	B.-Ph.	300/250	7 Feb. 69	12 Mar. 73
Pennsylvania Farmer	N.-Ph.	250/220	14 Mar. 69	C.E.P., 24 Aug. 69
Wallworth	D.-Ph.	250/300	11 May 70	12 Mar. 73
George	D.-Ph.	200/250	21 Aug. 70	26 Mar. 71
Prince of Wales	B.-N.Y.	250/100	22 Mar. 71	Treasury 64/312, 21 Mar. 71
Prince of Wales	B.-N.Y.	200/300	28 Mar. 71	23 Jun. 73
Ann	D.-Ph.	250/300	5 Jul. 71	20 Jun. 73
Robert	N.-N.Y.	300/350	23 Jul. 71	19 Feb. 73
Prince of Wales	D.-Ph.	300/350	28 Jun. 71	8 Jun. 73
Minerva	N.-Ph.&Ba.	350/400	12 Feb. 73	3 Mar. 75
Waddell	B.-N.C.	400/450	7 May 73 14 Apr. 75	14 Sep. 73
Catherine	B.-Ph.	300/260	31 Aug. 73	24 Aug. 74
Hope	B.-Md.	450/400	22 Jul. 74	20 Sep. 74
Lord Dunluce	L.-Ne.&Ba.	400/450	19 Aug. 74	14 Mar. 75

APPENDIX C

The Number of Emigrants Carried by Certain Vessels from North Irish Ports to Colonial America

---

COMPARATIVELY little information concerning the number of emigrants carried by vessels from north Irish ports is available. This Appendix comprises a complete list of all instances which have come to my attention. The number of passengers was sometimes variously reported by two or three sources. In such cases the alternative figures are given thus: 300/250.

The *New York Journal*, *Pennsylvania Gazette* and *Pennsylvania Packet* sources are cited from O'Brien, *Hidden phase*, pp. 276–84. The South Carolina sources are either the *South Carolina Gazette* and the *South Carolina Advertiser and General Magazine* in C.O. 5-380 or Revill, S.C.

The explanation of the difference in the two reports of the *Wallworth* in 1773 is that the vessel sailed first to Philadelphia, discharging some passengers there and took the remainder to Charleston (*B.N.L.* 29 June 1773; *S.C. Gaz.*, 31 Aug. 1773).

Year	Vessel	Voyage	Tons	Passengers	Source (*B.N.L.* unless otherwise stated)
1718	McCullom	D.-Bo.	70	100	C.O. 5/848, f.82
	Dolphin	D.-Bo	70	34	Ibid.
	Mary & Elizabeth	D.-Bo.	45	100	Ibid. f.83
1739	William	D.-N.Y.	120	186	C.O. 5/1226, f.56
1741	William	B.-N.Y.	120	6	Ibid. f.149
1762	Providence	P.-Ne. & N.Y. c.300	300	14 Jan. 63

Year	Vessel	Voyage	Tons	Passengers	Source (B.N.L. unless otherwise stated)
1763	Marquis of Granby	B.-Ph. & N.Y.	250	212	20 May 63
	Prince of Wales	B.-Ch.	240	170	C.O. 5/511, 20 Jan. 64
	Falls	B.-Ch.	over 200	80	Ibid. 9 Jan. 64
	King of Prussia	N.-Ph.	250	221	24 May 63
	Venus	N.-N.Y.	140	22	C.O. 5/1228, 24 Oct. 63
1764	Prince of Wales	B.-N.Y.	240	170	Ibid. 15 Jun. 64
1765	Prince of Wales	B.-Ch.	240	59	C.O. 5/511, 29 Mar. 66
1766	Belfast Pacquet	B.-Ch.	250	78	Ibid. 24 Oct. 66
	William	N.-Bo.	—	71	Donovan, *Ir. in Mass.*, p. 36
1767	Prince of Wales	B.-Ch.	240	210	C.O. 5/511, 27 May 67
	Nancy	B.-Ch.	300	c.300/287	Ibid. 25 June 67/ Revill, *S.C.*, pp. 74-80
	Britannia	B.-Ch.	300	174/99 redemptioners	C.O. 5/511, 31 Aug. 67/ Revill, *S.C.*, pp. 83-4
	James & Mary	L.-Ch.	—	183	Revill *S.C.*, pp. 99-103
	Admiral Hawke	D.-Ch.	—	93	Ibid., pp. 97-8
	Chichester	B.-Ch.	—	147	Ibid., pp. 93-5
1768	Prince George	B.-Sa.	—	c.170	O'Brien, *Hidden phase*, p. 170
	Providence	P.-N.Y.	300	c.25	3 Feb. 69
1771	Britannia	B.-Sa.	300	200	1 Nov. 71
	Pennsylvania Farmer	N.-Ph.	300	300	24 Jul. 72
1772	Friendship	B.-Ph.	250	250	3 Apr. 72
	Prince of Wales	B.-Ph.	400	400	12 May 72
	Philadelphia	B.-Ph.	250	240/380	21 Aug. 72/N.Y.J. 29 Aug. 72
	John & James	B.-P.E.I.	150	190	L.J. 17 Jun. 72
	Elizabeth	B.-Sa.	250	190/300	20 Nov. 72/L.J., 4 May 73
	Jupiter	D.-Ph.	300	430	N.Y.J. 25 Jun. 72
	Rose	D.-Ph.	300	340	18 Sep. 72
	Wallworth	D.-Ph.	250	300	Pa. Gaz. 9 Sep. 72

Year	Vessel	Voyage	Tons	Passengers	Source
					(B.N.L. unless otherwise stated)
	Hannah	D.-Ph.	400	400	*L.J.* 20 Jun. 72
	General Wolfe	D.-Ph.	300	250/300/ 400	*N.Y.J.* 29 Oct. 72/ 15 Dec. 72/*L.J.* 24 Jun. 72
	Prince of Wales	D.-Ba. & Ph.	300	over 350	18 Sep. 72
	Robert	N.-N.Y.	300	300	17 Apr. 72
	Phebe & Peggy	N.-Ph.	300	400/423	*N.Y.J.* 10 Sep. 72/ 12 Mar. 73
	Jupiter	L.-Ch.	250	200	12 May 72
	Lord Dunluce	L.-Ch.	400	near 400	9 Oct. 72
1773	*Friendship*	B.-Ph.	300	250	*Pa. Gaz.* 5 May 73
	Agnes	B.-Ph.	200	210/220	14 Sep. 73/ 14 May 73
	Peggy	B.-Ph.	200	207	30 Apr. 73
	Alexander	D.-Ph.	400	530/546/ 630	29 Jun. 73/*Pa. Gaz.* 11 Aug. 73/*F.D.J.* 5 Oct. 73
	Hannah	D.-Ph.	400	500/520/ 580	*Pa. Gaz.* 11 Aug. 73/29 Jun. 73/*F.D.J.* 5 Oct. 73
	Wallworth	D.-Ph.	300	300/450	*S.C. Gaz.* 31 Aug. 73/29 Jun. 73
	Jupiter	D.-Ph.	300	450/513	29 Jun. 73/*F.D.J.* 5 Oct. 73
	Prince of Wales	B.-Sa.	350	200	*Pa. Gaz.* 8 Nov. 73
	Betsy	N.-Ph.	300	360/361	14 Sep. 73/7 May 73
	Needham	N.-Ph.	400	400/near 500/509	18 Mar. 74/21 May 73/*C.E.P.* 23 Sep. 73
	Robert	N.-Ph.	350	300/420	*Pa. Packet* ? Jul. 73/ 21 May 73
	Newry Assistance	N.-Ph.	300	270	*Pa. Gaz.* 4 Aug. 73
	Helena	D.-Ch.	200	120	*S.C. Gaz.* 15 Sep. 73
	Elliot	N.-Ch.	300	200	*S.C. Adv.* 20 Aug. 73
	Minerva	N.-Ph.	350	near 420	7 May 73
1774	*Peace & Plenty*	B.-Ph. & N.Y.	400	400	13 May 74
	Glorious Memory	B.-Ph. & Ba.	400	70/117	14 Oct. 74/16 Sep. 74
	Prosperity	B.-Ph.	500	200	16 Sep. 74
	Hannah	D.-Ph.	400	400	27 Sep. 74
	Hope	N.-Ph.	350	200/220	Ezra Stiles, Newport (R.I.) to—, 9 Aug 1774 (O'Brien

Year	Vessel	Voyage	Tons	Passengers	Source
					(B.N.L. unless otherwise stated)
					Hidden phase, p. 284); Diary of Christopher Marshall (O'Brien, *Washington's Irish Assoc.*, p. 236)
	Renown	N.-Ph.	450	350	27 Sep. 74
	Needham	N.-Ph.	400	300	27 Sep. 74
	Jupiter	L.-Ch. & Ba	250	150	*S.C. Gaz.*, 12 Apr. 74
1775	*Prosperity*	B.-Ph.	500	480	25 Apr. 75
	John	B.-Ba.	450	30	28 Apr. 75

The arrival at Charleston of the following vessels with Irish protestants on board was noted in the Journal of the South Carolina Council—

Year	Vessel	Voyage	Tons	Passengers	Source
1766	*Earl of Hillsborough*	—	—	229	Revill, *S.C.*, pp. 67-70
1767	*Betty Gregg*	—	—	156	Ibid., pp. 108-11
	Lord Dungannon	—	—	139	Ibid., pp. 104-6
	Earl of Donegal	—	—	297	Ibid., pp. 93-6

APPENDIX D

A Synopsis of Advertisements of Emigrant Shipping, 1771–1775

THE following summaries illustrate many of the features of the organization of the emigration trade examined in this book. The period 1771–5 has been selected not only because north Irish emigration reached a new high level in those years, but because the organization of the trade had, by then, also reached a new high level.

The Belfast News Letter is the source of information except where otherwise stated. All dates in brackets are the DATES OF ISSUE of newspapers.

BELFAST 1771

BRIG POLLY: 200 tons.

Master:	Dd. McCutchion; well known for humanity
Agent:	Wm. & John Brown, merchants.
Destination:	Philadelphia.
Advertised:	1 Feb.
To Sail:	15 Feb.
Sailed:	—
Arrived:	1 May after voyage of 7 weeks.

Arr. from Phil. with flaxseed (Jan. 29); stout new ship; good acc. for passengers (Feb. 1); arr. at Phil.; all pass. in good health and spirits (June 4). Made second voyage from Belfast to Philadelphia in 1771.

PHILADELPHIA: 300 tons.

Master:	Jas. Malcolm; one of best passenger masters.
Agent:	Thos. & J. Greg, Waddell Cunningham, merchants.
Destination:	Philadelphia.
Advertised:	1 Mar.
To Sail:	1, 15, 26 Apr.
Sailed:	(7 May)
Arrived:	On or before 4 July.

Arr. from Phil. with flaxseed and flour (Feb. 12); special encouragement to young and recommended servants (Apr. 5); sailed with pork, beef, cloth (May 7); letter of thanks to master and agents, signed by 46 and dated Delaware Bay, July 4 (Nov. 26) Other voyages — 1769, Belfast - Phil. - Cork-Phil. (Apr. 11, *C.E.P.*, Oct. 10 & Nov. 10); 1770, Belfast-Phil. (Apr. 13)—see 1772.

Appendix D

PRINCE OF WALES: 250 tons.
Master: Ch. McKenzie.
Agent: Thos. & J. Greg, Waddell
            Cunningham, merchants.
Destination: New York.
Advertised: 22 Mar.
To Sail: 10, 15 Apr.
Sailed: (23 Apr.)
Arrived: —

Prince of Wales of Belfast, 100 tons, arr. there from N.Y. on Mar. 21 (Treasury, 64/312); arr. from N.Y. with flaxseed and flour (Mar. 26); pass. to be on board by Apr. 13 (Apr. 5); sailed with cloth, coals (Apr. 23). Other voyages—see 1772.

KITTY AND PEGGY: 300 tons.
Master: Duncan Ferguson; tender-
            ness and humanity.
Agent: Wm. Burgess, merchant.
Destination: Philadelphia.
Advertised: 26 Mar.
To Sail: 20 Apr., 14 May.
Sailed: (21 May).
Arrived: 19 Aug.

Kitty and Peggy, 120 tons, arr. Belfast from Phil. (Treasury, 64/312); flaxseed and flour imported in, to be sold (Mar. 26); sailed with beef, cloth (May 21); all pass. landed in good health (Oct. 25).

BRIG POLLY: 200 tons.
Master: Dd. McCutchon; humanity
            and good nature.
Agent: Wm. & John Brown,
            merchants.
Destination: Philadelphia.
Advertised: 14 June.
To Sail: 25 July, 5, 20 Aug.
Sailed: (23 Aug.)
Arrived: —

Right good vessel; shortly expected; will be fitted out for pass.; master in the trade for a 'series of years' (June 14); arr. from Phil. with flour; greatest plenty of water and best of provisions promised (July 9). Other voyage—see above.

HOPEWELL: 250 tons.
Master: Thos. Ash; well
            acquainted with the trade.
Agent: Wm. Beatty, merchant.
Destination: Charleston & Savannah.
Advertised: 30 July.
To Sail: 1, 20 Sep., 2, 10 Oct.
Sailed: 29 Oct.
Arrived: —

Hourly expected; good attention to provisions (July 30); arr. from Norway with deals (Aug. 9); postponed because of late harvest (Oct. 2); arr. all pass. well (10 Mar. 1771). Other voyages— 1769, Belfast-Savannah (Aug. 11); 1770, Belfast-Phil. (July 13); 1772, Phil.-Belfast, but ran aground in Belfast Lough (Feb. 14).

BRITANNIA: 300 tons; (See Appendix C)
Master: Jas. Clendinan; many
            years' experience.
Agent: Jas. Getty, Dd. Gaussan
            (Newry), merchants,
            Matt. Rea (Drumbo).
Destination: Savannah.

Long advert. re lands available, Rea to visit Belfast, Lisburn; Banbridge, Armagh; vessel now at Newry; pass. must be well. recommended (Aug. 6); arr. at Belfast (Aug. 23); still room for a

Advertised:	6 Aug.	
To Sail:	20 Sep., 7, 17 Oct.	
Sailed:	28 Oct.	
Arrived:	On or before 18 Jan 1772.	

certain number (Oct. 1); sailed with beef, cloth (Oct. 18); sailed on Oct. 28 with fair wind; all pass. in good health and spirits (Nov. 1); letter of thanks signed by 60, 14 of whom were 'a committee' dated Savannah, Jan. 18, 1772 (Mar. 13, 1772). Other voyages—1766, Newry-N.Y. (May 6); 1767, Newry-Charleston (Mar. 13); 1768, Newry-N.Y. and Phil.-Newry-Phil. (Mar. 29, July 5); 1769, Newry-Baltimore (Mar. 21) —see 1772.

LONDONDERRY 1771

EAGLE: 300 tons.
Master: Richard Green.
Agent: Geo. Sealy & Son, merchant.
Destination: New York.
Advertised: 5 Feb.
To Sail: In 20 days.
Sailed: —
Arrived: —

Fine, commodious, fast-sailing good ship (Feb. 5).

WALLWORTH: 250 tons.
Master: Conolly McCausland; well acquainted with the the trade; civil.
Agent: Abraham McCausland, Jas. Mitchell, merchants, Jas. Stirling.
Destination: Philadelphia.
Advertised: 5 Feb.
To Sail: 1st week Apr., 1 May.
Sailed: —
Arrived: —

Made voyage home from Phil. in 23 days; will take reasonable no. of pass. (Feb. 5); arr. safely at Phil. (Oct. 1). Other voyages— 1768, L'Derry-Charleston (May 21); 1769, N.C.-Liverpool (C.E.P., Sep. 4); 1770, Londonderry-Phil. —see 1772, 1773.

JUPITER: 300 tons.
Master: Alex. Ewing.
Agent: Andrew Greg, Jas. Mitchell, merchants.
Destination: Philadelphia.
Advertised 15 Mar.
To Sail: 1 May.
Sailed: —
Arrived: —

Good treatment promised (Mar. 15); spoken to, 40° 49′ N, 60° W, with servants on board; all well (*Dublin Chronicle*, Sep. 10). Other voyages—see 1772, 1773, 1774.

Appendix D

ADMIRAL HAWK: 300 tons.
Master: — McCadden.
Agent: Caldwell, Vance and
Caldwell, merchants.
Destination: Philadelphia.
Advertised: 15 Mar.
To Sail: 1 Apr.
Sailed: —
Arrived: —

Other voyages—1765, L'Derry-
Halifax (May 31); 1766, L'Derry-
Phil. (Mar. 18); 1767, L'Derry-
Charleston (Aug. 18).

MARQUIS OF GRANBY: 300 tons.
Master: Arch. McIlwaine.
Agent: John Maulevery, Thos.
Beesley, Dickson
Cunningham, merchants.
Destination: Philadelphia.
Advertised: 22 Mar.
To Sail: 1st week Apr.
Sailed: —
Arrived: —

Best usage to pass. as in past
(Mar. 22). Other voyages—1765,
L'Derry-Phil. (Mar. 22); 1766,
same (Mar. 28); 1767, same
(Aug. 4).

HENRY: 350 tons.
Master: Saml. Hunter.
Agent: — Alexander, merchant
(owner).
Destination: Philadelphia.
Advertised: 19 Mar.
To Sail: 1st week May, 30 May.
Sailed: —
Arrived: 4 Sep. after 8 weeks.

Remarkably high between decks;
limited no. of pass. will be taken
(Mar. 19); will be plentifully supplied with provisions of highest
quality (Mar. 26); arr. at Phil. after
agreeable voyage; pass. in good
spirits (Nov. 4).

GEORGE: 250 tons.
Master: Richard Paul.
Agent: Jas. Miller, Saml. Corry,
merchants.
Destination: Philadelphia.
Advertised: 26 Mar.
To Sail: 10 May.
Sailed: —
Arrived: —

Other voyages—1770, L'Derry-
Phil. (Aug. 21)—see 1773, 1775.

PHENIX: 300 tons.
Master: Jas. Mitchell; character
well established by series
of successful voyages.
Agent: Caldwell, Vance &
Caldwell, merchants,
Jas. Stirling.
Destination: Philadelphia.

Any who missed passage on
Wallworth will have their earnest
allowed on the *Phoenix* (May 21);
arr. at Phil.; all well (Oct. 29).
Other voyages—1767, L'Derry-
Phil. (Jan. 13); 1769, same (Mar.
21); 1770, same (Feb. 25).

Advertised:	12 Apr.
To Sail:	1 June.
Sailed:	—
Arrived:	8 weeks after sailing.

ROSE: 300 tons.
Master: Wm. Dysart.
Agent: Jas. Harvey, Thos. Moore, Saml. Curry, Wm. Hope, merchants.
Destination: Philadelphia.
Advertised: 11 June.
To Sail: 5, 15 July.
Sailed: —
Arrived: (21 Oct.).

Now in port; remarkable for quick voyages (June 11). Other voyages — 1766, Belfast-Phil. (Mar. 25); 1769, L'Derry-Phil. (June 2); 1770, same (May 29)—see 1772, 1773.

HOPEWELL: 250 tons.
Master: Neal McGowan.
Agent: Caldwell, Vance & Caldwell, merchants.
Destination: Halifax & Philadelphia.
Advertised: 21 June.
To Sail: 10 July, 1 Aug.
Sailed: (13 Aug.)
Arrived: —

C. V. and C. will send vessel to N.S. if reasonable no. of pass. agree and pay one guinea earnest (May 17); people may become landlords instead of tenants; good no. already agreed; will continue to Phil. for sake of servants (June 21). Other voyages — 1766, L'Derry-N.S. (Mar. 25)—see 1772.

MINERVA: 400 tons.
Master: Francis Fearis.
Agent: Caldwell, Vance & Caldwell, merchants.
Destination: Philadelphia.
Advertised: 28 June.
To Sail: 20 July.
Sailed: —
Arrived: —

Most comfortable acc.; hourly expected from Phil. and will return there with utmost expedition (June 28). Other voyages—see 1773, 1774.

PRINCE OF WALES: 300 tons.
Master: Thos. Morrison.
Agent: Jas. Thompson, merchant.
Destination: Philadelphia.
Advertised: 18 June.
To Sail: 20 July.
Sailed: —
Arrived: —

Extremely roomy between decks (June 28). Other voyages—1768, L'Derry-N.Y. (July 29); 1769, L'Derry-Phil. (Aug. 11); 1770, same (Aug. 10)—1772, 1773.

ANN: 250 tons.
Master: Pat. Miller.
Agent: Robt. Alexander, Jas. Harvey, merchants.

Other voyages—see 1772, 1773, 1774.

Destination:	Philadelphia.
Advertised:	5 July.
To Sail:	15 July.
Sailed:	—
Arrived:	—

BETTY:	200 tons.	Entirely calculated for pass. trade
Master:	Jas. McCay.	(July 9); now at quay discharging
Agent:	Abraham McCausland,	(Aug. 2). Other voyages—1769,
	Robt. Houston, Maxwell	Baltimore-Cork-Maryland(*C.E.P.*,
	Kennedy, merchants.	July 25 & Aug. 29).
Destination:	Wilmington.	
Advertised:	9 July.	
To Sail:	1, 20 Aug.	
Sailed:	—	
Arrived:	—	

NEWRY 1771

NEWRY PACKET:	300 tons.	Now at Warrenpoint; servants
Master:	Ch. Robinson, well	will be taken on board and receive
	acquainted with the trade.	full provisions from Mar. 1 (Feb.
Agent:	John Dickson, Hamilton	5); servants will be outfitted and
	Pringle, John Robinson,	clothed according to agreement
	merchants.	(Mar. 5). Other voyages—1767,
Destination:	Philadelphia.	Newry-Phil. (Apr. 21); 1769,
Advertised:	5 Feb.	L'Derry-Phil. (Feb. 10); 1770,
To Sail:	10 Mar., 15 Apr.	Newry-Phil. (Feb. 20).
Sailed:	—	
Arrived:	—	

BRIG DOLPHIN:	300 tons.	New vessel; abundance of best
Master:	Thos. Finlay.	provisions (Feb. 8).
Agent:	Wm. & John Ogle,	
	merchants, Robt. Shewell	
	(owner—Belfast)	
Destination:	Philadelphia.	
Advertised:	8 Feb.	
To Sail:	28 Feb., 15 Mar.	
Sailed:	—	
Arrived:	—	

PENNSYLVANIA FARMER:	250 tons (see Appendix C).	
Master:	Robt. Johnston; noted for	Forty persons already engaged
	humanity.	(Feb. 12). Other voyages—1769,
Agent:	Wm. & John Ogle,	Newry-Phil.-Cork-Phil. (Mar. 14;
	merchants.	*C.E.P.*, July 21 & Sep. 22).
Destination:	Philadelphia.	
Advertised:	12 Feb.	

To Sail: 25 Mar.
Sailed: —
Arrived: —

BETSY:	250 tons.	Not more than 10 male and 10
Master:	Gerald Brown.	female servants wanted (Feb. 12).
Agent:	Wm. & John Ogle, merchants.	
Destination:	Baltimore & Charleston.	
Advertised:	12 Feb.	
To Sail:	1 Mar.	
Sailed:	—	
Arrived:	—	

JENNY AND POLLY:	300 tons.	Special encouragement to trades-
Master:	Daniel Lawrence.	men (Apr. 9).
Agent:	Wm. & John Ogle, merchants.	
Destination:	Baltimore, Annapolis & Charleston.	
Advertised:	9 Apr.	
To Sail:	10, 20 May.	
Sailed:	—	
Arrived:	—	

BRIG VENUS:	250 tons.	Baltimore, a new town, improving
Master:	John Lloyd.	daily, is near Phil. — passage
Agent:	Gaussan & Bailie, Gregs & Cunningham (Belfast), merchants.	thence costs 6s. (June 4).
Destination:	Baltimore & Charleston.	
Advertised:	4 June.	
To Sail:	1 July.	
Sailed:	—	
Arrived:	—	

FRANKLIN:	400 tons.	Very fine and remarkably speedy
Master:	Moses Rankin.	vessel; uncommonly lofty in
Agent:	Geo., Wm. & John Glenny, Hill Wilson, Wm. Beath, George Anderson, merchants.	cabin, steerage, and between decks; few will be taken; goods will be carefully shipped (June 18).
Destination:	New York.	
Advertised:	18 June.	
To Sail:	mid. July.	
Sailed:	—	
Arrived:	—	

PEGGY:	about 300 tons.	Arr. with flour from America for
Master:	— Forsyth.	agents named (July 19).
Agent:	Wm. & John Ogle, merchants.	
Destination:	Maryland.	
Advertised:	19 July.	
To Sail:	10 Aug.	
Sailed	—	
Arrived:	—	

ROBERT:	300 tons.	Good acc. for pass.; can depend
Master:	Matt. Russell.	on being well treated (July 23).
Agent:	Andrew Thompson, merchant.	Other voyages—1748, Newry-N.Y. (June 21); 1770, same (Mar.
Destination:	New York.	9)—see 1772, 1773, 1774.
Advertised:	23 July.	
To Sail:	1 Sep.	
Sailed:	—	
Arrived:	—	

NEWRY ASSISTANCE:	300 tons.	Both master and vessel well
Master:	Wm. Cheevers; well known in the trade.	known in pass. trade; hourly expected, send goods to Dickson's
Agent:	John Dickson, John Pringle, merchants, John Hoope (Markethill), Joshua Adams (Moneymore).	warehouse (Aug. 13); six prisoners sentenced to transportation escaped from, at Newry, Oct. 1771 (June 26, 1772). Other voyages—1768, Newry-Phil. (Apr.
Destination:	Philadelphia.	22); 1769, Newry-Phil.-Cork-Phil.
Advertised:	13 Aug.	(Feb. 20; *C.E.P.*, July 11 and 22)—
To Sail:	1 Sep.	see 1772, 1773.
Sailed:	Oct.	
Arrived:	—	

LARNE 1771

JUPITER:	250 tons.	Considerable number already engaged; others must give at least
Master:	John Allen.	one guinea earnest (Apr. 26); arr.
Agent:	John Montgomery, merchant, Thos. Barklie (Ballymena on Saturdays).	Belfast from Gottenburgh with herrings (*L.J.* Apr. 26); arr. at Charleston, capt. Shutter (*sic*);
Destination:	Charleston.	pass. given grants of land (Jan. 10,
Advertised:	26 Apr.	1772). Other voyages — 1769,
To Sail:	25 June, 25 July.	Larne-Phil. (Aug. 21)—see 1772,
Sailed:	—	1773, 1774.
Arrived:	16 Oct.	

JAMES AND MARY: 250 tons.
Master: John Workman.
Agent: Jas. McVicker, John Moore, merchants.
Destination: New York.
Advertised: 6 Aug.
To Sail: 10, 25 Sep., 7, 15 Oct.
Sailed: —
Arrived: —

Other voyages — 1765, Larne-N.Y. (June 21); 1766, same (July 18); 1767, same (July 14); 1770, Larne-N.Y.-Larne-N.Y. (Mar. 20, Aug. 14)—see 1772, 1773, 1774, 1775.

PORTRUSH 1771

RAINBOW: 250 tons.
Master: Jas. Caldwell.
Agent: John & Ch. Gault, Alex. Lawrence, merchants (all of Coleraine).
Destination: New York.
Advertised: 5 July.
To Sail: 1, 20 Aug.
Sailed: —
Arrived: —

Other voyages—1765, Belfast and Portrush-Phil. (May 21); 1766, Belfast and Portrush-Phil.-Belfast and Portrush-Phil. (Feb. 7, July 1); 1767, Belfast and Portrush-Phil. (Feb. 24); 1769, Portrush-N.Y. (July 4); 1770, same (July 10)—see 1772.

BELFAST 1772

FRIENDSHIP: 250 tons (see Appendix C).
Master: Wm. McCulloch.
Agent: Wm. Burgess, merchant.
Destination: Philadelphia.
Advertised: 31 Jan.
To Sail: 15, 25 Mar.
Sailed: (31 Mar.)
Arrived: After 5 weeks.

Arr. Belfast from Phil.; remarkably fast sailer; well fitted for pass. trade (Jan. 31); sufficient pass. engaged, so must be punctual (Feb. 13); twice complement of pass. applied (Apr. 3); arr. Phil., all well (June 26). Other voyages —1769, Belfast-Phil. (Feb. 7)—see 1773.

PRINCE OF WALES: 400 tons (see Appendix C).
Master: Ch. McKenzie; long in emigrant trade from Newry.
Agent: Thos. & John Greg, Waddell Cunningham, merchants.
Destination: Philadelphia.
Advertised: 31 Mar.
To Sail: 23 Apr., 1 May.
Sailed: (12 May).
Arrived: 22 July.

Third voyage since launched; prime sailer; well fitted (Mar. 31); arr. Belfast from N.Y. with flaxseed and flour (Apr. 17); arr. in America; all well (Sept. 1). Other voyage—see 1771.

PHILADELPHIA: 250 tons (see Appendix C).

Master:	Jas. Malcolm.
Agent:	Thos. Greg, Waddell Cunningham, merchants.
Destination:	Philadelphia.
Advertised:	21 Apr.
To Sail:	20, 26 May.
Sailed:	(12 June).
Arrived:	—

Expected every day; well known; will fill up very quickly (Apr. 21); now arrived (Apr. 28); about 20 more will be taken; best rum for sale to pass. at 3s. 9½d. per gall. (May 12); sailed with beef, cloth, etc. (June 12). Other voyage— see 1771.

JOHN AND JAMES: 150 tons (see Appendix C).

Master:	John Baker.
Agent:	(Thos. Desbrisay).
Destination:	St John's Gulf.
Advertised:	28 Apr.
To Sail:	7 May.
Sailed:	19 May (30 May from Newry).
Arrived:	After 10 weeks and 4 days

Third voyage; will call at Newry (Apr. 28); sailed from Belfast; pass. in high spirits (May 29); arr. after tedious voyage; pass. unsuccessfully pleaded to be taken to N.S. (*F.D.J.*, Jan. 7, 1773).

BRITANNIA: 300 tons.

Master:	Jas. Clendenen.
Agent:	Jas. Getty, Dd. Gaussan (Newry), merchants, Arch. McCune (Richhill).
Destination:	Charleston and Savannah. Later changed to Halifax and New York. Later changed to Charleston.
Advertised:	3 July.
To Sail:	1 Sep. 1, 6, 20 Oct.
Sailed:	(6 Nov.) for Charleston.
Arrived:	Petitioned S.C. Council for land on 23 Jan. 1773.

Blacksmiths, carpenters, coopers wanted (July 3); voyage changed by request (Aug. 18); voyage reverted to Charleston by request (Sep. 1); letter of thanks from pass. of 1771 (Sep. 4); now in Newry (Sep. 15); has water on board, other provisions soon; pass. to be on board on Oct. 15 (Oct. 2); sailed with beef, butter, etc. (Nov. 6); 48 passengers petitioned S.C. Council for land (100 to 350 acres each). Seven stated to be 'able to pay for their Warr'ts' and remainder described as 'poor people who have severally sworn they are not worth five pounds sterling' (Revill, *S.C.*, p. 128). Other voyages—see 1771, 1773; wrecked on voyage from Md. to Newry (*L.J.*, Apr. 13).

FRIENDSHIP: 250 tons.

Master:	Wm. McCulloch.
Agent:	Wm. Burgess, merchant.
Destination:	Philadelphia.
Advertised:	7 July.
To Sail:	15 Aug.
Sailed:	(1 Sep.)
Arrived:	—

Daily expected; fine voyage to Phil. in spring (July 7); arr. from Phil. via Cork (July 21); sailed with rum and herrings (Sep. 1).

Appendix D

ELIZABETH: 250 tons (see Appendix C).

Master:	Dd. Brown.
Agent:	Arch. Scott, merchant, Capt. Barnett, Matthew Rea (Drumbo).
Destination:	Savannah.
Advertised:	23 June.
To Sail:	15, 20 Sep., 25 Oct.
Sailed:	(10 Nov. (*sic*)).
Arrived:	After 8 weeks.

Will leave L'Derry for Phil. on Aug 20; agent named—alderman Wm. Lecky (*L.J.*, July 29); will arr. Belfast from L'Derry about Aug. 20; long account of S.C. (Aug. 14); now in Belfast (Oct. 6); complaints of miserable condition of 190 pass. on board (Nov. 13); inspected by sovereign of Belfast (Nov. 17); letter signed by 41 stressing good treatment (Nov. 20); two children died on voyage, four born (May 4, 1773); all well and in great spirits; highly pleased with treatment (*L.J.*, May 4, 1773). Other voyages—1769, Cork-Phil. (*C.E.P.*, July 20)—see 1773.

HOPEWELL: 250 tons.

Master:	J. Ash; care, success, humane treatment.
Agent:	Wm. Beatty, merchant.
Destination:	Charleston.
Advertised:	10 Mar.
To Sail:	15 Aug., 15 Sep., 1, 5 Oct.
Sailed:	19 Oct.
Arrived:	23 Dec.

Aug. is proper season to emigrate to S.C. (Mar. 10); arr. England from S.C.; a minister urgently needed (June 16); arr. Belfast from Norway (Sep. 15); sailed, capt. Martin, with beef, etc. (Oct. 20); 63 pass. petitioned S.C. Council for land; 10 could afford to pay for warrants and 53 could not (Revill, *S.C.*, p. 124); arr. Charleston; all in perfect health (Feb. 5, 1773). Other voyages—see 1771.

PENNSYLVANIA FARMER: 350 tons.

Master:	C. Robinson; humanity and kind treatment greatly applauded.
Agent:	John Ewing, S. Brown, merchants. Later added Rev. John Logue (Broughshane).
Destination:	Philadelphia. Later changed to Charleston.
Advertised:	24 July.
To Sail:	20 Sep. 6, 10, 23 Oct.
Sailed:	(16 Oct.).
Arrived:	Petitioned S.C. Council for land on 6 Jan. 1773.

Arr. from Baltimore with wheat and flour for Ewing and Brown (Aug. 25); changed to Charleston; will be single-berthed; comfortable and agreeable passage (Aug. 28); postponed till Oct. 6 to allow farmers to dispose of crops (Sep. 11); postponed till Oct. 23 as did not arrive sooner (Oct. 6); sailed to Phil. with beef, etc. (Oct. 16); 86 (including 63 who were unable to pay for warrants) petitioned S.C. Council for land. 'John Logue' was granted 400 acres (Revill, *S.C.*, p. 125).

Appendix D

JUPITER: 300 tons (see Appendix C).
Master: Alex. Ewing; success well known.
Agent: Andrew Gregg, J. Thompson, merchants.
Destination: Philadelphia.
Advertised: 7 Feb.
To Sail: 1, 10, 25 Apr.
Sailed: 11 May.
Arrived: Voyage of 27 days.

Noted for short passages (Feb. 7); pass. landed in good health and great spirits (Aug. 7). Other voyages—see 1771, 1773, 1774.

ROSE: 300 tons (see Appendix C).
Master: Robt. George; well acquainted in the trade.
Agent: Jas. Harvey, Thos. Moore, Saml. Curry, Wm. Hope, merchants, Wm. Neely (Ballygawley).
Destination: Philadelphia.
Advertised: 17 Mar.
To Sail: 15, 25 Apr.
Sailed: —
Arrived: 12 July.

Best of treatment; quick passages; comfortable (Mar. 17); arr. at Phil. (Sep. 22). Other voyages— see 1771, 1773.

HANNAH: 400 tons (see Appendix C).
Master: Jas. Mitchell; 33 successful voyages to America.
Agent: Jas. Stirling; Jas. Harvey, merchant.
Destination: Philadelphia.
Advertised: 21 Apr.
To Sail: 10 May, 1 June.
Sailed: (18 June).
Arrived: Voyage of 8 weeks.

New; built last season in America for passenger trade; every conceivable convenience for health (Apr. 21); arr. Phil.; all well (Oct. 16). Other voyages—see 1773, 1774, 1775.

WALLWORTH: 250 tons
Master: Connolly McCausland; humane and civil.
Agent: Jas. Mitchell, Abraham McCausland, merchants, Jas. Stirling.
Destination: Philadelphia.
Advertised: 21 Apr.
To Sail: 10 May, 1 June.
Sailed: 22 June.
Arrived: Voyage of 8 weeks.

Stout ship; almost new; good acc.; fast sailer (Apr. 21); sailed with pass. and provisions (L.J., June 22); arr. Phil.; all healthy and well (Nov. 13). Other voyages—see 1771, 1773.

ANN: 250 tons
Master: Pat Miller.
Agent: Robt. Alexander, Jas. Harvey, merchants (owners)
Destination: Charleston.
Advertised: 28 Apr.
To Sail: 20 May, 1 July.
Sailed: (15 July).
Arrived: —

Proper encouragement to emigrants; well manned and victualled (Apr. 28); by contract with 12 decent and discreet families, will sail July 1 (May 1). Other voyages—see 1771, 1773, 1774.

UNNAMED: 250 tons.
Master: Unnamed.
Agent: Unnamed.
Destination: St John's Island.
Advertised: 2 June.
To Sail: 25 June.
Sailed: —
Arrived: —

NANCY: 300 tons.
Master: Norman Cheevers.
Agent: Wm. Caldwell, merchant. Added later—John Caldwell, jnr., (Ballymoney)
Destination: Nova Scotia & Wilmington. Later changed to Wilmington & Charleston.
Advertised: 30 June.
To Sail: 26 July, 10, 24, 31 Aug.
Sailed: (3 Oct.).
Arrived: —

Will go on to Wilmington if 80-100 persons desire; best acc. in every respect (June 30); Wilmington and Charleston (July 21); arr. from L'pool (Aug. 15); passengers to be on board Aug. 31 (Aug. 25); At meeting of S.C. Council on Nov. 8 seventy-three passengers on vessel recently arr. from Ireland petitioned for land; these included 'John Caldwell, Jun'r' who was granted 100 acres (Revill, *S.C.*, p. 118). Other voyages — 1769, L'Derry-N.S. (Apr. 19); 1770, Loch Tarbert-Amer. with 302 pass. (S.P. 54/45, no. 167); 1771, same, with 300 pass. (ibid.).

HOPEWELL: 250 tons.
Master: Jas. Campbell; changed to —Winning.
Agent: Wm. Caldwell, merchant, Andrew McFarlane (Eskreagh).
Destination: Philadelphia.
Advertised: 30 June.
To Sail: 20 July, 15 Aug.
Sailed: (26 Aug.)
Arrived: —

Hourly expected from Cork (June 30); sailed in ballast (*L.J.*, Aug. 26). Other voyages—see 1771.

Appendix D

PRINCE OF WALES: 300 tons (see Appendix C).

Master:	Thos. Morrison; well acquainted in pass. trade.
Agent:	Jas. Thompson, merchant.
Destination:	Baltimore & Philadelphia.
Advertised:	14 July.
To Sail:	1, 14 Aug.
Sailed:	(2 Sep.).
Arrived:	—

Arr. L'Derry from Baltic (*L.J.*, July 8); now in L'Derry; short passages (July 14). Other voyages —see 1771, 1773.

JUPITER: 300 tons.

Master:	Alex. Ewing.
Agent:	Andrew Gregg, Jas. Thompson, merchants.
Destination:	Philadelphia.
Advertised:	7 Aug.
To Sail:	20 Aug.
Sailed:	—
Arrived:	Voyage of 7 weeks.

Just arr. Belfast from Phil. via Dublin (July 27); arr. L'Derry from Phil.; voyage of 27 days in spring was fastest ever from L'Derry to Phil. (*L.J.*, July 31); arr. Phil. (*L.J.*, Jan. 19, 1773).

BOSCAWEN: 250 tons.

Master:	Geo. Marshall.
Agent:	Walter & Thos. Marshall, Stephen Bennett, Robert Houston, merchants.
Destination:	Philadelphia.
Advertised:	(27 June).
To Sail:	15 July, 1 Aug.
Sailed:	(15 Aug.).
Arrived:	—

Hourly expected from Norway; will sail as near time as possible (*L.J.*, June 27); arr. from Norway (*L.J.*, July 1). Other voyage—see 1773.

NEWRY 1772

ROBERT: 300 tons (see Appendix C).

Master:	Matthew Russell.
Agent:	Andrew Thompson, merchant.
Destination:	New York.
Advertised:	10 Mar.
To Sail:	1 Apr.
Sailed:	—
Arrived:	19 July.

Other voyages—see 1771, 1773, 1774.

ROYAL WILLIAM: — tons

Master:	John Thompson.
Agent:	Wm. Beath, Geo. Anderson, merchants.

Those parts of peace and plenty; well victualled and manned to make passage short and comfortable; servants of good character

251

Appendix D

Destination:	Baltimore & Georgetown.	wanted; a few miles from Pa.
Advertised:	17 Apr.	where lands are remarkably fertile
To Sail:	1 June.	and cheap (Apr. 17); now in port;
Sailed:	13 July.	pay passage money before May 25
Arrived:	—	(May 19).

PHEBE AND PEGGY 300 tons (see Appendix C).

Master:	Dd. McCulloch.	Fine new vessel, built for emig.
Agent:	Dd. Gaussan, Saml. Park	trade; every necessity provided to
	(Stewartstown), merchants,	make passage comfortable; spec-
	Ed. Patterson (Cookstown),	ial encouragement to servants
	Michael Johnston	(Apr. 28).
	(Moneymore), Jas.	
	McCulloch to attend at	
	Banbridge and Rathfriland.	
Destination:	Philadelphia.	
Advertised:	28 Apr.	
To Sail:	20 May, 1 June.	
Sailed:	—	
Arrived:	—	

NEEDHAM: 400 tons.

Master:	Wm. Cheevers.	One of the finest emigrant vessels;
Agent:	Dd. Gaussan, J., W., & G.	2 mths. old (July 4); arr. Newry
	Glenny, Hill Wilson,	(July 28). finest vessel that ever
	George Anderson, Wm.	took pass. from Newry (Aug. 28).
	Beath, merchants (owners).	Other voyages—see 1773, 1774.
Destination:	Philadelphia.	
Advertised:	14 July.	
To Sail:	20 Aug., 10 Sep.	
Sailed:	—	
Arrived:	—	

FREEMASON: 250 tons.

Master:	John Semple.	Well calculated for pass. trade
Agent:	J., W., & G. Glenny, Hill	(July 14); arr. from Antigua with
	Wilson, Geo. Anderson,	rum (Aug. 4); now in port; re-
	Wm. Beath, merchants	markably lofty between decks;
	(owners).	pass. must give earnest before
Destination:	Charleston.	Sep. 5 to enable owners to
Advertised:	14 July.	victual ship (Sep. 1); arr. Charles-
To Sail:	20 Aug., 1, 10, 20 Sep.	ton; pass. highly pleased (Feb. 5
Sailed:	27 Oct.	1773); 55 pass. (including 48 who
Arrived:	22 Dec.	were unable to pay for survey
		warrants) petitioned S.C. Council
		for land (Revill, *S.C.*, p. 126).
		Other voyages—1768, Newry-
		Phil. (July 12); 1769, Newry-
		N.Y. (Oct. 2)—see 1774.

NEWRY ASSISTANCE: 300 tons.
Master: Robt. Conyngham.
Agent: John Dickson, merchant.
Destination: Philadelphia.
Advertised: 29 July.
To Sail: 15, 28 Aug.
Sailed: —
Arrived: —

Now arr.; remarkably well known; provisions, firing, water now ready to be taken on board; free victuals if delayed longer; passage money will not exceed £3; send boxes to Dickson who will store and ship them free (July 29). Other voyages—see 1771, 1773.

LARNE 1772

JUPITER: 250 tons (see Appendix C).
Master: R. Shuter.
Agent: John Montgomery, Thos. Barclay, Andrew Thompson (Newry), merchants, Alex. Allen (Ballymena on Saturdays).
Destination: Charleston.
Advertised: 10 Mar.
To Sail: 15, 25, 28 Apr.
Sailed: (12 May).
Arrived: Voyage of 8 weeks.

Vessel and master well known, needless to say more (Mar. 10); arr. Charleston, all well. Letter of thanks to master from pass., signed by 65, states three children died during voyage and three born (Sep. 15). Other voyages—see 1771, 1773, 1774.

JAMES AND MARY: 200 tons.
Master: J. Workman.
Agent: Jas. McVicker, John Moore, merchants.
Destination: Charleston.
Advertised: 13 Mar.
To Sail: 15 Apr., 10 July, 8 Aug.
Sailed: 25 Aug.
Arrived: 16 Oct.

Will leave punctually on Apr. 15, but if not full no. of pass. will sail on July 10 (Mar. 13); arr. Belfast from N.Y. and 55 casks rum seized (Apr. 28); arr. Belfast from Sweden with herrings (July 14); hoped that pass. would be punctual and allow vessel to sail on Aug. 8 (July 29); letter of thanks to capt., signed by 35; five children died (Dec. 22); quarantined over seven weeks (*Chesney Journal*, p. 3).

BETTY: 250 tons.
Master: A. Woodside.
Agent: John & Saml. Montgomery, Thos. Barklie, merchants, Robt. McKedy (Ballymena).
Destination: Charleston.
Advertised: 28 Apr.
To Sail: 1 May, 1 Aug.
Sailed: —
Arrived: —

Other voyages—see 1773, 1774, 1775.

LORD DUNLUCE: 400 tons (see Appendix C).

Master:	Jas. Gillis; late mate to Robt. Shuter.	Arr. Belfast from Sweden with herrings (July 14); pass. to be
Agent:	John Montgomery, merchant, Rev. Wm. Martin (Kellswater), Wm. Barklie (Ballymena on Saturdays).	punctual on Aug. 15 (July 29); arr. Belfast from London with sugar (Aug. 21); pass. to give earnest before Sep. 5 as greater
Destination:	Charleston.	no. have offered than can be
Advertised:	29 May.	taken (Aug. 28); some families
To Sail:	15 Aug., 20, 22 Sep.	drawn back, so can acc. 200 pass.
Sailed:	4 Oct.	more (Sep. 15); sailed; pass., in-
Arrived:	20 Dec.	cluding Martin whose character

is defended, in high spirits (Oct. 9); arr. Charleston; one man and no. of children died of small-pox (Feb. 9, 1773); 184 petitioned S.C. Council for survey warrants; warrants for between 100 and 450 acres granted to each petitioner. 'Rev'd. William Martyn' granted 400 acres (Revill, *S.C.*, pp. 121-4); long letter of thanks to Gillis & Martin, signed by 51 (June 8, 1773). Other voyages—see 1773, 1774, 1775.

PORTRUSH 1772

RAINBOW: 250 tons.

Master:	Jas. Caldwell.
Agent:	John & Ch. Galt, Alex. Lawrance, John Allen (Ballymena on Saturdays), merchants.
Destination:	Newcastle & New York.
Advertised:	3 July.
To Sail:	1, 15 Aug.
Sailed:	—
Arrived:	—

Other voyages—see 1771.

BELFAST 1773

FRIENDSHIP: 300 tons (see Appendix C).

Master:	Wm. McCullogh.	Good treatment as always; high
Agent:	Wm. Burgess, merchant.	between decks; arr. from Phil.
Destination:	Philadelphia.	(Jan. 12); sailed with beef, etc.
Advertised:	12 Jan.	(Mar. 23). Other voyages—see
To Sail:	15 Mar.	1772.
Sailed:	(23 Mar.).	
Arrived:	Voyage of 30 days.	

BRIG AGNES: 200 tons (see Appendix C).

Master:	Robt. Ewing.
Agent:	Saml. Brown, merchant, later added Edward Hopes, Ballymena.
Destination:	Charleston & later Philadelphia and on to Baltimore.
Advertised:	5 Feb.
To Sail:	1, 20 Apr.
Sailed:	(30 Apr.).
Arrived:	After 49 days.

Now in Glasgow; high between decks (Feb. 5); sailed with beef, cloth, etc. (Apr. 30); letter from Saml. Brown informing friends of his arr. at Phil. (Aug. 20); letter signed by 56 thanking capt. for care and tenderness and Brown for plentiful provisions (Sep. 10). Other voyages—see 1774.

BRIG PEGGY: 200 tons (see Appendix C).

Master:	Ch. McKenzie; long good treatment.
Agent:	Waddell Cunningham, merchant, Jas. Barnett.
Destination:	Philadelphia.
Advertised:	9 Feb.
To Sail:	25 Mar., 6, 15 Apr.
Sailed:	(23 Apr.).
Arrived:	Mid June.

Will sail from L'Derry to Belfast (*L.J.*, Feb. 6); sailed to Phil. with beef, cloth, etc. (Apr. 23); letter signed by 30 thanking capt. Cunningham (Aug. 10); sailed in May 1773 (Jan. 4, 1774).

YAWARD: 350 tons.

Master:	Richard Bower.
Agent:	Wm. Rogers.
Destination:	Nova Scotia and St John's Island.
Advertised:	20 Apr.
To Sail:	In 10 days.
Sailed:	(7 May).
Arrived:	—

For Rogers' tenants (Apr. 20); also engaged to carry Desbrisay's tenants (Apr. 30); sailed with 50 head of passengers together with women and children and several skilled farmers to secure lands for 'selves and neighbours' (May 7).

WADDELL: 400 tons; later 450

Master:	Wm. Reid.
Agent:	Waddell Cunningham, merchant, later added Matthew Rea (Drumbo).
Destination:	Cape Fear and Wilmington, later Savannah.
Advertised:	7 May.
To Sail:	10, 31 Aug., 10, 20 Oct., 10, 13 Nov.
Sailed:	(23 Nov.).
Arrived:	Early in Feb. 1774.

More convenient ports than Phil. for settlement in back parts of Carolinas; will sail provided a sufficient no. of pass. engage; not yet 18 mths. old; rum on board at 3s. 9½d. gall. (May 7); 3 mill. acres for settlement near Augusta; 100 acres each head of family and 50 for others; Rea will attend at Banbridge, Lisburn and Castleblaney (Sep. 14); postponed at request of Castleblaney passengers; Rea will attend at Dromore, Ballynahinch, Drumbo (Oct. 22); testimonial to Reid signed by 32 at Savannah (June 17, 1774). Other voyages—see 1775.

BRIG *TWO BROTHERS:* 200 tons.
Master: John Bruce.
Agent: John Ewing, merchant.
Destination: Baltimore.
Advertised: 15 June.
To Sail: 8 July.
Sailed: (23 July).
Arrived: —

Arr. from Baltimore with flour for Ewing (June 11); stout new brig. (June 15); sailed with pork, etc. (July 23).

BETTY GREGG: 200 tons.
Master: Wm. Scott; well acquainted in the trade.
Agent: Thos. Greg, Waddell Cunningham, merchants, Capt. Jas. Barnett.
Destination: Philadelphia & Baltimore, later Georgetown & Baltimore.
Advertised: 6 July.
To Sail: 1 Aug.
Sailed: —
Arrived: —

Arr. from Baltimore (July 2). Other voyages—1765, Barbados-Belfast-Barbados (Oct. 8, Dec. 13); 1767, Barbados-Belfast-Charleston (Sep. 8, Oct. 6); 1768, Belfast-Charleston (Oct. 4); 1769, Belfast - Charleston - Belfast - Petersburg - Belfast - Barbados (Oct. 9, Dec. 8; *C.E.P.,* Jan 21); 1770, Belfast - Madeira - Belfast - Barbados-Belfast (July 3, Dec. 24); 1771, Belfast - Barbados-Belfast - Petersburg - Belfast - Antigua (Feb. 12, Sep. 13, Nov. 22; *L.J.,* Sep. 26); 1772, Antigua-Belfast - Petersburg - Belfast - Dominica (Mar. 15, Sep. 18, Dec. 24)—see 1774.

FRIENDSHIP: 300 tons.
Master: Wm. McCulloch.
Agent: Wm. Burgess, merchant.
Destination: Philadelphia.
Advertised: 9 July.
To Sail: 10, 20 Aug.
Sailed: (23 Aug.).
Arrived: —

Sailed full of pass. in March; has arr. back after voyage of 24 days (July 6); sailed with beef and linen cloth (Aug. 23).

LORD BANGOR: 200 tons.
Master: Samuel Piper.
Agent: Waddell Cunningham, merchant, James McCleary, Portaferry, Richard Callwell (L'Derry).
Destination: Cape Fear & Wilmington.
Advertised: 20 July.
To Sail: 20 Sep.
Sailed: —
Arrived: —

Arr. from London (Mar. 26); voyage of *Waddell* changed, so those engaged to sail in that vessel to take *Lord Bangor* instead (July 20); arr. Cork from St. Ubes (*C.E.P.,* Sep. 21); leaves Cork for Belfast (ibid., Sep. 25). Other voyages—1772, Belfast - Antigua (May 26). 1774, Alicante-Belfast - Danzig - Belfast - Leghorn (Mar. 30, Sep. 16, Oct. 21).

CHARMING MOLLY: 250 tons.

Master:	Chas. Poaug.
Agent:	John Ewing, Nathan Moore (Larne), merchants, Wm. Adams (Dungannon).
Destination:	Baltimore.
Advertised:	27 July.
To Sail:	1 Sep.
Sailed:	—
Arrived:	—

Arr. from Barbados (July 13); Thos. Ewing has land for sale in Virginia to which province carts go daily from Baltimore (July 27); John Poaug, merchant in Charleston, has been engaged in passenger trade from North Ireland for 15 years; mentions *Wallworth* and *Helen,* both from L'Derry as among Poaug's interests (Nov. 26). Other voyages—1766, Antigua-Belfast (Nov. 28); 1769, Belfast-Barbados (Dec. 29); 1770, Barbados - Belfast - Barbados - Belfast (May 15, June 5, Nov. 6); 1771, West Indies - Belfast - Barbados (June 4, Oct. 22); 1772, Barbados-Belfast (June 2).

LIBERTY AND PROPERTY: 250 tons.

Master:	John Martin.
Agent:	Wm. Beatty, merchant.
Destination:	Charleston.
Advertised:	6 Aug.
To Sail:	15 Sep., 1, 25 Oct.
Sailed:	(2 Nov.).
Arrived:	—

Beatty well knows the oppression that abounds, so will give all reasonable assistance and encouragement to relieve people from their present distress (Aug. 6); sailed with beef, butter, etc. (Nov. 2). Other voyages—see 1774.

LORD CHATHAM: 240 tons.

Master:	John Griffith.
Agent:	Jas. Patterson, Jas. Templeton, John Henderson, merchants (owners), Robt. Stewart (Lurgan), merchant, Joseph McClure (Newry), Blaney Adair (Galgorm).
Destination:	Charleston.
Advertised:	10 Aug.
To Sail:	20 Sep., 20 Oct., 5 Nov.
Sailed:	(16 Nov. to Barbados (*sic*))
Arrived:	—

Arr. Cork from Belfast en route to Barbados (*C.E.P.*, June 16); arr. from Barbados (*sic*) (June 22); will sail if proper no. of pass. come forward, but not too many will be taken (Aug. 10); still plenty of room (Oct. 8); sailed to Barbados with pork, butter, beef (Nov. 16); leaves Cork for Grenada (*C.E.P.*, Dec. 4). Other voyages—1767, W. Indies-Belfast (Sep. 29); 1768, same (Dec. 9); 1769, Belfast-W. Indies-Belfast-Gottenburgh - Belfast - Barbados (Feb. 14, July 28, Aug. 29, Oct. 24, Dec. 29; *C.E.P.*, Mar. 9); 1770, Belfast-Barbados (July 20); 1771, Baltimore - Belfast - Barbados - Belfast - Barbados (Mar. 4, Sep. 24, Dec. 6); 1772 Barbados -

BRIG BETTY: 200 tons.
Master: Michael Russell.
Agent: Jesse Taylor, merchant, Jas. Sufferan.
Destination: Philadelphia.
Advertised: 20 Aug.
To Sail: 5, 24 Sep.
Sailed: (30 Sep.).
Arrived: —

Belfast - Liverpool - St Ubes - Belfast (June 2, June 23, July 28, Oct. 16); 1774, Barbados-Belfast (June 28).

Heightened at great expense; is now full 5 ft. between decks, so very comfortable (Aug. 20); will sail first fair wind (Sep. 24); sailed with beef, etc. (Sep. 30); sailed latter end October (*sic*), all landed in great spirits (Feb. 15, 1773). Other voyage—1773, Waterford-Baltimore (Aug. 31).

CATHERINE: 300 tons.
Master: Robert Torrens; well acquainted in the trade.
Agent: John Ewing, Nathan Moore (Larne), merchants, Joseph McClure (Newry).
Destination: Philadelphia.
Advertised: 31 Aug.
To Sail: 20 Sep.
Sailed: —
Arrived: —

Arr. from Baltimore with flour (Aug. 27); of 260 tons, for sale, if not sold, will be fitted to sail for Charleston or Phil. if 60 people give earnest before Sep. 2 (Aug. 24); high between decks, plenty of provisions (Aug. 31).

LONDONDERRY 1773

JENNY: 250 tons.
Master: Archibald McIlwaine; long known in the trade.
Agent: David & Wm. Ross, Wm. Lecky, Ninian Boggs.
Destination: Philadelphia.
Advertised: 2 Mar.
To Sail: 20 Mar., 17 Apr.
Sailed: —
Arrived: Voyage of 5 weeks & 3 days

Arr. from Phil. (*L.J.*, Feb. 2); safe arr. after pleasant voyage; all well, one born on voyage (Aug. 17); similar report (Aug. 31).

ALEXANDER: 400 tons (see Appendix C).
Master: James Hunter; previously commanded *Henry*.
Agent: Robert Alexander, merchant.
Destination: Philadelphia.
Advertised: 8 Mar.
To Sail: 15 Apr.
Sailed: 7 June.
Arrived: Voyage of 7 weeks.

Arr. from Phil. (*L.J.*, Mar. 9); six mths. old; at least 6 ft. between decks; well victualled and watered; finest ship in the kingdom (Mar. 9); Capt. assures public he is not the Hunter wrecked off Wexford(*L.J.*, Apr. 13); arr. Phil.; all well (Oct. 1). Other voyage—see 1774.

HANNAH: 400 tons (see Appendix C).

Master:	Jas. Mitchell; well established in the trade.
Agent:	Jas. Stirling.
Destination:	Philadelphia.
Advertised:	12 Mar.
To Sail:	10 Apr., 1, 16 May.
Sailed:	7 June.
Arrived:	Voyage of 7 weeks.

Arr. from Phil. (*L.J.*, Mar. 5); left Cork for Dublin with flaxseed (*C.E.P.*, Mar. 18); lofty between decks; one year old; pass. from co. Antrim to come to Ballykelly where boats will be provided (Mar. 12); arr. Cork from Phil. with lumber (*C.E.P.*, Sep. 21). Other voyages—see 1772, 1774, 1775.

WALLWORTH: 300 tons (see Appendix C).

Master:	Conolly McCausland.
Agent:	Jas. Mitchell, Andrew McCausland, merchants, Jas. Stirling.
Destination:	Philadelphia, later Charleston and Cape Fear.
Advertised:	12 Mar.
To Sail:	6 Apr., 10 May.
Sailed:	7 June.
Arrived:	—

Arr. Lough Swilly from Phil. (*L.J.*, Jan. 19); water casks ready to fill; excellent stout ship, almost new (Mar. 12); destination changed at request of some very respectable families (Apr. 6); arr. Charleston (*S.C. Gazette*, Aug. 31). Other voyages—see 1771, 1772.

JUPITER: 300 tons (see Appendix C).

Master:	Alex. Ewing.
Agent:	And. Gregg, Jas. Thompson, merchants.
Destination:	Philadelphia.
Advertised:	26 Mar.
To Sail:	20 Apr., 10, 12 May.
Sailed:	7 June.
Arrived:	—

Arr. Phil. after voyage of 7 weeks from L'Derry in 1772; will sail back *circa* Dec. 25 loaded with wheat, flour, flaxseed (*L.J.*, Jan. 19); arr. from Phil. (*L.J.*, Mar. 5); now at Culmore Point (Apr. 28). Other voyages—see 1771, 1772, 1774.

BRIG LOUISA: 200 tons.

Master:	Isaac Kirkpatrick.
Agent:	Robt. Alexander, merchant (owner).
Destination:	Charleston.
Advertised:	9 Apr.
To Sail:	1 May.
Sailed:	—
Arrived:	—

Completely finished; special encouragement to single men and women servants (Apr. 9); arr. Charleston (*S.C. Gazette*, Sep. 15).

BRIG HELLEN: 200 tons (see Appendix C).

Master:	Jas. Ramage.
Agent:	—Dickson,—Coningham, Abraham McCausland, merchants (owners).

Single men and women servants encouraged (Apr. 27); wrecked off Wexford in Feb. 1774 (Customs 1/126, p. 54).

Destination: Charleston & Cape Fear.
Advertised: 27 Apr.
To Sail: 20 May
Sailed: —
Arrived: *c.* 15 Sep.

ROSE: 300 tons.
Master: Robt. George; long experienced.
Agent: Samuel Curry, William Hope, merchants.
Destination: Philadelphia.
Advertised: 1 June.
To sail: 15 June
Sailed: —
Arrived: —

Arr. from Christiansund with deals (*L.J.*, May 18). Other voyages—see 1771, 1772.

GEORGE: 250 tons.
Master: Wm. Pinkerton; well acquainted in the trade.
Agent: Samuel Curry, Jas. Miller, merchants.
Destination: Charleston.
Advertised: 1 June.
To Sail: 1 July, 1 Aug.
Sailed: —
Arrived: Probably Dec.

Arr. Phil. (*Pa. Journal*, Dec. 22). Other voyages—1771, Belfast-St. Ubes (*L.J.*, Sep. 30)—see 1771, 1775.

PRINCE OF WALES: 350 tons (see Appendix C).
Master: Thos. Morrison; long experienced.
Agent: Jas. Thompson, merchant.
Destination: Baltimore.
Advertised: 8 June
To Sail: 1 July.
Sailed: (9 July).
Arrived: 15 Oct.

Arr. from Baltimore (Mar. 12); sailed to Christiansund (Apr. 13); arr. from Christiansund (*L.J.*, May 25); arr. Baltimore with about 200 passengers (25 Jan., 1774). Other voyages—see 1771, 1772.

ANN: 300 tons.
Master: Pat Miller.
Agent: Robt. Alexander, merchant (owner).
Destination: Charleston.
Advertised: 20 June.
To Sail: 20 July.
Sailed: —
Arrived: —

Arr. from Christiansund with deals (*L.J.*, May 18); early application advised as is mostly engaged to creditable number of families (June 20). Other voyages —see 1771, 1772, 1774.

PHILADELPHIA: 250 tons.
Master: John Winning.
Agent: Master.
Destination: Philadelphia.
Advertised: 6 July.
To Sail: 6 Aug.
Sailed: —
Arrived: —

BOSCAWEN: 250 tons.
Master: Geo. Marshall.
Agent: Walter & Thos. Marshall, Stephen Bennett, Robert Houston.
Destination: Philadelphia.
Advertised: 3 Aug.
To Sail: 25 Aug.
Sailed: —
Arrived: —

Left Phil. on 18 Nov. 1772 (*F.D.J.*, Jan. 14); arr. from Phil. after voyage of 27 days (*L.J.*, Feb. 18); sailed to Baltimore in ballast (*L.J.*, Mar. 30); spoken to by *Betty Gregg* off Annapolis (Maryland) on 20 May, seven weeks out from Londonderry (July 2); agent will visit Coleraine (Aug. 3). Other voyage—see 1772.

ELIZABETH: 250 tons.
Master: Robt. Johnston.
Agent: Wm. Lecky.
Destination: Charleston or Cape Fear. Savannah later substituted for Cape Fear.
Advertised: 10 Aug.
To Sail: 8, 15 Sep.
Sailed: —
Arrived: —

To Charleston, but could continue to Cape Fear if 50 or 60 pass. so wished (Aug. 10); letter dated Georgia 2 Mar. 1774 telling of arr. of *Elizabeth*, 50 of whose pass. presented memorial to council and were granted £80 to carry them to the Queensborough settlement (June 10, 1774). Other voyage—see 1772.

BETTY: 250 tons.
Master: Rch. Hunter.
Agent: —Patterson,—Fletcher, Nathaniel Hunter.
Destination: Baltimore.
Advertised: (9 Mar.)
To Sail: In 10 days.
Sailed: —
Arrived: —

'Every encouragement' to pass.; will definitely sail on time (*L.J.*, Mar. 9). Other voyage—see 1774.

NEWRY 1773

BRIG CHARLOTTE: 250 tons.
Master: Robt. Montgomery.
Agent: Andrew Thompson, merchant.

Maximum of 100 pass. (Feb. 19). Other voyage—see 1775.

Destination:	Philadelphia.
Advertised:	19 Feb.
To Sail:	10 Apr.
Sailed:	—
Arrived:	—

BETSY:	300 tons (see Appendix C).	Owners will sail on the vessel (Apr. 6); sailed (May 14); arr. at Phil.; daily expected back to take emig. to Phil. (Sep. 14).
Master:	Dd. McCutchon; long in American trade.	
Agent:	Jas. Patterson, Henry Oakman, merchants (owners), Moyrick Bell (Dungannon), Wm. Oakman & John Irwin (Lurgan).	
Destination:	Philadelphia.	
Advertised:	23 Feb.	
To Sail:	20 Mar., 1, 30 Apr.	
Sailed:	7 May.	
Arrived:	6 July.	

NEEDHAM:	400 tons (see Appendix C).	
Master:	Wm. Cheevers.	Long description of N.Y.; vessel built for pass.; 6 ft. between decks; all pass. guaranteed as many acres as they wish (Feb. 23); same advert. (*F.D.J.*, Feb. 24); Capt. to visit Monaghan, Castleblaney, Clones, Cootehill, Ballybay, Caledon, Armagh, Stewartstown, Dungannon (Mar. 26); will return in spring for more emig. (Sep. 14); ref. to 1773 voyage (Mar. 18, 1774). Other voyages—1773, N.Y.—Cork—N.Y. (*C.E.P.*, Sep. 19, Nov. 1)—see 1772, 1774.
Agent:	Dd. Gaussan, Geo., Wm., & John Glenny, Wm. Beath, Hill Wilson, Geo. Anderson, merchants (owners).	
Destination:	Philadelphia & New York.	
Advertised:	23 Feb.	
To Sail:	20 Apr., 4 May.	
Sailed:	(21 May).	
Arrived:	9 July.	

ROBERT:	350 tons (see Appendix C).	5 ft. 6 in. between decks (Mar. 9); same advert. (*F.D.J.*, Mar. 1); some pass. landed at Amboy on way to lands in Jersey and Pa.; rest going to N.Y.; most skilled in linen trade (Sep. 7). Other voyages—see 1771, 1772, 1774.
Master:	Matthew Russell; long in American trade.	
Agent:	Andrew & Acheson Thompson, merchants (owners).	
Destination:	Philadelphia.	
Advertised:	9 Mar.	
To Sail:	1 May:	
Sailed:	(21 May).	
Arrived:	19 July.	

Appendix D

NEWRY ASSISTANCE: 300 tons (see Appendix C).

Master:	Robt. Conyngham; well known in the trade.	Will be settled among owners' friends (Mar. 12); arr. at Phil;
Agent:	John Dickson (owner), Thos. Johnston (Coalisland), Joseph Adams (Cookstown), Henry Evans (Castledawson), merchants.	all well (Sep. 7). Other voyages—see 1771, 1772.
Destination:	Philadelphia.	
Advertised:	12 Mar.	
To Sail:	1 May.	
Sailed:	—	
Arrived:	28 July.	

MINERVA: more than 350 tons (see Appendix C).

Master:	Francis Fearis. Later changed to Dd. McCullough; well known in the trade.	New ship, this her third voyage; 5 ft. 4 in. between decks; (Feb. 12); near 6ft. between decks; Mc-
Agent:	Wm. & John Ogle, but changed to Dd. Gaussan, merchants.	Cullough carried 423 emig. safely from Newry last season and is determined to continue in the trade; servants encouraged, espec-
Destination:	Philadelphia, Baltimore later added.	ially tradesmen (Apr. 10); same advert. (*L.J.*, Feb. 12); ref.
Advertised:	12 Feb.	to 1773 voyage (Mar. 1, 1774).
To Sail:	10 Apr.	Other voyages—see 1771, 1774.
Sailed:	28 Apr.	
Arrived:	—	

ELLIOTT:	300 tons (see Appendix C).	Accounted fastest sailing vessel
Master:	John Waring.	belonging to Ireland (Apr. 23);
Agent:	Thos. Waring, merchant.	arr. Charleston (Oct. 22). Other
Destination:	Charleston.	voyages—see 1774.
Advertised:	23 Apr.	
To Sail:	25 May.	
Sailed:	—	
Arrived:	*c.* 15 Aug.	

BETSY:	300 tons.	Ref. to voyage in May; has
Master:	Sam. Kyle; humanity well known.	returned to Newry in 26 days; plenty of good victuals; stout
Agent:	Dd. Gaussan, Moyrick Bell (Dungannon), merchants, Jas. Carson (Stewartstown), Hugh Kyle (Belfast).	new ship (Sep. 10). Other voyages—see 1771, 1773 and 1774.
Destination:	Philadelphia.	

Advertised: 10 Sep.
To Sail: 26 Sep.
Sailed: —
Arrived: —

LARNE 1773

JUPITER: 250 tons.
Master: Robt. Shutter; well known.
Agent: John Montgomery, Andrew Thompson (Newry), merchants, Thos. Barklie (Ballymena on Saturdays).
Destination: Baltimore, later Charleston and then on to Baltimore.
Advertised: 2 Mar.
To Sail: 11 May, 15 June, 25 July.
Sailed: —
Arrived: At Charleston after 9 weeks.

Ship and master well known (Mar. 2); voyage postponed; pass. will be informed of her arr. (May 18); arr. Cork from Md. (*C.E.P.*, June 16); Newry with flour; will sail to Larne in 4 days (June 22); change in voyage announced (July 6); arr. Charleston; all well; two born (Dec. 17). Other voyages—see 1771, 1772, 1774.

JAMES AND MARY: 250 tons.
Master: John Workman; well known.
Agent: Jas. McVickar, John Moore, merchants, John McVickar (Ballymena).
Destination: Charleston.
Advertised: 16 Apr.
To Sail: 15 May, 20 July, 3, 12 Aug.
Sailed: —
Arrived: —

Ship and master well known (Apr. 16); arr. from Christiansund (July 2). Other voyages—see 1771, 1772, 1774, 1775.

LORD DUNLUCE: 400 tons.
Master: Jas. Gillis; later changed to Robt. Shutter.
Agent: John Montgomery, Thos. Barklie, Robt. McKedy (Ballymena), merchants, John Campbell (Belfast) later added.
Destination: Charleston, later Baltimore.
Advertised: 18 May.
To Sail: 1, 20 Sep., 20 Dec., 10 Jan. 1774.
Sailed: —
Arrived: —

Now at Cowes; 'great encouragement' to servants; expected to arr. Larne at beginning July; not 2 years old (May 18); Shutter to attend at Ballymena on Saturdays (Aug. 31). Other voyages—1772, London-Belfast (Aug. 7); see 1772, 1774, 1775.

BETTY:	250 tons.	Abundance of water and good
Master:	Abraham Woodside.	provisions; rum at 3s. 9½d. gall.
Agent:	Saml. Montgomery, Robt.	(Sep. 10); has arr. at Larne (Oct.
	McKedy (Ballymena),	11); master to visit Ballymena on
	merchants.	Nov. 16(Nov. 5). Other voyages—
Destination:	Charleston.	see 1772, 1774, 1775.
Advertised:	10 Sep.	
To Sail:	5, 25 Oct., end Nov.	
Sailed:	—	
Arrived:	—	

BELFAST 1774

BETTY GREGG:	200 tons.	Arr. from Baltimore with flour
Master:	Wm. Scott; noted for kind	and wheat; fine vessel, British
	treatment.	built; fast sailer; fine acc. for
Agent:	Thos. & John Greg,	pass.; Capt. to visit Ballymena
	Waddell Cunningham,	and Magherafelt (Jan. 25); arr.
	merchants, Capt. Jas.	Belfast from Alexandria (Md.)
	Barnett.	(Sep. 6). Other voyages—see
Destination:	Philadelphia.	1773, 1774, Maryland-Belfast-
Advertised:	25 Jan.	Madeira (Sep. 6 and 30).
To Sail:	5 Mar.	
Sailed:	—	
Arrived:	—	

PROSPERITY:	500 tons.	Cleared from Phil. for Belfast
Master:	Wm. McCulloch; well	(C.O. 5/1285) (*Pa. Journal*, 15
	known for success in	Dec. 1773); new ship; built pur-
	Friendship.	posely for pass. trade under
Agent:	Wm. Burgess, merchant.	supervision of McCulloch (Jan.
Destination:	Philadelphia.	28); sailed with beef, etc. (Apr.
Advertised:	28 Jan.	15); arr. Phil. after pleasant voy-
To Sail:	10 Mar., 1, 10 Apr.	age (July 5).
Sailed:	(15 Apr.)	
Arrived:	20 May.	

SNOW BALTIMORE:	250 tons.	Arr. from Baltimore with flaxseed
Master:	Robt. White; great	& flour (Feb. 1); one of finest
	applause for kind and	vessels in the trade; high between
	humane treatment.	decks; fast sailer; Capt.'s success
Agent:	Saml. Brown, merchant,	from Larne in 1773 and now
	Wm. White (Larne).	means to take his family and
Destination:	Baltimore.	friends; plenty of good provi-
Advertised:	8 Feb.	sions; Capt. to visit Larne and
To Sail:	20 Mar., 6 Apr. (Belfast)	vessel will call there (Feb. 8);
	and 8 Apr. (Larne).	Capt. will visit Larne every Mon-
Sailed:	—	day and Tuesday (Mar. 1); arr.
Arrived:	—	Baltimore; all well (Sep. 6).

Appendix D

PEACE AND PLENTY: 400 tons (see Appendix C).

Master: Ch. McKenzie; short passages and good treatment.
Agent: Waddell Cunningham, merchant (owner), Matt. Rea (Drumbo).
Destination: Philadelphia & New York.
Advertised: 15 Feb.
To Sail: 15, 20 Apr., 2, 12 May.
Sailed: 12 May.
Arrived: —

High between decks; every convenience; Cunningham will, as usual, ensure plenty of good provisions and water; rum 3s. 9½d. gall.; one of finest vessels in the kingdom in the trade (Feb. 15); arr. from N.Y. with flaxseed (Mar. 4); sailed (May 13); arr. Phil.; all well (Sep. 27). Other voyage—see 1775.

BETTY: — tons.
Master: —
Agent: Jesse Taylor.
Destination: Philadelphia & Baltimore.
Advertised: 15 Feb. (prelim. notice).
To Sail: —
Sailed: —
Arrived: —

Hourly expected back after last last year's success (Feb. 15); *Betty*, of Belfast, wrecked on Apr. 6 near Wexford on voyage home from Phil. with flaxseed, flour, biscuit; one hand, a woman and a child drowned (Apr. 15).

LIBERTY: 450 tons.
Master: John Malcom; quick passages, good treatment known to many thousands.
Agent: Jas. Templeton, Jesse Taylor, John Woolsey (Portadown), merchants, Jas. Templeton (Loughbrickland), John Stewart (Ballymena).
Destination: Philadelphia & New York.
Advertised: 22 Mar.
To Sail: 20 May, 1 June, 4, 9 July.
Sailed: —
Arrived: At N.Y. in 7 weeks.

New; expected about Apr. 1 (Mar. 22); only 4 mths. old; is in Dublin but daily expected in Belfast; built of best materials specially for pass. trade under supervision of able judges; full 6 ft. between decks; port holes 'to let out the foul, and in the fresh air for want of which Disorders frequently happen on board Passenger Vessels'; N.Y. owners will give advice and utmost assistance to pass. (Apr. 8); still time to engage (June 24); postponed on account of Capt.'s health (July 5); arr. N.Y.; agreeable passage; all well (Nov. 29).

PEGGY: 200 tons.
Master: James March (or Marsh); experienced.
Agent: Waddell Cunningham, later added Coslet Patterson (Magheralin).
Destination: Philadelphia & New York.
Advertised: 26 Apr.

Arr. from N.Y. with flaxseed, flour (Apr. 8); not 3 mths. old; fast sailer; fitted for pass.; best provisions provided (Apr. 26); out with beef, etc. (June 24).

To Sail: 25 May, 1, 15 June.
Sailed: (24 June).
Arrived: —

LIBERTY AND PROPERTY: 250 tons.

Master:	John Martin, later Ch. McKenzie; well known for humanity.
Agent:	Wm. Beatty, merchant (owner), John Montgomery, Thos. Johnston (Ballynahinch), Henry Johnston (Loughbrickland), Jas. Martin (Dromore), Jas. Barr (Templepatrick), Hugh McCartan (Saintfield).
Destination:	Charleston & Savannah.
Advertised:	17 May.
To Sail:	23 Aug., Sept., 15 Sep., 10 Oct.
Sailed:	(28 Oct.).
Arrived:	—

Will arr. early in July; successful voyages in past; Capt.'s former pass. have written letters to friends in cos. Antrim and Down; strict attention to choice and quality of provisions (May 17); arr. from Baltic with deals (Aug. 23); must agree quickly to enable proper quantity of provisions to be provided (Sept. 23); sailed for Charleston with beef, butter, etc. (Oct. 28). Other voyage—see 1773.

BRIG AGNES: 250 tons.

Master:	Jos. Mathers; well acquainted in the trade.
Agent:	Saml. Brown, Robt. McKedy (Ballymena) merchants.
Destination:	Philadelphia.
Advertised:	17 May.
To Sail:	Shortly after arrival, 25, 30 June.
Sailed:	(1 July).
Arrived:	—

Daily expected from Bristol; stout, well-built vessel; high between decks; good provisions; Capt. taking his wife and family (May 17); arr. from Bristol (June 3). Other voyages—see 1773.

GLORIOUS MEMORY   400 tons (see Appendix C).

Master:	Wm. Stewart.
Agent:	Jesse Taylor, merchant.
Destination:	Philadelphia & Baltimore.
Advertised:	21 June.
To Sail:	1, 20 Aug.
Sailed:	(16 Sep.).
Arrived:	—

Plenty of best provisions and water; no expense spared to make voyage agreeable and comfortable; remarkably fast; near 6 ft. between decks; will be completely fitted out; Capt. was first mate to Capt. Malcom for years; no more pass. than can be accommodated with the greatest ease (June 21);

Taylor and family sailing on vessel to settle at Phil. (July 22); arr. from Bristol with glass (Aug. 30); sailed to Phil. with beef, oatmeal, etc. (Sep. 16); put into Plymouth—sails lost and cargo shifted; four pass. killed (Oct. 14).

PROSPERITY: 500 tons (see Appendix C).

Master:	Wm. McCulloch.
Agent:	Wm. Burgess, merchant.
Destination:	Philadelphia.
Advertised:	5 July.
To Sail:	15 Aug., 1 Sep.
Sailed:	(5 Sep.).
Arrived:	Voyage of 38 days.

This fortunate vessel expected back immediately (July 5); has arr. at Cork from Phil. in 20 days (July 12); arr. Belfast from Phil. (July 22); arr. Phil.; all well; expected back immediately and will return to Phil. (Dec. 30). Other voyage—see 1775.

HOPE:	450 tons, changed to 400.
Master:	Thos. Ash; long in the trade.
Agent:	John Henderson, Francis Tagert, merchants.
Destination:	Charleston & Savannah, later Charleston, later Maryland.
Advertised:	22 July.
To Sail:	15 Oct.
Sailed:	(28 Oct.) for Madeira.
Arrived:	—

Not 9 mths. old (Sep.30); arr. Maryland (Jan. 31, 1775).

LONDONDERRY 1774

ALEXANDER:	400 tons.
Master:	Jas Hunter; remarkable for bountiful distribution of provisions.
Agent:	Robt. Alexander, Henry Newtown (Coleraine), merchants. Alex. Clerk Esq. (Maghera).
Destination:	Philadelphia.
Advertised:	1 Feb.
To Sail:	20 Apr., 1 May.
Sailed:	—
Arrived:	—

Arr. from Phil. with flaxseed & about 80 pass. (Jan. 28); calculated for acc. of pass.; especial care to supply very best provisions of their kind; not 2 years old (Feb. 1); 6 ft. between decks; not 1 year old; provisions include beef & pork (Apr. 8). Other voyages—see 1773.

HANNAH: 400 tons (see Appendix C).

Master:	Jas. Mitchell; great success.
Agent:	Jas. Sterling.
Destination:	Philadelphia.
Advertised:	11 Mar.
To Sail:	10 Apr., 1 May.
Sailed:	—
Arrived:	In 8 weeks.

Air holes between decks; well known good ship; every convenience requisite for health and convenience; ease and comfort for pass.; as usual, plenty of water and very best provisions to make voyage comfortable, healthful and agreeable (Mar. 11); arr. Phil.; all well (Sep. 27). Other voyages— see 1772, 1773, 1775.

MARY:	350 tons.
Master:	Robert George.
Agent:	Wm. Hope, Wm. Glen, Thos. Chambers, Abraham McCausland, merchants (owners), Jos. Adams (Cookstown), John Alexander (Maghera), Andrew Cochrane (Omagh).
Destination:	Philadelphia.
Advertised:	15 Mar.
To Sail:	10 Apr., 1 May.
Sailed:	—
Arrived:	—

Only 3 mths. old; built for pass. trade; lofty between decks; 6 air ports on each side; well watered and victualled (Mar. 15).

JUPITER:	350 tons.
Master:	Alex. Ewing; humanity.
Agent:	Andrew Gregg, Jas. Thompson, merchants (owners).
Destination:	Philadelphia.
Advertised:	1 Apr.
To Sail:	20 Apr., 1, 12 May.
Sailed:	—
Arrived:	—

Remarkable for fast sailing and short passages; people should embrace this early and good opportunity; best provisions (Apr. 1); now at Culmore; will sail on May 12 regardless of how many pass. are on board (Apr. 29). Other voyages—see 1771, 1772, 1773.

HILL:	300 tons.
Master:	Geo. Marshall; well known for humanity.
Agent:	Robt. Houston, Wm. Gregg (Coleraine), merchants.
Destination:	Philadelphia & New York.
Advertised:	19 Apr.
To Sail:	10 May.
Sailed:	—
Arrived:	—

Only 2 mths. old; very high between decks; Capt.'s previous voyages; best provisions will be on board (Apr. 19).

MINERVA: 500 tons.
Master: Robt. Macky; rose by his merit.
Agent: Andrew Gregg, Jas. Thompson, merchants (owners).
Destination: Philadelphia.
Advertised: 19 Apr.
To Sail: 10 May, 20 June.
Sailed: —
Arrived: —

Built last summer at great expense for pass. trade; 8 ft. in cabin, 7 ft. in steerage, 6 ft. between decks (Apr. 19); now arr.; no cost or pains will be spared to establish the vessel in pass. trade and have laid in plentiful stores for that purpose (June 10). Other voyage—see 1775.

BETTY: 250 tons.
Master: Geo. Campbell; well acquainted with pass. trade.
Agent: Patterson and Fletcher, Wm. Hunter, merchants (owner).
Destination: Charleston.
Advertised: 7 June.
To Sail: 20 July.
Sailed: —
Arrived: —

Will have plentiful provisions; every accom. to make passage agreeable; Capt. may be seen at his lodgings (June 7). Other voyage—see 1773.

ANN: 300 tons.
Master: Pat Miller.
Agent: Robt. Alexander, Henry Newtown (Coleraine), merchants, Alex. Clark, Esq. (Maghera).
Destination: Charleston.
Advertised: 28 June.
To Sail: 10 July, 20 Aug.
Sailed: —
Arrived: —

Best provisions (June 28). Other voyages—1771, 1772, 1773.

NEWRY 1774

LIBERTY: 300 tons.
Master: Ch. Johnston, later Ch. Thompson.
Agent: Dd. Gaussan, merchant, Robt. Park (Stewartstown), Ed. Patterson (Cookstown), Michael Johnston (Moneymore).
Destination: Philadelphia.

Every tide expected; will be completely fitted out with provisions and water; owners in Phil. have large tract of land and will sell or let it (Feb. 15); arr.; Capt. Thompson; Dd. Duncan, one of her owners, on board, will see justice done (May 24).

Advertised:	15 Feb.
To Sail:	1 June.
Sailed:	—
Arrived:	—
HOPE:	350 tons (see Appendix C).
Master:	Robt. McClenaghan; no need to mention character.
Agent:	Andrew Thompson, merchant.
Destination:	Philadelphia.
Advertised:	1 Mar.
To Sail:	1 June.
Sailed:	—
Arrived:	25 July.

Coffee seized off, at Wexford (Customs 1/126, Feb. 15); new vessel, prime sailer; well calculated for pass. trade; now arr.; Capt. is 'a young man and purposes establishing his character in the trade'; plenty of provisions; can go on to N.Y. or Baltimore for additional 5s. (Mar. 1); same advert. (*F.D.J.*, Apr. 1); arr. Phil. with 200 pass. (O'Brien, *Hidden phase*, p. 254); arr. Newcastle with 200 pass. (O'Brien, *Washington's Irish assoc.*, p. 236).

MINERVA:	350 tons.
Master:	Dd. McCullagh; means to stay in the trade.
Agent:	Dd. Gaussan, merchant.
Destination:	Philadelphia.
Advertised:	1 Mar.
To Sail:	10 Apr.
Sailed:	—
Arrived:	—

Prime sailer; her voyage last year was speediest ever made from Newry; well calculated for the trade; near 6 ft. between decks; not too many pass. will be taken; well provisioned; pass. can go on to Baltimore for 6s. 6d. extra (Mar. 1). Other voyages—see 1771, 1773.

BALTIMORE PACKET:	350 tons.
Master:	Alex. Kennedy; well known for care.
Agent:	Dd. Gaussan, merchant, J. Woolley (Portadown), Thos. McCabe (Belfast).
Destination:	Baltimore.
Advertised:	4 Mar.
To Sail:	1 Apr.
Sailed:	—
Arrived:	—

Not 20 mths. old; built for pass. trade; near 6 ft. between decks; Capt. has been trading on American coast for 20 years; pleasure of former pass.; cheap land in Maryland; most convenient ports for back parts of Pa. (Mar. 4).

RENOWN:	450 tons (see Appendix C).
Master:	Wm. Keith.
Agent:	Andrew Thompson, merchant, John Bell (Armagh on Tuesdays), Joseph Adams (Cookstown), John Hyndman (Belfast).
Destination:	Philadelphia.

Not 18 mths. old; 6 ft. between decks; 'commodious Rooms that pass. may live separate'; 'compleatest ship in the kingdom' (Mar. 11); same advert. with two Dublin agents added (*F.D.J.*, Apr. 20). Other voyages—see 1775.

Advertised:	11 Mar.
To Sail:	20 Apr.
Sailed:	—
Arrived:	—

ELLIOTT:	300 tons.	Same good usage as those who went last year (Mar. 11). Other voyage—see 1773.
Master:	John Waring; master and owner.	
Agent:	Thos. Waring.	
Destination:	Charleston and Cape Fear.	
Advertised:	11 Mar.	
To Sail:	10 May.	
Sailed:	—	
Arrived:	—	

ROBERT:	350 tons.	Same advert. as in *B.N.L.(F.D.J.*, Apr. 1). Other voyages—see 1771, 1772, 1773.
Master:	Matt Russell	
Agent:	Andrew & Acheson Thompson, merchants.	
Destination:	New York.	
Advertised:	15 Mar.	
To Sail:	1 Apr.	
Sailed:	—	
Arrived:	—	

NEEDHAM:	400 tons (see Appendix C).	
Master:	Wm. Cheevers.	Built at Newry specially for pass. trade; near 6 ft. between decks; no expense spared to make passage comfortable and agreeable; previous successful voyages; pass. will get as much land as they want, in accordance with the American advt. dispersed throughout North of Ireland (Mar. 18); a few servants still wanted; now in harbour (Apr. 29); times of servants of both sexes to be disposed of to pay for their passages (*Rivington's Gazette*, Aug. 4). Other voyages—see 1772, 1773.
Agent:	Dd. Gaussan, Geo. Anderson, J., W., & G. Glenny, Wm. Beath, Hill Wilson, merchants (owners).	
Destination:	Philadelphia.	
Advertised:	18 Mar.	
To Sail:	20 Apr., 5 May.	
Sailed:	—	
Arrived:	—	

WILLIAM:	250 tons.	Only 10 mths. old; now in harbour; well fitted out; provisions and acc. of highest quality; farmers and tradesmen wanted (Apr. 12).
Master:	Bartholomew McCann.	
Agent:	Wm. & John Ogle.	
Destination:	Charleston and Cape Fear.	
Advertised:	12 Apr.	
To Sail:	20 May, 1 June.	
Sailed:	—	
Arrived:	—	

BRIG SPARROW: 200 tons.
Master: Moses Sawyer.
Agent: Geo. Anderson, merchant.
Destination: New York.
Advertised: 19 Apr.
To Sail: 1 May.
Sailed: —
Arrived: —

Good stout ship; only 50 persons will be taken; usual passage money; pass. will have freedom of whole vessel (Apr. 19).

BETSEY: 300 tons.
Master: Samuel Kyle; so successful last season.
Agent: Dd. Gaussan, Wm. Oakman (Armagh), John Patterson touring Dungannon, Stewartstown, Cootehill, Belfast.
Destination: Philadelphia.
Advertised: 16 Apr.
To Sail: 15 May, 1 June.
Sailed: —
Arrived: —

Now in port (May 24). Other voyage—see 1773.

FREEMASON: 300 tons.
Master: John Semple.
Agent: J., W., & G. Glenny, Wm. Beath, Geo. Anderson, merchants (owners).
Destination: Philadelphia & New York.
Advertised: 27 May.
To Sail: 20 Aug., 10 Oct.
Sailed: —
Arrived: —

Well victualled and manned; great encouragement promised to those engaging on behalf of a number of pass. (May 27); arr. from Antigua with rum for agents named (Sep. 20). Other voyages—see 1772.

ELLIOTT: 300 tons.
Master: John Waring, master and owner.
Agent: Thos. Waring.
Destination: Charleston, Savannah added later.
Advertised: 16 Aug.
To Sail: End Sep., 10, 28 Oct.
Sailed: —
Arrived: —

Will have great comfort on voyage (Aug. 16); sail to Savannah also (Sep. 2).

LARNE 1774

JUPITER: 250 tons (see Appendix C).
Master: Saml. Brown.

Arr. Larne Feb. 6 from Phil. and Charleston; has to discharge

Agent:	John Montgomery, Robt. McKedy (Ballymena), And. Thompson (Newry), merchants, Thos. Barklie.	part of cargo at Newry; any intending emigrants living there can have goods brought free to Larne (Feb. 11); arr. Baltimore
Destination:	Charleston & Baltimore.	(*N.Y. Gaz*.). Other voyages—see
Advertised:	11 Feb.	1771, 1772, 1773.
To Sail:	1, 25 Apr., 12 May.	
Sailed:	—	
Arrived:	Early in Sep.	

SNOW JAMES AND MARY: 250 tons.

Master:	John Moore.	Expected every day; people must
Agent:	Jas. McVickar, merchant, Rev. Isaac Patton (Templepatrick), Rev. Dd. Arrot (Markethill), Mrs Susanna Moody (Limavady).	engage at once as many have already done so; Patton has relatives in Novia Scotia and can show 'most inviting letters' from them (Feb. 18); arr. Belfast on
Destination:	Fort Cumberland (N.S.).	Feb. 27 with flaxseed from N.Y.
Advertised:	18 Feb.	(Mar. 1); more than one vessel
To Sail:	End Mar., 1 Apr.	will sail; *J. & M*'s complement
Sailed:	—	already agreed (Mar. 4). Other
Arrived:	—	voyages—see below and 1771, 1772, 1773, 1775.

SNOW JAMES AND MARY: 250 tons.

Master:	John Workman; well known.	Both vessel and master well known (May 27).
Agent:	Jas. McVickar, merchant, John Moore, John McVickar (Ballymena).	
Destination:	Newcastle & New York.	
Advertised:	27 May.	
To Sail:	15 July, 1, 10 Aug.	
Sailed:	—	
Arrived:	—	

LORD DUNLUCE: 400 tons.

Master:	Robert Shutter; humane treatment well known.	Remarkably well calculated for pass. trade; very high between
Agent:	John Montgomery, merchant, Thos. Barklie (Ballymena on Saturdays).	decks; greatest care to make passage agreeable; now at Cork (June 28); arr. from Baltimore
Destination:	Newcastle & Baltimore.	and L'pool (Aug. 16). Other
Advertised:	28 June.	voyages—see 1772, 1773, 1775.
To Sail:	20 Aug., 6 Sep.	
Sailed:	—	
Arrived:	—	

Appendix D

BETTY:	250 tons.	Best water and provisions (Aug. 5); arr. at Belfast on way to L'pool (Sep. 2); arr. Larne (Oct. 11). Other voyages—see 1772, 1773, 1775.
Master:	Abraham Woodside; humane treatment.	
Agent:	Saml. Montgomery, Robt. McKedy (Ballymena), merchants, Hugh Harrison (Ballycastle).	
Destination:	Charleston.	
Advertised:	5 Aug.	
To Sail:	20 Sep., 25 Oct.	
Sailed:	—	
Arrived:	—	

MINERVA:	300 tons.	Built in London river; not one yr. old; as fine a vessel as is in the trade; now at Bristol (Nov. 1); master will visit Ballymena and Lisburn (Dec. 2).
Master:	Arthur Hill.	
Agent:	Arthur Hill. Later added Nathan Moore, John Ewing (Belfast), merchants, Joshua Shepherd (Lisburn).	
Destination:	Charleston.	
Advertised:	1 Nov.	
To Sail:	15, 25 Nov., 20 Dec.	
Sailed:	—	
Arrived:	—	

PORTRUSH 1774

BRIG MARY ANN:	250 tons.
Master:	John Breen.
Agent:	John & Ch. Galt, Alex. Laurence, merchants (all of Coleraine).
Destination:	Newcastle & New York.
Advertised:	22 Apr.
To Sail:	15 May, 1 June.
Sailed:	—
Arrived:	—

BELFAST 1775

JENNY:	160 tons.	Stout, fast sailing vessel; only a few will be taken (Dec. 16, 1774).
Master:	John Brown; well acquainted with American trade.	
Agent:	Saml. Brown (owner).	
Destination:	Baltimore.	
Advertised:	16 Dec., 1774.	
To Sail:	15 Jan.	
Sailed:	—	
Arrived:	—	

Appendix D

PROSPERITY: 500 tons (see Appendix C).

Master:	Wm. McCulloch.
Agent:	Henry McCulloch, Jos. McCulloch at Capt. Hawthorn's, Robt. McKedy, John McCulloch (both of Ballymena).
Destination:	Philadelphia.
Advertised:	20 Jan.
To Sail:	15 Mar., end of Apr.
Sailed:	19 Apr.
Arrived:	7 June.

Arr. from Phil. after voyage of 24 days; best provisions and water provided (Jan. 20); maliciously reported that vessel will call at Cork for troops; can take 300 pass. more than have engaged; master to visit Ballymena and Ballymoney (Feb. 24); Rev. Martin, Newtownards, and family to sail on (Mar. 14); arr. at Phil.; letter of thanks for good treatment signed by 23; will soon be back for more emigrants (July 21) Other voyage—see 1774.

CHARLOTTE: 500 tons.

Master:	Thos. Egger, Jnr.; chief mate to McCulloch.
Agent:	Jesse Taylor, merchant.
Destination:	Philadelphia.
Advertised:	3 Feb.
To Sail:	30 Mar., 20 Apr., 5 May.
Sailed:	—
Arrived:	—

Expected daily; not 2 mths. old; built for pass. trade between Belfast and Phil. (Feb. 3); arr. Sligo from N.Y. after voyage of 18 days; will sail at once to Belfast (Mar. 3); shortly expected (Apr. 3); master will visit Newtownards & Ballymena (Apr. 18); arr. from N.Y. with flaxseed (Apr. 21); to ensure health of pass., master has got 12 air ports cut in vessel's side (May 5).

PEACE AND PLENTY: 400 tons.

Master:	Ch. McKenzie.
Agent:	Waddell Cunningham, merchant.
Destination:	Philadelphia, New York added later.
Advertised:	21 Feb.
To Sail:	15 Apr., 20, 26 June, 6, 15 July.
Sailed:	—
Arrived:	—

Daily expected; as good treatment as enjoyed by pass. in previous years (Feb. 21); daily expected from London (May 9); arr. with barilla ashes from London; ship's boat available every Mon., Wed., Fri., for use of any wishing to see the ship's accom.; master will visit Ballymena and Ballynahinch on market days; rum and vinegar will be sold cheaply to pass. (May 30); will sail from Campbletown on July 1; lighter will sail from Belfast on June 26 (June 20); pass. be in town July 6 (June 27); last notice as the vessel is now in Belfast lough (July 7). Other voyage—see 1774.

JOHN: 450 tons (see Appendix C).
Master: Ch. Poaug.
Agent: John Ewing, merchant, Saml. Brown, John Bashford.
Destination: Annapolis & Baltimore.
Advertised: 3 Mar.
To Sail: 3 weeks after arrival 1 Apr., 23 Apr.
Sailed: 23 Apr.
Arrived: —

Daily expected; no extra delay for pass.; none will be taken unless agree and give earnest 8 days before sailing; 3 or 4 stout apprentices needed for the vessel (Mar. 3); arr. from Baltimore with wheat and flour; plenty of room; no stinting of provisions; stout new ship (Mar. 10); arr. Md. (Sep. 5).

WADDELL: 400 tons.
Master: —Scott.
Agent: Waddell Cunningham, merchant, Wm. Reed (Newry).
Destination: Alexandria, Georgetown and Baltimore.
Advertised: 14 Apr.
To Sail: 1 May.
Sailed: (12 May for Madeira).
Arrived: —

Arr. from Alexandria (Md.) with wheat, flaxseed; Alexandria very convenient to N.C.; visits to vessel can be arranged (Apr. 14); sailed to Madeira with wine (May 12). Other voyages—see 1773, 1774, Baltic - Belfast - St Eustatia (Oct. 11, Nov. 8).

UNNAMED: — tons
Master: Unnamed.
Agent: Jesse Taylor, merchant.
Destination: Charleston.
Advertised: 30 June.
To Sail: 10 Sep.
Sailed: —
Arrived: —

Stout vessel; full 6 ft. between decks; will sail only if more than 100 people engage for voyage; best provisions and water (June 30).

LONDONDERRY 1775

HANNAH: 400 tons.
Master: Jas. Ramage; well acquainted in the trade.
Agent: Jas. Sterling, Capt. Jas. Mitchell, Wm. Neely (Ballygawley).
Destination: Philadelphia.
Advertised: 7 Mar.
To Sail: 10 Apr., 1 May.
Sailed: —
Arrived: —

Well known to be a stout and roomy vessel; great plenty of provisions and water, so pass. need not fear being stinted (Mar. 7). Other voyages—see 1772, 1773, 1774.

MINERVA: 500 tons.
Master: Alex. Ewing; great success for several years.
Agent: Jas. Thompson, Andrew Gregg (owners).
Destination: Philadelphia.
Advertised: 7 Mar.
To Sail: 20 Apr., 15 May.
Sailed: —
Arrived: —

One of most complete pass. vessels in the trade; 8 ft. high in cabin, 7 ft. in steerage; 6 ft. between decks; plentiful store of provisions; 1 yr. old (Mar. 7). Other voyage—see 1774.

GEORGE: 250 tons.
Master: Wm. Pinkerton.
Agent: Jas. Mitchell, Saml. Curry.
Destination: Philadelphia.
Advertised: 21 Mar.
To Sail: —
Sailed: —
Arrived: —

Good provisions as those who have gone hitherto have experienced (Mar. 21). Other voyages—see 1771, 1773.

NEWRY 1775

CHARLOTTE: 250 tons.
Master: Jas. Montgomery.
Agent: Andrew Thompson.
Destination: Philadelphia.
Advertised: 10 Feb.
To Sail: 15 Apr.
Sailed: —
Arrived: —

Noted for fast passages; not more than 100 pass. will be taken (Feb. 10). Other voyage—see 1773.

RENOWN: 450 tons.
Master: Wm. Keith.
Agent: Andrew Thompson, John Bell (Armagh), Jas. Adams (Cookstown), John Hagan (Ballyronan).
Destination: Philadelphia.
Advertised: 20 Jan.
To Sail: 10, 20 Apr.
Sailed: —
Arrived: —

Arr. from Phil. after voyage of 26 days with flaxseed and flour for Thompson (Jan. 20); well calculated for pass. trade 18 mths. old; 6 ft. between decks; has commodious rooms that pass. may sleep separate; most complete vessel ever in pass. trade (Feb. 10). Other voyage—see 1774.

MINERVA: 400 tons.
Master: Ch. Forrest.
Agent: Andrew Thompson.
Destination: Philadelphia.

Noted for short passages, good acc., and plenty of food and provisions (Mar. 3).

Advertised:	3 Mar.
To Sail:	10 Apr.
Sailed:	—
Arrived:	—

LIBERTY:	500 tons.	Now arr. after passage of 19
Master:	Thos. Lowden.	days; not quite 14 mths. old; full
Agent:	Jas. Ogle, John Hoope	6 ft. between decks; Rea, Hoope's
	(owner, Lurgan), John	brother-in-law, will sail in the
	Rea (at Newry, Banbridge,	vessel and make it his study to
	Tandragee).	ensure comfortable passage (Mar.
Destination:	Philadelphia.	3).
Advertised:	3 Mar.	
To Sail:	1, 10 Apr.	
Sailed:	—	
Arrived:	—	

JULIANA:	500 tons.	Not quite 12 mths. old; not more
Master:	Robt. Montgomery.	than 150 pass. will be taken; is
Agent:	Andrew Thompson.	certainly finest vessel ever known
Destination:	Philadelphia.	in the pass. trade (Mar. 10).
Advertised:	10 Mar.	
To Sail:	10 May.	
Sailed:	—	
Arrived:	—	

RECOVERY:	500 tons.	Built under master's supervision
Master:	Dd. McCullough.	for pass.; new type of vessel being
Agent:	Jas. Giles	7 ft. between decks and having
Destination:	Philadelphia.	tier of portholes to admit light
Advertised:	14 Mar.	and cause a refreshing circulation
To Sail:	25 Mar.	of air; most complete vessel in
Sailed:	—	the pass. trade; many false reports
Arrived:	—	spread to injure master's reputa-
		tion, but intending pass. may get
		names of former pass. who have
		returned, from Giles (Mar. 14).

BRITANNIA:	500 tons.	Fine new vessel; air ports and
Master:	Saml. Kyle; character well	every acc. as in a London trader;
	known.	Gaussan will, as usual, supply
Agent:	Dd. Gaussan, John	plenty of provisions and water;
	Graham, Saml. Kyle	Graham has large tract of land
	(Belfast), Thos. Cuming	for pass. (Mar. 28); excellent fast
	(Stewartstown). Later	vessel; sailed from Phil. to Cork
	added Ed. Hanna (Belfast),	in 21 days; 6 ft. between decks;
	Wm. & Isaac Oakman	separate rooms; has provisioned
	(Armagh), Saml. Park,	at Cork for voyage; best beef,
	Adam Foreman, Francis	butter and oatmeal (Apr. 7); pass.

Young (Stewartstown)
—Boyd (Charlemont),
Theophilis Erwin (Gribly),
John Lackey (Monaghan),
Joshua Thornton
(Cootehill), Alex. Chambers
(Ballybay), —Walker
(Ballymena), Thos.
Cummin (Coagh).

Destination: Philadelphia.
Advertised: 28 Mar.
To Sail: 20 May or sooner.
Sailed: —
Arrived: —

will have full allowance of provisions from May 16 weekly
allowance from then and during
voyage will be 6 lb. beef, 6 lb.
bread (shipped at Phil.) or 6 lb.
oatmeal, 1 lb. butter or 1
pint of treacle and molasses and
14 qts. water; plenty of potatoes
also; pass. from Phil. can testify
to quality of provisions; bonds
for faithful performance of this
scale of provisions will be given
to each pass.; baggage will be
carried free to vessel (May 2).

DUKE OF LEINSTER: 500 tons.
Master: Hugh Hamilton.
Agent: Wm. & John Ogle, Thos.
McFarin, A. Donnelly
(Blackwatertown), Geo.
Carooth (Coalisland),
Francis Armstrong
(Richhill), Geo. Ramsey
(Moneymore), Henry
Thompson (Belturbet),
Thos. Trouton (Armagh,
Dungannon, Aughnacloy).
Destination: Newcastle & New York.
Advertised: 14 Apr.
To Sail: 1 May.
Sailed: —
Arrived: —

Best vessel in pass. trade from
Newry; fully 6 ft. 3 in. between
decks; cabin elegantly finished
and is large enough to acc. 50
pass.; best provisions; some of
the agents going on board; pass.
to be ready by Apr. 25 (Apr. 14).

LARNE 1775

LORD DUNLUCE: 450 tons.
Master: Robt. Shutter.
Agent: John Montgomery, Thos.
Barklie (Ballymena on
Saturdays), Andrew
Thompson (Newry).
Destination: Newcastle & Baltimore.
Advertised: 14 Mar.
To Sail: 10 Apr.
Sailed: —
Arrived: —

Discharging cargo; any there can
be taken on board and brought to
Larne without expense (Mar. 14);
arr. Larne; sail at appointed time
(Mar. 31). Other voyages—see
1772, 1773, 1774.

JANE AND ISABELLA: 450 tons.
Master: John Moore.
Agent: John & Nathan Moore, John McVickar (Bally-mena), Waddell Cunningham (Belfast).
Destination: New York.
Advertised: 21 Mar.
To Sail: 10 Apr.
Sailed: —
Arrived: —

Arr. from N.Y. with flaxseed; not 4 mths. old; owners will make it their study to render passage as agreeable as possible; plentiful provisions and water (Mar. 21).

SNOW JAMES AND MARY: 250 tons.
Master: John Manfoad.
Agent: Jas. McVickar, John Moore, John McVickar (Ballymena)
Destination: Newcastle & New York.
Advertised: 2 May.
To Sail: 1 June.
Sailed: —
Arrived: —

Best provisions and water; must sail at appointed time so will be comfortable as will not be more than half full (May 2). Other voyages—see 1771, 1772, 1773, 1774.

BETTY: 250 tons.
Master: —Woodside; character well known.
Agent: Saml. Montgomery, Robt. McKedy (Ballymena), Hugh Harrison (Ballycastle).
Destination: Charleston.
Advertised: 23 June.
To Sail: 10 Sep.
Sailed: —
Arrived: —

Greatest care to provide plentiful water and provisions (June 23). Other voyages—see 1772, 1773, 1774.

PORTRUSH 1775

BETTY AND HELEN: 300 tons.
Master: Pat McCormick.
Agent: John & Ch. Galt, Alex. Laurence.
Destination: Philadelphia.
Advertised: 14 Apr.
To Sail: 1 May.
Sailed: —
Arrived: —

Best treatment assured; owners resolved to fit out vessel in most plentiful way; will sail on time be there many or few pass. (Apr. 14).

APPENDIX E

The Destination of Emigrant Vessels from the North Irish Ports, 1750–1775

COMPILED from advertisements of emigrant shipping in the *B.N.L.* and *Londonderry Journal*. In cases where an emigrant vessel was advertised to call at two ports for emigrants, the voyage has been shared between these ports. In each of the middle columns, the name of the colony is followed by the port or ports of destination, where stated.

BELFAST

Date	Total Vessels	Pa. Ph.	N.Y. N.Y.	S.C. Ch.	Md. Ba. An.	Other Voyages
1750	3	2				1 N.Y. & Pa.
1751		No copies of *B.N.L.*				
1752	1½	1				½ N.Y. & Pa.ᵃ
1753	3	2				1 Wi. & C.F.
1754	2½		1			1½ Wi. & C.Fᵇ.
1755	3					3 Wi. & C.F.
1756	—					
1757	3	1	1			1 Va.
1758	5	2	2			1 Ja.
1759	—					
1760	1	1				

BELFAST—*continued*

Date	Total Vessels	Pa. / Ph.	N.Y. / N.Y.	S.C. / Ch.	Md. / Ba. An.	Other Voyages
1761	4	1½ᵃ	2½ᵃ			
1762	4½	1½ᵃ	2	1		
1763	5½	2½ᵇ		2		1 N.Y. & Pa.
1764	6½	3	3½ᵃ			
1765	10½	4ᶜ		3		1 Qu.
						½ De. & N.Y.ᵃ
						1 Bar. & N.Y.
						1 N.S., Mas., S.C.
1766	9½	7½ᵇ	1	1		
1767	12	3½ᵇ	1	6	1	½ De. & N.Y.ᵇ
1768	7	3	1	1	1	1 Sa.
1769	8	3	1		1	1 Sa.
						1 S.C. & Ga.
						1 Md. & Va.
1770	7	3	2		1	1 Va.
1771	7	4	1			1 Sa.
						1 S.C. & Ga.
1772	8	4		2		½ Sa.ᵉ
						½ Ha. & Ct.ᵈ
						1 N.Y. & N.S.
1773	14	5		2	3	1 Ha. & Ct.
						1 Wi. & C.F.
						1 Sa.
						1 Pa. & Md.
1774	10½	4			1½ᵃ	3 Pa. & N.Y.
						1 Pa. & Md.
						1 S.C. & Ga.
1775	7	2		1	3	1 Pa. & N.Y.
Totals		60½	19	19	11½	
Part voyages		4¼	4¾	1⅝	1½	
Grand Totals	143	64¾	23¾	20⅝	13	2⅓ N.S. & P.E.I.; 6½ N.C.; 6 Ga.; 2½ Va.; ⅓ Mas.; ½ De.; 1 Qu.; 1½ W. Indies

ᵃ Sailing shared with Larne
ᵇ Sailing shared with Portrush
ᶜ Two sailing shared with Portrush
ᵈ Sailing shared with Newry
ᵉ Sailing shared with Londonderry

LONDONDERRY

Date	Total Vessels	Pa. Ph.	N.Y. N.Y.	S.C. Ch.	N.S. & P.E.I. Ha. Ct.	Other Voyages
1750	3	3				
1751		No copies of *B.N.L.*				
1752	−					
1753	2	2				
1754	1	1				
1755	−					
1756	1	1				
1757	3	3				
1758	−					
1759	−					
1760	3	3				
1761	6	4			2	
1762	7	6			1	
1763	6	6				
1764	4	4				
1765	5	4			1	
1766	10	8			2	
1767	7	5		1	1	
1768	5	2	1	1	1	
1769	5	5				
1770	8	7				1 Wi.
1771	14	11	1			1 Wi.
1772	11½	7½ᵃ		1	1	1 N.S. & Pa. 1 S.C. & N.C. 1 Md. & Pa.
1773	15	7		3		2 Ba. 1 S.C. & Ga. 2 S.C. & N.C.
1774	8	5		2		1 Pa. & N.Y.
1775	3	3				
Totals		97½	2	8	9	
Part voyages		1½	½	2	½	
Grand totals	127½	99	2½	10	9½	3½ N.C.; 2¼ Md.; ¼ Ga.

ᵃ Sailing shared with Belfast

Appendix E

NEWRY

Date	Total Ves-sels	Pa.	N.Y.	S.C.	Md.	Other Voyages
		Ph.	N.Y.	Ch.	Ba. An.	
1750	–					
1751		No cop	ies of	*B.N.L.*		
1752	–					
1753	–					
1754	2	2				
1755	–					
1756	1		1			
1757	–					
1758	–					
1759	–					
1760	1	1				
1761	–					
1762	1					1 Pa. & N.Y.
1763	4	3	1			
1764	2		2			
1765	3	1	2			
1766	3	½[a]	2			½Bo[b].
1767	5½	1½[a]	2	1		1 N.S., Mas., Pa., N.Y.
1768	7	2	2			1 Wi. 1 De. & N.Y. 1 Pa. & N.Y.
1769	7	3	2		1	1 S.C. & N.C.
1770	2	1	1			
1771	10	4	2		1	3 S.C. & Md.
1772	6½	3	1	1	1	½ N.S. & P.E.I.[c]
1773	8	5		1		1 Pa. & Md. 1 Pa. & N.Y.
1774	13	6	2		1	2 S.C. & N.C. 1 Pa. & N.Y. 1 S.C. & Ga.
1775	8	7				1 De. & N.Y.
Totals		40	20	3	4	
Part voyages		2¾	3¼	3½	2	
Grand totals	84	42¾	23¼	6½	6	2½ N.C.; ¾ Mas.; ¾ N.S. & P.E.I.; 1 De.; ½ Ga.

[a] Sailing shared with Larne
[b] Sailing shared with Portrush
[c] Sailing shared with Belfast

LARNE

Date	Total Vessels	Pa. / Ph.	N.Y. / N.Y.	S.C.	Md.	Other Voyages
1750	1		1			
1751		No cop	ies of *B.N.L.*			
1752	1½	1				½ Pa. & N.Y.ᵃ
1753	1					1 Pa. & N.Y.
1754	2	1				1 Pa. & N.Y.
1755	1	1				
1756	2		2			
1757	2	2				
1758	1					1 Pa. & N.Y.
1759	3	2				1 Pa. & N.Y.
1760	4	2	2			
1761	3	1½ᵃ	1½ᵃ			
1762	1½	½ᵃ	1			
1763	3	2				1 De. & N.Y.
1764	1½		1½ᵃ			
1765	½					½ De. & N.Y.ᵃ
1766	2½	1½ᵇ	1			
1767	2½	½ᵇ	1	1		
1768	1		1			
1769	–					
1770	3	1	2			
1771	2		1	1		
1772	4			4		
1773	4			2	1	1 S.C. & Md.
1774	6½			2	½ᵃ	1 N.S.
						1 De. & N.Y.
						1 De. & Md.
						1 S.C. & Md.
1775	4		1	1		1 De. & N.Y.
						1 De. & Md.
Totals		16	16	11	1½	
Part voyages		2¼	4	1	2	
Grand totals	57½	18¼	20	12	3½	1 N.S.; 2¼ De.

ᵃ Sailing shared with Belfast
ᵇ Sailing shared with Newry

PORTRUSH

Date	Total Vessels	Pa. Ph.	N.Y. N.Y.	Mas. Bo.	N.C. Wi and C.F.	Other Voyages
1750	4	1		3		
1751		No copies of B.N.L.				
1752	1	1				
1753	1	1				
1754	1½	1			½ᵃ	
1755	1	1				
1756	–					
1757	1		1			
1758	1	1				
1759	–					
1760	1		1			
1761	–					
1762	2	1				1 N.Y. & De.
1763	1½	½ᵃ				1 N.Y. & De.
1764	2	1	1			
1765	2	1ᵇ	1			
1766	2	½ᵃ	1		½ᶜ	
1767	2	½ᵃ	1			½ N.Y. & De.ᵃ
1768	1		1			
1769	1		1			
1770	1		1			
1771	1		1			
1772	1					1 N.Y. & De.
1773	–					
1774	1					1 N.Y. & De.
1775	1	1				
Totals		11½	10	3½	½	
Part voyages			2¼			
Grand totals	30	11½	12¼	3½	½	2¼ De.

ᵃ Sailing shared with Belfast
ᵇ Two sailings shared with Belfast
ᶜ Sailing shared with Newry

APPENDIX F

Two Accounts of Voyages from the North of Ireland to Colonial America

---

(a) *Sally*, James Taylor or Turner, Belfast to Philadelphia, 1762.

THE vessel was advertised to sail on April 15 and was declared to be one of the finest belonging to North America. Ample provisions were promised and, as the master was stated to be well known and experienced, passengers were assured of the very best treatment (*B.N.L.*, Mar. 2). The letter was published in the *B.N.L.* on 13 May 1763.

> To the Printers, etc.   Greyabbey, April 23, 1763
> Gentlemen,
>   As many of my Friends and Countrymen are about to go to some of the Provinces of North-America, I thought it my Duty to them, in Order, if possible, to prevent their being treated, in the Passage, in so barbarious and inhumane a Manner, as many were, last Year, who went on Board the S————y from Belfast, Capt. T————r, Commander; and to deter any such Ship-Captains or others, concerned in transporting Passengers to America, who might be capable of such horrid Villainy, from attempting it; by laying before the Publick a faithful Account of what his Crew of Passengers suffered: Being a Letter from my own Son (who was one of those unhappy People) a true Copy of which I herewith send you, begging you may communicate it to the World, for the Good of Mankind, thro' the Channel of your very useful News-Letter; I have the Original, which I know to be genuine, and am ready to produce it, for the Satisfaction of any Person of Worth, if required.—There are many Letters in the Country, from others, to the same Purpose.
>   I am, etc.
>   Robert Smilie

Appendix F

Honoured Father,

I account it my Honour and Duty, to give you an Account of myself and my Proceedings since I left you; which have, I confess, been a little extraordinary. On the next Tuesday after I left you, I came on Board the S——y, on the Monday following, being the 24th of May last, we sailed for America: On the 31st we lost Sight of Ireland, having been detained 'till then by Calms and contrary Winds, which seemed to be the doleful Presages of our after unhappy Voyage. We had our full Allowance of Bread and Water, only for the first Fortnight; then we were reduced to three Pints of Water per day, and three Pounds and a Half of Bread per Week, to each Person; which it never afterwards exceeded the whole Passage. We had a South-west Wind, which drove us so far North, that our Weather became extremely cold, with much Rain and hard Gales of Wind: On the 5th of July we had a hard Squal of Wind which lasted 3 Hours, and caused us to lie to; on the 6th we had a Storm which continued 9 Hours, and obliged us to lie to under bare Poles; on the 12th we espied a Mountain of Ice of prodigious Size; on the 13th our Weather became more moderate; on the 16th we espied a Sail, which was along Side of us before either saw the other; she, having the Wind right aft, crowded Sail, and bore away; we gave her Chase, and fired six Guns at her but the Fog soon hid her from us. In this manner did the Captain behave, giving Chace to all Ships he saw, whether they bore off us East or West, it was all alike, the Motives of which caused various Conjectures. August the first our Weather became extremely warm, and the Crew very weak: The 10th Day our Allowance of Bread came to two Pounds and a Half per week to each Passenger; next Week we had only one Pound and a Half; and the next twelve Days we lived upon two Biscuits and a half for that Time, and half a Naggin of Barley each, which we ate raw, for want of Water to boil it in: We had Beef, but could make no Use of it, for Thirst; for we were a Week that we had but half a Pint of Water per Day for each Person. Hunger and Thirst had now reduced our Crew to the last Extremity; nothing was now to be heard aboard our Ship but the Cries of distressed children, and of their distressed Mothers, unable to relieve them. Our Ship now was truly a real Spectacle of Horror! Never a Day passed without one or two of our Crew put over Board; many kill'd themselves by drinking Salt Water; and their own Urine was a common Drink; yet in the midst of all our Miseries, our Captain shewed not the least Remorse or Pity. We were now out of Hopes of ever seeing land. August 29th we had only one Pint of Water for each Person, which was all we Passengers would have got, and our Bread was done: But on that Day the Lord was pleased to sent the greatest Shower of Rain I ever saw, which was the Means of preserving our Lives. After this we had fair Winds, and, for most Part, Rains every Day; and tho' we had no Bread, yet, we thought, we lived well. On the first of September we sounded, and found ourselves in forty Fathom Water, and the next Morning, about eight o'clock, we saw Land, to the inexpressible Joy of all our Ship's Crew; and on Sunday Morning the 4th of Sept. we came to an Anchor off Newcastle; so that we had a Passage of fourteen Weeks and five Days. You may judge of Capt T———'s Temper and Character by this, that, notwithstanding all the Straits we were in for Bread and Water, neither he, nor his Mistress, nor five others that were his Favourites, ever came to Allowance. We had now, since the Time of our setting sail, lost sixty-four of our Crew by Death. Monday the fifth I came on Shore, and by the Blessing of God, in three Weeks Time I got perfectly well; but indeed, few of our Ship's Crew were so strong as I; for notwithstanding all I suffered I enjoyed a good State of Health the whole Passage.

I am your dutiful Son,
John Smilie

(b) *Lord Dunluce,* James Gillis, Larne to Charleston, 1773.
Advertised in *B.N.L.,* May 18. The letter was published in the *B.N.L.* on 4-8 June 1773.
For the Belfast News Letter.   Charlestown, 15 January, 1773.

We the undernamed Subscribers, think it is a duty incumbent upon us to acquaint the Publick in general and our Friends in particular, that we went on board from Larne the Ship Lord Dunlace, a stout commodious Vessel, James Gillis, Master; and after eleven Weeks Passage we arrived at Charlestown in South Carolina (our passage being prolonged by contrary Winds, which beat us so far North, and continuing to blow from the South West, detained us near three Weeks out of our way, notwithstanding all the Care and unwearied Diligence of our Captain, who did not fail to take all safe Advantage, in order to expedite our Way.) But the Tediousness of our Voyage was rendered as agreeable to us as possible by the humane treatment of our worthy Captain, and agreeable Company, together with the useful and timely Admonitions of our respected Friend, the Revd. William Martin, who never failed when the Weather and Time would permit, to preach the everlasting Gospel to us, the which we esteemed a singular Blessing. We had Plenty of Provisions of good Quality, and so would have had as agreeable a Passage, notwithstanding the Length of it, as any that ever was made from Ireland, had it not happened that the Small-pox broke out in the Vessel, which continued for some Time, and occasioned the Death of some Children; during which Time our Worthy Captain, and the Revd. Mr. Martin were duly employed visiting the Sick, and administering Cordials to their several Necessities, etc which Disorder would have caused us (according to the Laws of the Land) to have road Quarantine six Weeks, had not our Captain, by his Application to a Friend of his, through whose kind Mediation we obtained Liberty to go ashore the Day before the grand Court met, and got the Favour of being called upon to get our Warrants before those that had landed before, with riding fifteen Days Quarantine, which was a Favour that not many have been favoured with. Again, our worthy Friend Captain Gillis and Mr Martin did not cease, at the Expiration of our Voyage, to continue their fatherly Care over us, but used their utmost Endeavours to obtain Money to carry us to our Plantations, etc. Therefore we invite all our Friends that intend to come to this Land, to sail with Captain Gillis if possible, as he is both a solid, cautious, and careful Captain as ever sailed in the Passenger Way; the which Opinion we were confirmed in by meeting with some Passengers who landed near the same Time, and hearing of their Treatment, concluded that we would rather pay Capt. Gillis something extraordinary, than sail with any other.

John HUEY	Abraham THOMSON
Samuel MILLER	Robert HANNA
Wm. FAIRIES	Charles BURNIT
Charles MILLER	John ROARKE
John CRAIG	John McQUILLEN
Wm. HUMPHREY	George CHERRY
Archibald McWILLIAMS	Thomas WEIR
James CRAWFORD	David McQUESTIN
John FLEMMING	James McQUESTIN
Richard WRIGHT	Wm. BARLOW
James SLOAN	Samuel FEAR
Francis ADAMS	Gilbert MENARY
Wm. ADAMS	James McLURKIN
Wm. MILLER	Richard McLURKIN
Samuel BARBER	Widow MEBIN
Hugh OWENS	Thomas McCLURKIN
Wm. GREG	James BLAIR
John GREG	Brice BLAIR
James BROWN	Thomas WILSON
John AGNEW	David MURRAY & Family
David MONTGOMERY	John McCLENAGHAN
John BAIRD	Archibald McNEEL
Alexander FLEMING	James WILSON
Matthew FLEMING	Robert JAMESON
Wm. CRAWFORD	Robert REED
	John HENRING

Critical Note on Authorities

REFERENCE has already been made to the lack of information regarding emigration in official departmental records. The State Papers relating to Ireland are especially disappointing for they are mainly concerned with political and military matters—with the exception of a few references to emigration between 1728 and 1731 and between 1771 and 1774, they consist largely of army lists and correspondence dealing with such matters as jobbery, patronage and political manœuvring. On the other hand, there are scattered references to Irish immigration into colonial America during most parts of the period in the Colonial Office Papers which also serve to give some idea of the colonial attitude to the Irish and of conditions that partly determined the direction of Irish emigration. As Alexander McNutt was the only person intimately concerned with Irish emigration who kept closely in touch with the British government, it is natural that the correspondence, instructions, etc. in the Nova Scotia papers should be the most fruitful single field of research in the Colonial Office Papers. Though McNutt's activities were confined to a few years and though his methods were not typical of the normal organisation of the emigration trade, a few of these papers have a wider significance as they state the official attitude to emigration in general and include references to the chartering of vessels for the conveyance of emigrants. The Treasury Papers throw some light on the causes of emigration from Great Britain in the few years before the outbreak of the American revolution and also on the attitude of the British government to the movement to America. Most information on the latter point, however, is to be found in the State Papers relating to Scotland, particularly in the correspondence between Miller and Suffolk, and in the Privy Council Registers with regard to emigration between 1728 and 1731. The Customs Papers are useful for statistics concerning Irish-American trade but the minutes of the commissioners of the Irish Customs have merely the negative value of demonstrating the resigned attitude of authority to a movement it disliked. A most useful, though not exhaustive, supplement to the incomplete official calendars is

Critical Note on Authorities

Andrews's *Guide to the materials for American history to 1783*, in the *P.R.O. of Gt. Britain*.

Few of the manuscripts examined in the British Museum have any direct bearing on the subject, the most relevant being letters dealing with social conditions in Ireland and in America, statistics of trade between the two countries and lists of Irish emigrants between 1803 and 1805, the earliest north Irish lists to be compiled.

The oft-stressed connection between emigration and rising rents and the surprising absence of any examination of north Irish rentals in the eighteenth century prompted a detailed study of rent-rolls and leases in the Public Record Office of Northern Ireland, the Londonderry Estate Office, Newtownards, and the Southwell Estate Office, Downpatrick. The leases of the Londonderry estate—now transferred to the Public Record Office of Northern Ireland—even though they are far from complete, are the most useful of the three sources for compiling a composite picture of the level of north Irish rents during the eighteenth century.

The Public Record Office of Northern Ireland contains three collections of manuscripts and transcripts of value in the present study, as well as rent-rolls and leases and transcripts of the State Papers relating to Ireland from 1715. The commercial papers of the Belfast merchant Daniel Mussenden contain many references to periods of famine and periods of plenty, to general Irish-American trade, to the chartering of vessels for the transatlantic trade and—most interesting of all—one paper detailing the cost of outfitting indentured servants and the preparations made for their voyage to America. It is unfortunate that some of the most valuable of the Mussenden papers have not been calendared. The Dobbs collection of letters gives some insight into the character and early plans of Arthur Dobbs but its usefulness from the present point of view practically ends with the departure of Dobbs for North Carolina. The transcripts of the papers of the Merchant Taylors Company are particularly valuable as it was from the proportion of that Company that the first large group of emigrants left the north of Ireland. The transcripts dealing with the period from 1715 to 1730 contain more of interest than those of the remainder of the century and enable a balanced judgment to be made of the causes of the earliest phase of emigration. Many of the Company's papers which have not been transcribed are letters illustrating the hardships indicated by the rent-rolls and petitions among the transcripts.

One would expect to find frequent references to emigration among presbyterian records not only because of the alleged connection between presbyterian disabilities and emigration but also because of the very practical effect that emigration must have had on many presbyterian congregations. Yet the only references to emigration in the *Records of the general synod of Ulster* are a few isolated and inconsequential entries recording the departure of a minister or calls for spiritual guidance from congregations in the plantations. McGregor's departure from Aghadowey merited only a line in the Aghadowey Session book baldly recording that he had gone. Only in the Minutes of the presbytery of Strabane is there a detailed account of proceedings arising out of the intention of a minister to emigrate. On the whole, the presbyteries were concerned with ministerial vacancies and finance while internal administration and dissensions occupied most of the time and energies of the synod.

The value of the letters of the time is limited because those which survive are overwhelmingly anti-presbyterian and are mostly confined to the years between 1715 and 1730. Archbishop Boulter's *Letters* contain information that is of importance for they represent the views not only of a liberal minded episcopalian but of a man who was virtually the chief executive in Ireland at the time. Archbishop King never reached the eminence of toleration or influence attained by Boulter, but some pertinent points are included in his letters printed in C. S. King's *A great archbishop of Dublin* and Mant's *History of the Church of Ireland*. There are a few letters dealing with Irish social life and the Hearts of Steel insurrection in the Townshend collections in the National Library, Dublin, and in the British Museum. A proclamation of the Hearts of Steel in the form of a letter to a member of the Irish parliament is among the Londonderry Estate Office Papers in the Northern Ireland Public Record Office. The value of this letter-proclamation lies in the detailed account it gives of the conditions that culminated in the agrarian unrest in the early 'seventies.

The eighteenth century was the golden age of pamphleteering in Ireland but none of the pamphlets examined deals directly with north Irish emigration. Almost all are concerned with trade restrictions, absentees and poverty or tread with tiresome repetition the well-worn paths of religious controversy. The most productive source of information for the present purpose is the newspapers of the time. These compensate in part for the paucity of other sources, for from them can be obtained a broad outline of the causes and extent of emigration and of the organisation of the emigration trade. Comparatively few direct comments on emigration are made—the summary of the extent of north Irish emigration between 1771 and 1773 in the *Belfast News Letter* of 6 April 1773 is a notable exception—but fluctuations in the number and type of shipping advertisements reflect reliably fluctuations in the volume of emigration. Conditions which in great measure determined the extent of emigration are discernible in reports of scarcities and in advertisements concerning the letting of land. As newspaper advertisements were the main means of contact between agent and emigrant their importance in the study of the organisation of the emigration trade is obvious. To all this is added, at times, the spice of correspondence in which emigration is extolled or condemned, America described as paradise or hell, and masters and vessels thanked or damned. The usefulness of newspaper sources is, however, limited. One has to depend largely on southern newspapers for information till the middle of the century. The price of food, with the exception of bread, is seldom to be found in the *Belfast News Letter* in the 'sixties or 'seventies. The port news printed in the southern newspapers is regular and detailed but its appearance is irregular in the *Belfast News Letter* and is obviously incomplete even when it does appear. It is impossible to gain any impression of the attitude of the authorities to the trade except for dark hints of opposition or suppression. But, despite these limitations, the importance of newspaper sources may be summed up by saying that the impressions they give are supported by official sources where the latter are available and the gaps they leave may be filled in from official sources.

There are three groups of secondary sources—Irish, American and Irish-American. The limitations of the works of Froude and Lecky have been indicated in the introduction of this book. G. O'Brien's suggestive *Economic History of Ireland in the eighteenth century* partly compensates for the omissions in the political works of the century but tends to read the present into the past and often accepts statements from propagandist works without sufficient examination. At any rate, it is inevitable that the broad sweep of

O'Brien's pen should be secured by sacrificing the examination of local conditions. The absence of a bibliography and the inadequacy of many of the references are added handicaps to the student of Irish economic history. Gill's *Rise of the Irish linen industry* and Murray's *Commercial and financial relations between England and Ireland* are excellent backgrounds in their own particular fields and Young's *Tour in Ireland*, despite a lack of balance in some of his conclusions, is the obvious starting point of any survey of social conditions in Ireland in the 'seventies. After a century, Reid's *History of the presbyterian church in Ireland* remains an indispensable guide to Irish presbyterianism and is worthily supplemented by Beckett's *Protestant dissent in Ireland 1687–1780*, dealing with relations between the Irish presbyterians and the government. The latter work gives a balanced judgment of the influence of religious disabilities on emigration between 1728 and 1731.

It is outside the scope of this work to detail general American histories of the eighteenth century but mention must be made of a few works of more particular interest. The understanding of the early phase of north Irish immigration into the New England colonies is made easier by the excellent account of land conditions in New England given in Akagi's *Town proprietors of the New England colonies* which also includes several direct references to north Irish immigration. Proper's *Colonial immigration laws* serves to complement a study of the attitude of the home authorities to emigration. The system of indentured labour is very adequately covered by a series of monographs in *The John Hopkins University studies in Historical and Political Sciences* (xii, xiii, xiv, xxii) and, though in a more incidental and less satisfactory manner, in the first volume of Hurd's *Freedom and bondage in the United States*.

There is an abundance of writings on the Irish and Scotch-Irish in colonial America but, unfortunately, history has largely degenerated into the tool of faction. Some of the articles in *The Scotch-Irish in America: Proceedings of the Scotch-Irish Congress* and the *Journal of the American Irish Historical Society* are both interesting and suggestive but they are often biased and seldom authenticated. Of the two publications, the former deals more exclusively with the period covered by this work but many of the articles in the latter are more informative and are obviously based on more intensive research. This is mainly due to the work of M. J. O'Brien who was historiographer of the American Irish Historical Society for many years and, despite the many times it has been necessary in this book to challenge his conclusions, the ardour of his industry must be acknowledged. There are three possible explanations of the doubtful value of the results of that industry—or ardour. First, it may be that the material available in America is misleading. For example, one of O'Brien's trump cards is the customs returns of the Philadelphia port officials, but the pre-eminence of Cork as the victualling port for Irish-American shipping may cause those returns to give a distorted view of Irish-American trade. Second, O'Brien's enthusiasm may have distorted his judgment. He attaches great weight, for example, to the surnames of immigrants in deciding whether they were 'north' or 'south' Irish (*Washington's Ir. assoc.*, p. 239). The dangers of the use of such a method are obvious but the dangers are increased by the acceptance of such names as Mitchell, Moore, Gillespie and English as 'obviously pure Irish' ('Burke's Garden, Virginia', in *Amer. Ir. Hist. Soc. Jn.*, xxvi.61). A third possible explanation is that O'Brien has distorted evidence to suit his own purpose. For example, when calculating the relative value of north and south Irish trade with New York and Philadelphia, he includes in the south Irish list, vessels which the official records state sailed to or from 'Ireland' (*Hidden phase*, p. 287). However, whatever the explanation of O'Brien's doubtful conclusions may be, the fact remains that the evidence unearthed by his patience is indispensable to the student of Irish emigration in the eighteenth century and is invaluable in substantiating and supplementing evidence available in the British Isles.

Some Scotch-Irish protagonists have all of O'Brien's faults without his virtues. Maude Glasgow's *The Scotch Irish in Northern Ireland and in the American colonies* bases an unoriginal past on an ill-understood and often misrepresented present. Nevertheless, the three best works dealing—though only as part of broader themes—with north Irish emigration to colonial America are written by Scotch-Irish historians. Ford's *Scotch-Irish pioneers in Ulster and America* must be commended for its balance though much of its value is lost by failure to cite sources. The other two works—Klett's *Presbyterians in colonial Pennsylvania* and Dunaway's *Scotch-Irish in colonial Pennsylvania*—do not suffer from this defect and the general conclusions of these writers on the earlier phases of north Irish emigration have been borne out by the examination of British and Irish sources on which this work is based.

Bibliography

I: PRIMARY SOURCES

A. MANUSCRIPT

i. British Museum

Add. MS 6117. Letters, Ed. Synge, abp. of Tuam.

Add. MS 15485. Account of shipping, imports, exports, value and character of articles carried to and from the American colonies, 1768–9.

Add. MSS 21122; 21123. Letters, Marmaduke Coghill to Ed. Southwell, 1722–34.

Add. MSS 24137; 24138. Abstracts, letters and papers relating to Ireland, 1724–83.

Add. MS 34778. Letters of T. Meldycott to Ed. Southwell, 1703–27.

Add. MS 35585. Hardwicke papers, 1728.

Add. MS 35932. Passenger lists, Ireland to America, 1803–6.

Add. MS 36219. Statements concerning brigantine *Providence* of Rhode Island.

Add. MS 38016. Carteret correspondence as Lord lieutenant of Ireland.

Add. MS 38497. Townshend papers relating to Ireland, 1698–1801.

ii. Church House, Belfast.

Aghadowey session book.

iii. Library of Magee University College, Londonderry

Minutes of the presbytery of Strabane, 1717–40
Minutes of the presbytery of Bangor, 1739–74.

iv. National Library, Dublin.

MS. 394. Letters and papers of George, 4th Visct. Townshend.

v. Merchant Taylors Company, London

Boxes 126–131. Letters relating to the Merchant Taylors and Cloth-workers proportion in Ireland.

vi. Public Record Office, London

Admiralty 1/3679. Letters relating to the Admiralty solicitor's department, 1767–75.
C.O. 5/114. Original correspondence, secretaries of state, 1768–71.
C.O. 5/138. Original correspondence, secretaries of state, 1771–5.
C.O. 5/216. Original correspondence, secretaries of state, 1761–9.
C.O. 5/276. Miscellaneous. MS. list of acts, 1704–59.
C.O. 5/297. North Carolina. Original correspondence, secretaries of state, 1750–7.
C.O. 5/323, 324. North Carolina. Commissions, instructions, etc., 1730–60.
C.O. 5/358–380. South Carolina. Original correspondence, board of trade, 1720–75.
C.O. 5/383–386. South Carolina. Original correspondence, secretaries of state, 1715–76.
C.O. 5/508–511. South Carolina. Shipping returns, 1716–19, 1721–67.
C.O. 5/752–754. Massachusetts. Original correspondence, secretaries of state, 1714–83.
C.O. 5/848. Massachusetts. Shipping returns, 1686–1719.
C.O. 5/1222–1228. New York. Naval office lists, 1713–65.
C.O. 5/1234. Pennsylvania. Letters from governors to secretaries of state, 1709–46.
C.O. 5/1267–1285. Proprieties. Original correspondence, secretaries of state, 1727–74.
C.O. 217/18–25. Nova Scotia. Original correspondence, board of trade, 1760–70.
C.O. 217/34. Nova Scotia. Original correspondence, secretaries of state, 1754–82.
C.O. 217/43–46. Nova Scotia. Original correspondence, secretaries of state, 1762–9.
C.O. 218/6. Nova Scotia. Entry book of commissions, instructions, correspondence, 1760–6.
C.O. 221/30–31. Nova Scotia. Shipping returns, 1758–65.
C.O. 226/1. Prince Edward Island. Original correspondence, board of trade, 1769–77.
C.O. 226/4–6. Prince Edward Island. Original correspondence, secretaries of state, 1769–77.
C.O. 227/1-2. Prince Edward Island. Entry books, commissions, instructions, etc., 1769–93, 1769–81.
C.O. 229/1. Prince Edward Island. Sessional papers, 1770–88.
C.O. 324/40. Plantations general. Instructions to governor, 1760–4.
C.O. 388/52. Board of trade. Commercial. Original correspondence, 1763–5.

C.O. 388/85–88. Board of trade. Commercial (Ireland). Original correspondence, 1697–1790.

C.O. 391. Board of trade. Minutes, 1675–1782.

Customs 1/14–129. Ireland. Commissioners of the Irish customs. Minutes, 1715–75.

Customs 15/76. Ireland. Ledgers, imports and exports, 1772–3.

Customs 16/1. America. Ledgers, imports and exports, 1768–73.

Customs 64/312. Correspondence concerning sailings to America, 1767–77.

Index 8310. Board of trade. Register of papers relating to Ireland, 1697–1731.

P.C. 1/48–50. Acts of the privy council. Unbound, 1725–75.

P.C. 2/85–119. Registers of the privy council, 1715–75.

S.P. 54/45–47. Scotland. Letters and papers, 1772–5.

S.P. 63/432, 436, 438–447. Ireland. Letters and papers, 1770–5.

S.P. 63/437A. Ireland. In—letters. Col. Blanquiere's register, 1772–6.

S.P. 63/437B. Ireland. Out—letters. Col. Blanquiere's register, 1772–6.

Treasury 1/500. Treasury board papers. In–letters, 1773.

Treasury 1/518. Treasury board papers. In–letters, 1775.

Treasury 1/523. Treasury board papers. In–letters, 1776.

Treasury 14/11–15. Ireland. Treasury board papers. Out–letters, 1723–78.

Treasury 29/43. Treasury board papers. Minutes, 1773–4.

Treasury 47/9–11. England and Wales. Emigration lists, 1773–6.

Treasury 47/12. Scotland. Emigration lists 1774–5.

Treasury 64/312. Exports from Ireland to America, 1767–77.

vii. Public Record Office of Northern Ireland, Belfast

D. 162. Dobbs papers.

D. 162/85. Lord Dungannon's estate: Rent-roll, 1765–6.

D. 207. Foster papers.

D. 235/20, 23. Town and manor of Dungannon: Rent-rolls, 1744–5, 1746–7.

D. 354. Mussenden papers.

D. 427/1 and 2 Hertford estate: Receipt book, 1719; Rent-roll, 1727–8.

D. 464/26, 28. Derrygonnelly estate: Rent-rolls, 1758–9, 1766–7.

D. 654. Marquis of Londonderry's Estate Office papers: Proclamations of the Hearts of Steel; Leases of Colville and Stewart estate; Correspondence and rent-rolls concerning Salter's proportion.

T.448, 519, 546, 580, 610, 659, 693. Transcripts of State Papers relating to Ireland, 1715–41.

T. 649/4. Mussenden papers. Petition to Geo. Macartney.

Bibliography

T. 656. Transcripts of Merchant Taylor's Company's Irish records.
T. 788. Transcripts of Vincent leases.

viii. Southwell Estate Office, Downpatrick.

Copy rental of part of Southwell estate, 1710.
Rent-roll of Southwell estate, 1751-2.

B. PRINTED

i. Newspapers

Belfast News Letter: 1739, 1746,[1] 1747,[1] 1749, 1750, 1751,[1] 1752,[1] 1753,[1] 1754, 1755,[1] 1756-75.
Cork Evening Post: 1757, 1758,[1] 1759, 1760,[1] 1762, 1763,[1] 1769, 1773.
Dublin Chronicle: 1770-1.
Dublin News Letter: 1737-8, 1739,[1] 1741-3.
Dublin Weekly Journal: 1725,[1] 1726, 1727,[1] 1728-31, 1747-51, 1752,[1]
Faulkner's Dublin Journal: 1728-65, 1767-8, 1773-5.
Freeman's Journal (Dublin): 1763-8, 1769,[1] 1770-5.
[1] Only a few copies.
Hybernian Chronicle (Cork): 1773
Limerick Chronicle: 1771.
Londonderry Journal: June, Oct. 1772; June 1773.
Public Journal: (Dublin) 1771-3.
Pue's Occurrences (Dublin): 1752.
Dublin Evening Post: 1732-6.

ii. Periodicals

Gentleman's Magazine, or, Monthly Intellingencer, 1731-75, London.
Scots Magazine, 1739-75, Edinburgh.

iii. Documentary collections

ABBOTT, E. (ed.), *Historical aspects of the immigration problems. Select documents*, Chicago, 1926.
ABBOTT, E. (ed.), *Immigration: select documents and case histories*, Chicago, 1924.
Acts of the privy council, colonial series, 1680-1783, 6 vols, London, 1910-12.

Calendar of home office papers, 1760–75, 4 vols, London, 1879–99.
Calendar of state papers, domestic series, 1689–90, London, 1895.
Calendar of treasury books and papers, 1729–30, London, 1897.
COMMONS, J. R., PHILLIPS, U.B., GILMORE, E.A., SUMNER, H.L., ANDERSON, J.B. (eds.), *A documentary history of American industrial society*, i, Cleveland, 1910.
Debates relating to the affairs of Ireland, in the years, 1763 and 1764. Taken by a military officer, 2 vols, London, 1764.
FORTESCUE, Sir J. (ed.), *The correspondence of King George the third, 1760–1783*, iii, London, 1928.

Historical Manuscripts Commission publications:
   Charlemont MSS, i, London, 1894.
   Laing MSS, ii, London, 1925.
   Second report, London, 1871.
   Stopford-Sackville MSS, i, London 1904.

Journals of the continental congress, i–iii, Washington, 1904–5.
Journals of the house of commons of the kingdom of Ireland, Dublin, 1782.
Journals of the house of lords of Ireland, Dublin, 1779.
Journals of the house of representatives of Massachusetts, 1715–45. 20 vols, Boston, 1919–46.
KING, C.S. (ed.), *A great archbishop of Dublin; William King, 1650–1729, his autobiography, family, and a selection from his correspondence*, London, 1906.
LEFLER, H.T. (ed.), *North Carolina history told by contemporaries*, Chapel Hill, 1934.
Letters written by his excellency Hugh Boulter, D.D., lord primate of all Ireland, etc. to several ministers of state in England . . ., 2 vols, Dublin, 1770.
MADDEN, D.O., *The speeches of the right hon. Henry Gratten*, Dublin, 1853.
O'CALLAGHAN, E.B. (ed.), *The documentary history of the state of New York*, 4 vols, Albany, 1849.
Parliamentary history of England from the earliest period to the year 1803, xvii, London, 1813.
The Parliamentary register; or history of the proceedings and debates in the house of commons of Ireland, iii, Dublin, 1790.
Precedents and abstracts from the journals of the trustees of the linen and hempen manufacture of Ireland, to the twenty-fifth of March, MDCCXXXVII, Dublin, 1784.
Records of the general synod of Ulster, 3 vols, Belfast, 1890, 1897, 1898.
Reports from committees of the house of commons, 1715–1801, London, n.d.
Report(s) of the Deputy Keeper of the Public Records of Northern Ireland, 1929, 1930, 1931, Belfast

Bibliography

REVILL, JANIE, *A compilation of the original lists of protestant immigrants to South Carolina, 1763-1773*, Columbia, S.C., 1939.

Ruffead's statutes at large of England and of Great Britian, 1225-1809, 22 vols, London, 1769-1809.

Statutes at large passed in the parliaments held in Ireland, 13 vols, Dublin, 1786.

Statutes of the United Kingdom of Great Britain and Ireland, i-xiv, London, 1810-37.

STOCK, L.F. (ed.), *Proceedings and debates of the British parliaments respecting North America, 1542-1754*, 5 vols, Washington, 1924-41.

iv. Contemporary and nearly contemporary works

ADAIR, P., *A true narrative of the rise and progress of the presbyterian church in Ireland, 1623-1670* (end 17th cent.), ed. W. D. Killen, Belfast, 1866.

An appeal to the Rev. Dean Swift, by way of a reply to the observer on seasonable remarks, Dublin, 1729.

BARBER, S., *Remarks on a pamphlet entitled the present state of the church of England by Richard lord bishop of Cloyne*, Dublin, 1787.

CRAWFORD, W. A. M., *History of Ireland from the earliest time, in a series of letters addressed to William Hamilton, esq.*, 2 vols, Strabane, 1783.

DE CREVECOEUR, J. H. ST. J., *Letters from an American farmer* (1782), London, 1940.

DOBBS, A., *An essay upon the trade and improvement of Ireland*, Dublin, 1729.

EDDIS, W., *Letters from America, historical and descriptive, 1769-77*, London, 1792.

FULLER, A., and HOLMS, T., *A compendious view of some extraordinary sufferings of the people called quakers, both in person and in substance, in the kingdom of Ireland; from the year 1655 to the end of the reign of King George I*, Dublin, 1731.

An historical account of the rise and progress of the colonies of South Carolina and Georgia, 2 vols, London, 1779.

A history of the new world called America, as discovered by the Spaniards; and of the first remarkable voyages of several Europeans to divers parts therein. With a view of the dominion of the crown of England in the West Indies, namely, Newfoundland, New England, Pennsylvania, ... Containing an account of the discovery, excellencies, and rarities of those countries, with the customs, religion, and manners of the Indians, Belfast, n.d.

JOHNSTON, G. M., *A short description of the province of South Carolina with an account of the air, wealth, and diseases of Charles-Town, written in the year 1763*, London, 1770. This is B.M., Add.MS 29973.

A letter upon the subject of taxing the absentees of Ireland, Dublin, 1773.

Letters which passed in Great Britain relative to the absentee tax, Dublin, 1773.

Bibliography

A list of the absentees of Ireland, and an estimate of the yearly value of their estates and incomes spent abroad; with observations on the trade and manufacture of Ireland and means to encourage, improve, and extend them; with some remarks why Great Britain should be more indulgent to Ireland in particular points of trade, Dublin, 1767.

MOORE, F., *Considerations on the exorbitant price of provisions, setting forth the pernicious effects which a real scarcity of the necessaries of life must eventually have upon the commerce, population, and power of Great Britain*, London, 1773.

Observations on the popery laws, Dublin, 1771.

Observations on the trade between Ireland, and the English and foreign colonies in America, London, 1731.

PATON, H. (ed.), *The lyon in mourning, or a collection of the speeches relating to Prince Charles Edward Stewart, by Rev. Robt. Forbes, bishop of Ross and Caithness, 1746–1775*, iii, Edinburgh, 1896.

PETTY, W., *The political anatomy of Ireland* (1672), Dublin, 1691.[1]

PETTY, W., *A treatise of Ireland* (1687).[1]

[1] From *The economic writings of Sir William Petty*, ed. C. H. Hull, 2 vols, Cambridge, 1899.

The post chaise companion, or travellers directory through Ireland (c.1780), 3rd ed., Dublin, 1803.

PRIOR, T., *A list of the absentees of Ireland, and the yearly value of their estates and incomes spent abroad* (1729), 3rd ed., Dublin, 1745.

Remarks on the decay of the linen manufacture of Ireland: by a general trader, and a traveller, Dublin, 1774.

RUTTY, J., *A chronological history of the weather and seasons, and of the prevailing diseases in Dublin*, London, 1770.

A scheme for utterly abolishing the present heavy and vexatious tax of tithe, Dublin, 1742.

Serious considerations of the present alarming state of agriculture and the linen trade by a farmer, Dublin, 1773.

SMITH, W., *The history of the province of New York, from the first discovery to the year MDCCXXXII. To which is annexed a description of the country, with a short account of the inhabitants, their trade, religious and political state, and the constitution of the courts of justice in that colony*, London, 1752.

(SWIFT. J.), *Consideration on two letters lately published. The first called seasonable remarks, etc. The other, an essay on trade in general, and that of Ireland in particular*, Dublin, 1729.

(SWIFT, J.), *An humble address to both houses of parliament*, Dublin.

SWIFT, J., *The present miserable state of Ireland*, Dublin, n.d. (1726).[1] 1905.

SWIFT, J., *A proposal for the universal use of Irish manufactures, in cloaths and*

Bibliography

furniture, etc., utterly rejecting and renouncing every thing wearable that comes from England, Dublin, 1720.[1]

[1]From *The prose works of Jonathan Swift, D.D.*, ed. T. Scott, vii, London.

TAYLOR, G. and SKINNER, A., *The post chaise*, Dublin, 1778.

YOUNG, A., *A tour in Ireland: with general observations on the present state of that kingdom: made in the years 1776, 1777, and 1778. And brought down to the end of 1779*, 2 vols, 2nd ed., London, 1780.

II. SECONDARY SOURCES, including bibliographies and guides

ADAMS, C. F., *The works of John Adams with a life of the author . . . by his grandson C. F. Adams*, iii, Boston, 1850.

ADAMS, J. T., *Provincial society, 1690–1763*, New York, 1927.

ADAMS, M. I., 'The highland emigration of 1770', in *Scot. Hist. Rev.*, xvi, Edinburgh, 1919.

ADAMS, W. F., *Ireland and Irish emigration to the new world from 1815 to the Famine*, New Haven, 1932. By far the best work dealing with any phase of Irish emigration.

AKAGI, R. H., *The town proprietors of the New England colonies*, Philadelphia, 1924.

ALLEN, R., *Scottish ecclesiastical influence upon Irish presbyterianism from the non-subscription controversy to the union of the synods*. Unpublished thesis for the M.A. degree, Queen's University, Belfast, 1940.

ANDREWS, C. M., *The colonial period of American history*, 4 vols, New Haven, 1934–8.

ANDREWS, C. M., *A guide to the materials for American history to 1783, in the Public Record Office of Great Britain*, 2 vols, Washington, 1912, 1914.

ANDREWS, C. M. and DAVENPORT, F. G., *Guide to the manuscripts for the history of the United States to 1783, in the British Museum, in minor London archives, and in the libraries of Oxford and Cambridge*, Washington 1908.

BAGENAL, P. H., *The American Irish and their influence on Irish politics*, London, 1882.

BASSETT, J. S., *Slavery and servitude in North Carolina*, Baltimore, 1896.

BECKETT, J. C., *Protestant dissent in Ireland 1687–1780*, London, 1948.

BEERS, H. P., *Bibliographies in American history*, New York, 1942.

BENN, G., *History of Belfast*, London, 1877.

BIDWELL, P. W. and FALCONER, J. I., *History of agriculture in the northern United States, 1620–1860*, Washington, 1925.

BIGGER, F. J., *The Ulster land war of 1770*, Dublin, 1910. A bitter attack on eighteenth-century landlordism, based mainly on *B.N.L.* extracts.

BINING, A. C., Brunhouse, R.L., and Wilkinson, N.B., *Writings on Pennsylvania history: a bibliography*, Harrisburg, 1946.

Bibliography

BOLTON, C. K., *Scotch Irish pioneers in Ulster and America*, Boston, 1910.

BOURINOT, J. G., 'Builders of Nova Scotia', in *Proc. and Trans. Roy. Soc. Canada*, series 2, v, Toronto, 1899.

BYRNE, S., *Irish emigration to the United States*, New York, 1873. Deals mainly with the nineteenth century.

CALHOUN, P., 'Scotch Irish in Georgia', in *Scotch-Ir. in Amer.*, iv. Nashville, 1892.

Cambridge modern history, vii, Cambridge, 1934.

CAMPBELL, D., *History of Prince Edward Island*, Charlottetown, 1875.

CAMPBELL, J. H., *History of the Friendly Sons of St. Patrick and the Hibernian Society for the Relief of Emigrants from Ireland*, March 17, 1771 – March 17, 1892, Philadelphia, 1892.

CARROTHERS, W. A., *Emigration from the British Isles with special reference to the development of the overseas dominions*, London, 1929.

CLARK, V. S., *History of manufactures in the United States, 1607–1860*, Washington, 1916.

CONDON, E. O' M., *The Irish in America*, New York, 1887. Little on the eighteenth century.

COWAN, H. I., *British emigration to British North America 1783–1837*, Toronto, 1928. Contains excellent accounts of conditions on the voyage to America and on the growth of state regulation of the emigration trade.

CRAIGHEAD, J. G., *Scotch and Irish seeds in American soil*, Philadelphia, 1878.

CRIMMINS, J. D., *Irish American historical miscellany*, New York, 1905.

Dictionary of American biography, ed. A. Johnson, London, 1928–44.

Dictionary of national biography, ed. L. Stephen, 63 vols., London, 1885–1900.

DONOVAN, G. F., *The pre-Revolutionary Irish in Massachusetts, 1620–1775*, Boston, 1831. Useful for details of arrival of vessels and class of immigrants.

DOYLE, J. A., *The English in America; Virginia, Maryland and the Carolinas*, London, 1882.

DUFFIELD, G., *One hundred years ago: an historical sermon delivered by Rev. George Duffield, D.D. during the centenary celebration of the first presbyterian church at Carlisle, Pa., July 1, 1857*, Carlisle (Pa.), 1858. Interesting but superficial.

DUNAWAY, W. F., *The Scotch-Irish of colonial Pennsylvania*, Chapel Hill, 1944.

EATON, A. W. H., 'The settling of Colchester county, Nova Scotia, by New England puritans and Ulster Scotsmen', in *Proc. and Trans. Roy. Soc. Can.*, series 3, vi, Toronto, 1912. An informative addendum to Raymond's work on Alexander McNutt.

FARNAM, H. W., *Chapters in the history of social legislation in the United States to 1860*, Washington, 1938.

Bibliography

FAYLE, C. E., *A short history of the world's shipping industry*, London, 1933.

FERENSI, I., *International migrations*, ed. W. F. Willcox, i, New York, 1929.

FLEMING, W. S., 'Scotch Irish settlers in South Carolina and their descendants in Maury country, Tennessee', in *Scotch-Ir. in Amer.*, i, Cincinatti, 1889.

FLOOD, W. H. C., 'Irish emigration to the American colonies', in *Amer.- Ir. Hist. Soc. Jn.*, xxvi, New York, 1927. Value is limited by brevity and unjustified assumptions.

FORD, H. J., *The Scotch-Irish in America*, Princetown, 1915.

FROUDE, J. A., *The English in Ireland in the eighteenth century*, London, 1872.

GILL, C., *The rise of the Irish linen industry*, Oxford, 1925.

GLASGOW, M., *The Scotch Irish in northern Ireland and in the American colonies*, New York, 1926.

GRAY, L. C., *History of agriculture in the southern United States to 1860*, i, Washington, 1933.

GREEN, E. R. R., 'The Scotch-Irish and the coming of the revolution in North Carolina', in *Irish Historical Studies*, vii. 77–86.

GREEN, S. S., 'The Scotch-Irish in America', in *Amer. Antiq. Soc. Proc.*, xxxviii, Worcester (Mass.), 1928.

GREENE, E. B., *The revolutionary generation, 1763–90*, New York, 1943.

GRIFFIN, G. G., *A guide to manuscripts relating to American history in British depositories reproduced for the division of manuscripts of the library of congress* (Washington), 1946.

GRIFFITH, G. T., *Population problems in the age of Malthus*, London, 1926. Includes a very concise chapter on Irish population.

HALIBURTON, T. C., *A historical and statistical account of Nova Scotia*, Halifax (N.S.), 1929.

HANNA, C. A., *The Scotch Irish: or, the Scot in North Britain, North Ireland, and North America*, 2 vols, New York, 1902.

HANSEN, M. L., *The Atlantic migration 1607–1860. A history of the continuing settlement of the United States*, Cambridge (Mass.), 1941.

HEMPTON, J. (ed.), *The siege and history of Londonderry*, Londonderry, 1861.

HOON, E. E., *The organisation of the English customs system 1696–1786*, New York, 1900.

HORNER, J., *The linen trade of Europe during the spinning wheel period*, Belfast, 1920.

HUGHSON, S. C., *The Carolina pirates and colonial commerce*, Baltimore, 1894.

HUNT, W. (ed.), *The Irish parliament, 1775*, Dublin, 1907.

HURD, J. C., *The law of freedom and bondage in the United States*, i, Boston, 1938.

ISAAC, J., *Economics of emigration*, London, 1947.

JERNEGAN, M. W., *Laboring and dependent classes in colonial America, 1607–1783*, Chicago, 1931.

JOHNSON, E. R., VAN METRE, T. W., HUEBNER, G. G., HANCHETT, D. S.,
History of the domestic and foreign commerce of the United States, i, Washington, 1915.

JOHNSTON, S. C., *A history of emigration from the United Kingdom to North America, 1763-1912*, London, 1913. Little on the colonial period.

JONES, E. A., (ed.), *The journal of Alexander Chesney, a South Carolina loyalist in the Revolution and after*, Columbus (Ohio), 1921.

KERNOGHAN, J. W., *Two Ulster parishes: Kilrea and Tamlaght O'Crilly* Coleraine, 1912. Brief, but includes some original material.

KERR, W. D., *Who persecuted?* Belfast, 1947. A clear and provocative account of relations between protestant espiscopalians and presbyterians in Ireland in the seventeenth and eighteenth centuries by the former bishop of Down and Dromore.

KILLEN, W. D., *The ecclesiastical history of Ireland from the earliest period to the present times*, 2 vols., London, 1875.

KLETT, G. S., *Presbyterians in colonial Pennsylvania*, Philadelphia, 1937.

KNITTLE, W. A., *The early eighteenth century Palatine emigration: a British government redemptioner project to manufacture naval stores*, Philadelphia, 1936.

LATIMER, W. T., *A history of the Irish presbyterians*, Belfast, 1902.

LATIMER, W. T., 'Ulster emigration to America', in *R.S.A.I. Jn.*, series 5, xii, Dublin 1903. Brief and rather superficial.

LECKY, A. G., *The Laggan and its presbyterianism*, Belfast, 1905.

LECKY, W. E. H., *A history of Ireland in the eighteenth century*, 5 vols, London, 1892.

LINCOLN, W. and BALDWIN, C. C. (eds.), *The Worcester Magazine and Historical Journal*, 2 vols, Worcester (Mass.), 1826.

LINDSAY, W. S., *History of merchant shipping and colonial commerce*, 4 vols, London, 1872-8.

LINN, R., 'Notes on some early Ulster emigrants to America', in *R.S.A.I. Jn.*, series 6, ii, Dublin, 1913. Bigger's notes on the article are interesting.

MACDONALD, N., *Canada, 1763-1841. Immigration and settlement: the administration of the imperial land regulations*, London, 1939.

MACK, R. C., *The Londonderry celebration, June 10, 1869*, Manchester (N.H.), 1930. Uncritical, but contains information about the descendants of the north Irish immigrants into New England.

MACKINNON, I. F., *Settlements and churches in Nova Scotia, 1749-76*, Halifax (N.S.), 1930.

MACPHERSON, D., *Annals of commerce, manufactures, fisheries, and navigation . . . containing the commercial transactions of the British Empire and other countries, from the earliest accounts to . . . January 1801, and comprehending the most valuable part of Mr Anderson's History of commerce, etc.*, 4 vols, London, 1805.

MAGINNISS, T. H., (jnr.), *The Irish contribution to America's independence*, Philadelphia, 1913. Written with a strong anti-Scotch-Irish bias.

MAGUIRE, J. F., *The Irish in America*, London, 1868. Deals mostly with the nineteenth century.

MANT, R., *History of the church of Ireland from the Revolution to the union of the churches of England and Ireland, January 1, 1801*, London, 1840.

MARMION, A., *The ancient and modern history of the maritime ports of Ireland*, London, 1855.

METZGER, C. H., *The Quebec act: a primary cause of the American revolution*, New York, 1936.

MOODY, T. W., 'Irish and Scotch-Irish in eighteenth century America', in *Studies*, xxxv, Dublin, 1946. This and the following article provide a reliable basis for more detailed investigation.

MOODY, T. W., 'The Ulster Scot in colonial and revolutionary America', in *Studies*, xxxiv, Dublin, 1945.

MURDOCK, B., *A history of Nova Scotia or Acadie*, Halifax (N.S.), 1865.

MURPHY, M. J., 'Ulster settlers in America. Some of the early colonists—their service in the American revolution', in *U.J.A.*, series 2, ii, Belfast, 1896.

MURRAY, A. E., *Commercial and financial relations between England and Ireland*, London, 1903.

MYERS, A. C., *Immigration of the Irish quakers into Pennsylvania, 1682–1750, with their early history in Ireland*, Swathmore, 1902.

MCCRADY, E., *The history of South Carolina under the royal government*, New York, 1899.

MCCORMAC, E. J., *White servitude in Maryland, 1634–1830*, Baltimore, 1904.

MCCRACKEN, J. L., *The undertakers in Ireland and their relations with the lords lieutenant, 1724–71.* Unpublished thesis for the Ph.D. degree, Queen's University, Belfast, 1948.

MCDOWELL, R. B., *Irish public opinion, 1750–1800*, London, 1943.

MCGEE, T. d'A., *A history of the Irish settlers in north America*, Boston, 1852. Very disappointing in view of its title.

MCGREGOR, J., *Historical and descriptive sketches of the maritime colonies of British North America*, London, 1828.

MCLEAN, J. P., *An historical account of the settlements of Scotch highlanders in America prior to the peace of 1763*, Cleveland, 1900.

MCLINTOCK, A. H., *The establishment of constitutional government in Newfoundland, 1783–1832*, London, 1941.

NEWENHAM, T., *A statistical and historical enquiry into the magnitude of the population of Ireland*, London, 1805.

NICHOLLS, G., *A history of the Irish poor law in connexion with the condition of the people*, London, 1856.

NIXON, J. A., 'Health and sickness', in *The trade winds*, ed. C. N. Parkinson, London, 1948.

NOLAN, J. B., *Benjamin Franklin in Scotland and Ireland, 1759 and 1771*, Philadelphia, 1938.

OSGOOD, H. L., *The American colonies in the eighteenth century*, 4 vols, New York, 1924.

O'BRIEN, G., *The economic history of Ireland in the eighteenth century*, Dublin, 1918.

O'BRIEN, M. J., 'Burke's Garden, Virginia', in *Amer. Ir. Hist. Soc. Jn.*, xxvi, New York, 1927.

O'BRIEN, M. J., 'Early Irish settlers in the Champlain valley', in *Amer. Ir. Hist. Soc. Jn.*, xxvi, New York, 1927.

O'BRIEN, M. J., *George Washington's associations with the Irish*, New York, 1937.

O'BRIEN, M. J., *A hidden phase of American history: Ireland's part in America's struggle for liberty*, New York, 1919.

O'BRIEN, M. J., *Pioneer Irish in New England*, New York, 1937.

O'BRIEN, M. J., 'Shipping statistics of the Philadelphia customs house, 1773 to 1774, refute the Scotch-Irish theory', in *Amer.-Ir. Hist. Soc. Jn.*, xxii, New York, 1923.

O'SULLIVAN, W., *The economic history of Cork city from the earliest times to the act of Union*, Cork, 1937.

PARKER, E. L., *The history of Londonderry, comprising the towns of Derry and Londonderry, N.H.*, Boston, 1851. Supplies much information about the early Scotch-Irish settlers in New England.

PLOWDEN, F., *An historical review of the state of Ireland, from the invasion of that country under Henry II to its union with Great Britain on 1st of January 1801*, 2 vols, London, 1803.

PROPER, E. E., *Colonial immigration laws*, New York, 1900.

PROUD, R., *The history of Pennsylvania . . . from the original institution and settlement of that province . . . in 1681, till after the year 1742*, 2 vols, Philadelphia, 1797–8.

PURCELL, R. J., 'The Irish contribution to colonial New York', in *Studies*, xxix and xxx, Dublin, 1940–1941.

PURCELL, R. J., 'The Irish emigrant society of New York', in *Studies*, xxvii, Dublin, 1938.

RAYMOND, W. O., 'Colonel Alexander McNutt and the pre-loyalist settlements of Nova Scotia', in *Proc. and Trans. Roy. Soc. Can.*, series 3, v and vi, Toronto, 1911, 1912.

The Recorder: bulletin of the American Irish Historical Society, iii, New York, 1926.

Bibliography

REID, J. S., *History of the presbyterian church in Ireland*, 3 vols, Belfast, 1851.

REID, W., *The Scot in Ulster and the Ulster Scot*, London, 1912.

ROSENBERGER, J. L., *The Pennsylvania Germans*, Chicago, 1923.

SAMPSON, G. V., *Statistical survey of the county of Londonderry with observations on the means of improvement; drawn up for the consideration, and under the direction of the Dublin Society*, Dublin, 1802.

SANFORD, E., *A history of the United States before the Revolution*, Philadelphia, 1819.

SELKIRK, the earl of, *Observations of the present state of the highlands of Scotland with a view of the causes and probable consequences of emigration*, London, 1805.

SLADE, R., *Narrative of a journey to the north of Ireland in the year 1802*, London, 1803.

STEVENS, W. B., *A history of Georgia from its first discovery by Europeans to the adoption of the present constitution*, 2 vols, New York, 1847.

STEVENSON, J., *Two centuries of life in Down 1600–1800*, Belfast, 1920. Contains copious extracts from documents in private collections.

SUTHERLAND, S. H., *Population distribution in colonial America*, New York, 1936.

THOMPSON, M. A., *The secretaries of state*, London, 1832.

TOOKE, T., *A history of prices and the state of the circulation, from 1793 to 1837; preceded by a brief sketch of the state of the corn trade in the last two centuries*, i, London, 1838.

TURNER, F. J., *The frontier in American history*, New York, 1920.

WARBURTON, A. B., *A history of Prince Edward Island, 1534–1831*, St. John, 1923.

WATSON, J. F., *Annals of Philadelphia and Pennsylvania*, 2 vols, Philadelphia, 1860.

WHITNEY, E. L., *The government of the colony of South Carolina*, Baltimore, 1895.

WITHEROW, T., *The historical and literary memorials of the presbyterians in Ireland*, series 2, Belfast, 1880. A guide to controversial presbyterian writings in the eighteenth century.

WOODBURN, J. B., *The Ulster Scot, his history and religion*, London n.d. (1914).

Index

Place names in America and Ulster have been classified in provinces and counties, respectively. The Appendices are not included in the Index.

Index

Lightning Source UK Ltd.
Milton Keynes UK
UKOW050913250113

205336UK00002B/7/P